冨樫義博

"IF I COULD BE REBORN AS ANYONE, WHO WOULD I BE?" PART 4: THE UNKNOWN FACE IN A COMMERCIAL. AN INSANE NUMBER OF VIEWER REQUESTS POURS IN ASKING WHO I AM AFTER I APPEAR ON SOME ELECTRICAL APPLIANCE MAKER'S TV COMMERCIAL. FOR A WHILE, I AM IN THE SPOTLIGHT, BUT MY AGE, GENDER, AND ORIGINS REMAIN COMPLETELY UNKNOWN. RUMORS ABOUND ABOUT ME IN SOCIETY: RUMORS THAT I AM THE CHILD OF A ENTERTAIN-MENT-COMPANY PRESIDENT BORN OUT OF WED-LOCK, RUMORS OF MY MENTAL BREAKDOWN AND SUICIDE, RUMORS OF MY GHOST BEING SEEN, RUMORS OF MY BEING AN ALIEN, ETC. I BECOME THE YEAR'S MOST TALKED-ABOUT PERSON IN THE "WHO THE HECK ARE YOU?" CATEGORY. BUT MY IDENTITY REMAINS UNKNOWN. IN REALITY, I AM NINE MONTHS PREGNANT, LIVING IN YAMAGATA PREFECTURE, MARRIED TO A FARMER THREE YEARS MY SENIOR, AND WORKING HARD AT GROWING RICE.

—YOSHIHIRO TOGASHI, 1991

Born in 1966, Yoshihiro Togashi won the prestigious Tezuka Award for new manga artists at the age of 20. He debuted in Japan's WEEKLY SHONEN JUMP magazine in 1988 with the romantic comedy manga **Tende Showaru Cupid**. His hit comic **YuYu Hakusho** ran in WEEKLY SHONEN JUMP from 1990 to 1994. Togashi's other manga include **I'm Not Afraid of Wolves!**, **Level E**, and **Hunter x Hunter**.

YUYU HAKUSHO VOL. 4
The SHONEN JUMP Graphic Novel Edition

This graphic novel contains material that was originally published in English in SHONEN JUMP #13-16.

STORY AND ART BY
YOSHIHIRO TOGASHI

English Adaptation/Gary Leach
Translation/Lillian Olsen
Touch-Up Art & Lettering/Bill Schuch
Graphics & Cover Design/Sean Lee
Supervising Editor/Jason Thompson
Editor/Shaenon K. Garrity

Managing Editor/Annette Roman
Production Manager/Noboru Watanabe
Executive V.P./Editor in Chief/Hyoe Narita
Sr. Director, Licensing and Acquisitions/Rika Inouye
V.P. of Marketing/Liza Coppola
V.P. of Strategic Development/Yumi Hoashi
Publisher/Seiji Horibuchi

PARENTAL ADVISORY
YUYU HAKUSHO is rated "T" for teens. It contains fantasy violence. It is recommended for ages 13 and up.

Printed in USA.

Published by VIZ, LLC
P.O. Box 77010 • San Francisco, CA 94107

SHONEN JUMP Graphic Novel Edition
10 9 8 7 6 5 4 3 2 1
First printing, May 2004

www.viz.com

THE WORLD'S MOST POPULAR MANGA

SHONEN JUMP
GRAPHIC NOVEL
www.shonenjump.com

SHONEN JUMP GRAPHIC NOVEL

YuYu HAKUSHO ™

Vol.4
Training Day

STORY AND ART BY
YOSHIHIRO TOGASHI

THE STORY SO FAR:

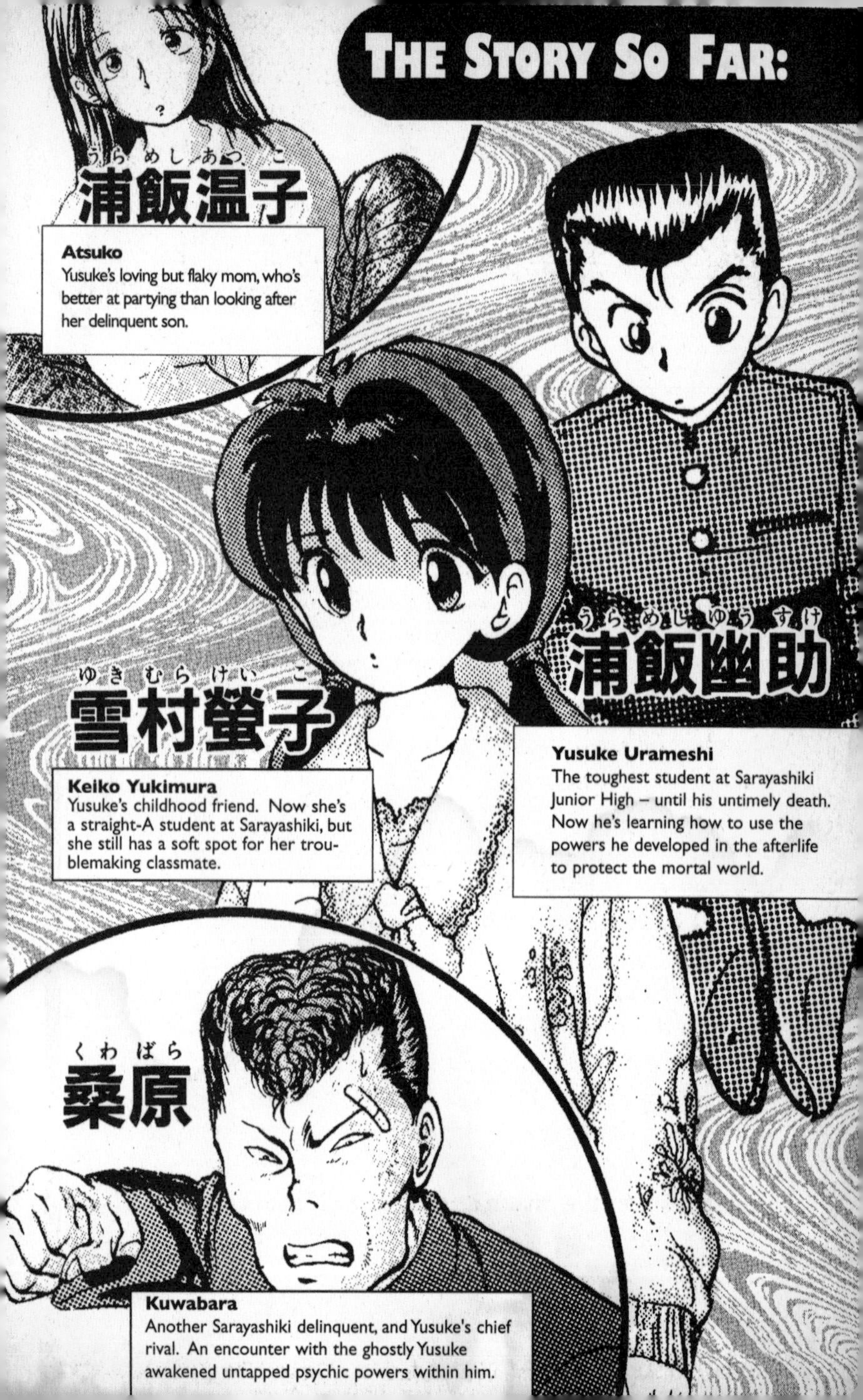

うらめしあつこ
浦飯温子
うらめしゆうすけ
浦飯幽助
ゆきむらけいこ
雪村螢子
くわばら
桑原

Atsuko
Yusuke's loving but flaky mom, who's better at partying than looking after her delinquent son.

Yusuke Urameshi
The toughest student at Sarayashiki Junior High – until his untimely death. Now he's learning how to use the powers he developed in the afterlife to protect the mortal world.

Keiko Yukimura
Yusuke's childhood friend. Now she's a straight-A student at Sarayashiki, but she still has a soft spot for her troublemaking classmate.

Kuwabara
Another Sarayashiki delinquent, and Yusuke's chief rival. An encounter with the ghostly Yusuke awakened untapped psychic powers within him.

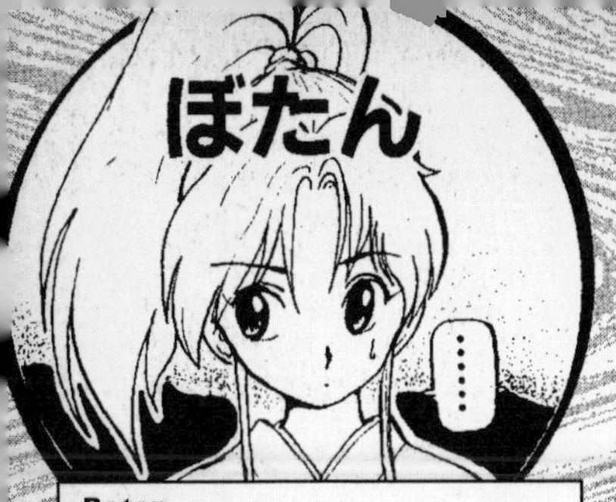
ぼたん
……

Botan
The ferrywoman of the Sanzu River (the River Styx in Western mythology), Botan delivers Yusuke's assignments from the Underworld.

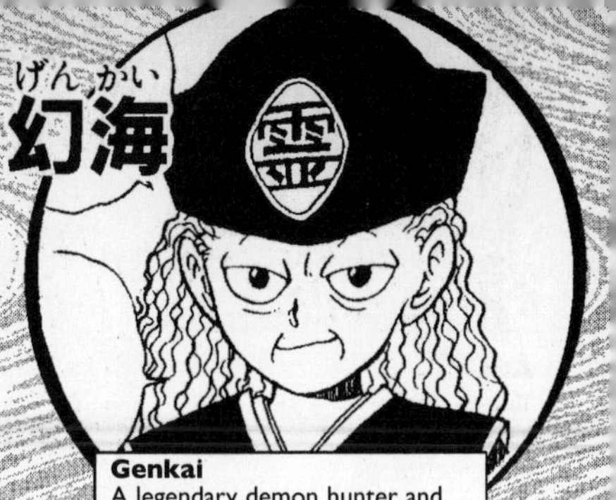
げんかい
幻海
霊

Genkai
A legendary demon hunter and master of *reiki*, she can heal or destroy with a touch… and humans and demons alike would love to learn her secrets.

When surly street punk Yusuke Urameshi died in an unexpected act of self-sacrifice, the Underworld decided to give him a second chance… and he returned to life a changed teenager, armed with supernatural powers and a new perspective. Now he's the Underworld's new supernatural detective, keeping the Earth clean of demonic scum.

Yusuke's current assignment is also his training: he's undercover at the dojo of elderly martial-arts master Genkai, competing with other tough guys for the right to learn her incredible demon-fighting techniques. According to Underworld intelligence, somewhere in the lineup is the demon Rando, who's already slaughtered ninety-nine masters of magic and martial arts in his quest for ultimate power. Unable to figure out which of the aspiring demon-slayers is Rando, Yusuke can think of only one solution: fight his way through the competition and unmask him in the final battle. And, as if Yusuke doesn't have enough headaches, his old rival Kuwabara is also in the competition…

YU YU HAKUSHO VOLUME 4 TRAINING DAY

CONTENTS

MORTAL MANEUVERS IN THE DARK!!

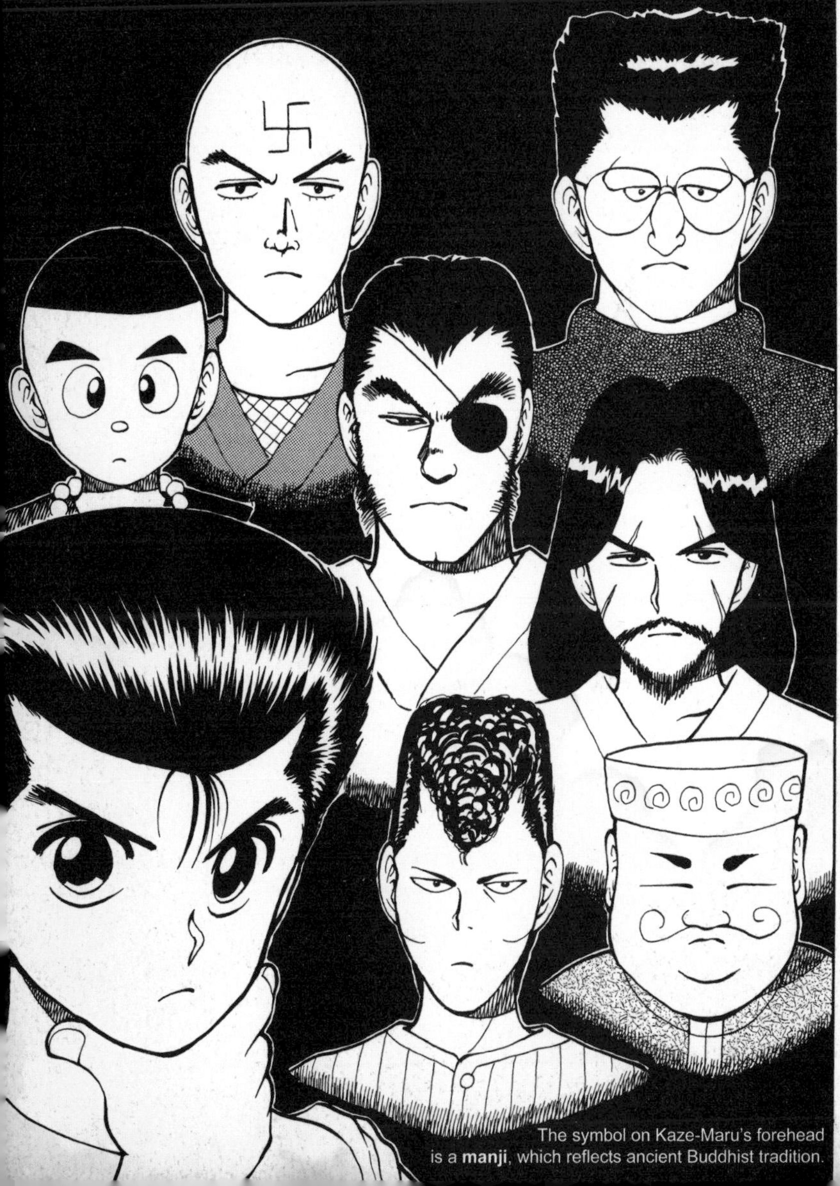

The symbol on Kaze-Maru's forehead is a **manji**, which reflects ancient Buddhist tradition.

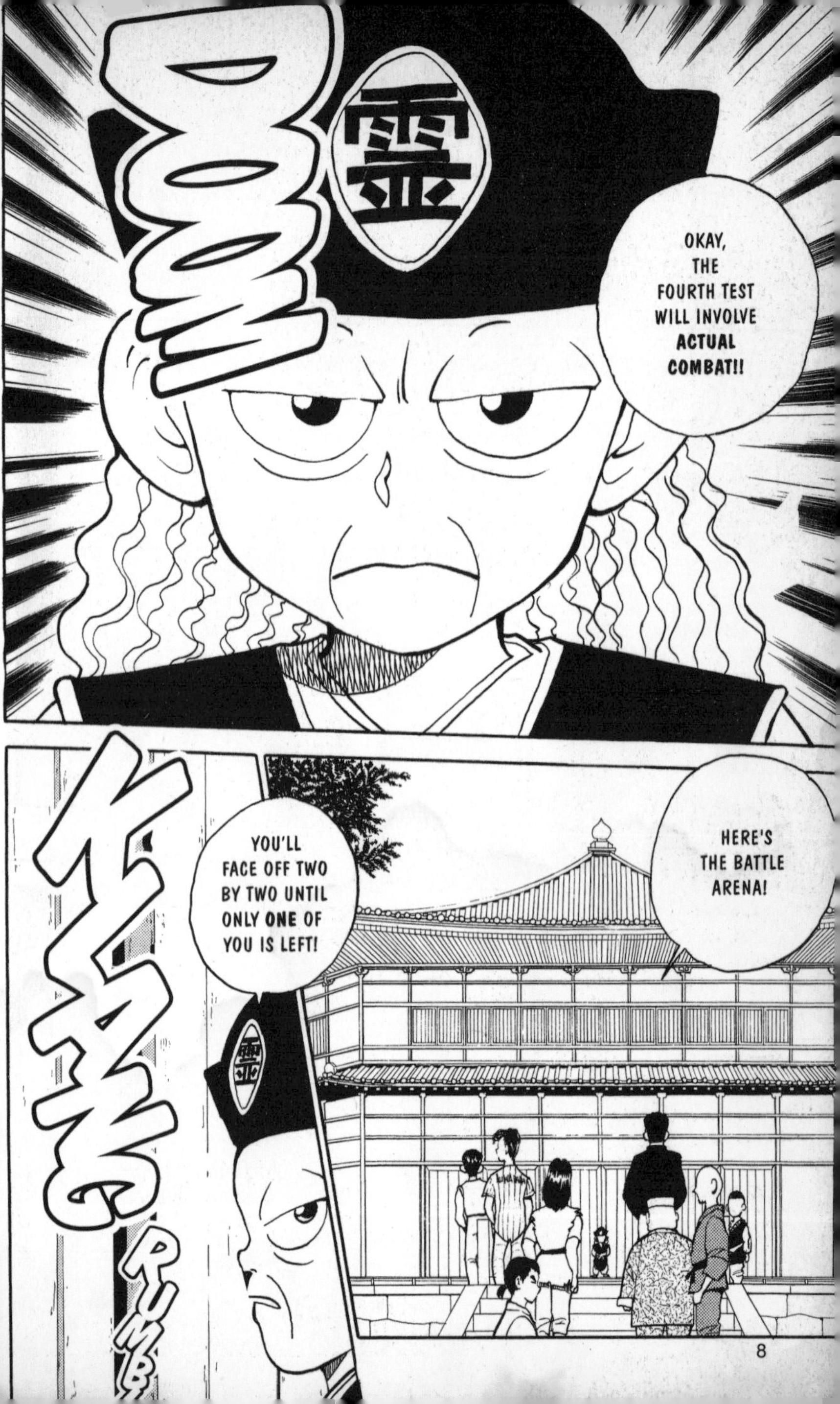
DOOM
OKAY, THE FOURTH TEST WILL INVOLVE ACTUAL COMBAT!!
HERE'S THE BATTLE ARENA!
YOU'LL FACE OFF TWO BY TWO UNTIL ONLY ONE OF YOU IS LEFT!
RUMB

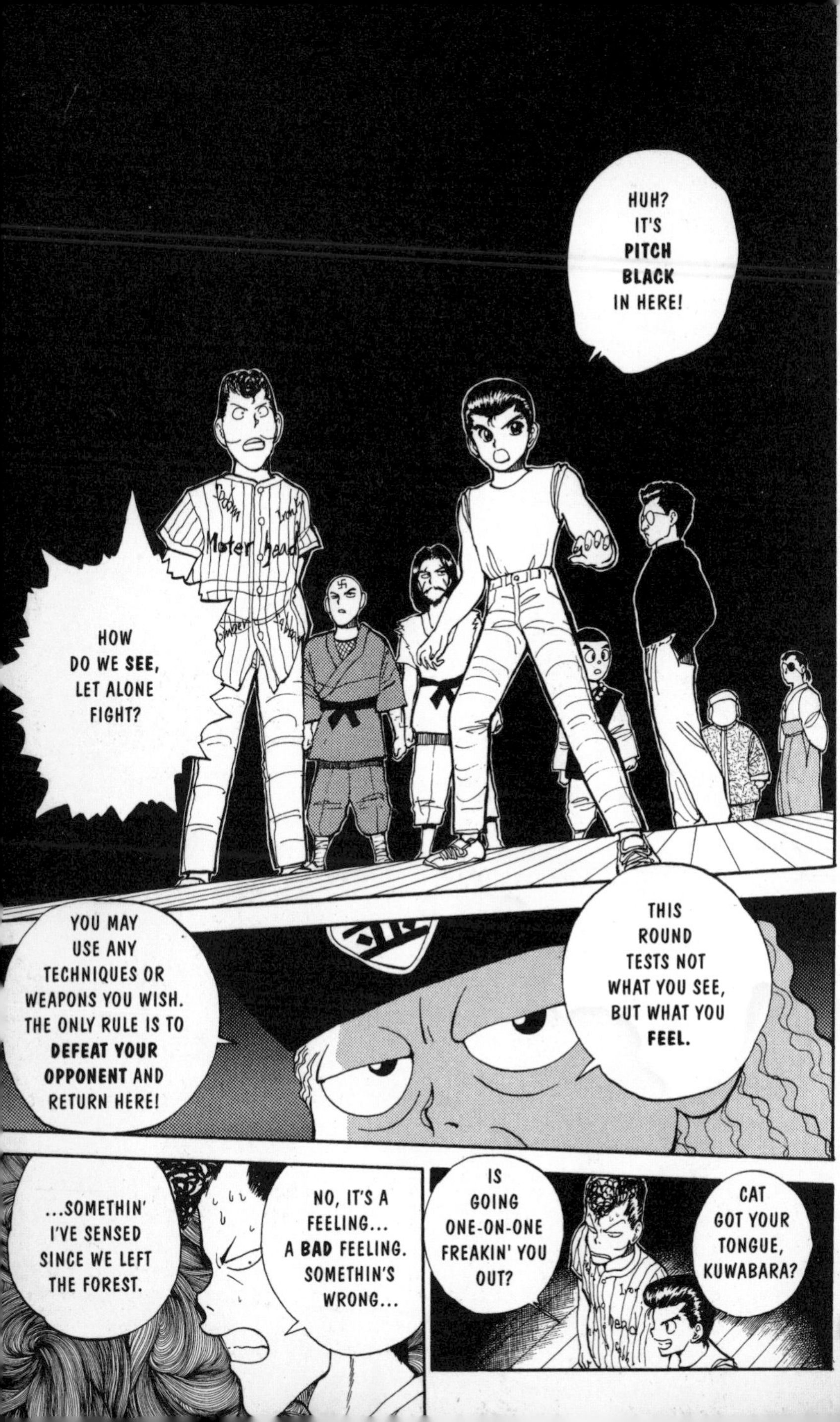
HUH? IT'S PITCH BLACK IN HERE!
HOW DO WE SEE, LET ALONE FIGHT?
THIS ROUND TESTS NOT WHAT YOU SEE, BUT WHAT YOU FEEL.
YOU MAY USE ANY TECHNIQUES OR WEAPONS YOU WISH. THE ONLY RULE IS TO DEFEAT YOUR OPPONENT AND RETURN HERE!
CAT GOT YOUR TONGUE, KUWABARA?
IS GOING ONE-ON-ONE FREAKIN' YOU OUT?
NO, IT'S A FEELING... A BAD FEELING. SOMETHIN'S WRONG...
...SOMETHIN' I'VE SENSED SINCE WE LEFT THE FOREST.

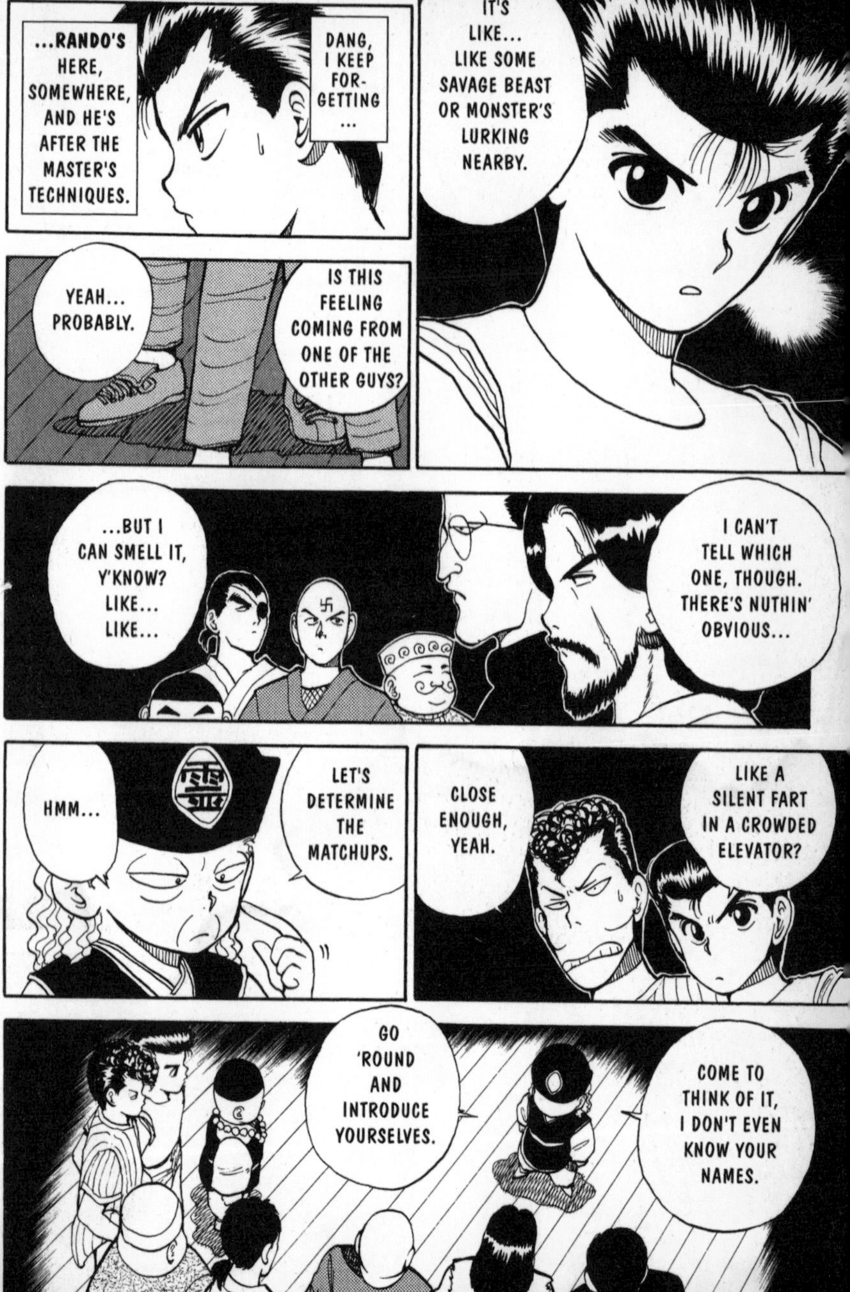
IT'S LIKE... LIKE SOME SAVAGE BEAST OR MONSTER'S LURKING NEARBY.
DANG, I KEEP FOR-GETTING ...
...RANDO'S HERE, SOMEWHERE, AND HE'S AFTER THE MASTER'S TECHNIQUES.
IS THIS FEELING COMING FROM ONE OF THE OTHER GUYS?
YEAH... PROBABLY.
I CAN'T TELL WHICH ONE, THOUGH. THERE'S NUTHIN' OBVIOUS...
...BUT I CAN SMELL IT, Y'KNOW? LIKE... LIKE...
LIKE A SILENT FART IN A CROWDED ELEVATOR?
CLOSE ENOUGH, YEAH.
LET'S DETERMINE THE MATCHUPS.
HMM...
COME TO THINK OF IT, I DON'T EVEN KNOW YOUR NAMES.
GO 'ROUND AND INTRODUCE YOURSELVES.

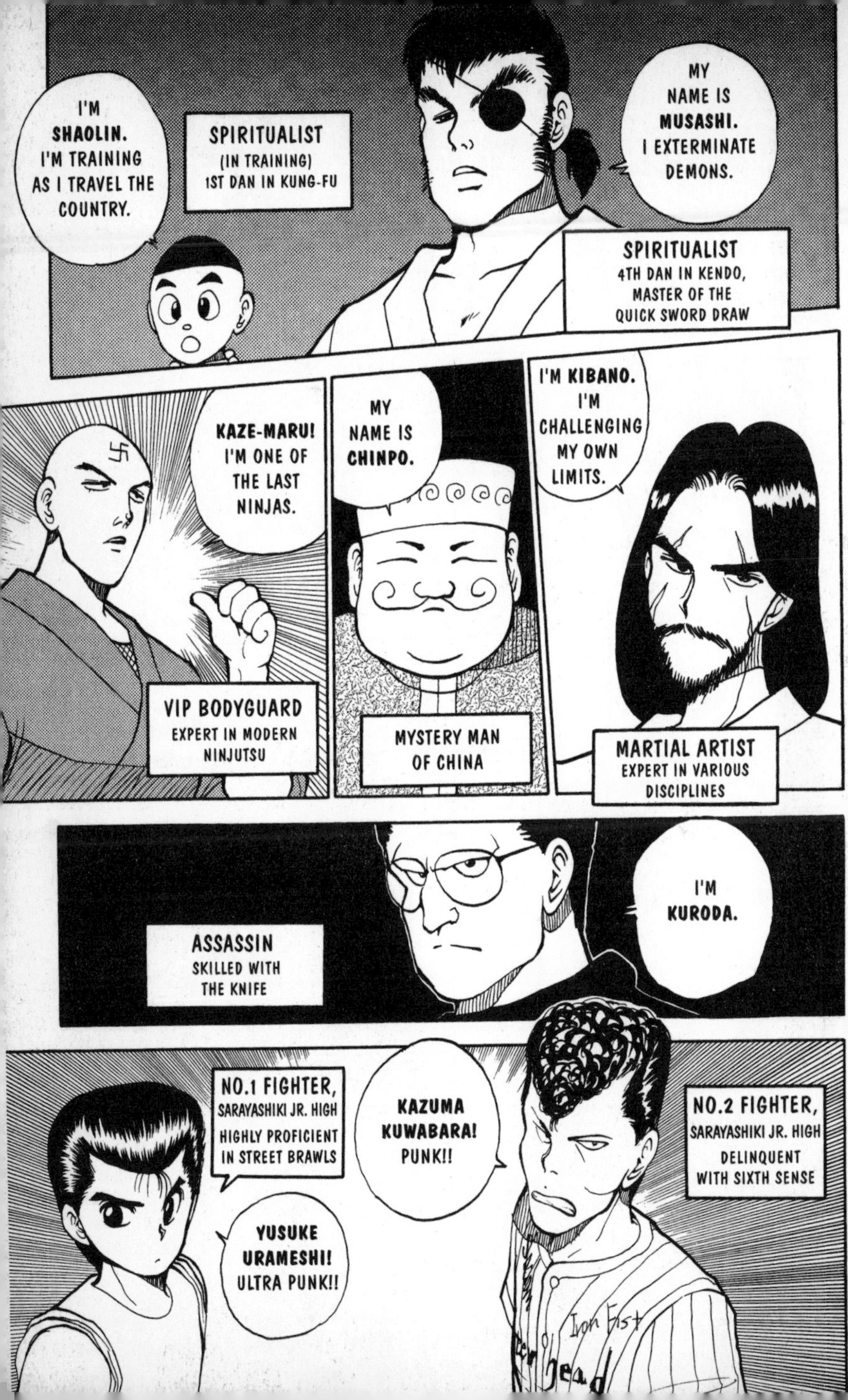
MY NAME IS MUSASHI. I EXTERMINATE DEMONS.
SPIRITUALIST 4TH DAN IN KENDO, MASTER OF THE QUICK SWORD DRAW
SPIRITUALIST (IN TRAINING) 1ST DAN IN KUNG-FU
I'M SHAOLIN. I'M TRAINING AS I TRAVEL THE COUNTRY.
I'M KIBANO. I'M CHALLENGING MY OWN LIMITS.
MARTIAL ARTIST EXPERT IN VARIOUS DISCIPLINES
MY NAME IS CHINPO.
MYSTERY MAN OF CHINA
KAZE-MARU! I'M ONE OF THE LAST NINJAS.
VIP BODYGUARD EXPERT IN MODERN NINJUTSU
I'M KURODA.
ASSASSIN SKILLED WITH THE KNIFE
NO.2 FIGHTER, SARAYASHIKI JR. HIGH DELINQUENT WITH SIXTH SENSE
KAZUMA KUWABARA! PUNK!!
Iron Fist
NO.1 FIGHTER, SARAYASHIKI JR. HIGH HIGHLY PROFICIENT IN STREET BRAWLS
YUSUKE URAMESHI! ULTRA PUNK!!

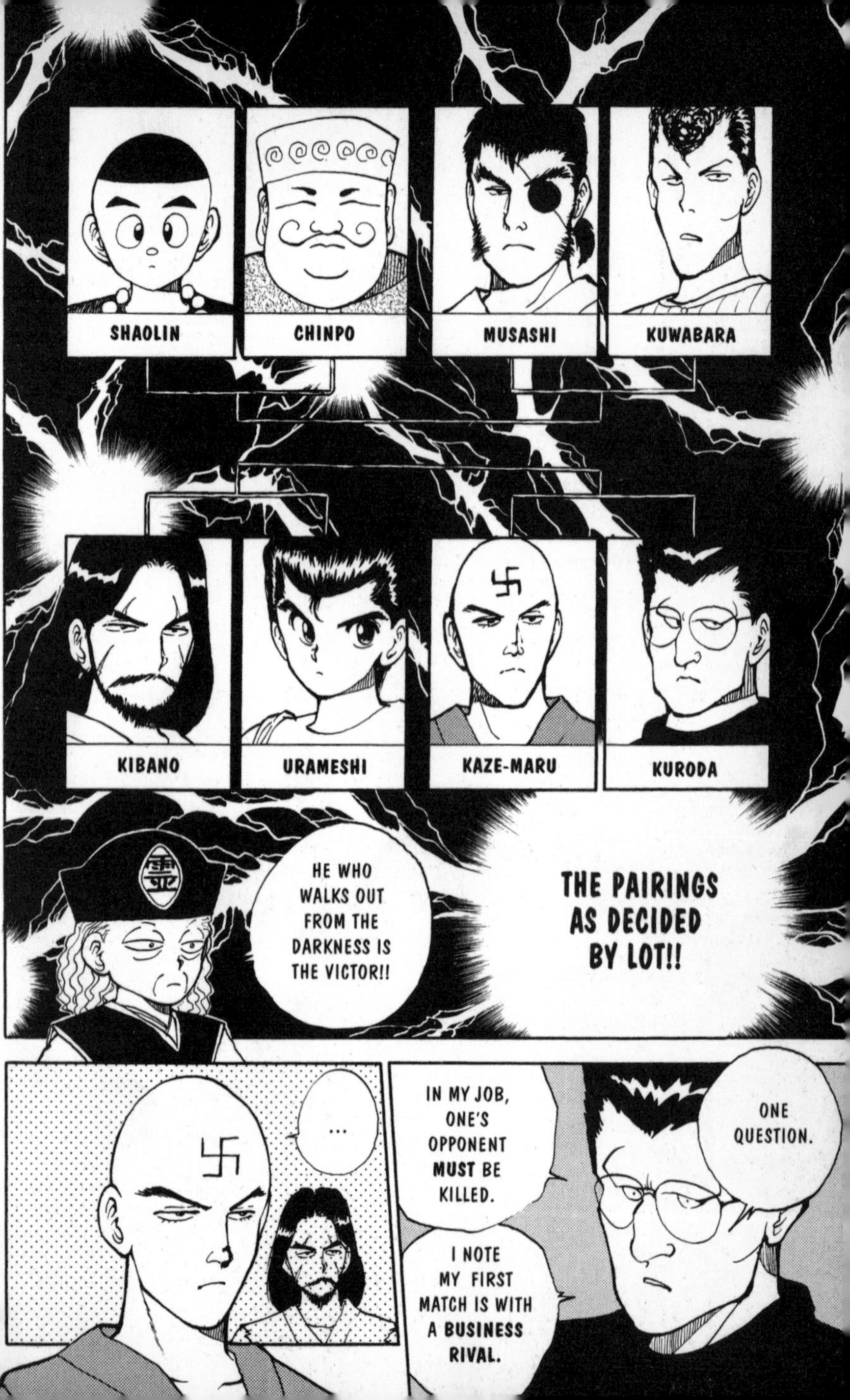
SHAOLIN
CHINPO
MUSASHI
KUWABARA
KIBANO
URAMESHI
KAZE-MARU
KURODA
THE PAIRINGS AS DECIDED BY LOT!!
HE WHO WALKS OUT FROM THE DARKNESS IS THE VICTOR!!
ONE QUESTION.
IN MY JOB, ONE'S OPPONENT MUST BE KILLED.
I NOTE MY FIRST MATCH IS WITH A BUSINESS RIVAL.
...

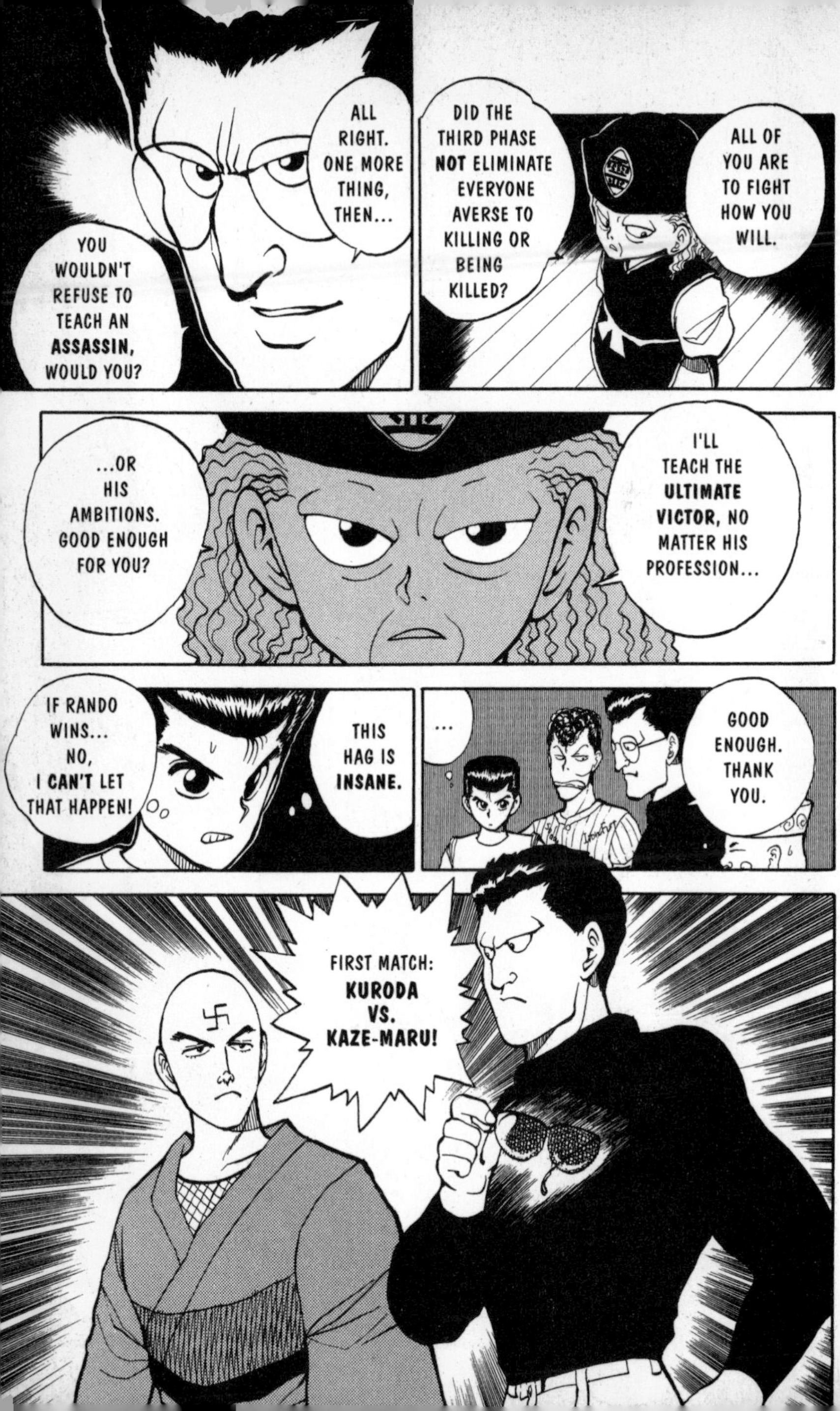
ALL OF YOU ARE TO FIGHT HOW YOU WILL.
DID THE THIRD PHASE **NOT** ELIMINATE EVERYONE AVERSE TO KILLING OR BEING KILLED?
ALL RIGHT. ONE MORE THING, THEN...
YOU WOULDN'T REFUSE TO TEACH AN **ASSASSIN,** WOULD YOU?
I'LL TEACH THE **ULTIMATE VICTOR,** NO MATTER HIS PROFESSION...
...OR HIS AMBITIONS. GOOD ENOUGH FOR YOU?
GOOD ENOUGH. THANK YOU.
...
THIS HAG IS **INSANE.**
IF RANDO WINS... NO, I **CAN'T** LET THAT HAPPEN!
FIRST MATCH: **KURODA VS. KAZE-MARU!**

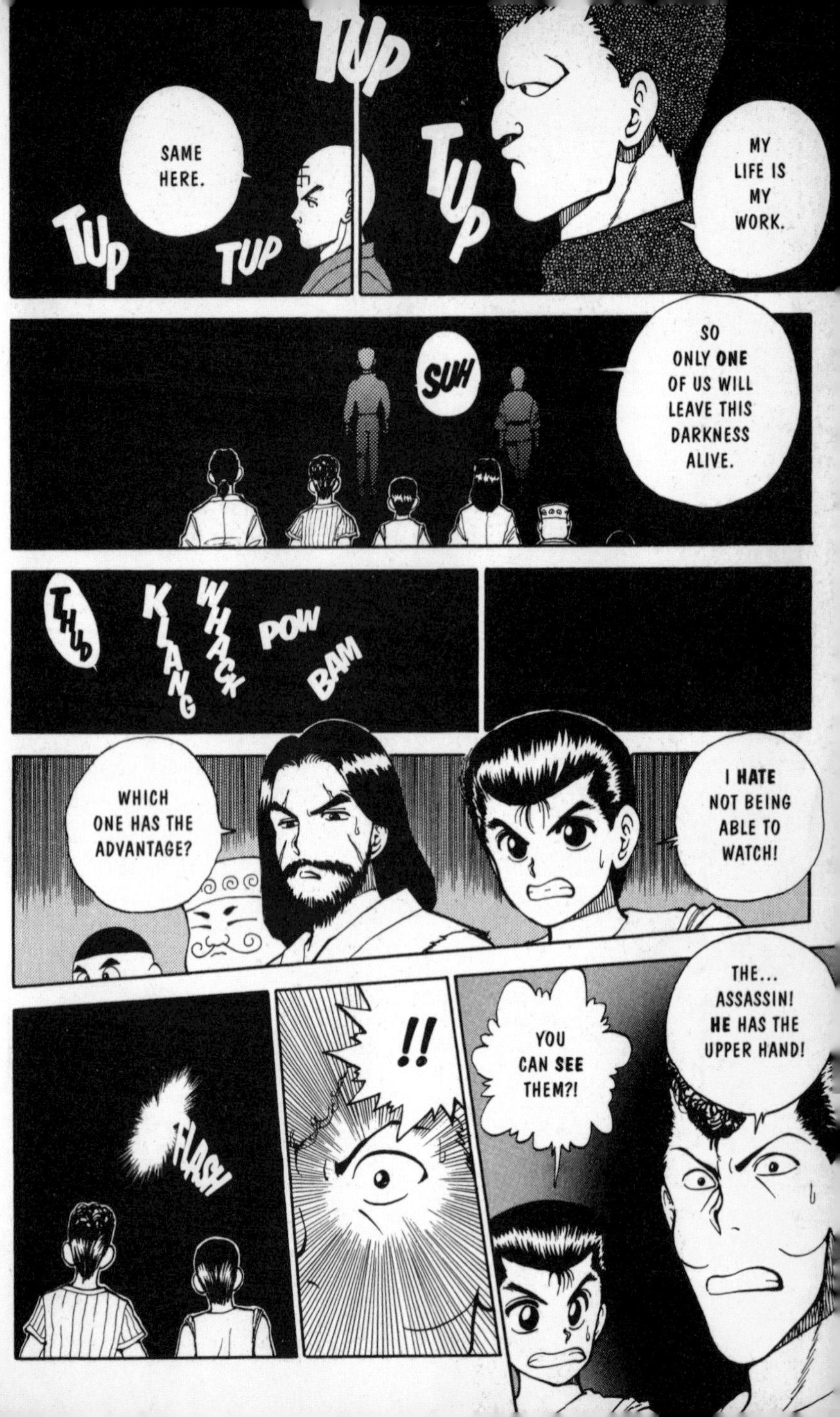
TUP
TUP
MY LIFE IS MY WORK.
SAME HERE.
TUP
TUP
SO ONLY ONE OF US WILL LEAVE THIS DARKNESS ALIVE.
SUH
THUD
KLANG
WHACK
POW
BAM
I HATE NOT BEING ABLE TO WATCH!
WHICH ONE HAS THE ADVANTAGE?
THE... ASSASSIN! HE HAS THE UPPER HAND!
YOU CAN SEE THEM?!
!!
FLASH

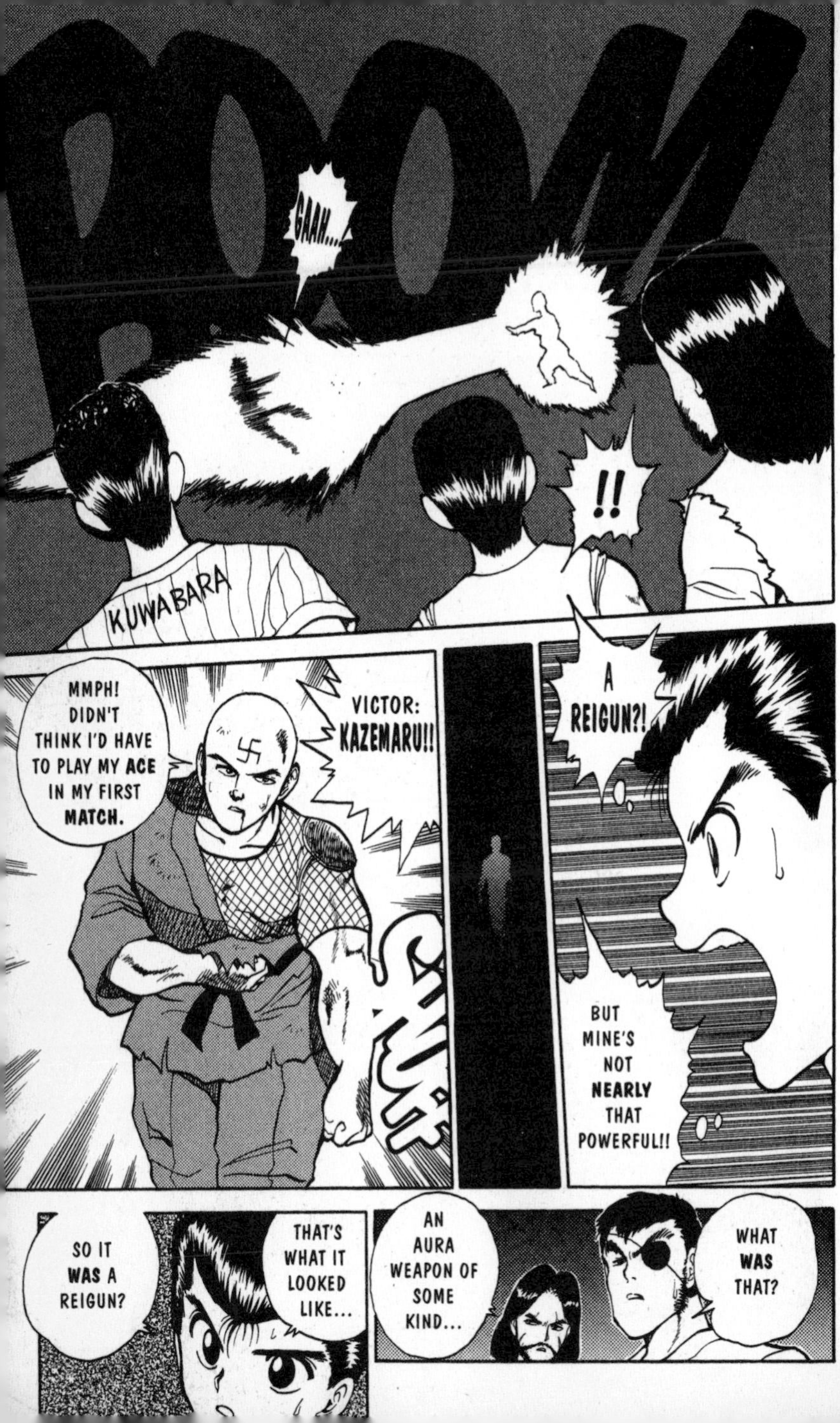
BOOM
GAAH...
!!
KUWABARA
A REIGUN?!
BUT MINE'S NOT NEARLY THAT POWERFUL!!
VICTOR: KAZEMARU!!
MMPH! DIDN'T THINK I'D HAVE TO PLAY MY ACE IN MY FIRST MATCH.
WHAT WAS THAT?
AN AURA WEAPON OF SOME KIND...
THAT'S WHAT IT LOOKED LIKE...
SO IT WAS A REIGUN?

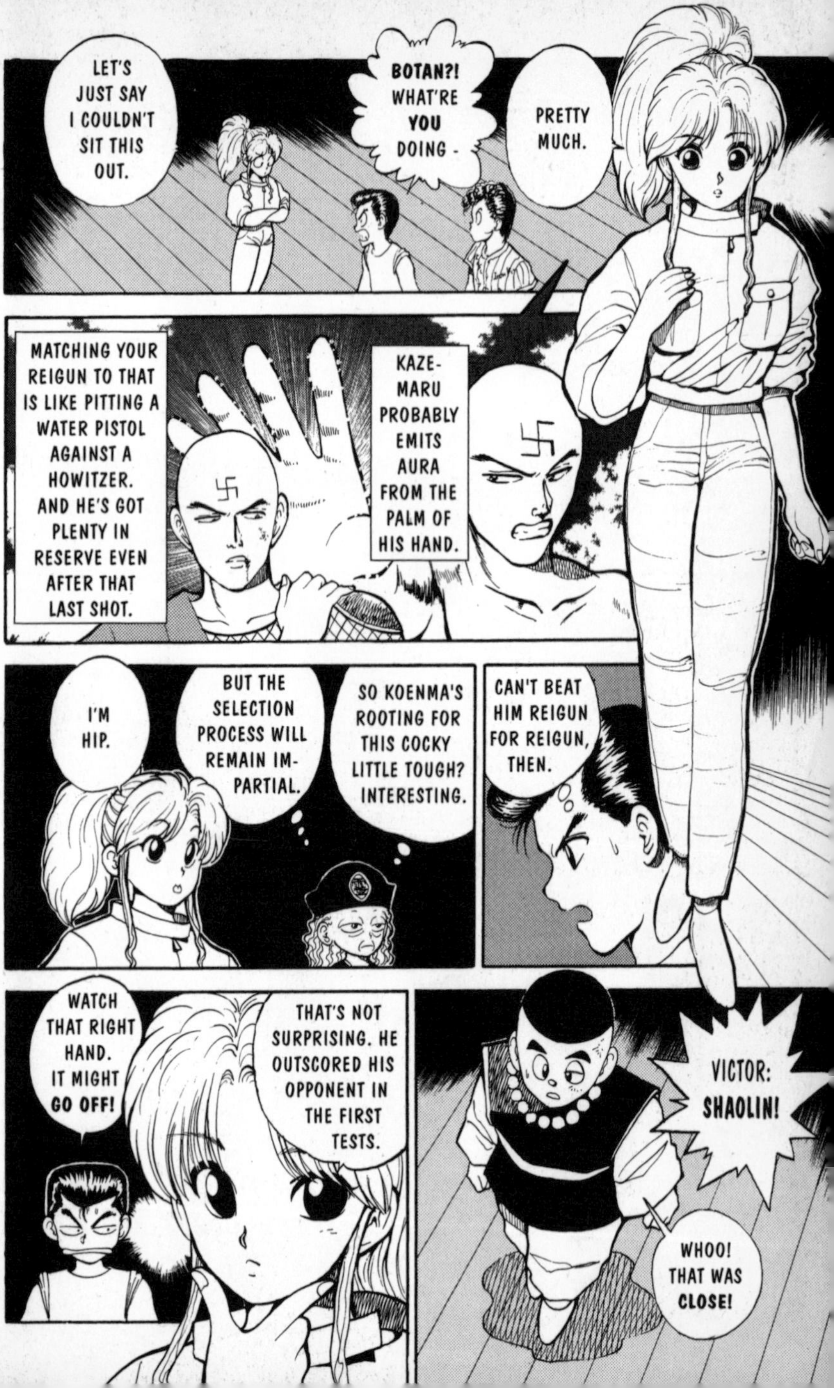
PRETTY MUCH.
BOTAN?! WHAT'RE YOU DOING -
LET'S JUST SAY I COULDN'T SIT THIS OUT.
KAZE-MARU PROBABLY EMITS AURA FROM THE PALM OF HIS HAND.
MATCHING YOUR REIGUN TO THAT IS LIKE PITTING A WATER PISTOL AGAINST A HOWITZER. AND HE'S GOT PLENTY IN RESERVE EVEN AFTER THAT LAST SHOT.
CAN'T BEAT HIM REIGUN FOR REIGUN, THEN.
SO KOENMA'S ROOTING FOR THIS COCKY LITTLE TOUGH? INTERESTING.
BUT THE SELECTION PROCESS WILL REMAIN IM-PARTIAL.
I'M HIP.
VICTOR: SHAOLIN!
WHOO! THAT WAS CLOSE!
THAT'S NOT SURPRISING. HE OUTSCORED HIS OPPONENT IN THE FIRST TESTS.
WATCH THAT RIGHT HAND. IT MIGHT GO OFF!

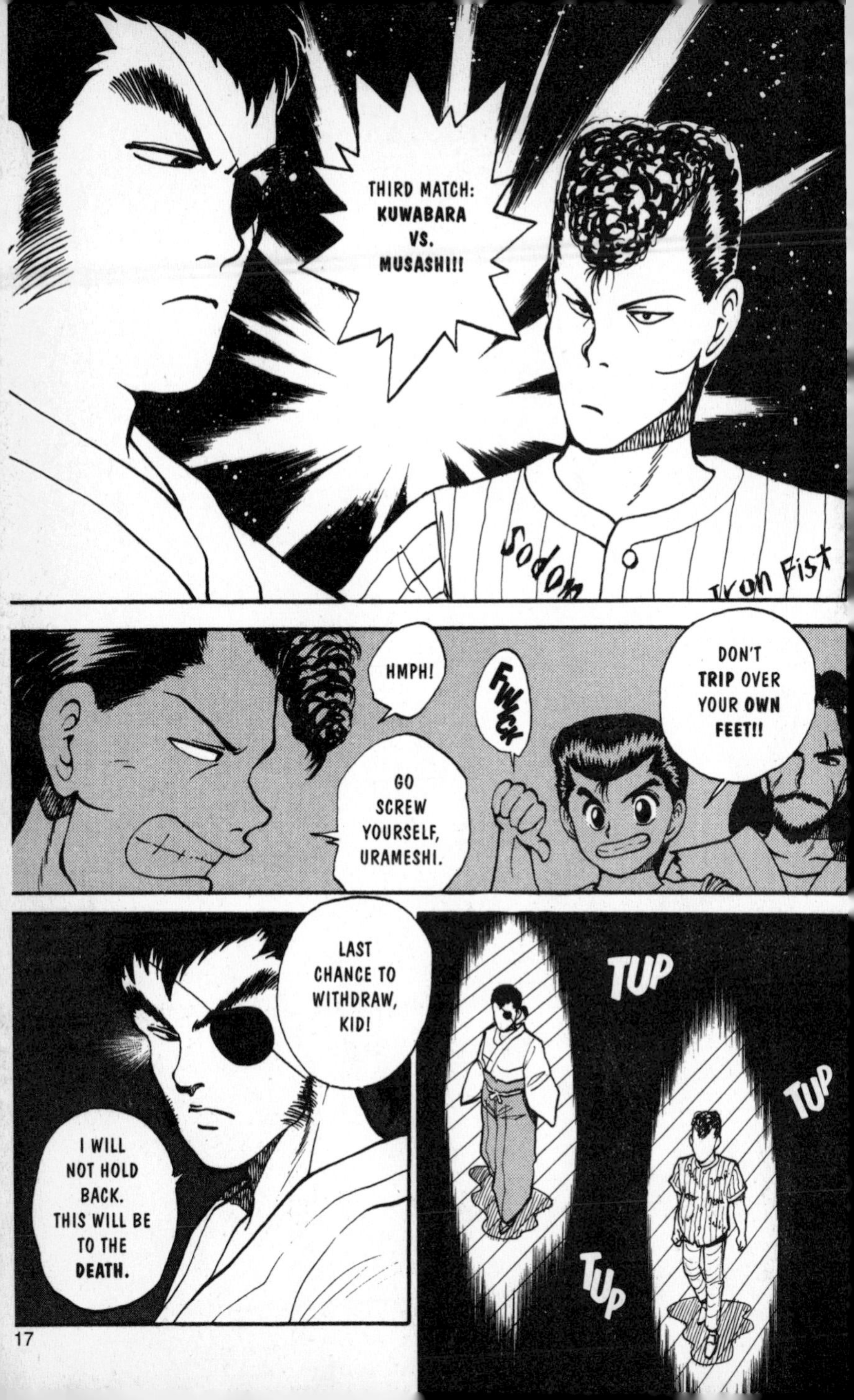
THIRD MATCH: KUWABARA VS. MUSASHI!!
Sodom
Iron Fist
DON'T TRIP OVER YOUR OWN FEET!!
FWACK
HMPH!
GO SCREW YOURSELF, URAMESHI.
TUP
TUP
TUP
LAST CHANCE TO WITHDRAW, KID!
I WILL NOT HOLD BACK. THIS WILL BE TO THE DEATH.

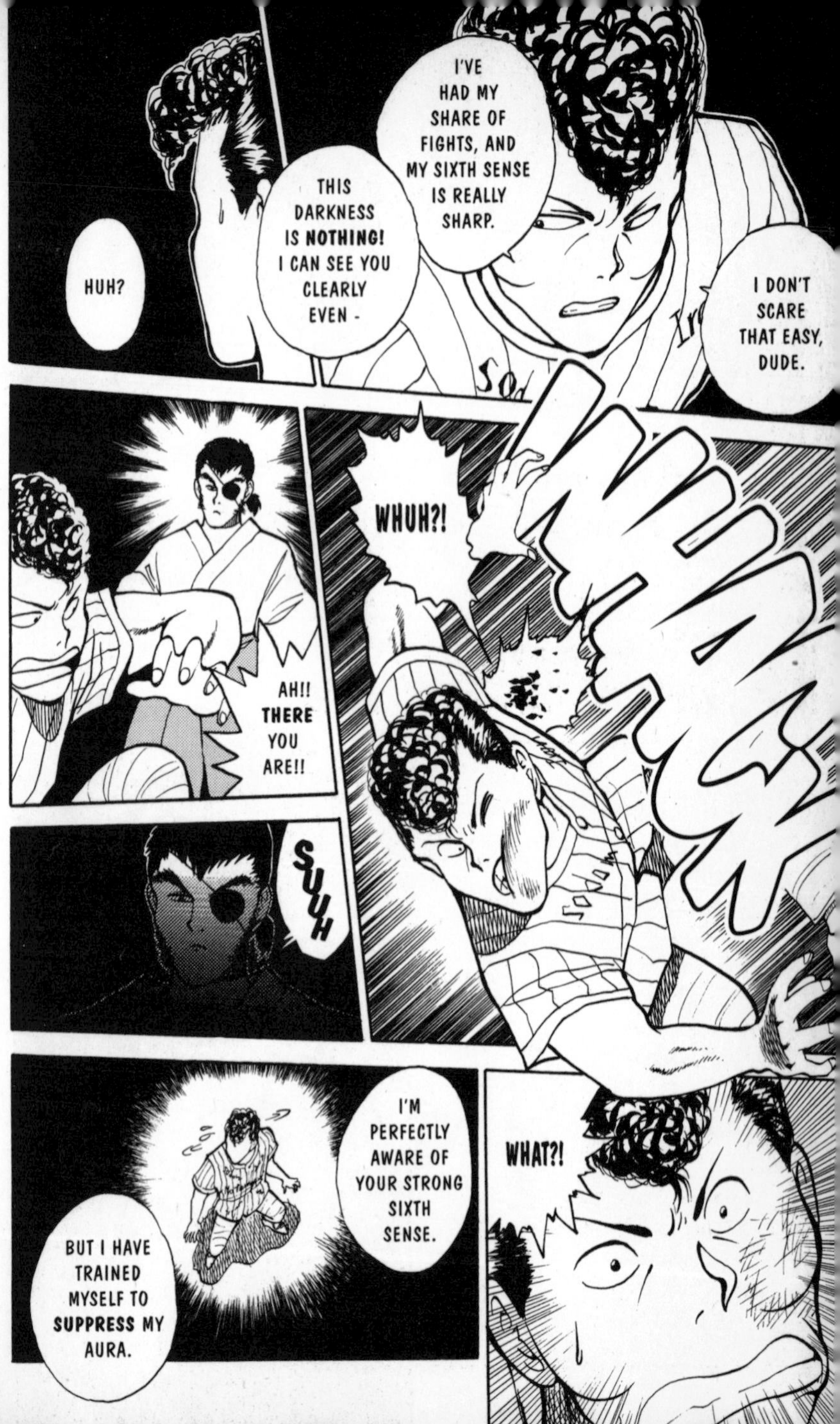
I DON'T SCARE THAT EASY, DUDE.
I'VE HAD MY SHARE OF FIGHTS, AND MY SIXTH SENSE IS REALLY SHARP.
THIS DARKNESS IS **NOTHING!** I CAN SEE YOU CLEARLY EVEN -
HUH?
WHUH?!
WHACK
AH!! **THERE** YOU ARE!!
SUUH
WHAT?!
I'M PERFECTLY AWARE OF YOUR STRONG SIXTH SENSE.
BUT I HAVE TRAINED MYSELF TO **SUPPRESS** MY AURA.

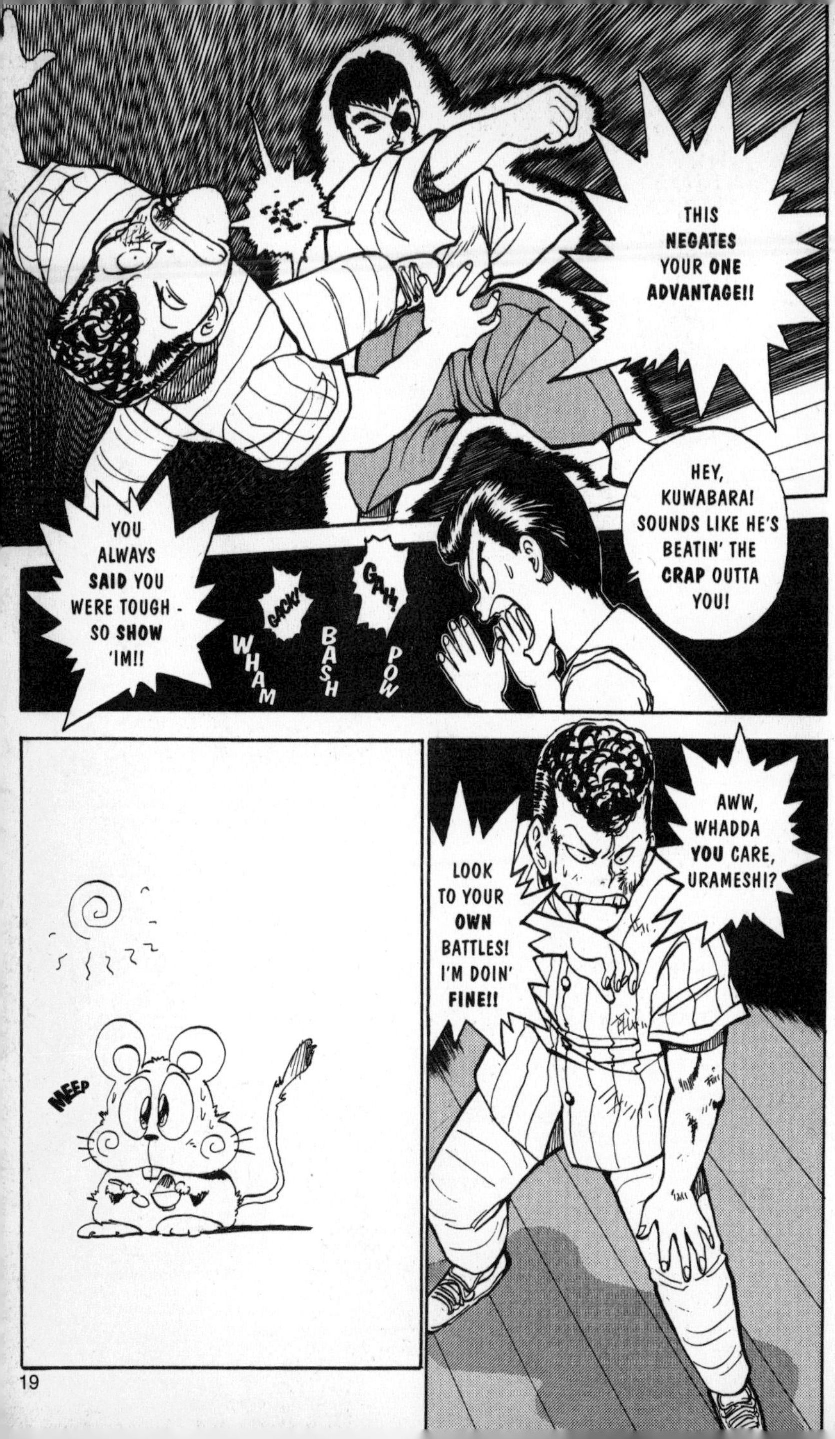

THIS NEGATES YOUR ONE ADVANTAGE!!
HEY, KUWABARA! SOUNDS LIKE HE'S BEATIN' THE CRAP OUTTA YOU!
POW
GPAH
BASH
GACK!
WHAM
YOU ALWAYS SAID YOU WERE TOUGH - SO SHOW 'IM!!
AWW, WHADDA YOU CARE, URAMESHI?
LOOK TO YOUR OWN BATTLES! I'M DOIN' FINE!!
MEEP

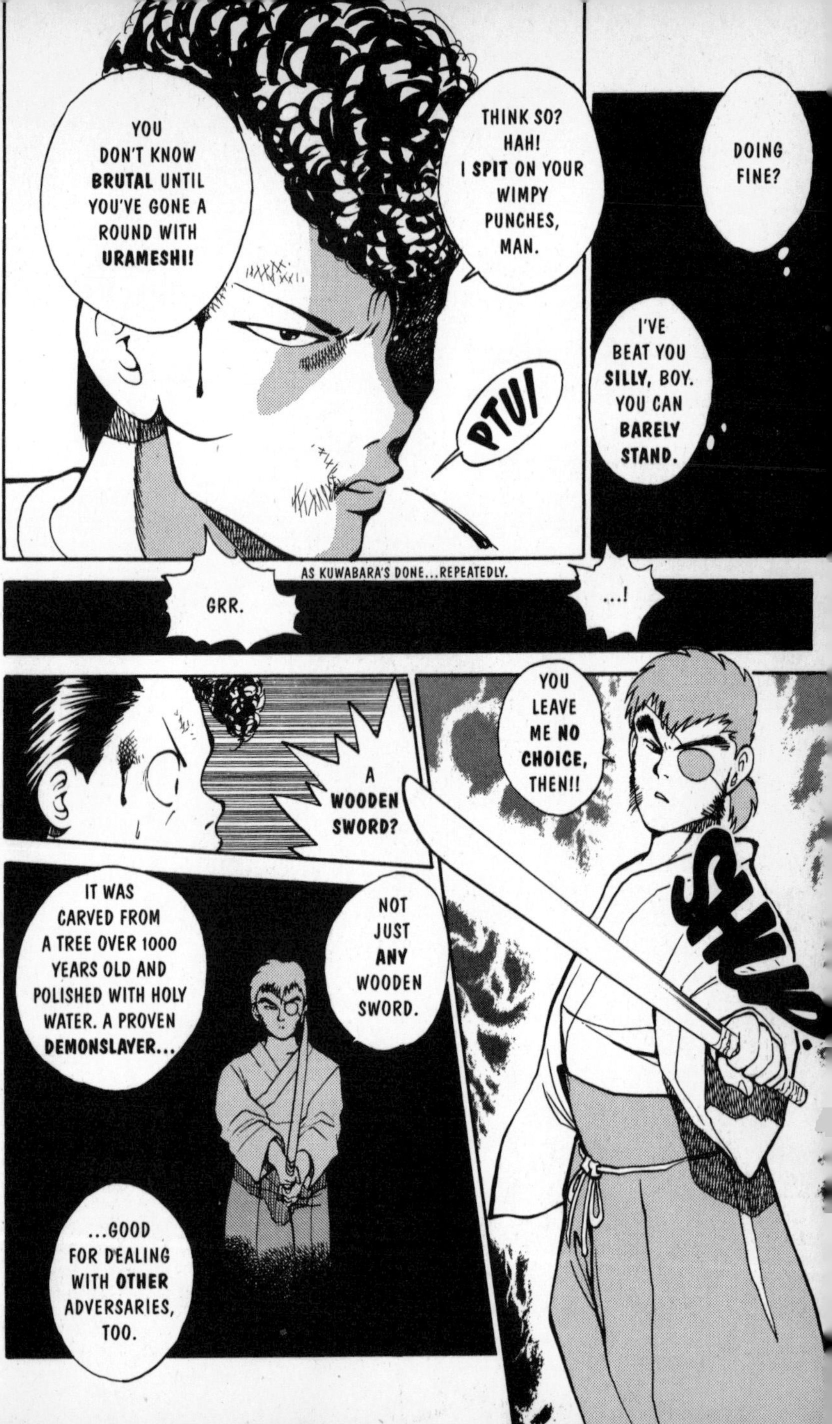
DOING FINE?
I'VE BEAT YOU SILLY, BOY. YOU CAN BARELY STAND.
THINK SO? HAH! I SPIT ON YOUR WIMPY PUNCHES, MAN.
PTUI
YOU DON'T KNOW BRUTAL UNTIL YOU'VE GONE A ROUND WITH URAMESHI!
...!
AS KUWABARA'S DONE...REPEATEDLY.
GRR.
YOU LEAVE ME NO CHOICE, THEN!!
A WOODEN SWORD?
NOT JUST ANY WOODEN SWORD.
IT WAS CARVED FROM A TREE OVER 1000 YEARS OLD AND POLISHED WITH HOLY WATER. A PROVEN DEMONSLAYER...
...GOOD FOR DEALING WITH OTHER ADVERSARIES, TOO.

READ THIS WAY

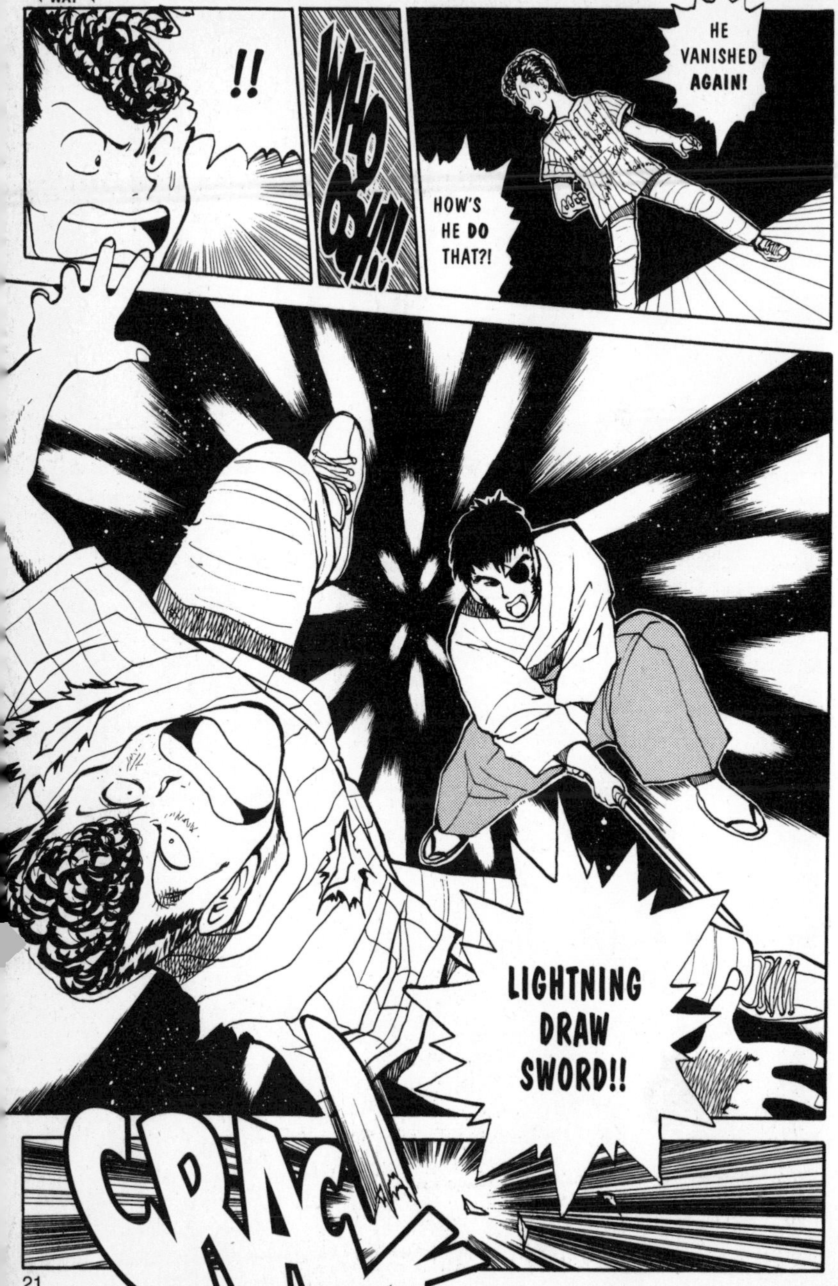
HE VANISHED AGAIN!
HOW'S HE DO THAT?!
WHOOSH!!
!!
LIGHTNING DRAW SWORD!!
CRACK

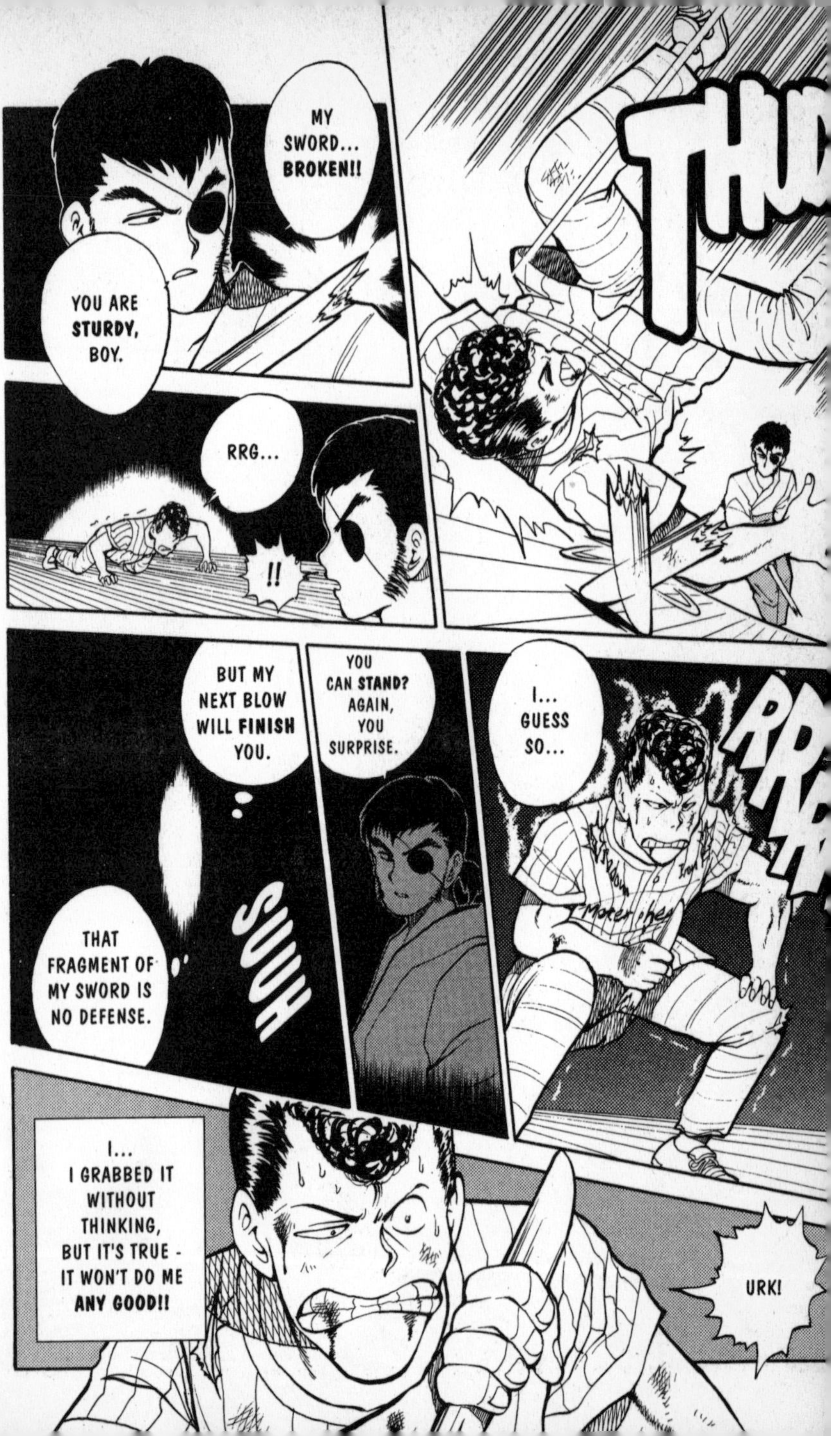

THU
MY SWORD... BROKEN!!
YOU ARE STURDY, BOY.
RRG...
!!
I... GUESS SO...
YOU CAN STAND? AGAIN, YOU SURPRISE.
SUUH
BUT MY NEXT BLOW WILL FINISH YOU.
THAT FRAGMENT OF MY SWORD IS NO DEFENSE.
URK!
I... I GRABBED IT WITHOUT THINKING, BUT IT'S TRUE - IT WON'T DO ME ANY GOOD!!

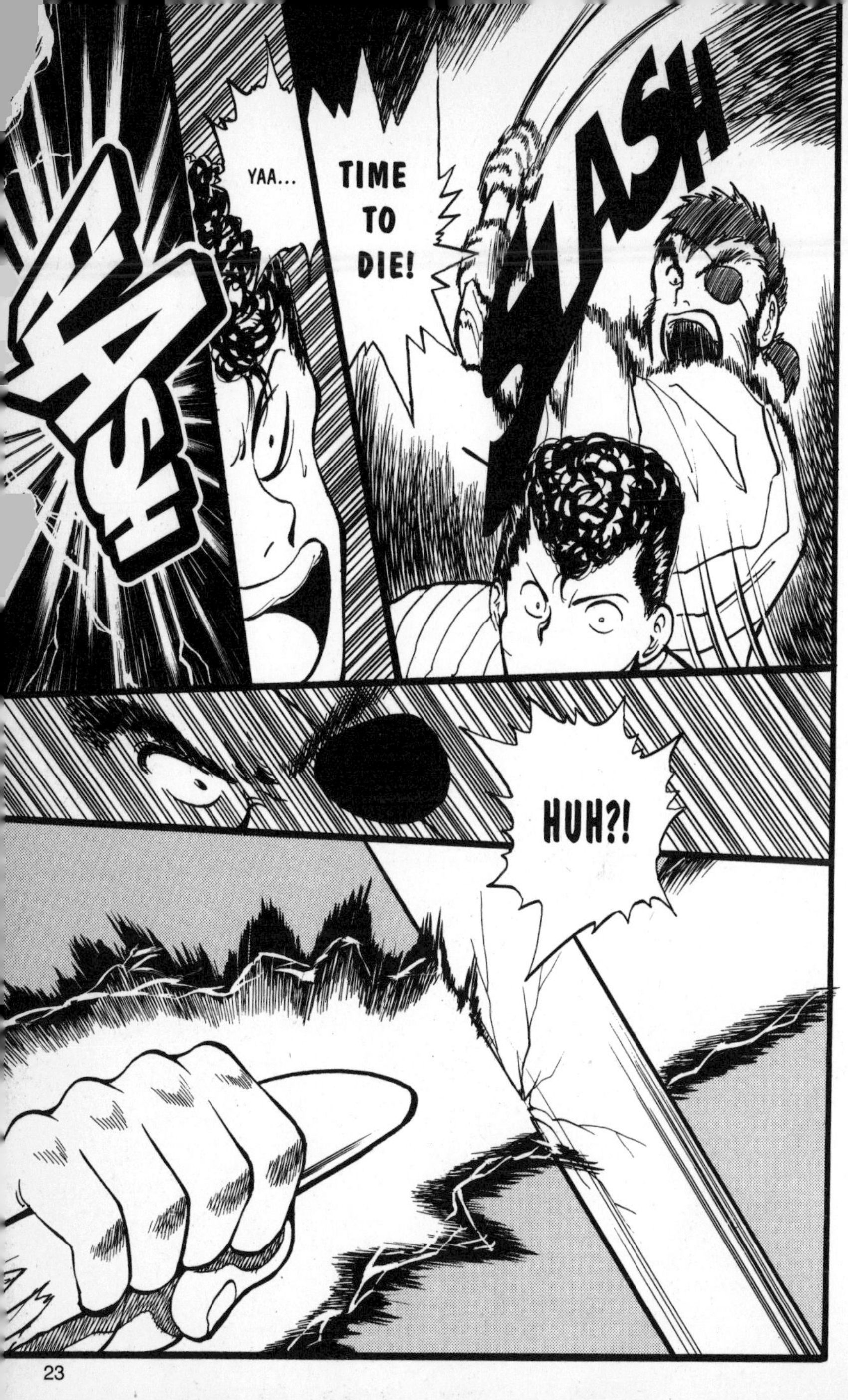
SLASH
TIME TO DIE!
YAA...
HUH?!

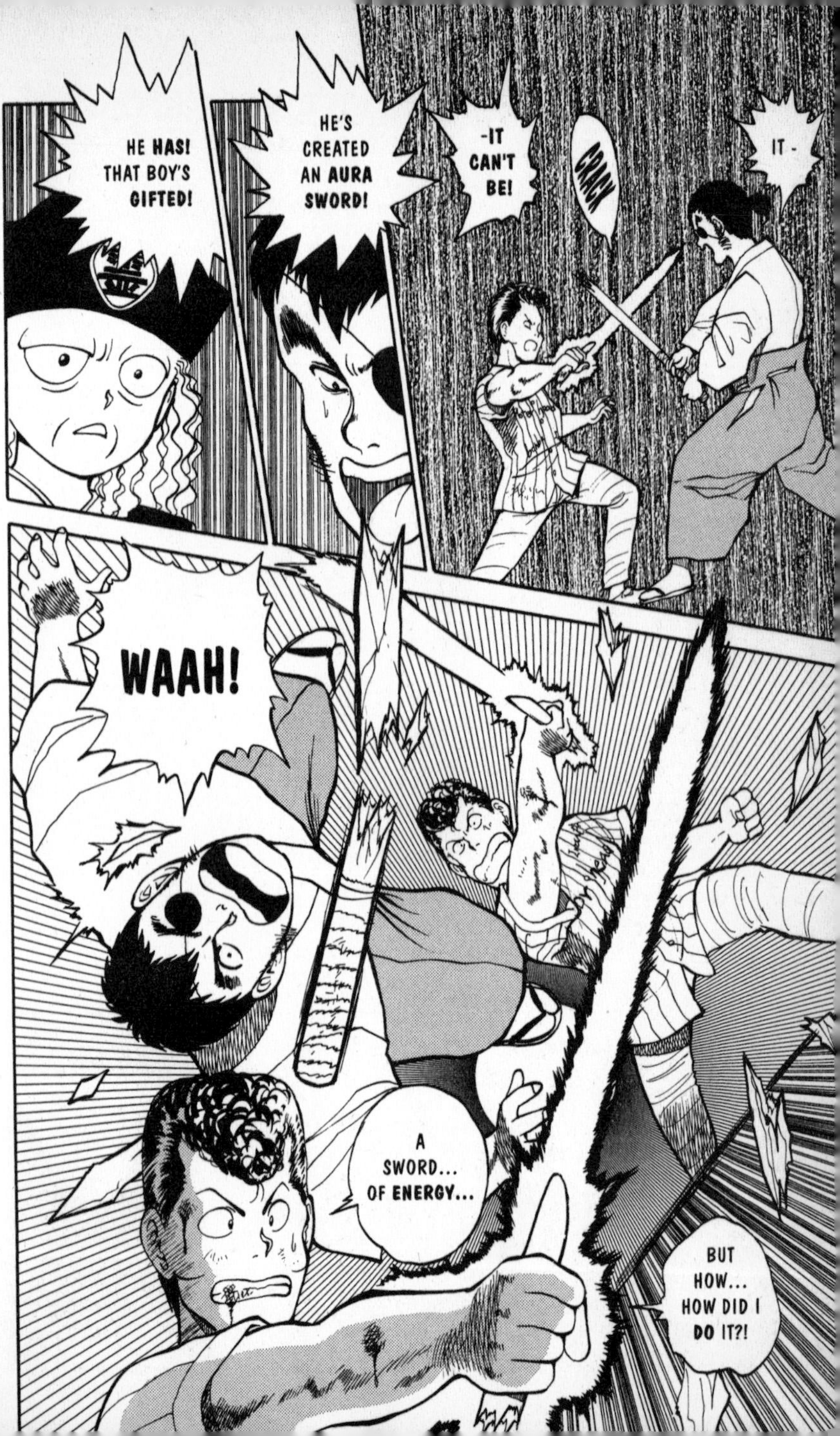
IT -
CRACK
-IT CAN'T BE!
HE'S CREATED AN AURA SWORD!
HE HAS! THAT BOY'S GIFTED!
WAAH!
A SWORD... OF ENERGY...
BUT HOW... HOW DID I DO IT?!

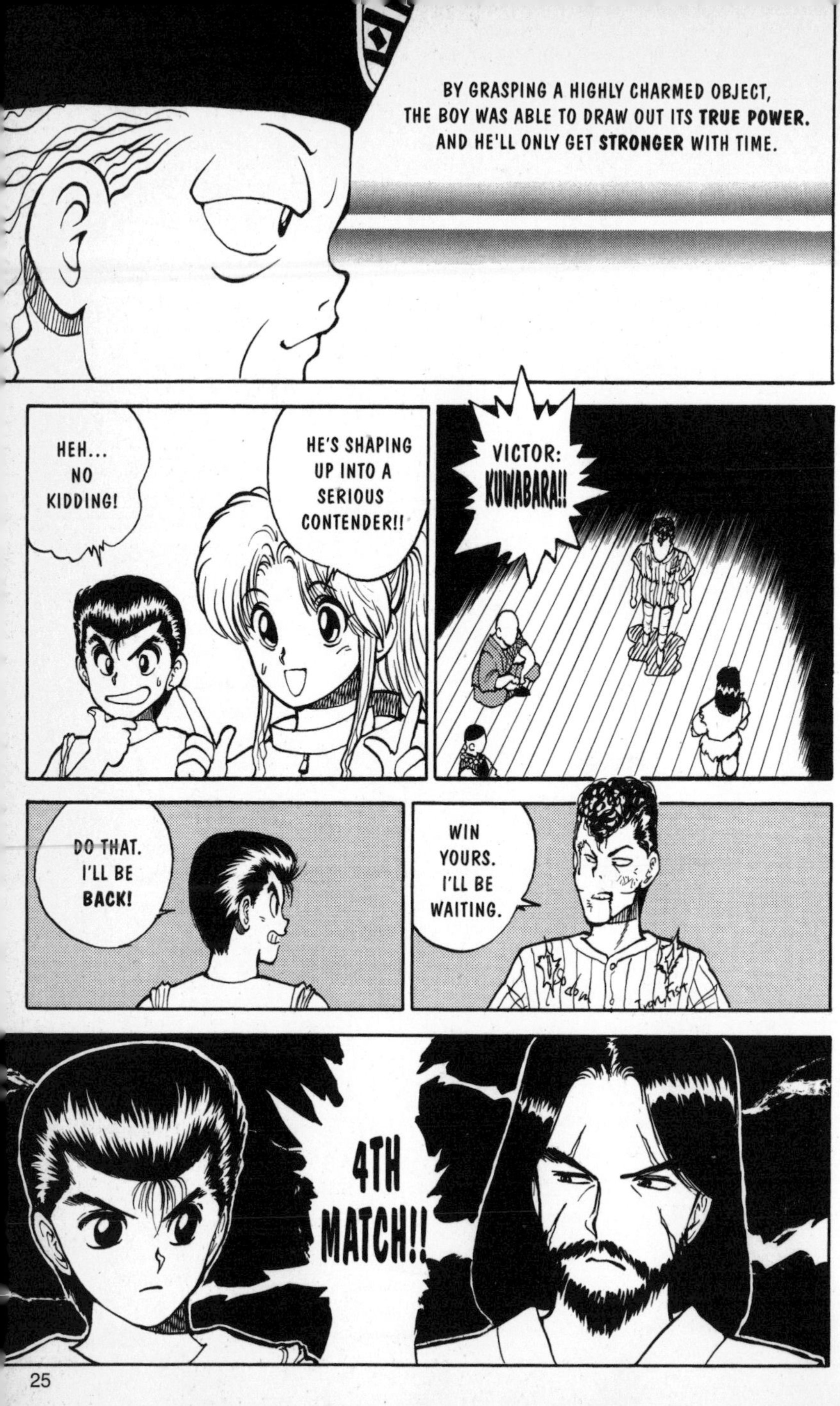
BY GRASPING A HIGHLY CHARMED OBJECT, THE BOY WAS ABLE TO DRAW OUT ITS TRUE POWER. AND HE'LL ONLY GET STRONGER WITH TIME.
VICTOR: KUWABARA!!
HE'S SHAPING UP INTO A SERIOUS CONTENDER!!
HEH... NO KIDDING!
WIN YOURS. I'LL BE WAITING.
DO THAT. I'LL BE BACK!
4TH MATCH!!

MY RAMBLING DIARY, PART 1

August '81

A Night I Freaked Out

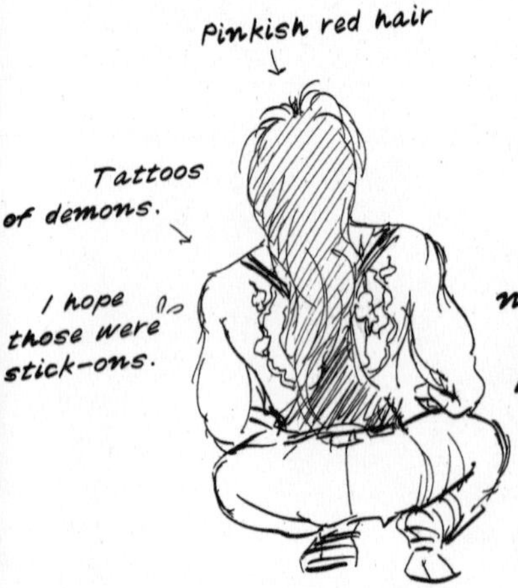
Pinkish red hair
Tattoos of demons.
I hope those were stick-ons.

I went to rent a video one night, and there was a real hard-core dude there. (It would've been scarier if he had been looking at teen idol concert videos.)

On my way back, at an intersection called Four Corners, a car beeped at another dude on a bicycle, who had run a red. This dude chased the car out to the middle of the intersection and started bashing its side. (A lot of cars were driving through, but he didn't care.)

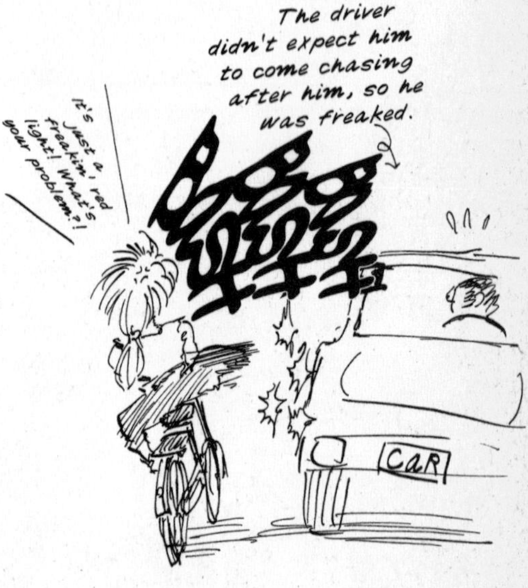
The driver didn't expect him to come chasing after him, so he was freaked.
It's just a freakin' red light! What's your problem?!
CAR

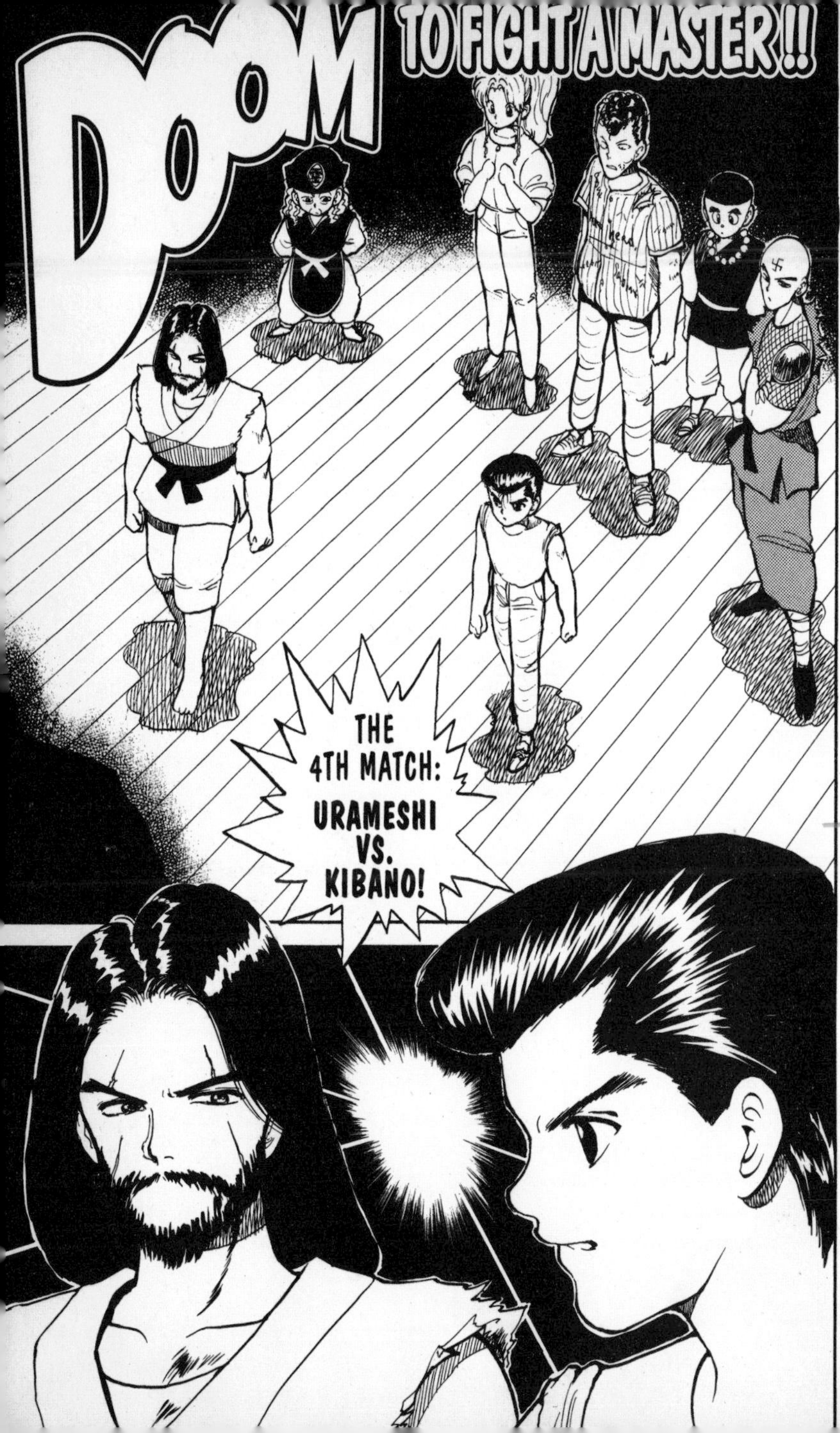
DOOM
TO FIGHT A MASTER!!
THE 4TH MATCH: URAMESHI VS. KIBANO!

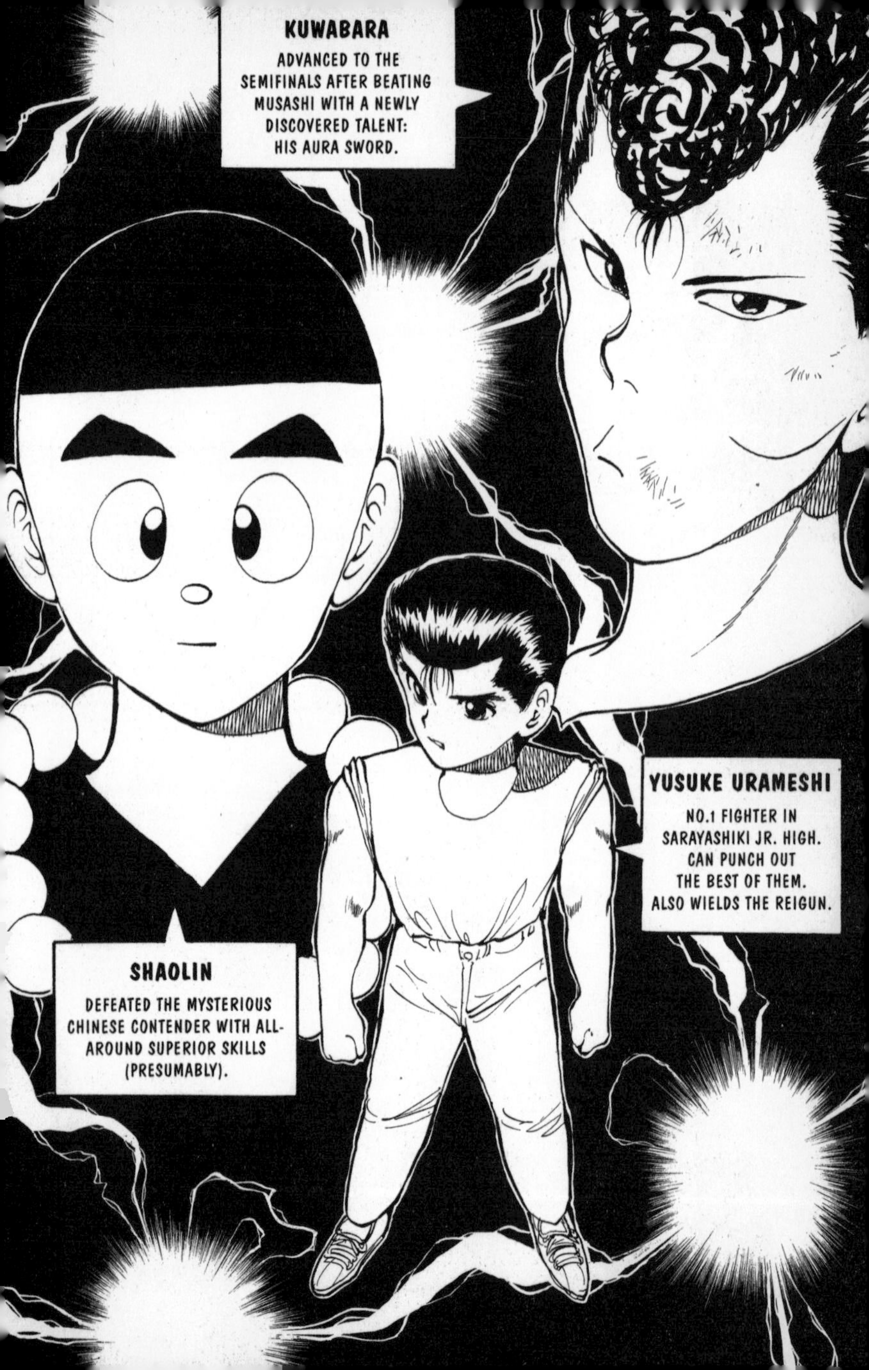
KUWABARA
ADVANCED TO THE SEMIFINALS AFTER BEATING MUSASHI WITH A NEWLY DISCOVERED TALENT: HIS AURA SWORD.
YUSUKE URAMESHI
NO.1 FIGHTER IN SARAYASHIKI JR. HIGH. CAN PUNCH OUT THE BEST OF THEM. ALSO WIELDS THE REIGUN.
SHAOLIN
DEFEATED THE MYSTERIOUS CHINESE CONTENDER WITH ALL-AROUND SUPERIOR SKILLS (PRESUMABLY).

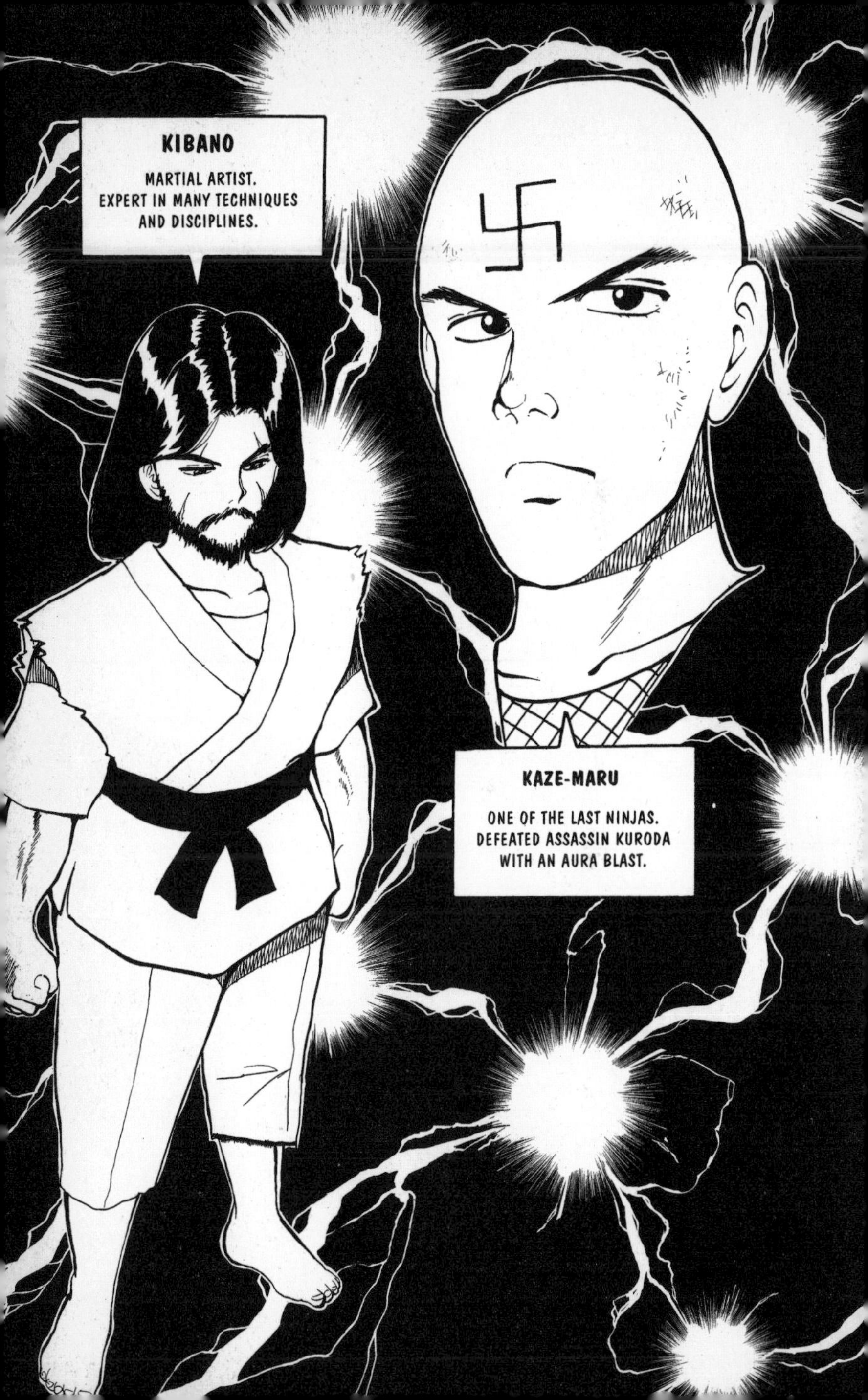
KIBANO
MARTIAL ARTIST. EXPERT IN MANY TECHNIQUES AND DISCIPLINES.
KAZE-MARU
ONE OF THE LAST NINJAS. DEFEATED ASSASSIN KURODA WITH AN AURA BLAST.

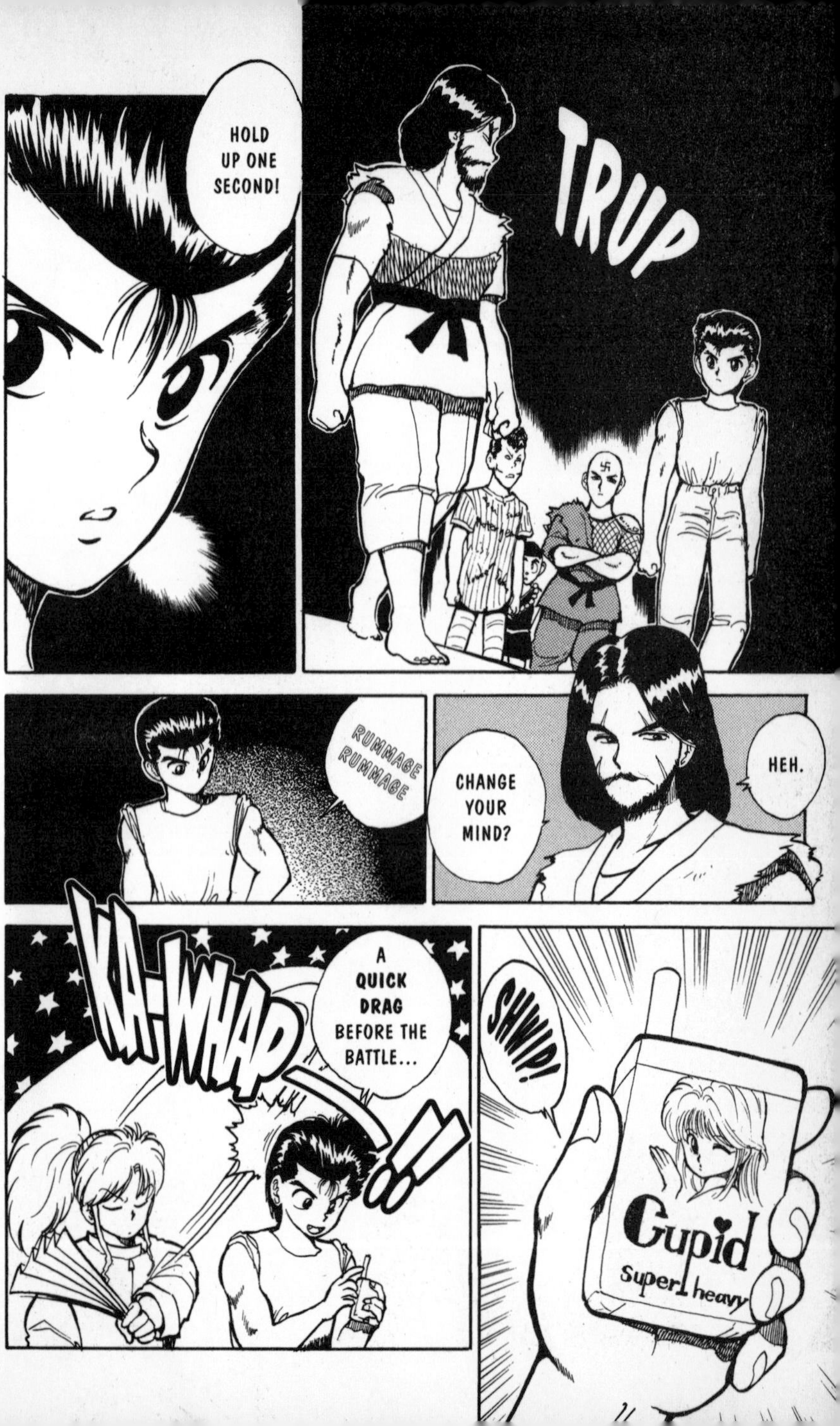
TRUP
HOLD UP ONE SECOND!
HEH.
CHANGE YOUR MIND?
RUMMAGE RUMMAGE
SHWIP!
Cupid Super heavy
A QUICK DRAG BEFORE THE BATTLE...
KA-WHAP

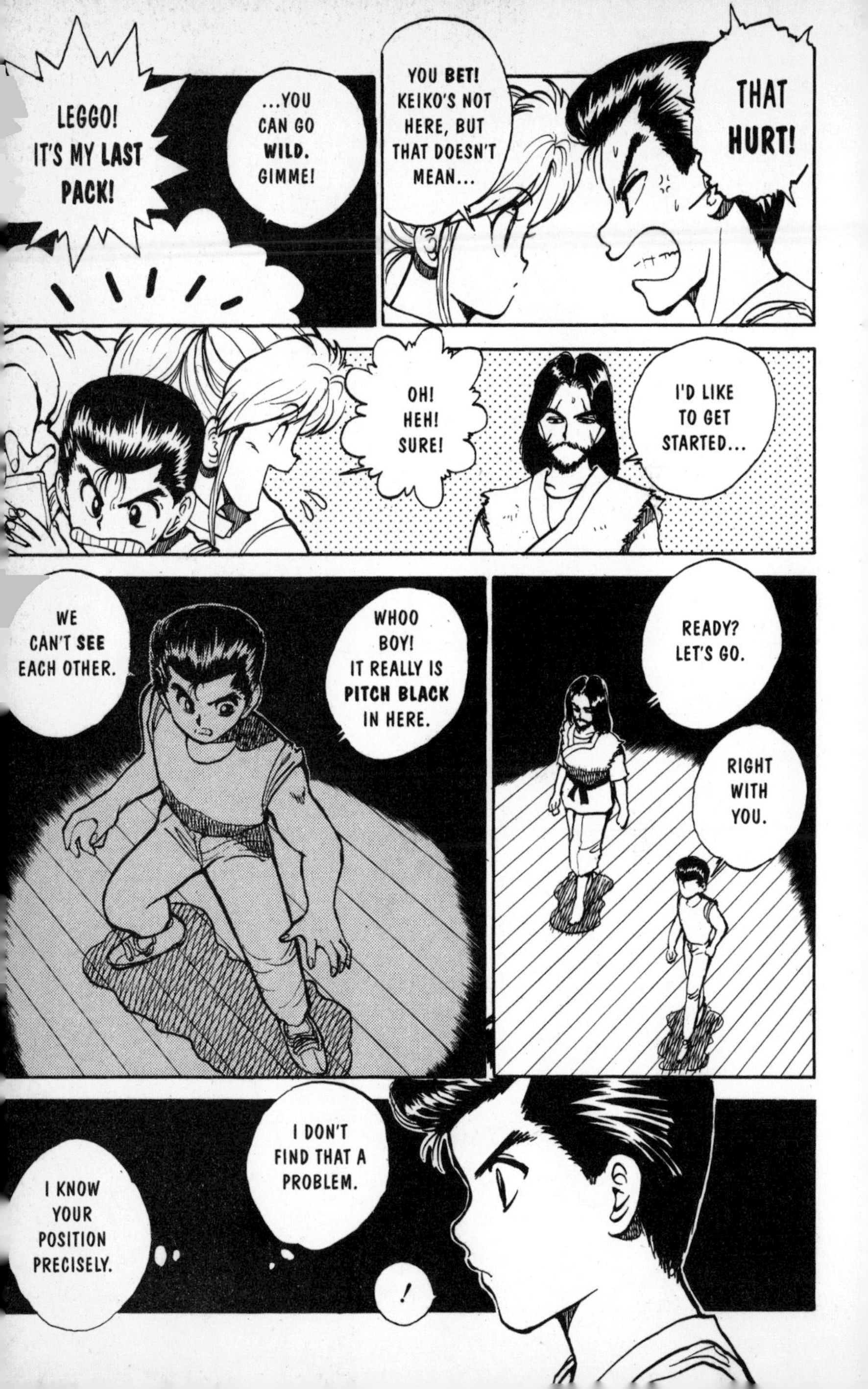
THAT HURT!
YOU BET! KEIKO'S NOT HERE, BUT THAT DOESN'T MEAN...
...YOU CAN GO WILD. GIMME!
LEGGO! IT'S MY LAST PACK!
I'D LIKE TO GET STARTED...
OH! HEH! SURE!
READY? LET'S GO.
RIGHT WITH YOU.
WHOO BOY! IT REALLY IS PITCH BLACK IN HERE.
WE CAN'T SEE EACH OTHER.
!
I DON'T FIND THAT A PROBLEM.
I KNOW YOUR POSITION PRECISELY.

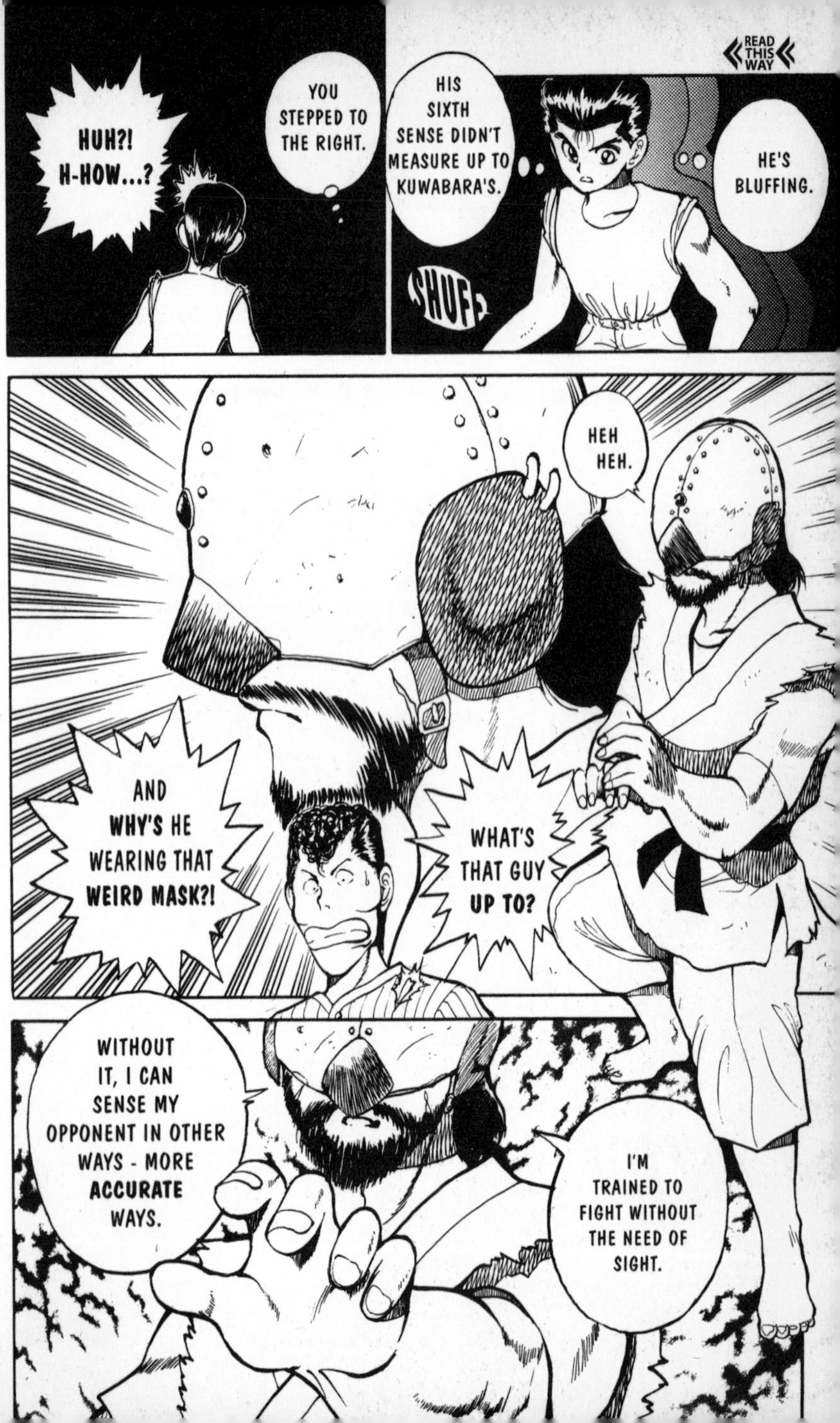
READ THIS WAY
HE'S BLUFFING.
HIS SIXTH SENSE DIDN'T MEASURE UP TO KUWABARA'S.
SHUF
YOU STEPPED TO THE RIGHT.
HUH?! H-HOW...?
HEH HEH.
WHAT'S THAT GUY UP TO?
AND WHY'S HE WEARING THAT WEIRD MASK?!
I'M TRAINED TO FIGHT WITHOUT THE NEED OF SIGHT.
WITHOUT IT, I CAN SENSE MY OPPONENT IN OTHER WAYS - MORE ACCURATE WAYS.

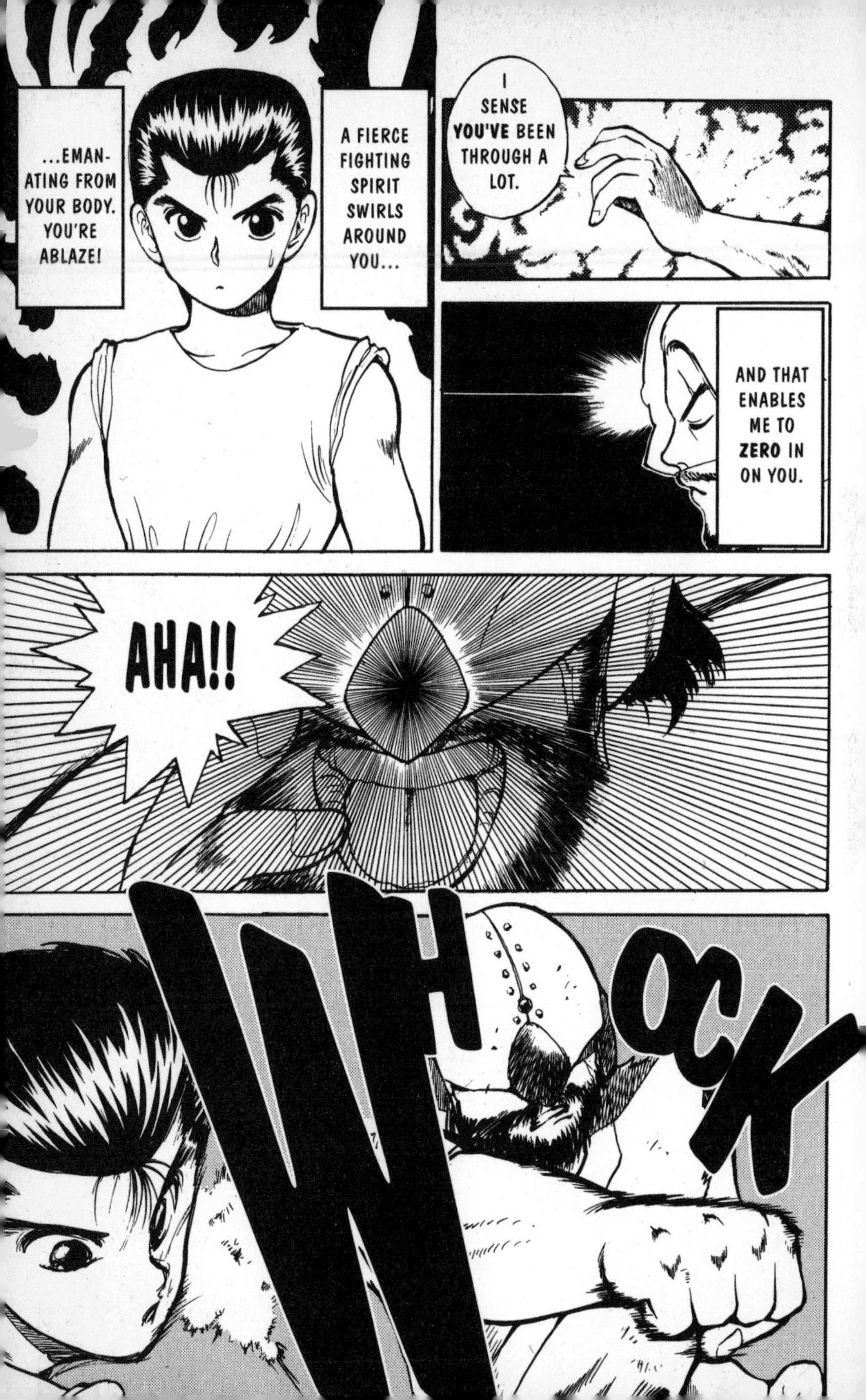

I SENSE YOU'VE BEEN THROUGH A LOT.
AND THAT ENABLES ME TO ZERO IN ON YOU.
A FIERCE FIGHTING SPIRIT SWIRLS AROUND YOU...
...EMAN-ATING FROM YOUR BODY. YOU'RE ABLAZE!
AHA!!
WHOCK

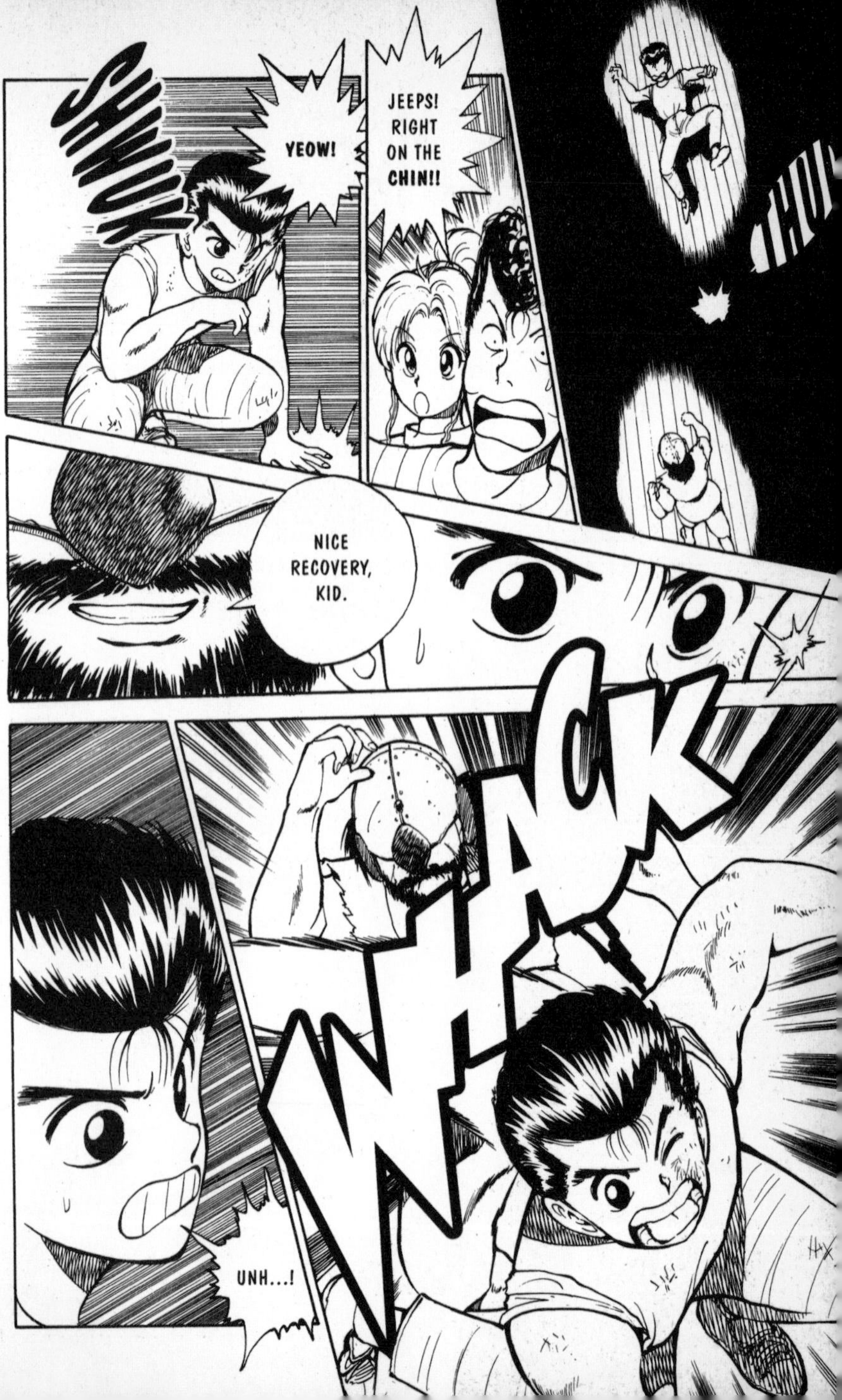
JEEPS! RIGHT ON THE CHIN!!
YEOW!
SHWOOK
NICE RECOVERY, KID.
WHACK
UNH...!

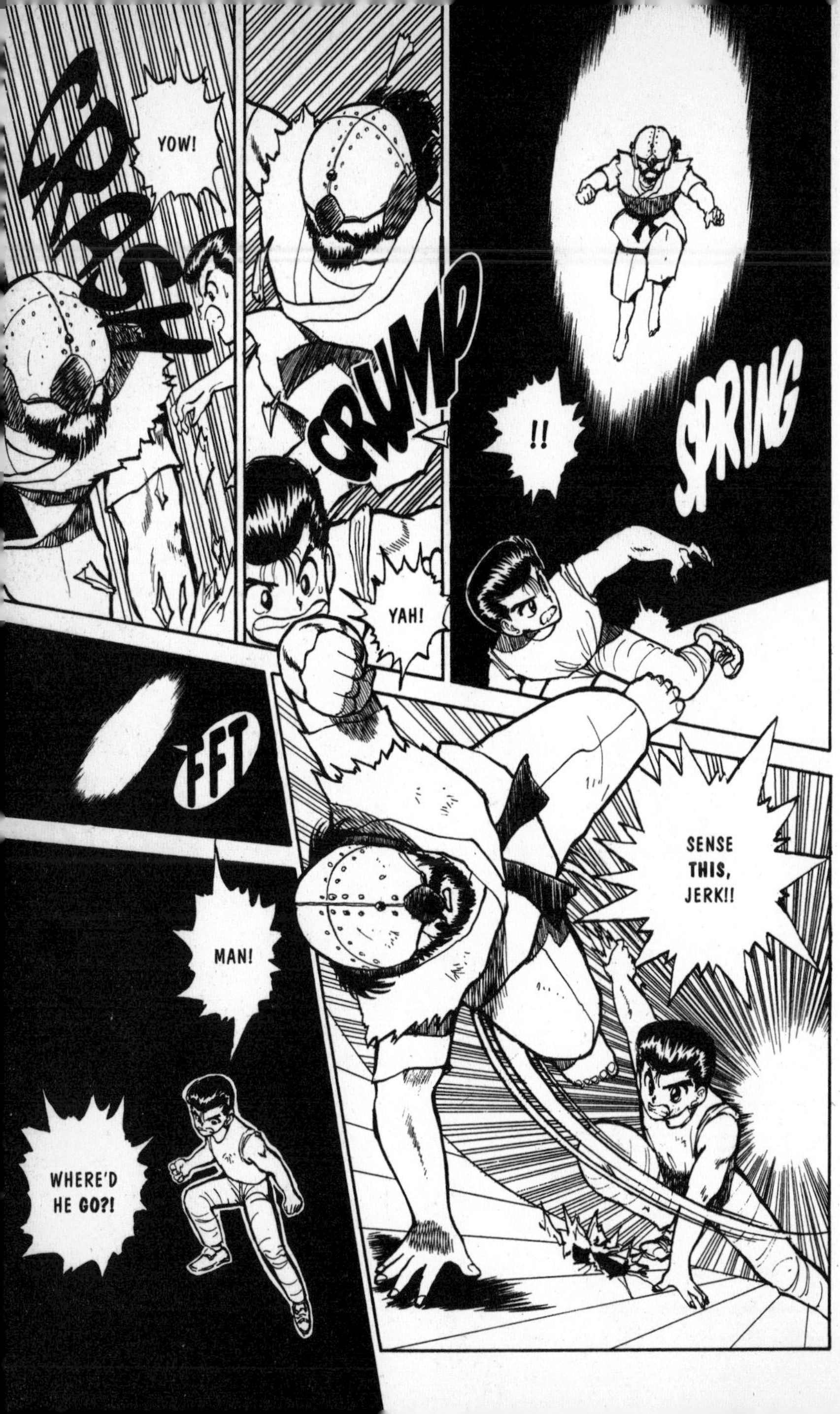
!!
SPRING
CRUMP
YAH!
YOW!
CRASH
SENSE THIS, JERK!!
FFT
MAN!
WHERE'D HE GO?!

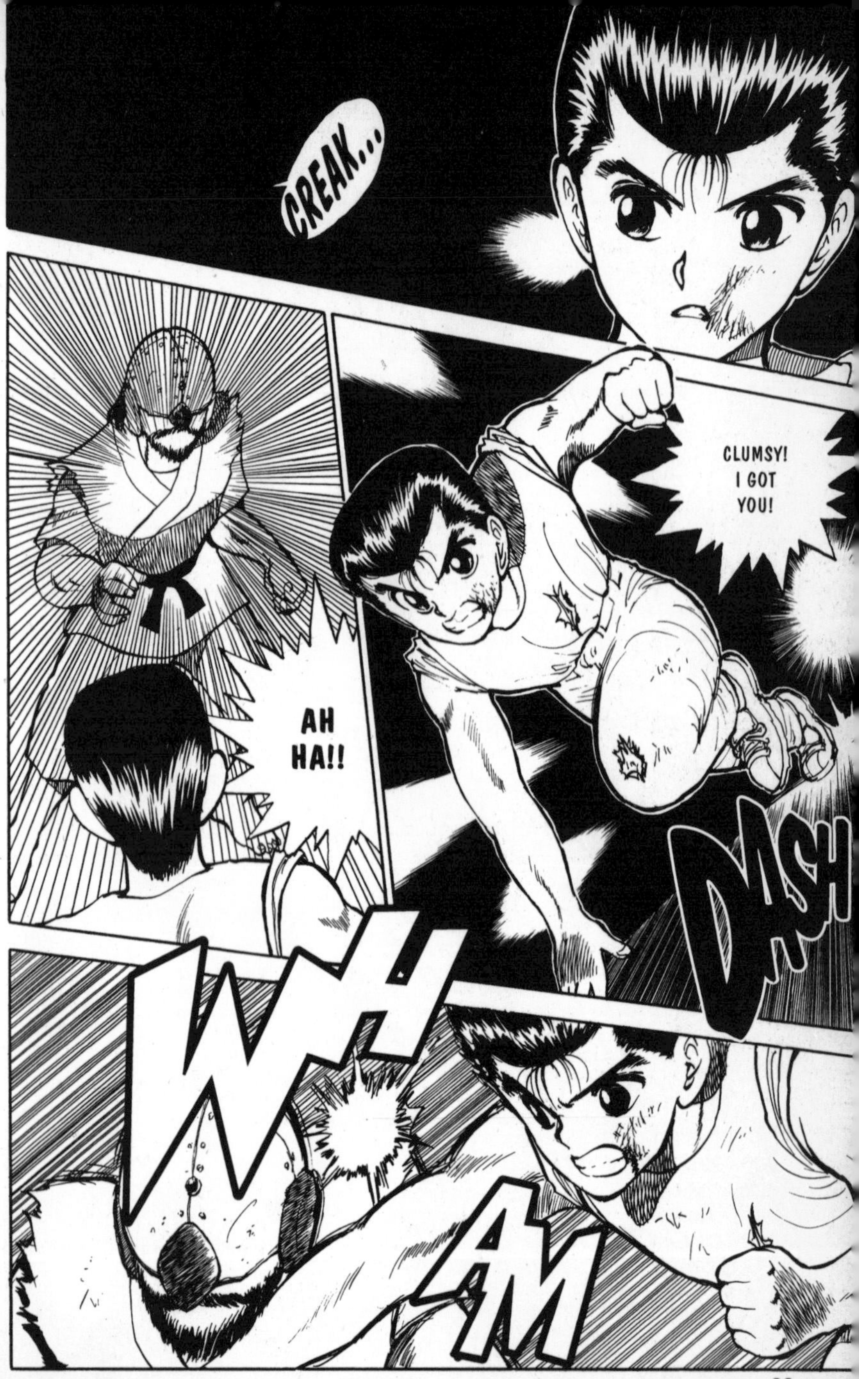
CREAK...
CLUMSY! I GOT YOU!
DASH
AH HA!!
WHAM

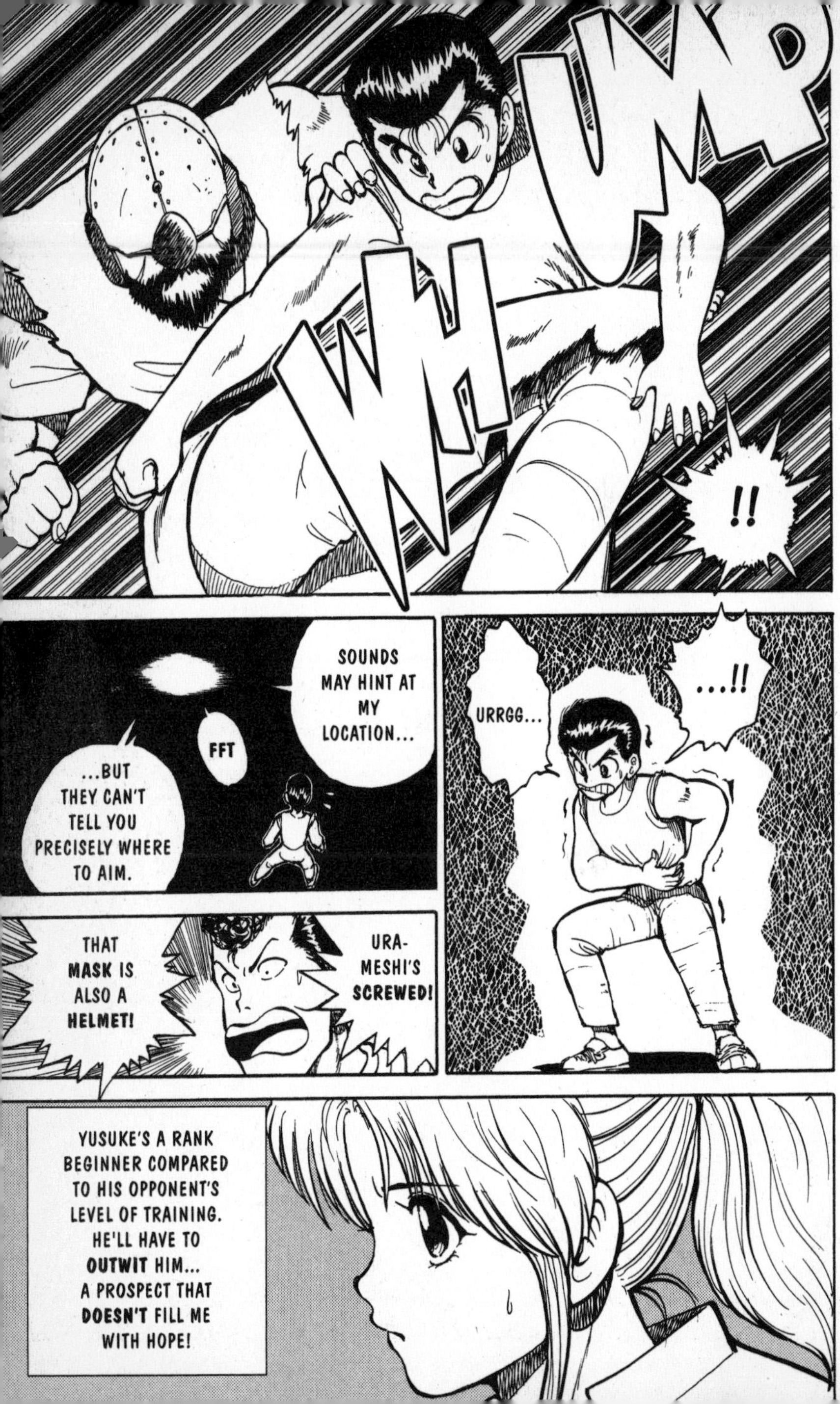
WHUMP
!!
...!!
URRGG...
SOUNDS MAY HINT AT MY LOCATION...
FFT
...BUT THEY CAN'T TELL YOU PRECISELY WHERE TO AIM.
URA-MESHI'S SCREWED!
THAT MASK IS ALSO A HELMET!
YUSUKE'S A RANK BEGINNER COMPARED TO HIS OPPONENT'S LEVEL OF TRAINING. HE'LL HAVE TO OUTWIT HIM... A PROSPECT THAT DOESN'T FILL ME WITH HOPE!

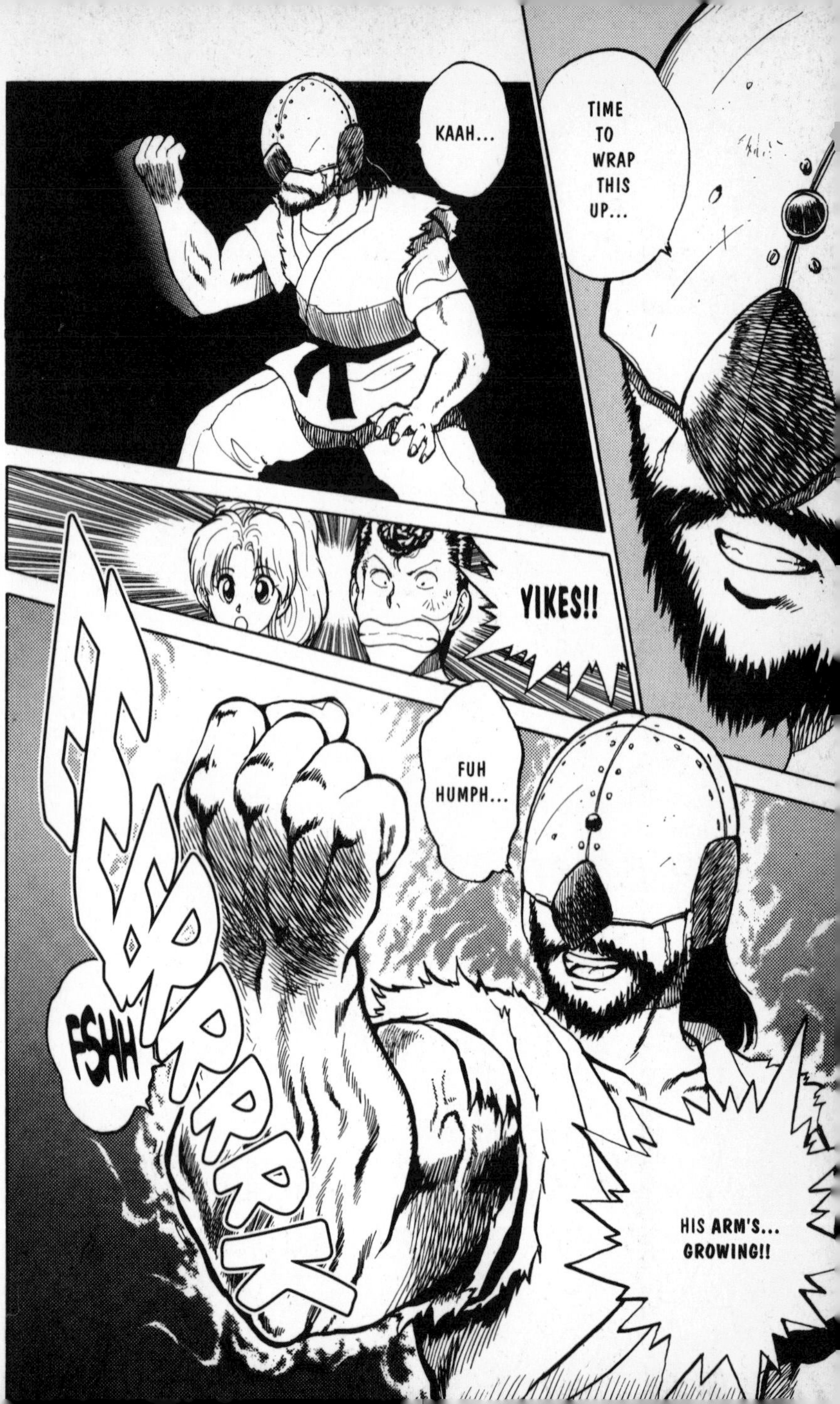
TIME TO WRAP THIS UP...
KAAH...
YIKES!!
FUH HUMPH...
HIS ARM'S... GROWING!!
FSHH

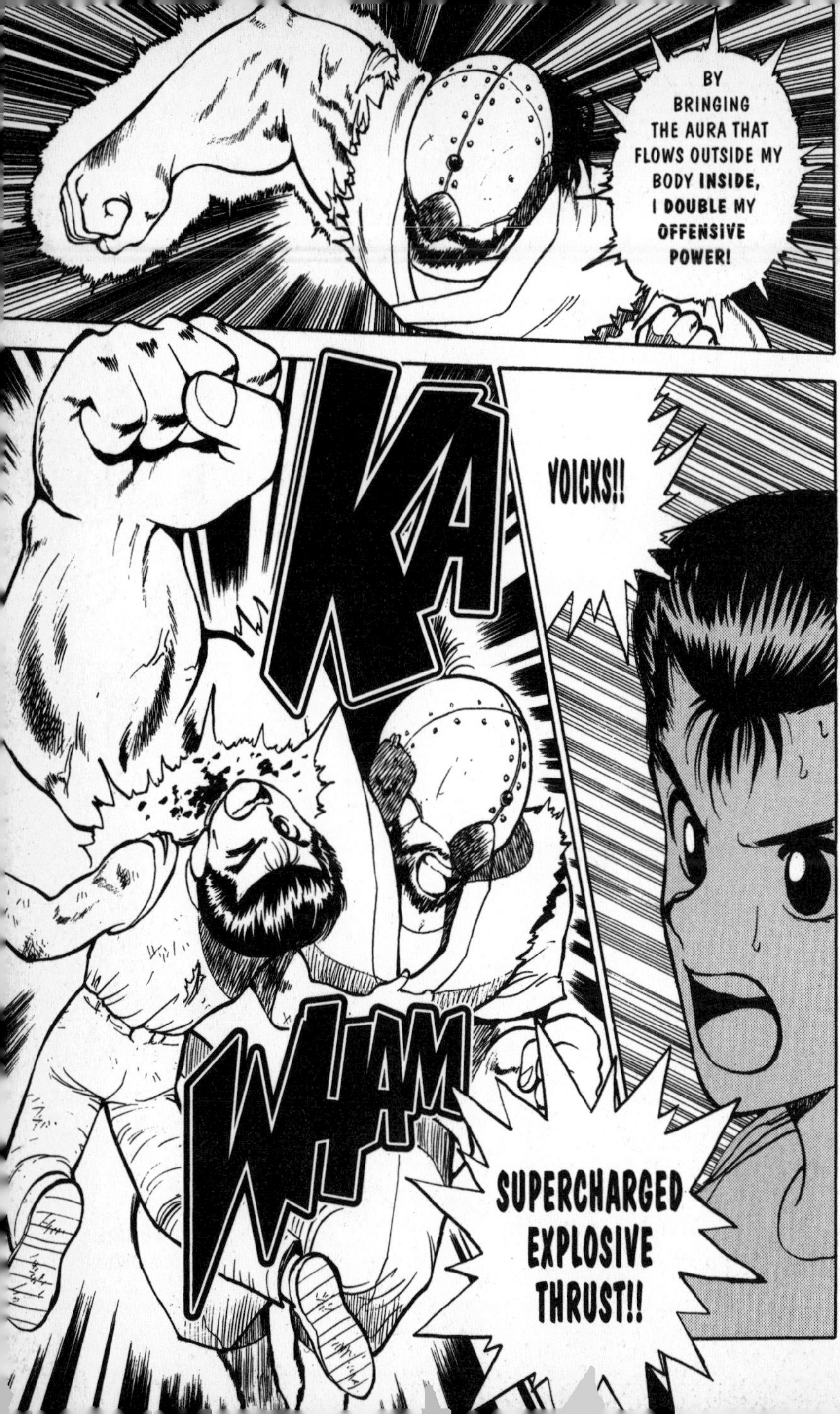
BY BRINGING THE AURA THAT FLOWS OUTSIDE MY BODY INSIDE, I DOUBLE MY OFFENSIVE POWER!
YOICKS!!
KA
WHAM
SUPERCHARGED EXPLOSIVE THRUST!!

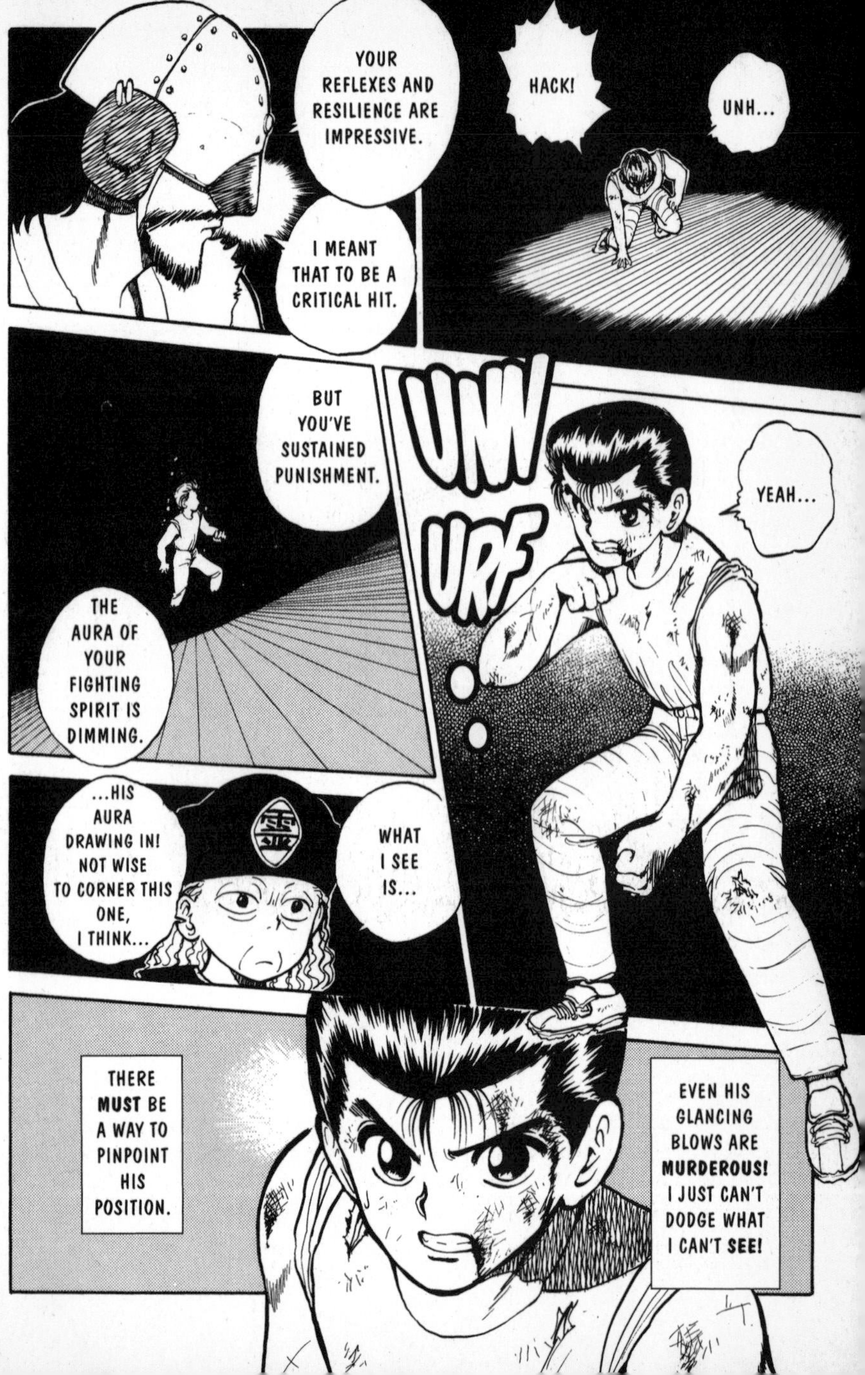
HACK!
UNH...
YOUR REFLEXES AND RESILIENCE ARE IMPRESSIVE.
I MEANT THAT TO BE A CRITICAL HIT.
UNN
URF
YEAH...
BUT YOU'VE SUSTAINED PUNISHMENT.
THE AURA OF YOUR FIGHTING SPIRIT IS DIMMING.
WHAT I SEE IS...
...HIS AURA DRAWING IN! NOT WISE TO CORNER THIS ONE, I THINK...
EVEN HIS GLANCING BLOWS ARE **MURDEROUS!** I JUST CAN'T DODGE WHAT I CAN'T **SEE!**
THERE **MUST** BE A WAY TO PINPOINT HIS POSITION.

READ THIS WAY

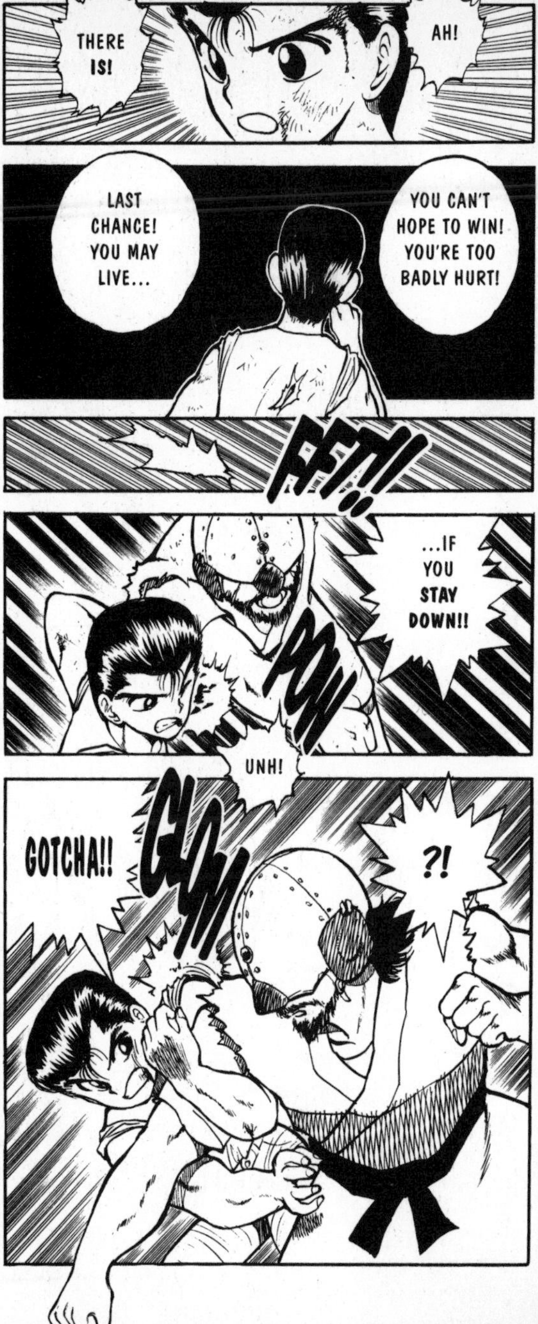
AH!
THERE IS!
YOU CAN'T HOPE TO WIN! YOU'RE TOO BADLY HURT!
LAST CHANCE! YOU MAY LIVE...
FFT!!
...IF YOU STAY DOWN!!
POW
UNH!
?!
GLOM
GOTCHA!!

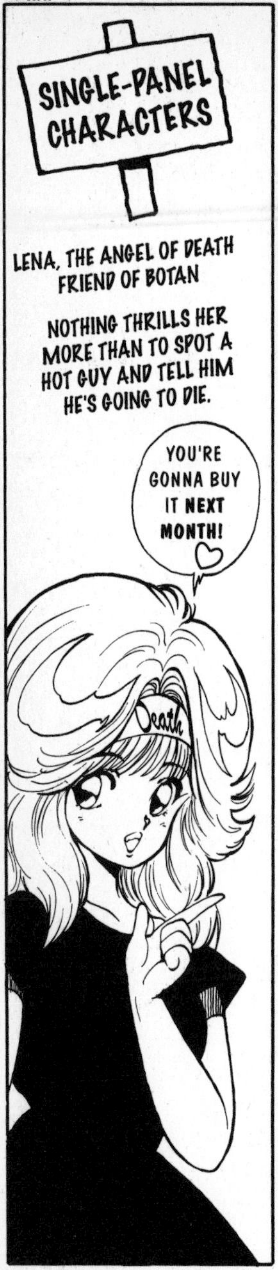
SINGLE-PANEL CHARACTERS
LENA, THE ANGEL OF DEATH
FRIEND OF BOTAN
NOTHING THRILLS HER MORE THAN TO SPOT A HOT GUY AND TELL HIM HE'S GOING TO DIE.
YOU'RE GONNA BUY IT **NEXT MONTH!**
Death

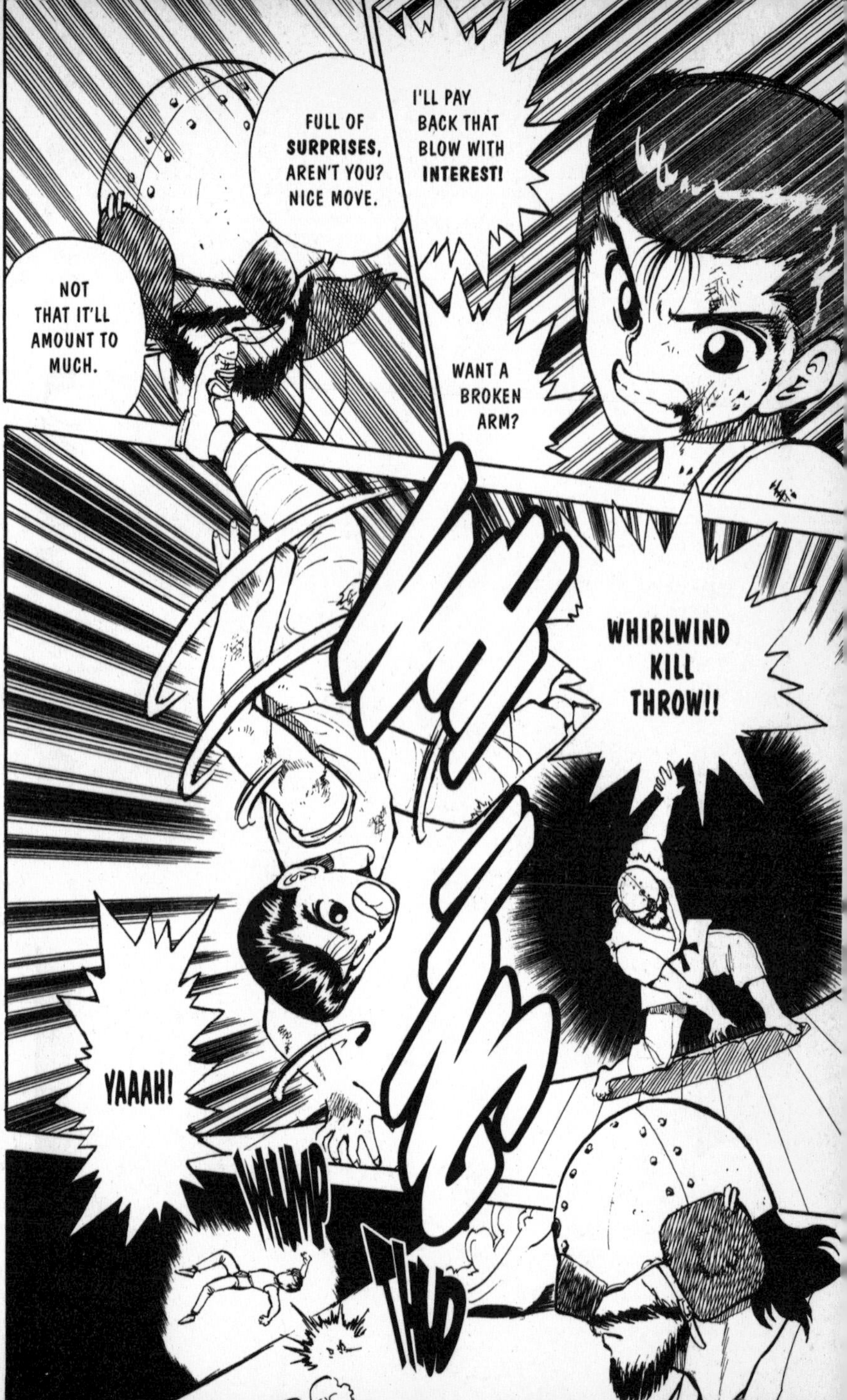
I'LL PAY BACK THAT BLOW WITH INTEREST!
WANT A BROKEN ARM?
FULL OF SURPRISES, AREN'T YOU? NICE MOVE.
NOT THAT IT'LL AMOUNT TO MUCH.
WHIRLWIND KILL THROW!!
YAAAH!
WHUMP
THUD

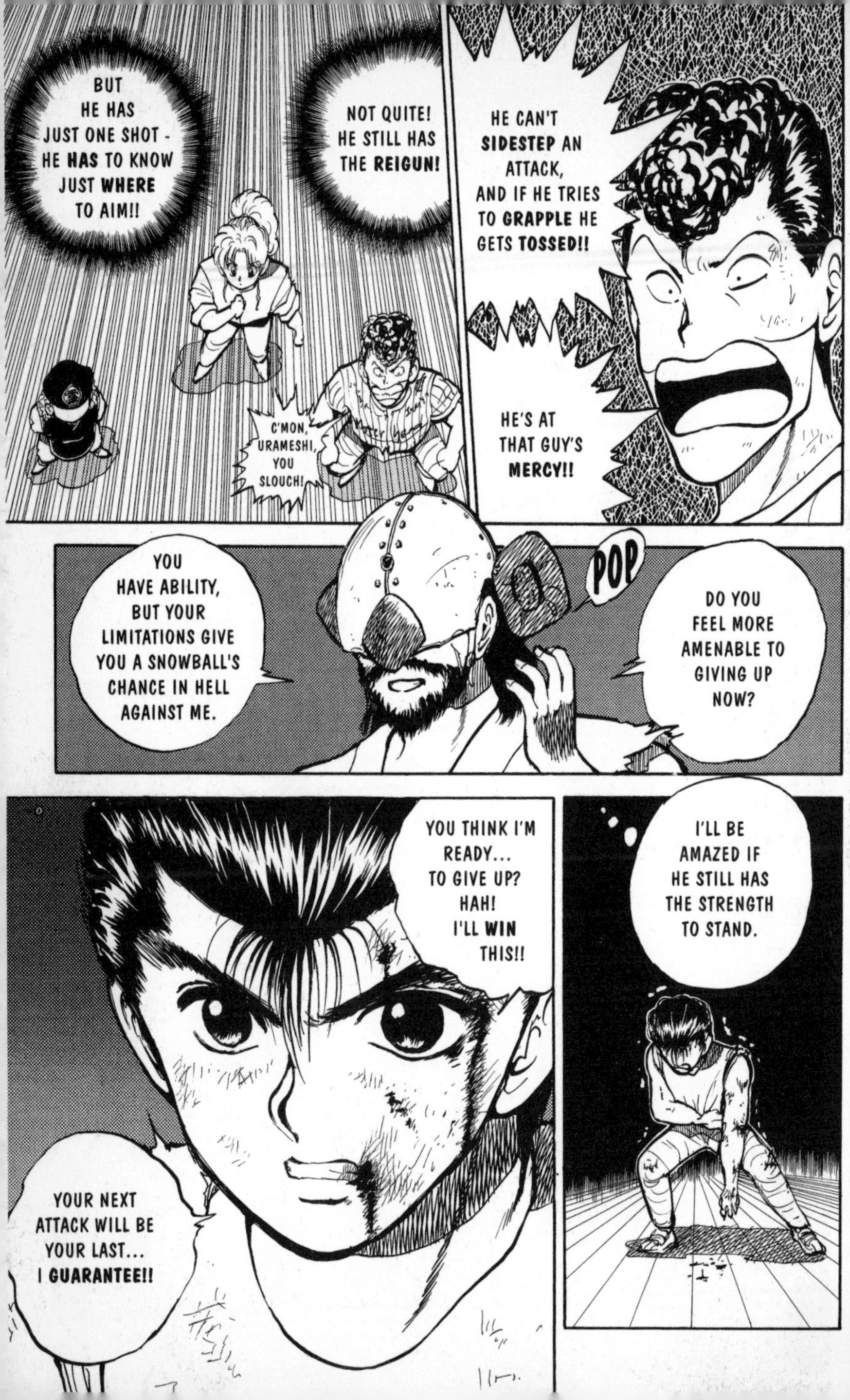
HE CAN'T SIDESTEP AN ATTACK, AND IF HE TRIES TO GRAPPLE HE GETS TOSSED!!
HE'S AT THAT GUY'S MERCY!!
NOT QUITE! HE STILL HAS THE REIGUN!
BUT HE HAS JUST ONE SHOT - HE HAS TO KNOW JUST WHERE TO AIM!!
C'MON, URAMESHI, YOU SLOUCH!
POP
DO YOU FEEL MORE AMENABLE TO GIVING UP NOW?
YOU HAVE ABILITY, BUT YOUR LIMITATIONS GIVE YOU A SNOWBALL'S CHANCE IN HELL AGAINST ME.
I'LL BE AMAZED IF HE STILL HAS THE STRENGTH TO STAND.
YOU THINK I'M READY... TO GIVE UP? HAH! I'LL WIN THIS!!
YOUR NEXT ATTACK WILL BE YOUR LAST... I GUARANTEE!!

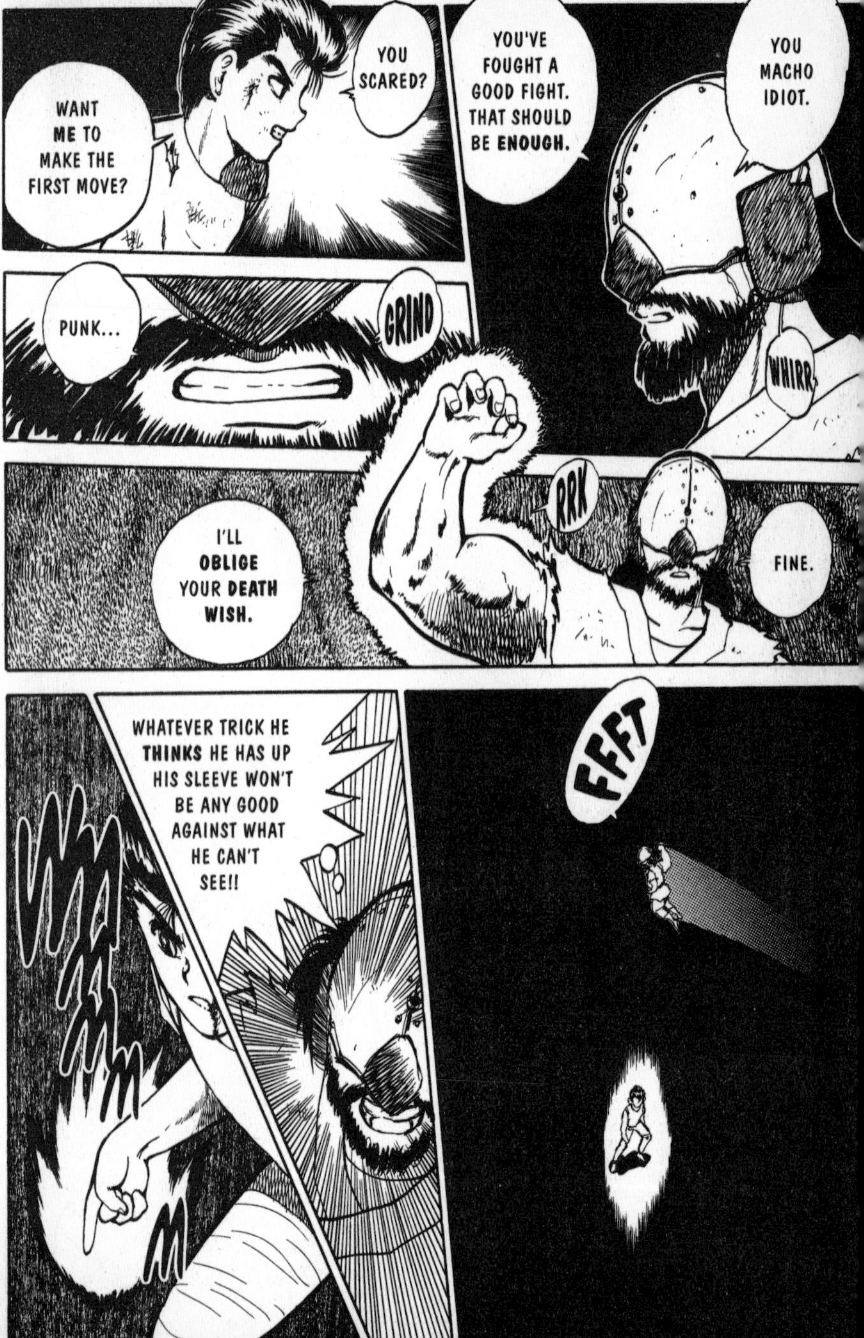
YOU MACHO IDIOT.
YOU'VE FOUGHT A GOOD FIGHT. THAT SHOULD BE ENOUGH.
WHIRR
YOU SCARED?
WANT ME TO MAKE THE FIRST MOVE?
GRIND
PUNK...
FINE.
RRK
I'LL OBLIGE YOUR DEATH WISH.
FFFT
WHATEVER TRICK HE THINKS HE HAS UP HIS SLEEVE WON'T BE ANY GOOD AGAINST WHAT HE CAN'T SEE!!

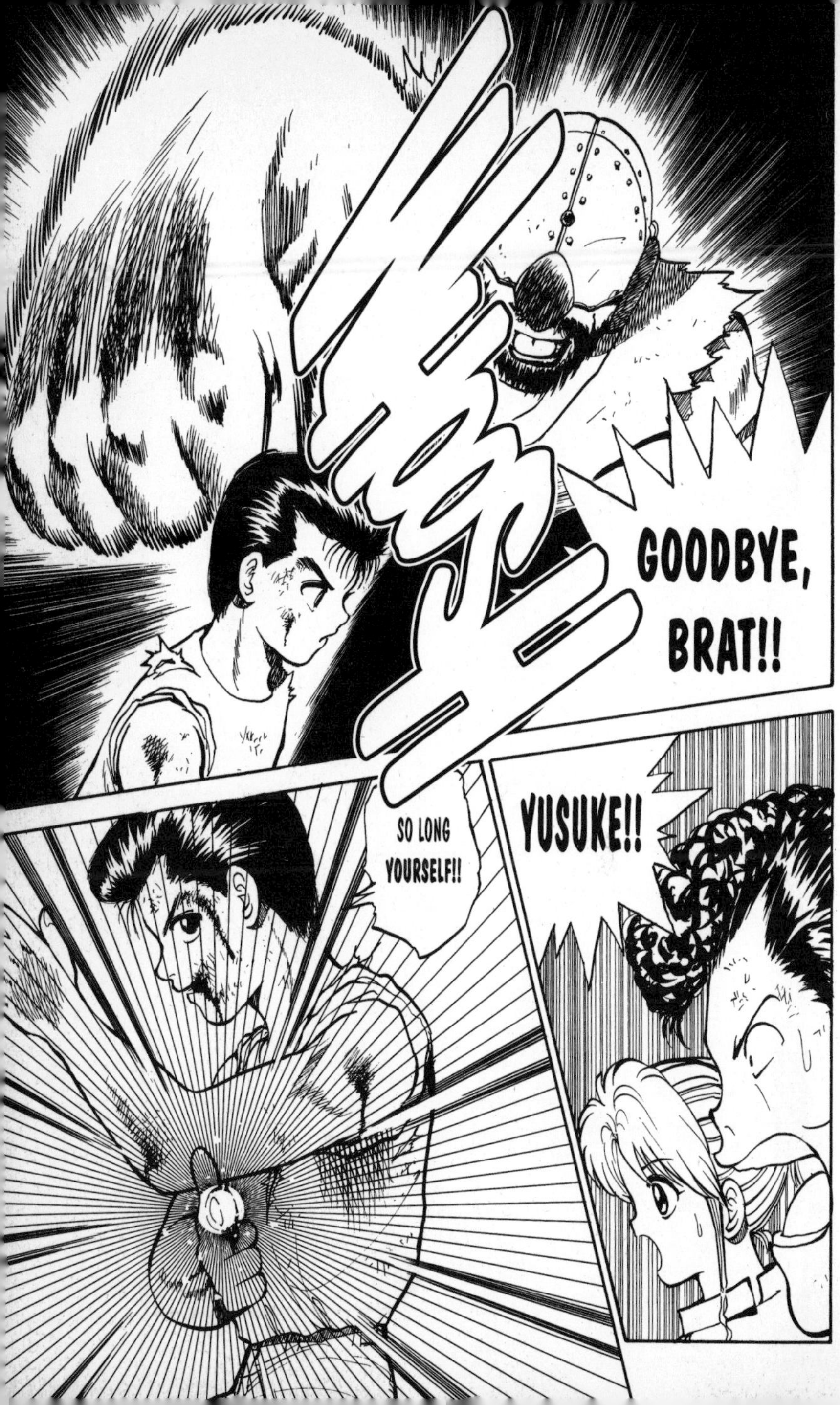
GOODBYE, BRAT!!
YUSUKE!!
SO LONG YOURSELF!!

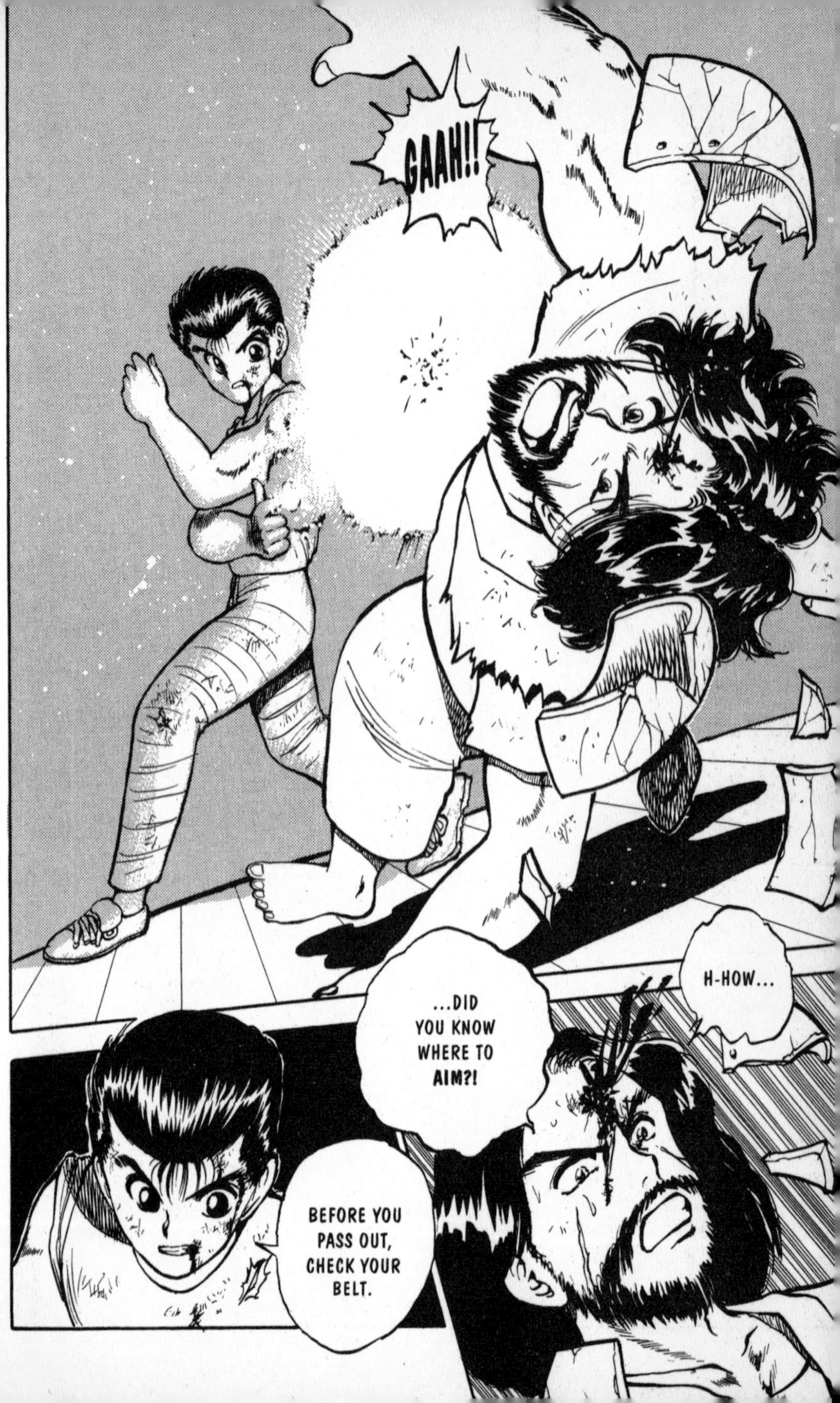
GAAH!!
H-HOW...
...DID YOU KNOW WHERE TO AIM?!
BEFORE YOU PASS OUT, CHECK YOUR BELT.

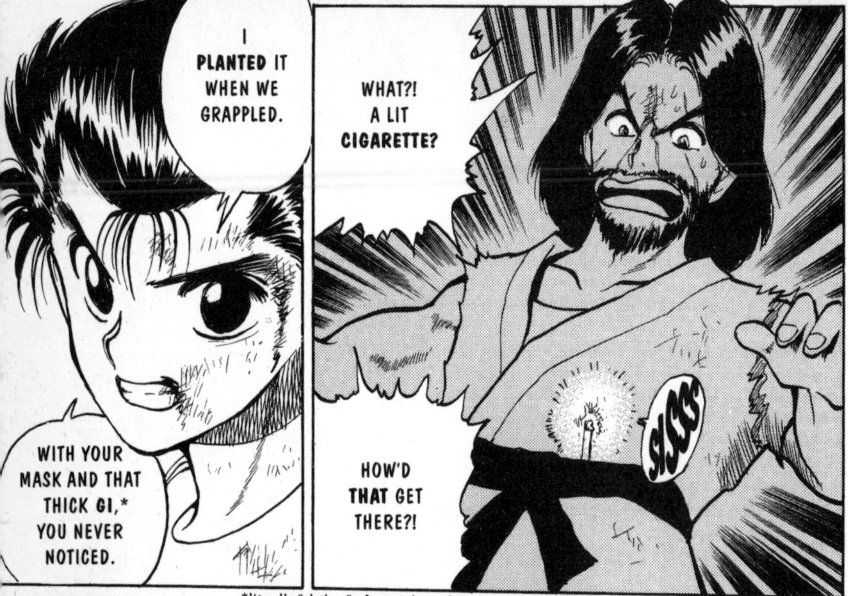
WHAT?! A LIT CIGARETTE?
SISSSS
HOW'D THAT GET THERE?!
I PLANTED IT WHEN WE GRAPPLED.
WITH YOUR MASK AND THAT THICK GI,* YOU NEVER NOTICED.

*literally "clothes," often used to refer to a martial arts uniform.

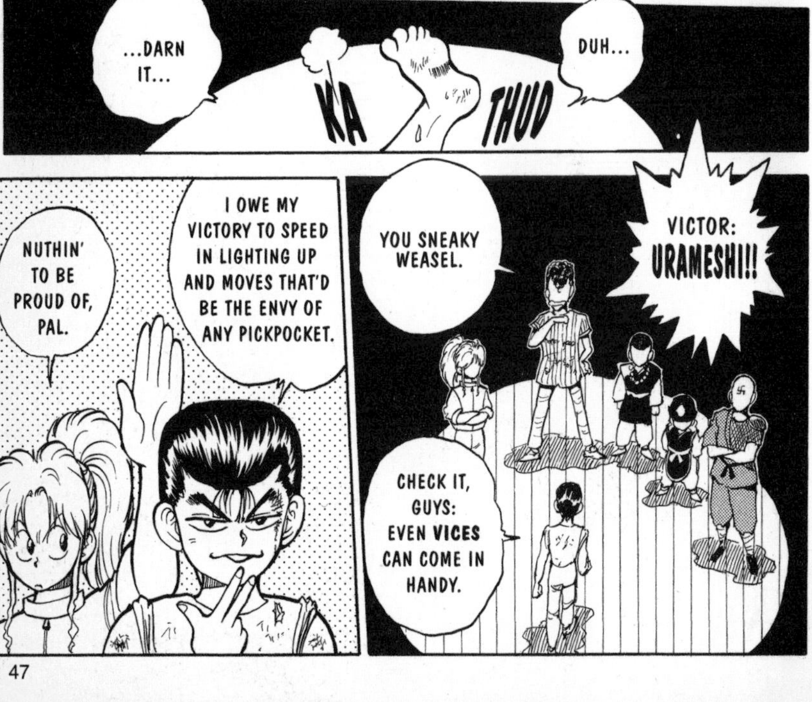
DUH...
KA THUD
...DARN IT...
VICTOR: URAMESHI!!
YOU SNEAKY WEASEL.
CHECK IT, GUYS: EVEN VICES CAN COME IN HANDY.
I OWE MY VICTORY TO SPEED IN LIGHTING UP AND MOVES THAT'D BE THE ENVY OF ANY PICKPOCKET.
NUTHIN' TO BE PROUD OF, PAL.

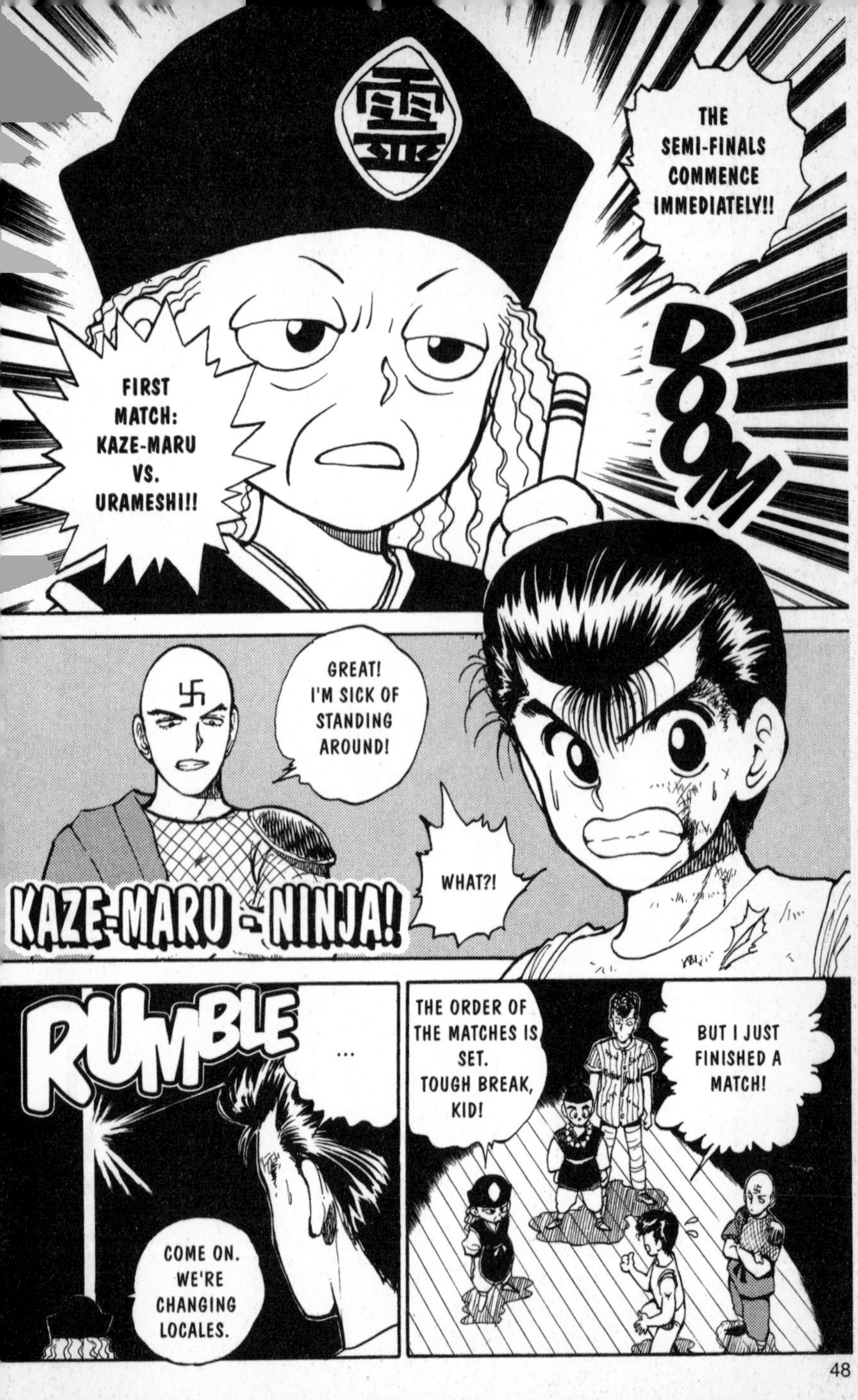
THE SEMI-FINALS COMMENCE IMMEDIATELY!!
DOOM
FIRST MATCH: KAZE-MARU VS. URAMESHI!!
GREAT! I'M SICK OF STANDING AROUND!
WHAT?!
KAZE-MARU - NINJA!
BUT I JUST FINISHED A MATCH!
THE ORDER OF THE MATCHES IS SET. TOUGH BREAK, KID!
...
RUMBLE
COME ON. WE'RE CHANGING LOCALES.

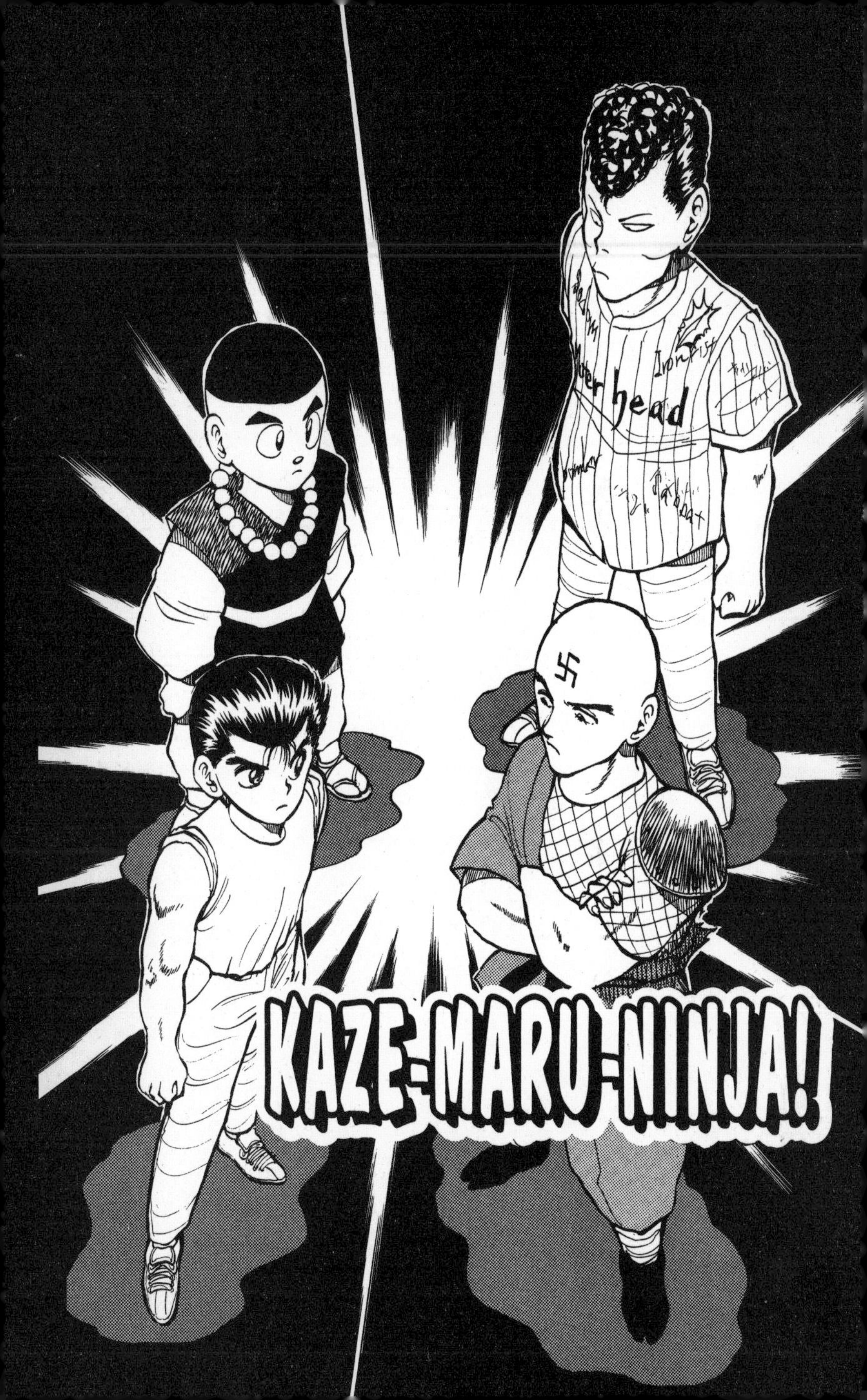
KAZE-MARU-NINJA!

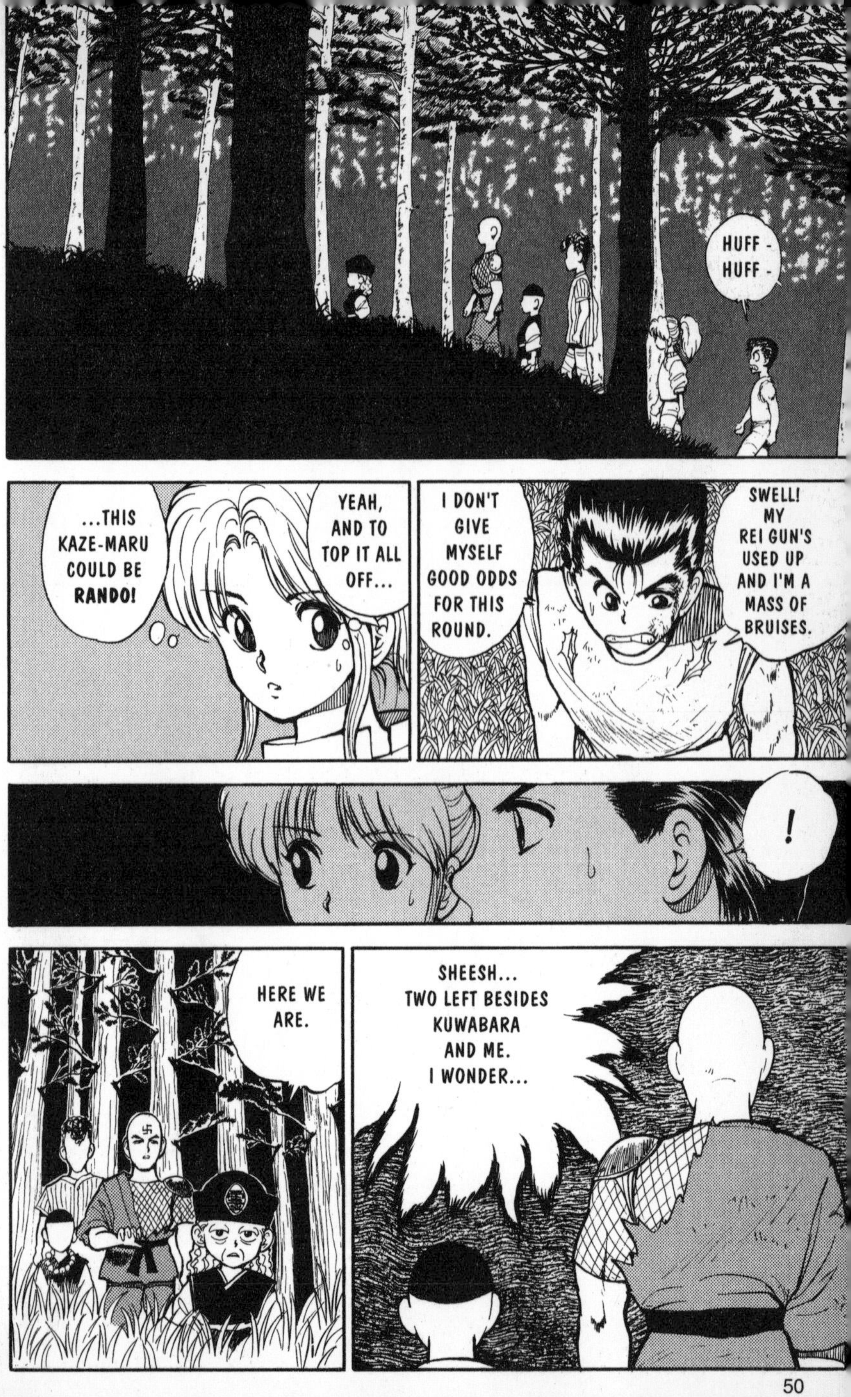
HUFF - HUFF -
SWELL! MY REI GUN'S USED UP AND I'M A MASS OF BRUISES.
I DON'T GIVE MYSELF GOOD ODDS FOR THIS ROUND.
YEAH, AND TO TOP IT ALL OFF...
...THIS KAZE-MARU COULD BE **RANDO!**
!
SHEESH... TWO LEFT BESIDES KUWABARA AND ME. I WONDER...
HERE WE ARE.

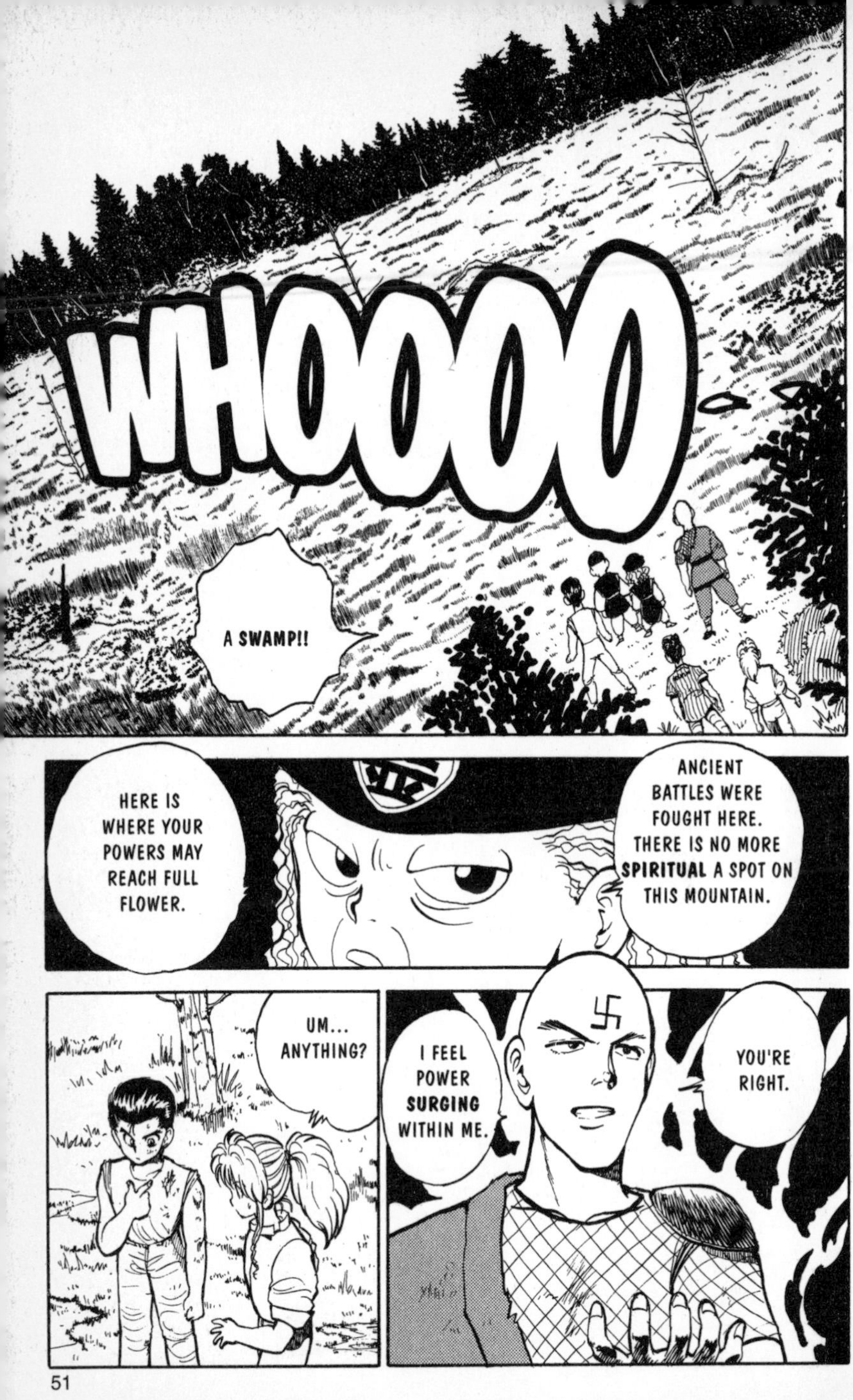
WHOOOO
A SWAMP!!
ANCIENT BATTLES WERE FOUGHT HERE. THERE IS NO MORE SPIRITUAL A SPOT ON THIS MOUNTAIN.
HERE IS WHERE YOUR POWERS MAY REACH FULL FLOWER.
YOU'RE RIGHT.
I FEEL POWER SURGING WITHIN ME.
UM... ANYTHING?

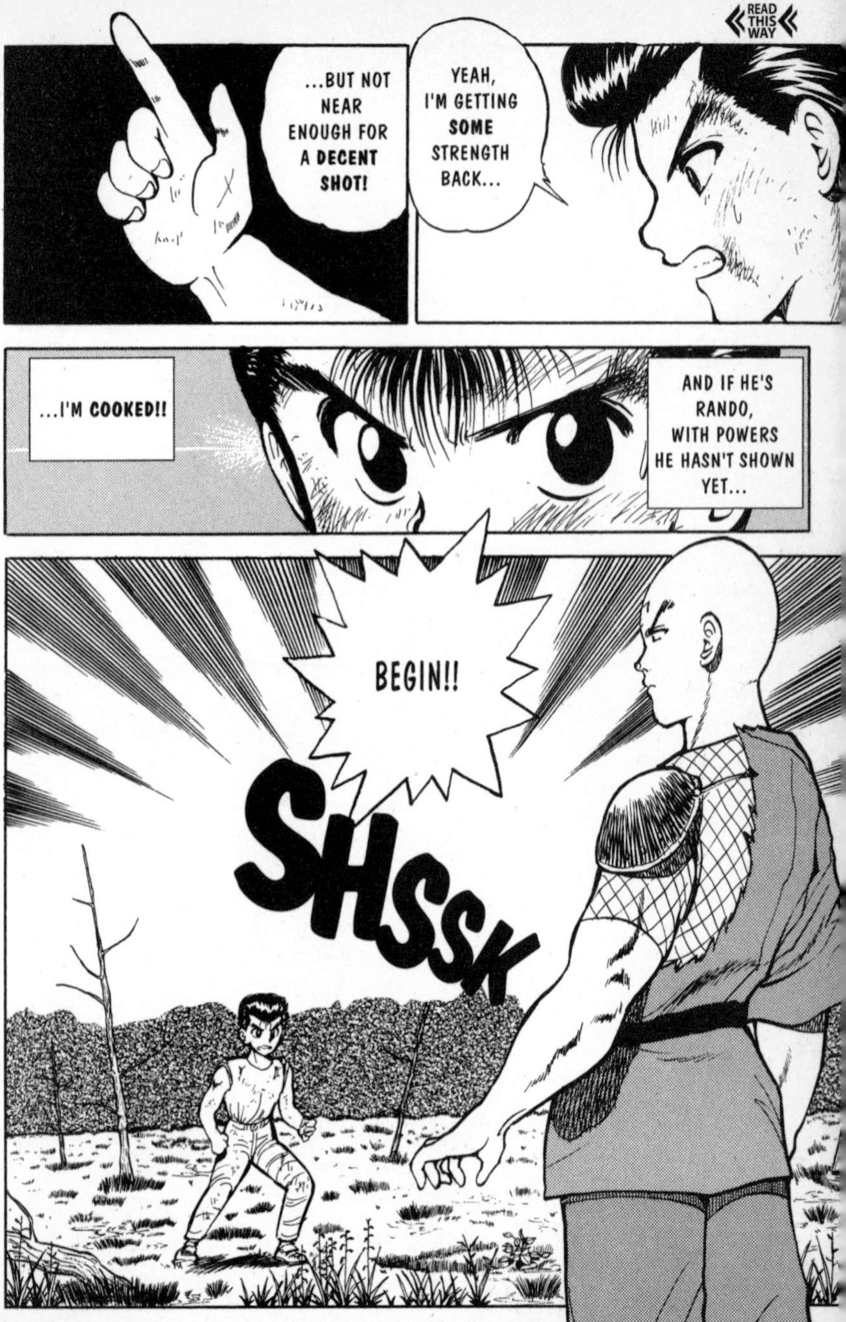
READ THIS WAY
YEAH, I'M GETTING SOME STRENGTH BACK...
...BUT NOT NEAR ENOUGH FOR A DECENT SHOT!
AND IF HE'S RANDO, WITH POWERS HE HASN'T SHOWN YET...
...I'M COOKED!!
BEGIN!!
SHSSK

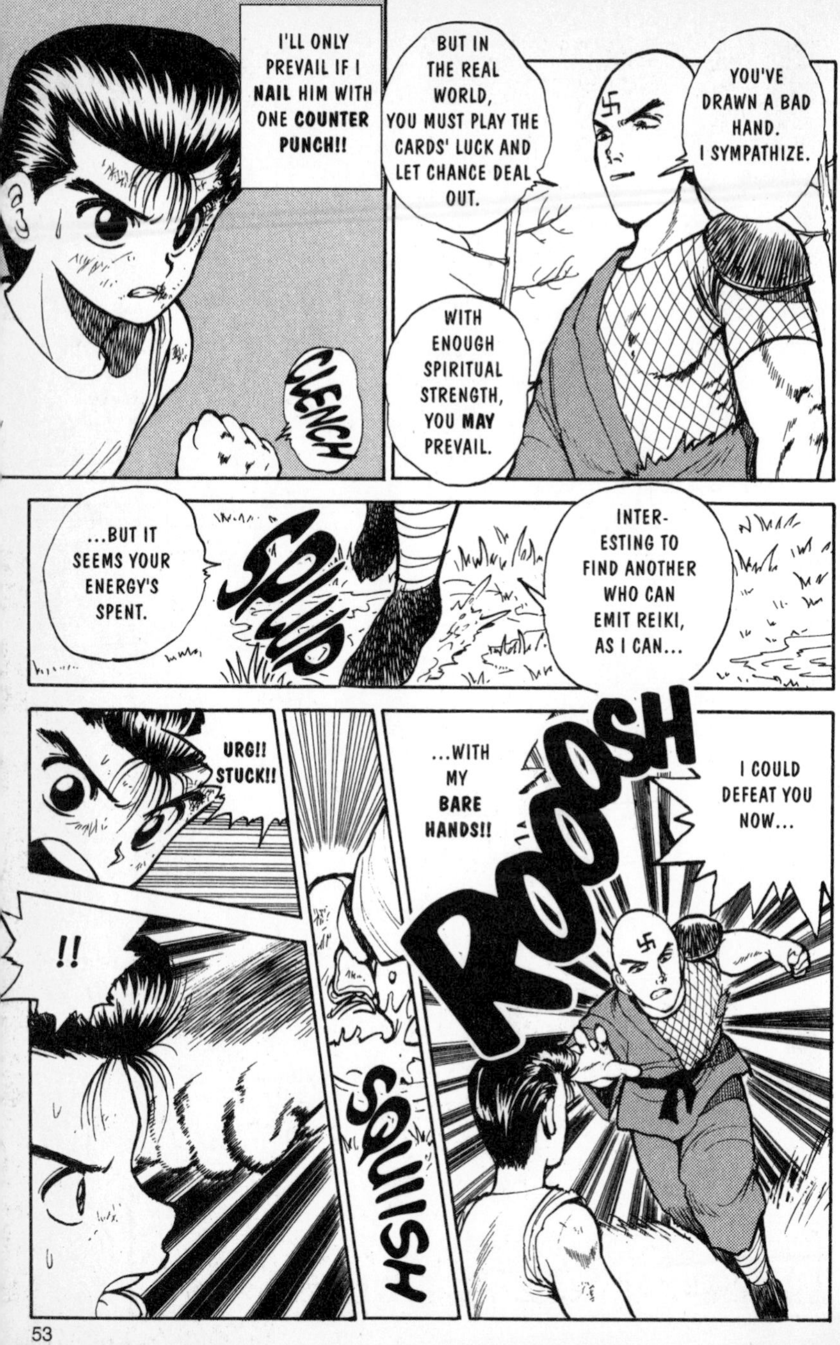
YOU'VE DRAWN A BAD HAND. I SYMPATHIZE.
BUT IN THE REAL WORLD, YOU MUST PLAY THE CARDS' LUCK AND LET CHANCE DEAL OUT.
WITH ENOUGH SPIRITUAL STRENGTH, YOU MAY PREVAIL.
I'LL ONLY PREVAIL IF I NAIL HIM WITH ONE COUNTER PUNCH!!
CLENCH
INTER-ESTING TO FIND ANOTHER WHO CAN EMIT REIKI, AS I CAN...
SPLUP
...BUT IT SEEMS YOUR ENERGY'S SPENT.
I COULD DEFEAT YOU NOW...
ROOOSH
...WITH MY BARE HANDS!!
SQUIISH
URG!! STUCK!!
!!

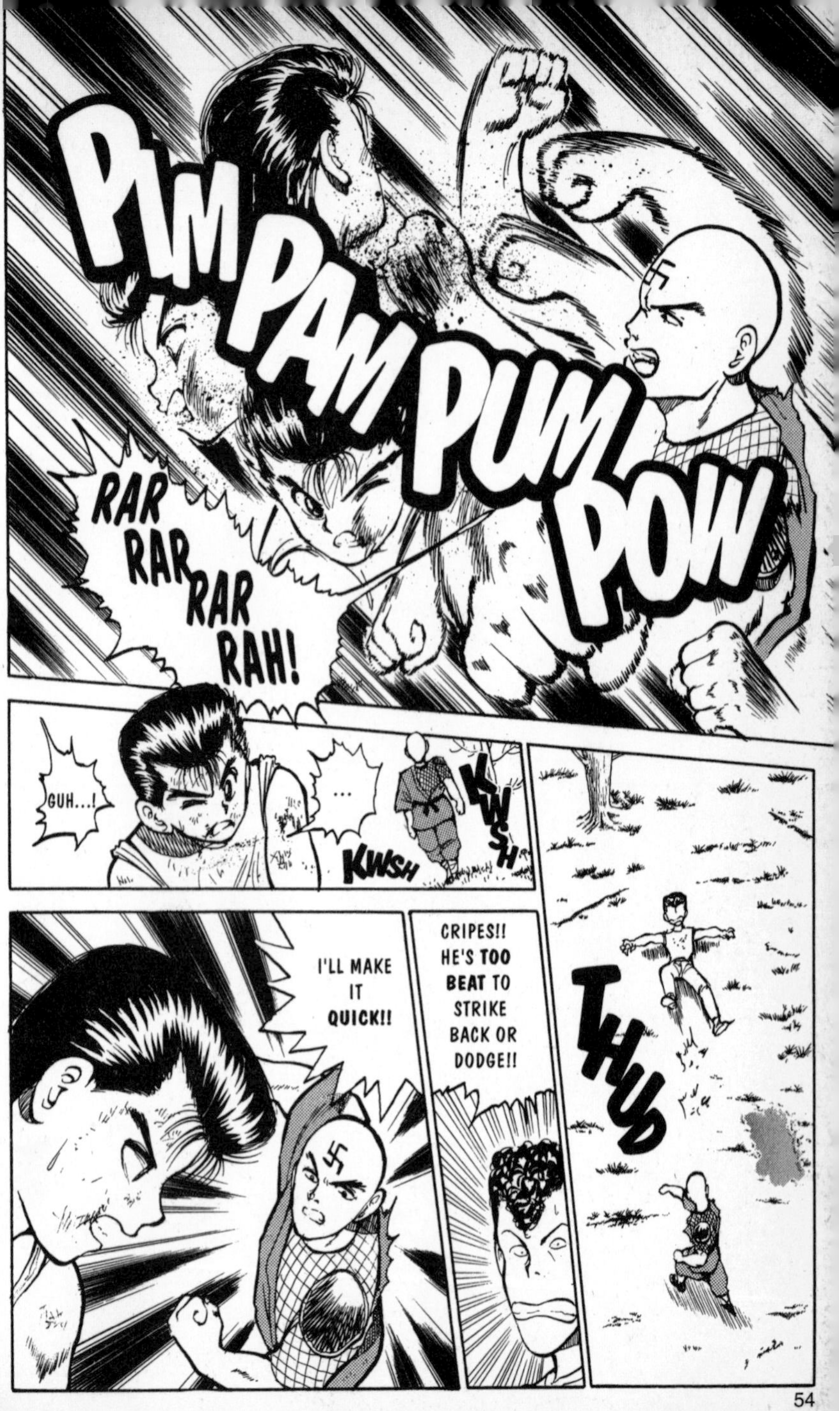
PIM PAM PUM POW
RAR RAR RAR RAH!
THUD
KWSH
...
KWSH
GUH...!
CRIPES!! HE'S TOO BEAT TO STRIKE BACK OR DODGE!!
I'LL MAKE IT QUICK!!

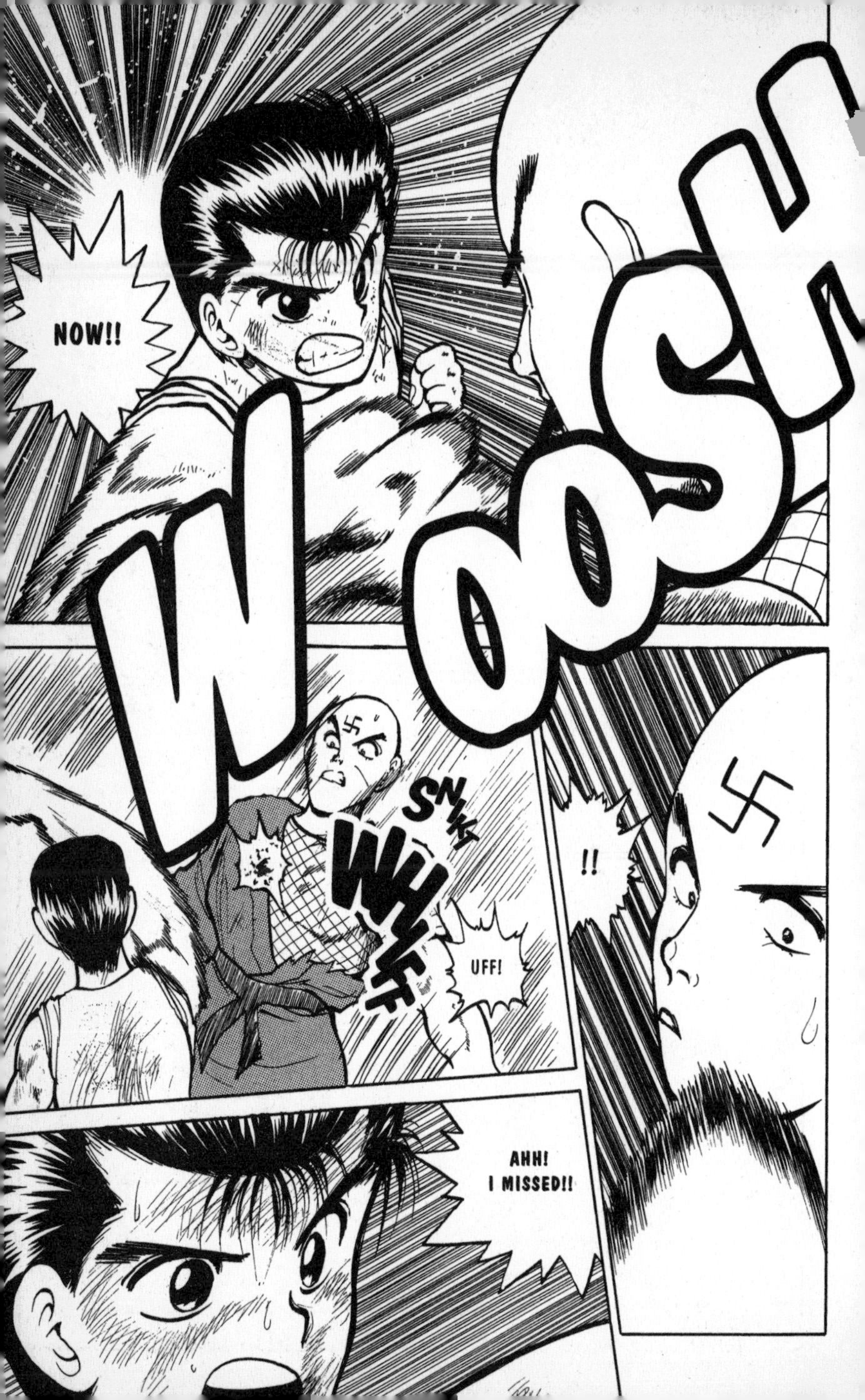
WHOOSH
NOW!!
!!
SNIKT
WHUFF
UFF!
AHH! I MISSED!!

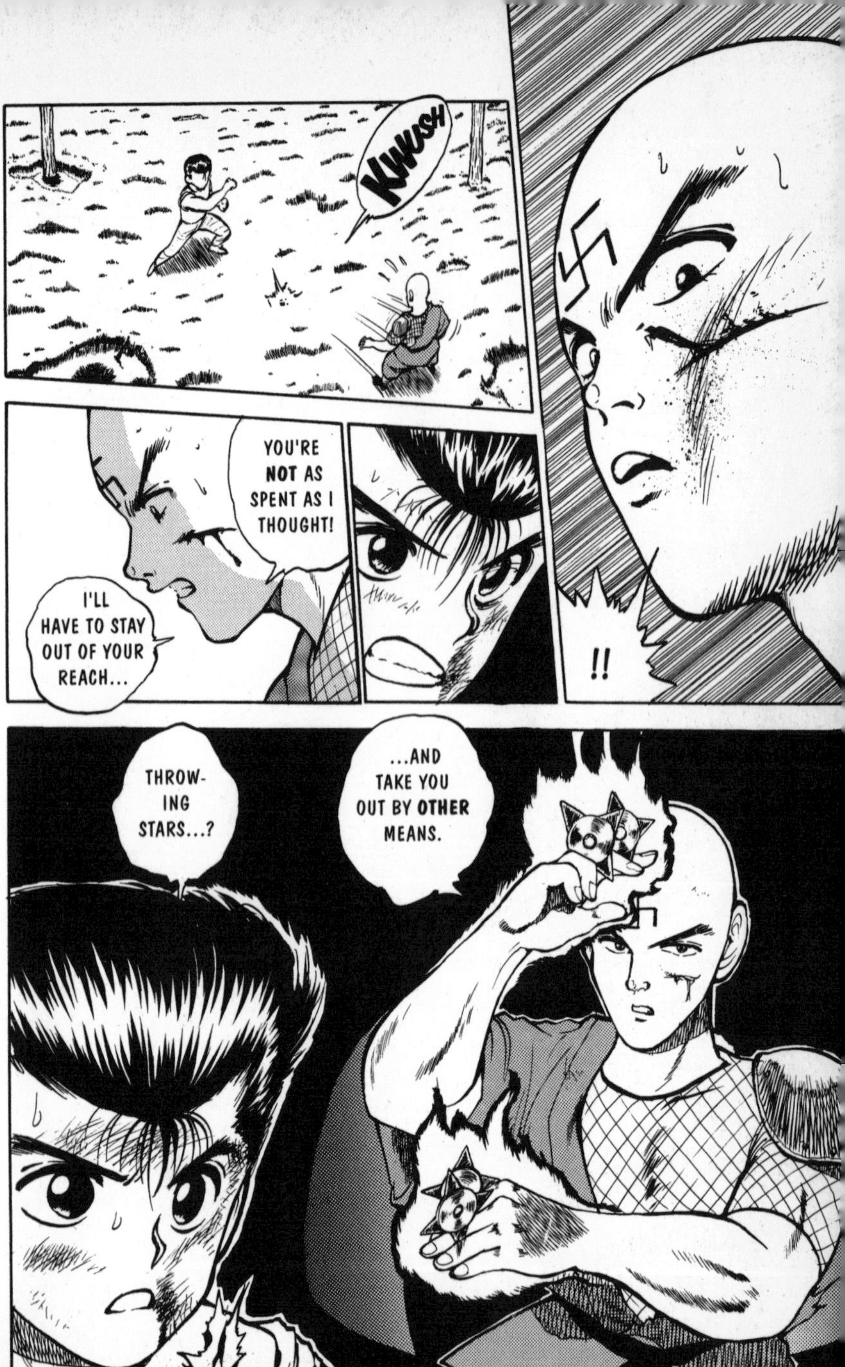
!!
KWUSH
YOU'RE NOT AS SPENT AS I THOUGHT!
I'LL HAVE TO STAY OUT OF YOUR REACH...
...AND TAKE YOU OUT BY OTHER MEANS.
THROW-ING STARS...?

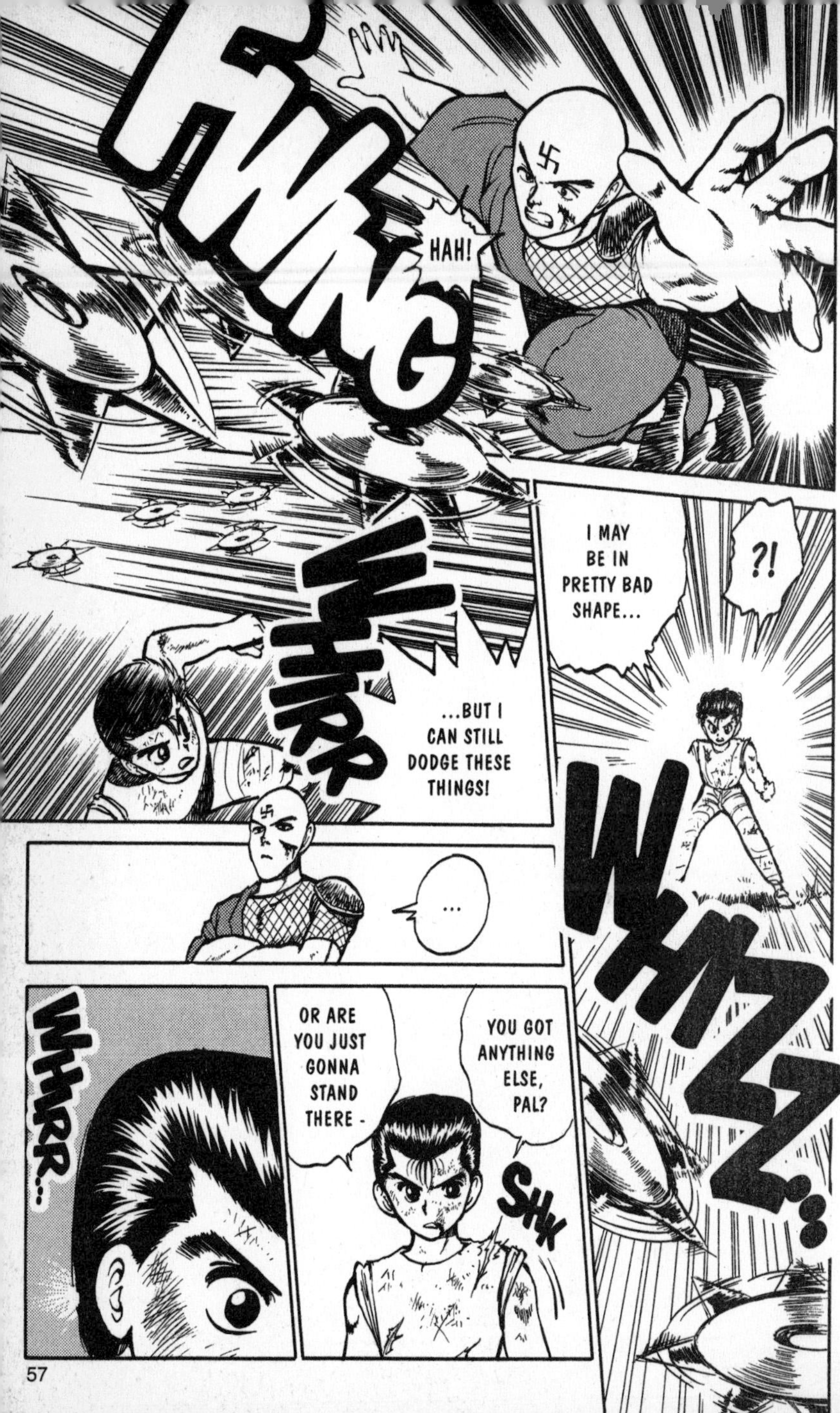
ZWING
HAH!
?!
I MAY BE IN PRETTY BAD SHAPE...
WHIZZ..
WHIRR
...BUT I CAN STILL DODGE THESE THINGS!
...
YOU GOT ANYTHING ELSE, PAL?
OR ARE YOU JUST GONNA STAND THERE -
SHK
WHIRR...

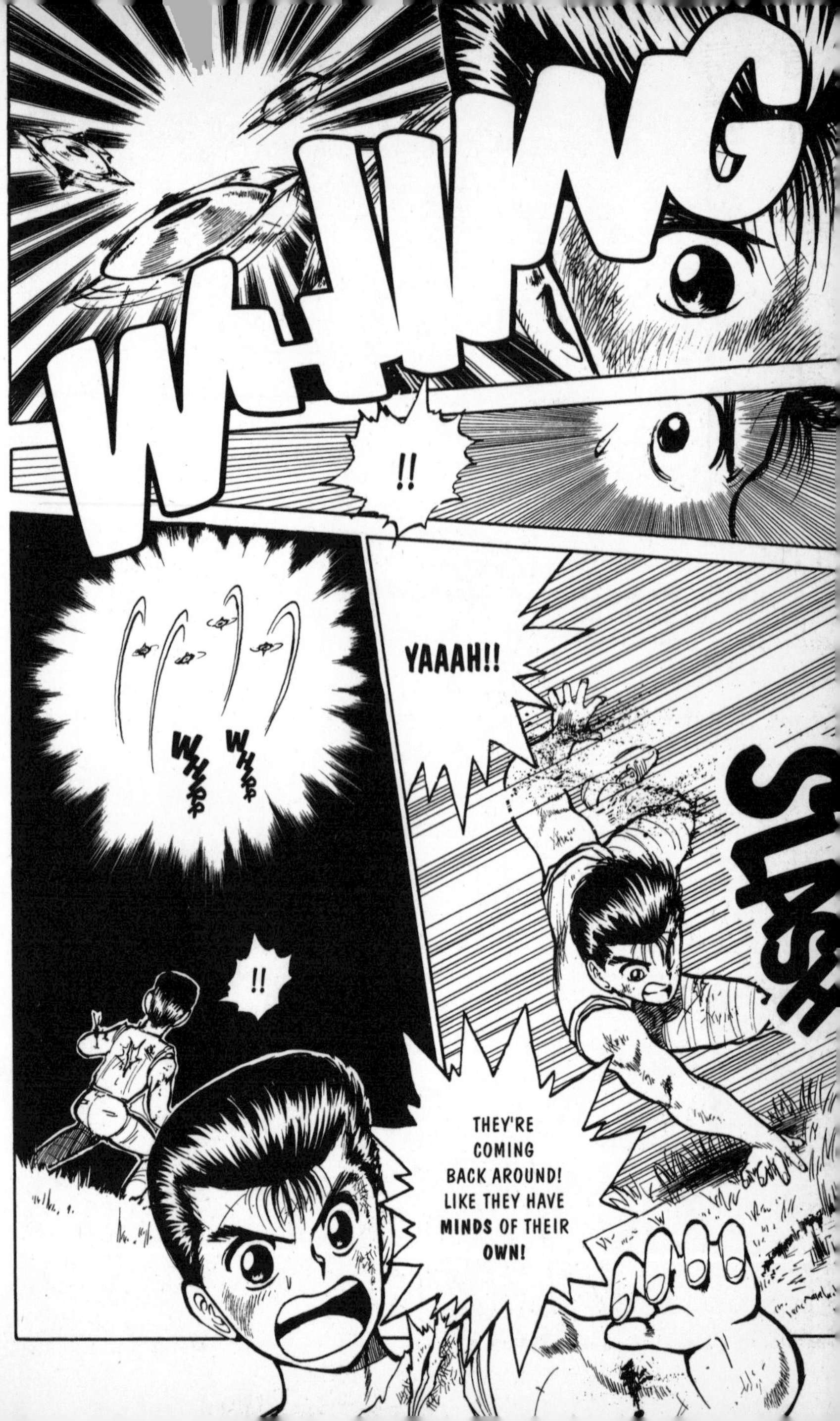
WHANG
!!
YAAAH!!
SLASH
!!
THEY'RE COMING BACK AROUND! LIKE THEY HAVE MINDS OF THEIR OWN!

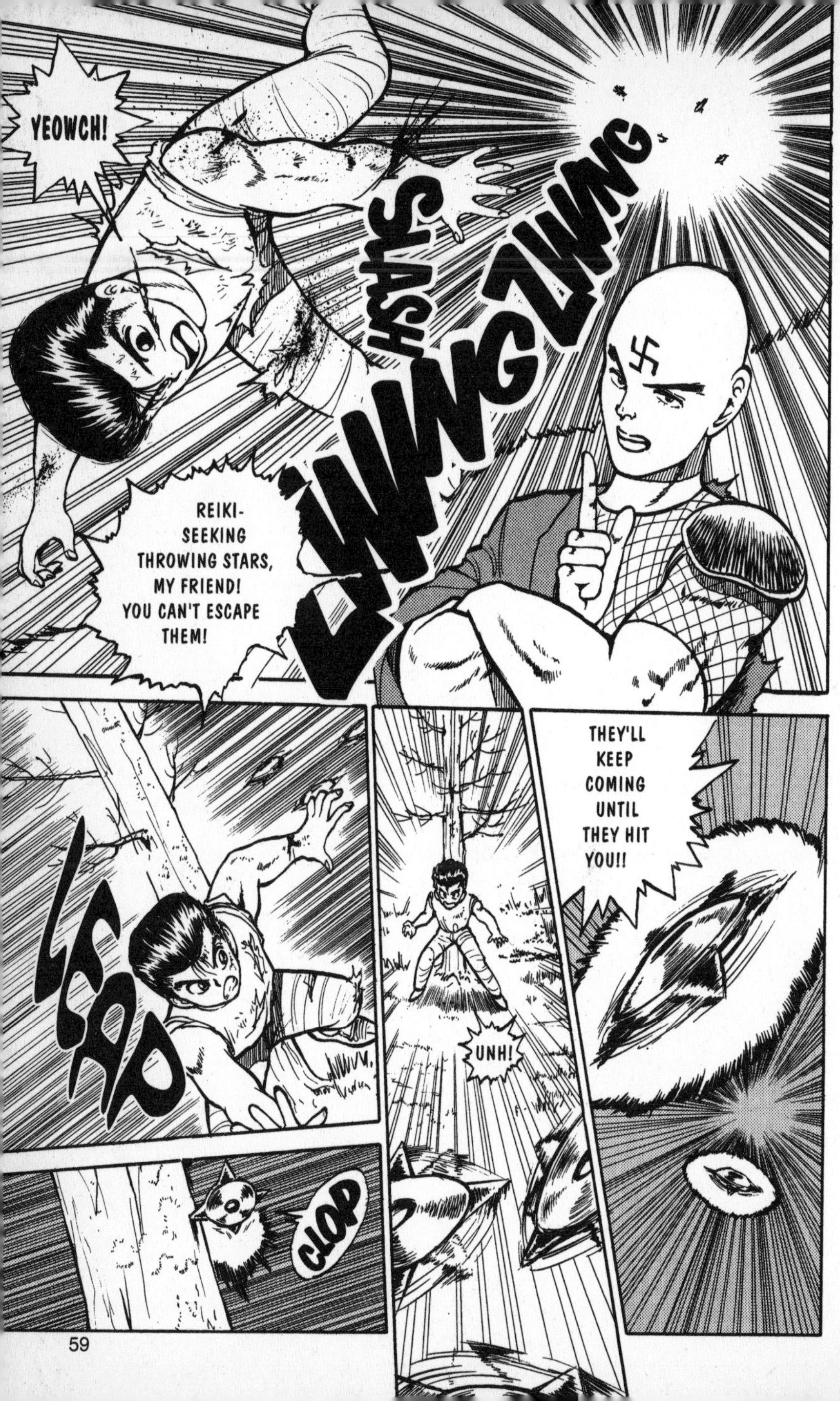
SLASH
WHIING ZWING
YEOWCH!
REIKI-SEEKING THROWING STARS, MY FRIEND! YOU CAN'T ESCAPE THEM!
THEY'LL KEEP COMING UNTIL THEY HIT YOU!!
UNH!
LEAP
CLOP

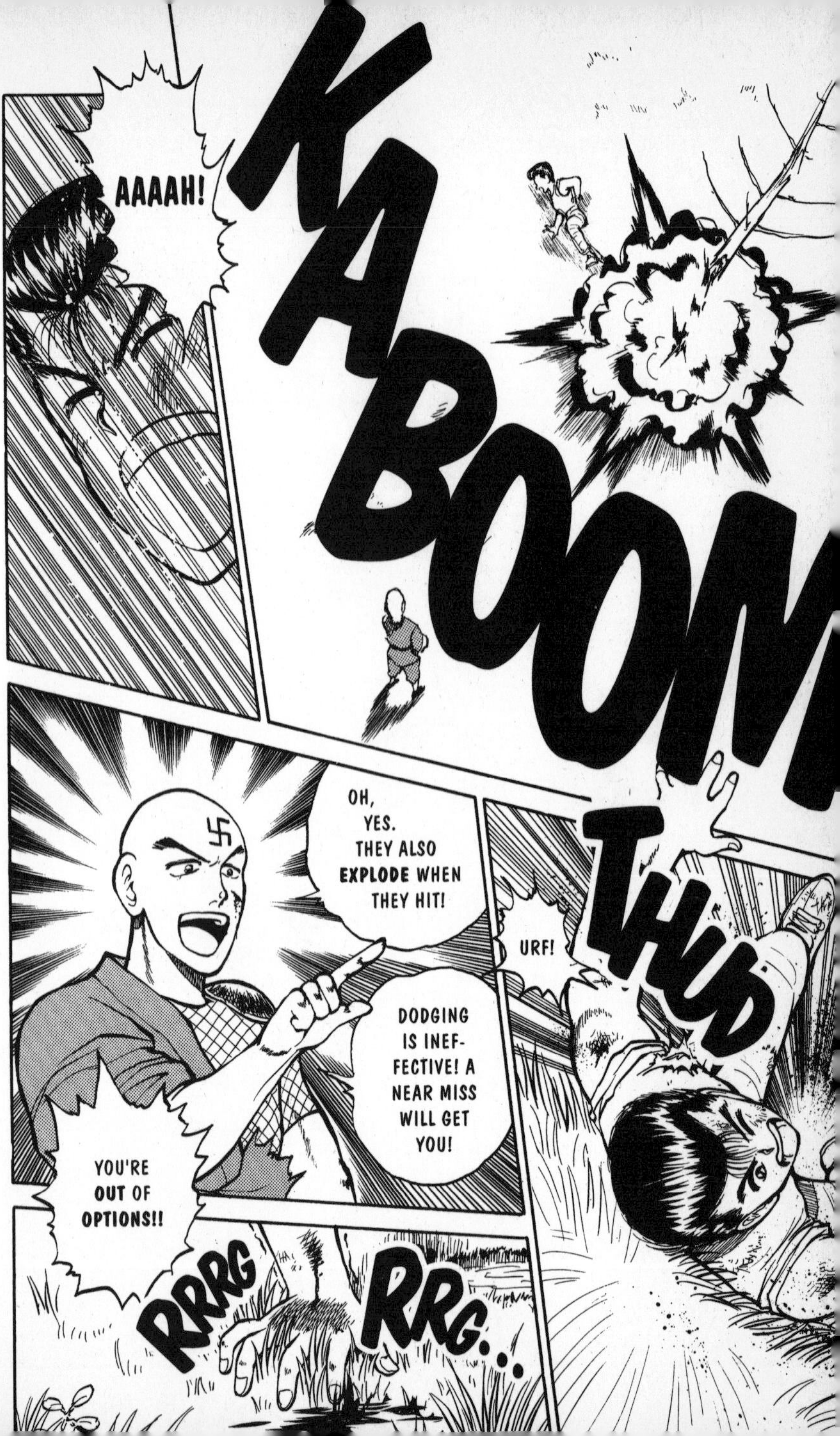
KABOOM
AAAAH!
THUD
URF!
OH, YES. THEY ALSO EXPLODE WHEN THEY HIT!
DODGING IS INEF- FECTIVE! A NEAR MISS WILL GET YOU!
YOU'RE OUT OF OPTIONS!!
RRRG
RRG...

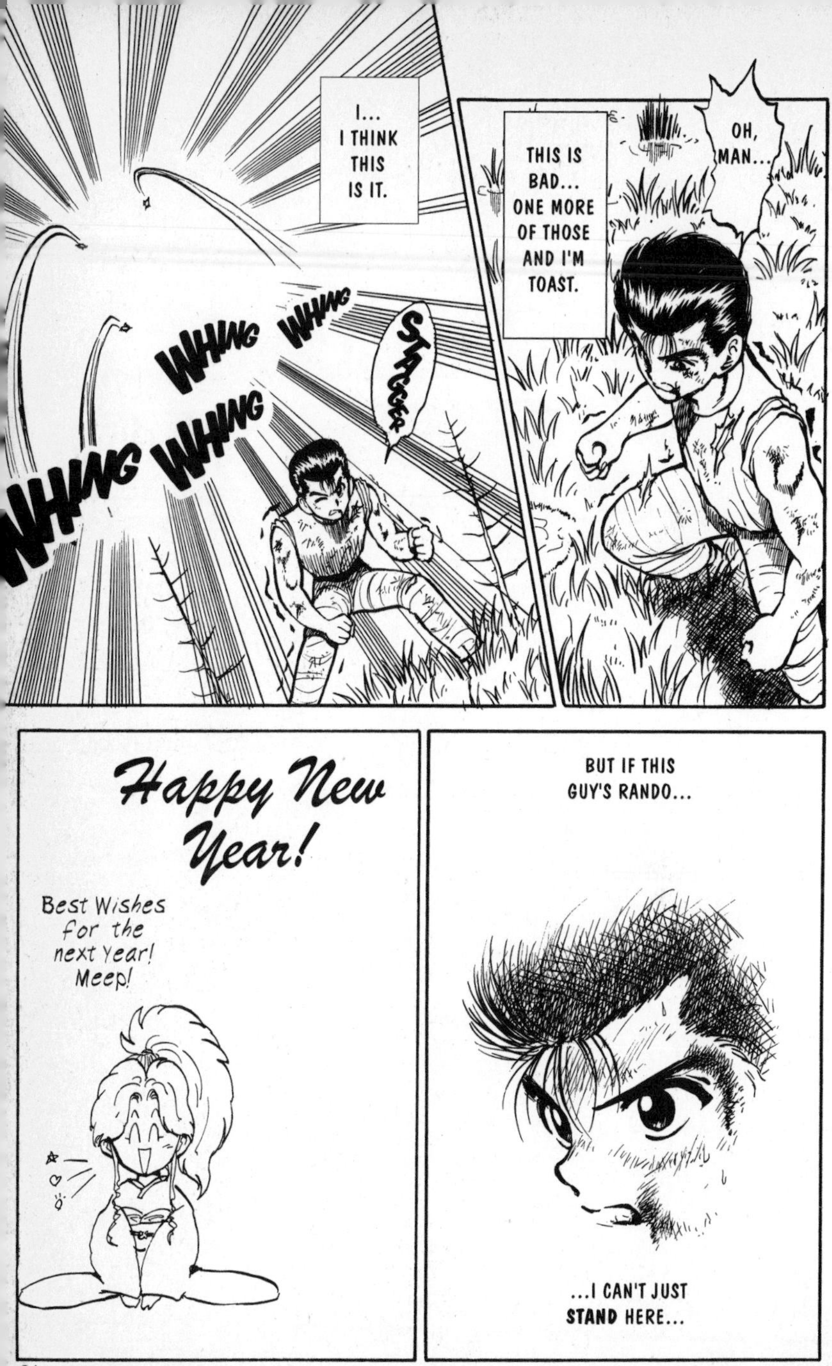
THIS IS BAD... ONE MORE OF THOSE AND I'M TOAST.
OH, MAN...
I... I THINK THIS IS IT.
STAGGER
WHING WHING
WHING WHING
WHING
BUT IF THIS GUY'S RANDO...
...I CAN'T JUST STAND HERE...
Happy New Year!
Best Wishes for the next Year! Meep!

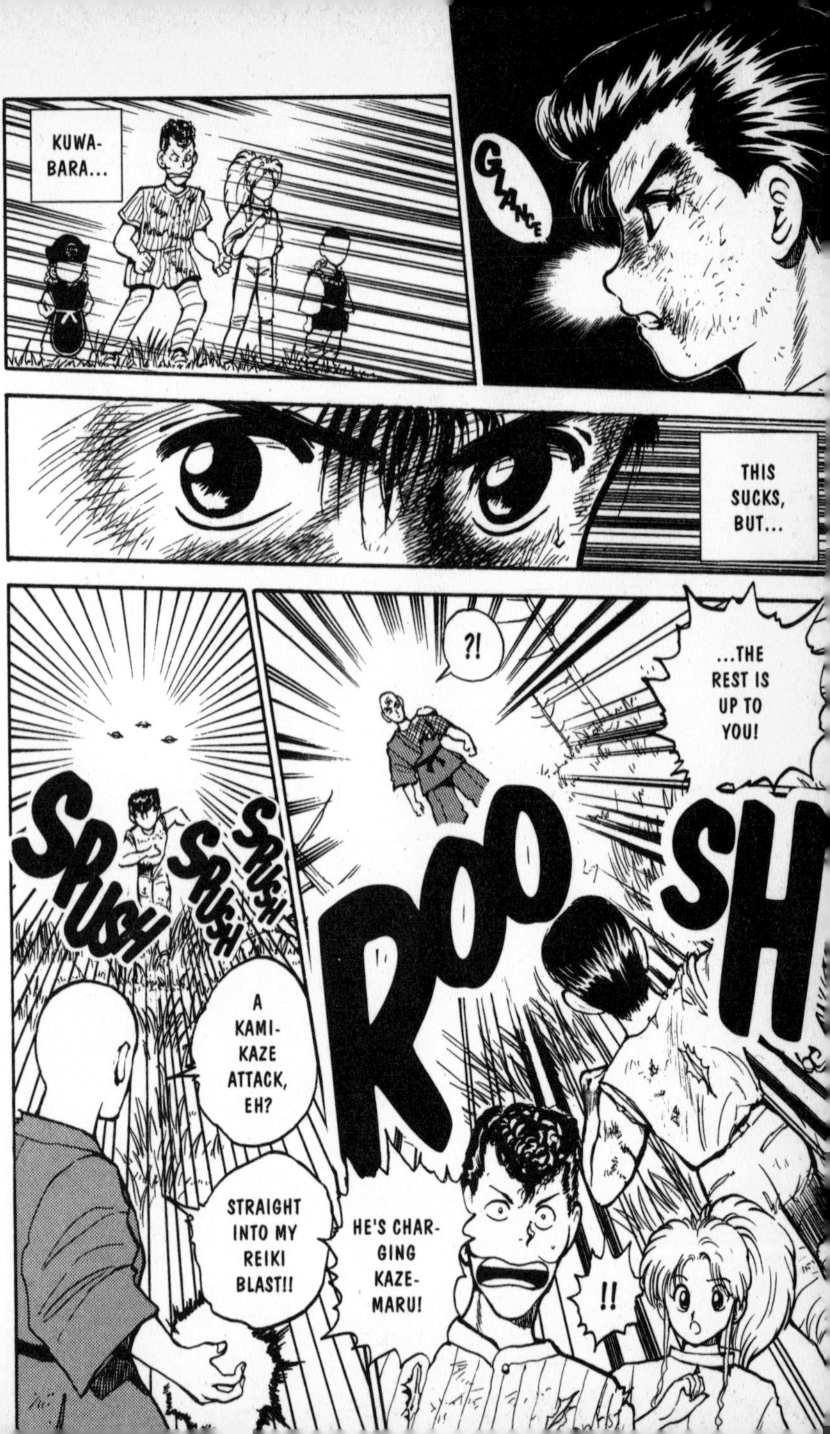
GLANCE
KUWA-BARA...
THIS SUCKS, BUT...
...THE REST IS UP TO YOU!
?!
ROOSH
!!
HE'S CHAR-GING KAZE-MARU!
SPLUSH SPLUSH SPLUSH
A KAMI-KAZE ATTACK, EH?
STRAIGHT INTO MY REIKI BLAST!!

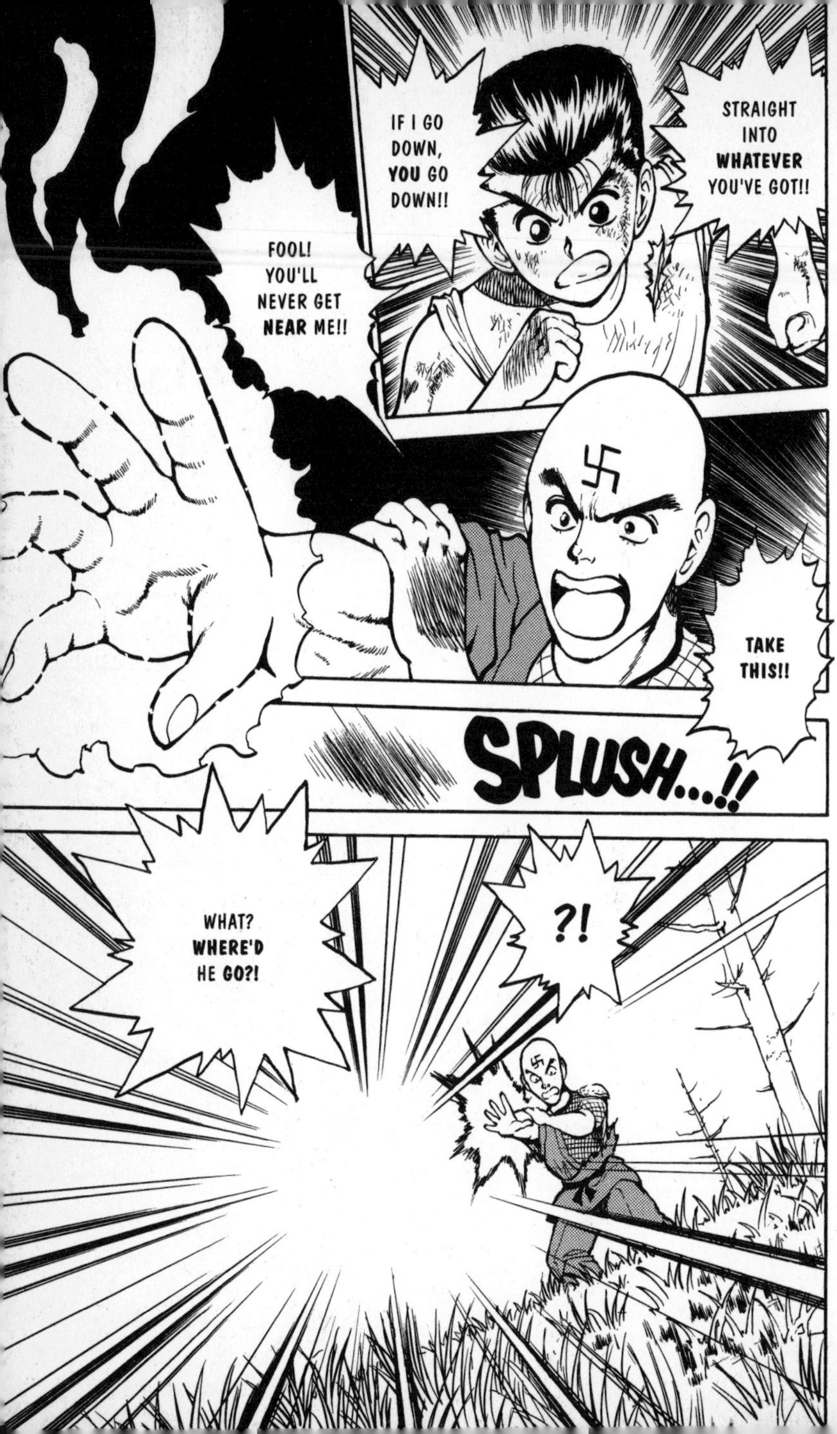
STRAIGHT INTO WHATEVER YOU'VE GOT!!
IF I GO DOWN, YOU GO DOWN!!
FOOL! YOU'LL NEVER GET NEAR ME!!
TAKE THIS!!
SPLUSH...!!
?!
WHAT? WHERE'D HE GO?!

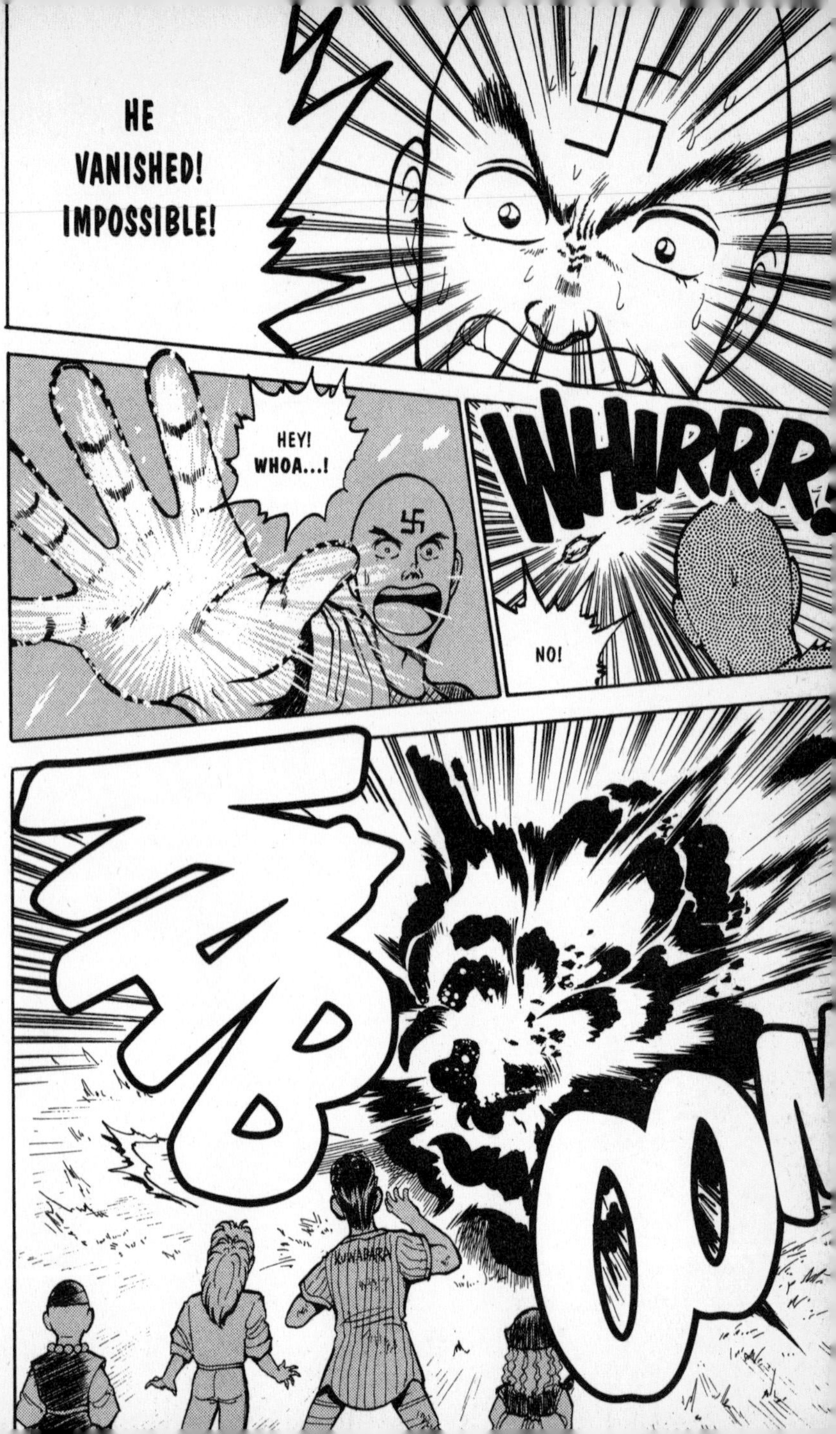
HE VANISHED! IMPOSSIBLE!
WHIRRR!
NO!
HEY! WHOA...!
BOO
KUWABARA

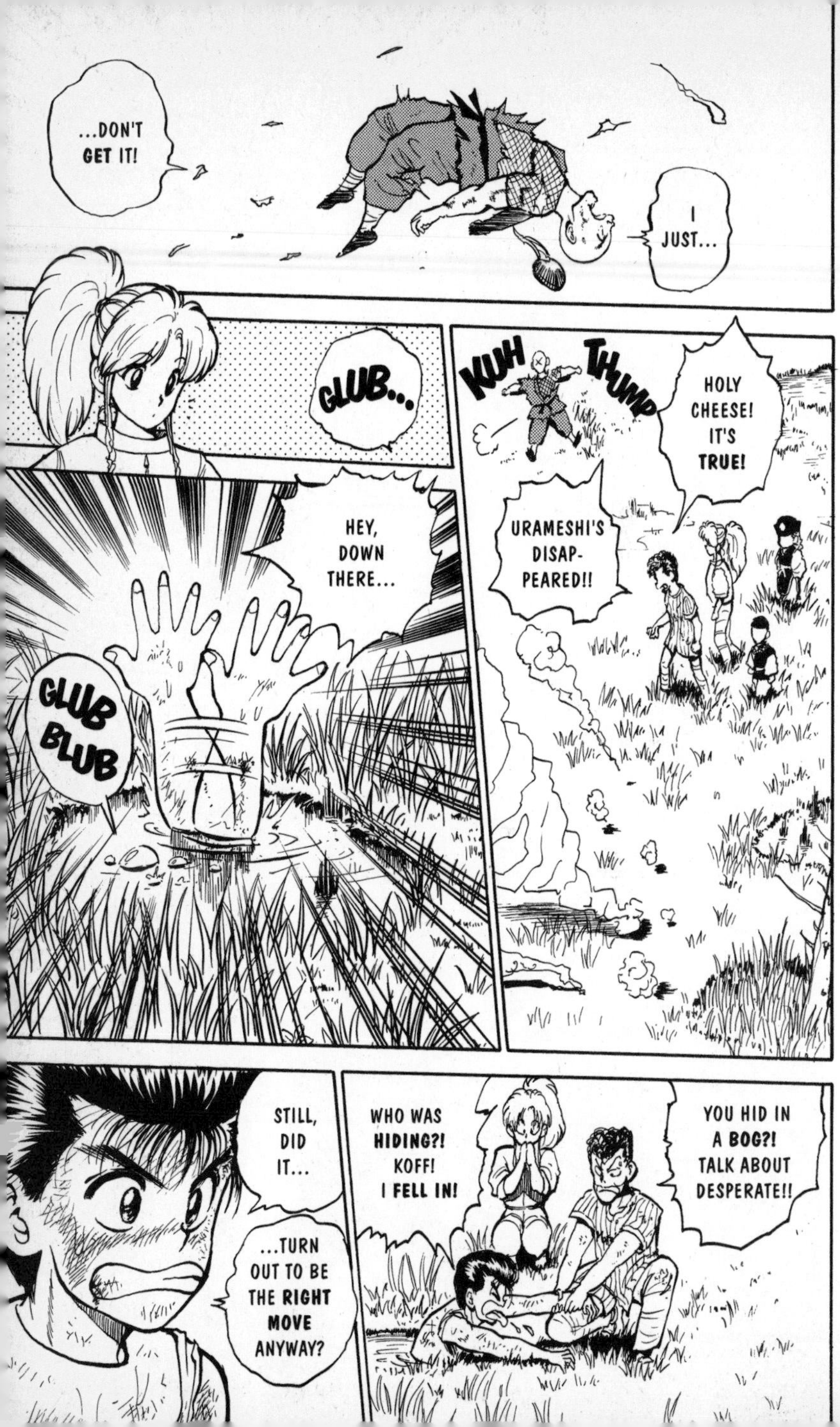
I JUST...
...DON'T GET IT!
KUH THUMP
HOLY CHEESE! IT'S TRUE!
URAMESHI'S DISAP-PEARED!!
GLUB...
HEY, DOWN THERE...
GLUB BLUB
YOU HID IN A BOG?! TALK ABOUT DESPERATE!!
WHO WAS HIDING?! KOFF! I FELL IN!
STILL, DID IT...
...TURN OUT TO BE THE RIGHT MOVE ANYWAY?

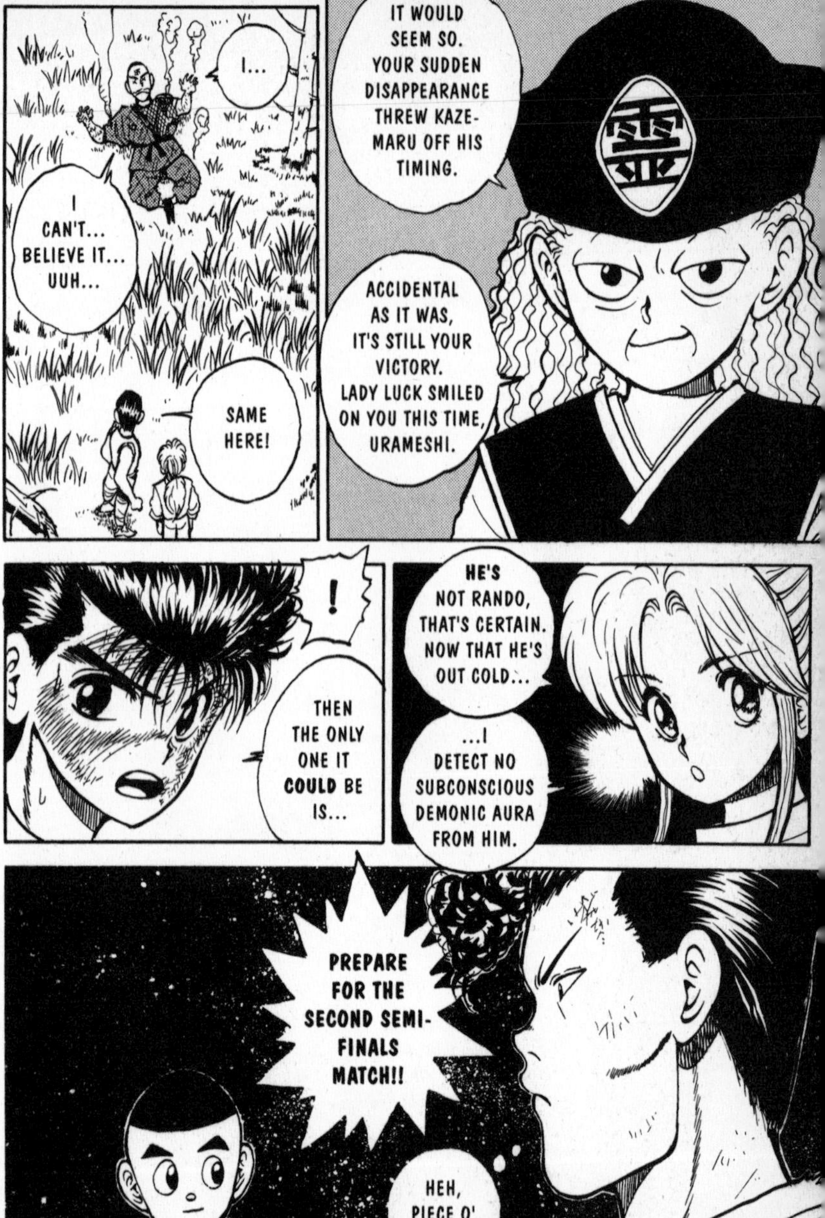
IT WOULD SEEM SO. YOUR SUDDEN DISAPPEARANCE THREW KAZE-MARU OFF HIS TIMING.
ACCIDENTAL AS IT WAS, IT'S STILL YOUR VICTORY. LADY LUCK SMILED ON YOU THIS TIME, URAMESHI.
I...
I CAN'T... BELIEVE IT... UUH...
SAME HERE!
HE'S NOT RANDO, THAT'S CERTAIN. NOW THAT HE'S OUT COLD...
...I DETECT NO SUBCONSCIOUS DEMONIC AURA FROM HIM.
!
THEN THE ONLY ONE IT COULD BE IS...
PREPARE FOR THE SECOND SEMI-FINALS MATCH!!
HEH, PIECE O' CAKE.

SHAOLIN = RANDO!?

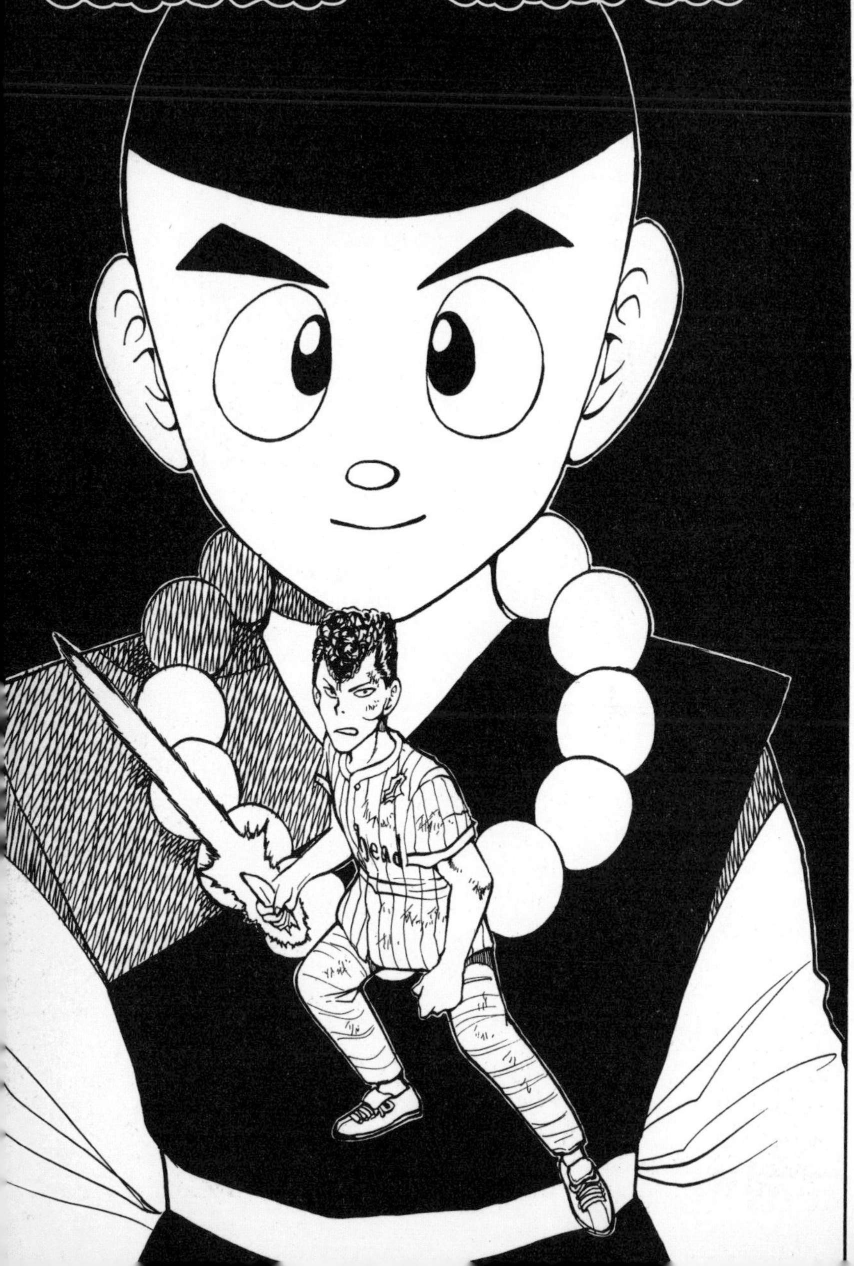

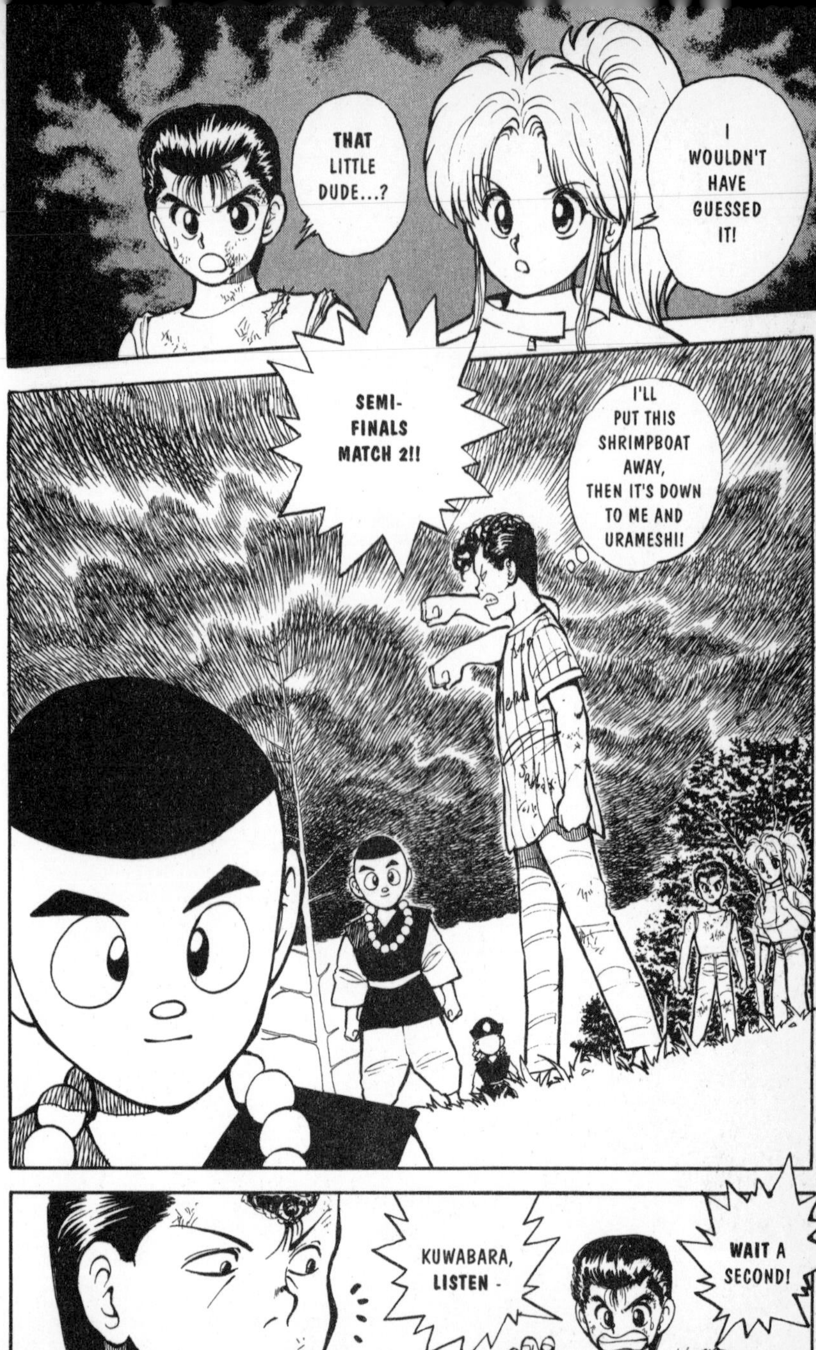
I WOULDN'T HAVE GUESSED IT!
THAT LITTLE DUDE...?
SEMI-FINALS MATCH 2!!
I'LL PUT THIS SHRIMPBOAT AWAY, THEN IT'S DOWN TO ME AND URAMESHI!
WAIT A SECOND!
KUWABARA, LISTEN -

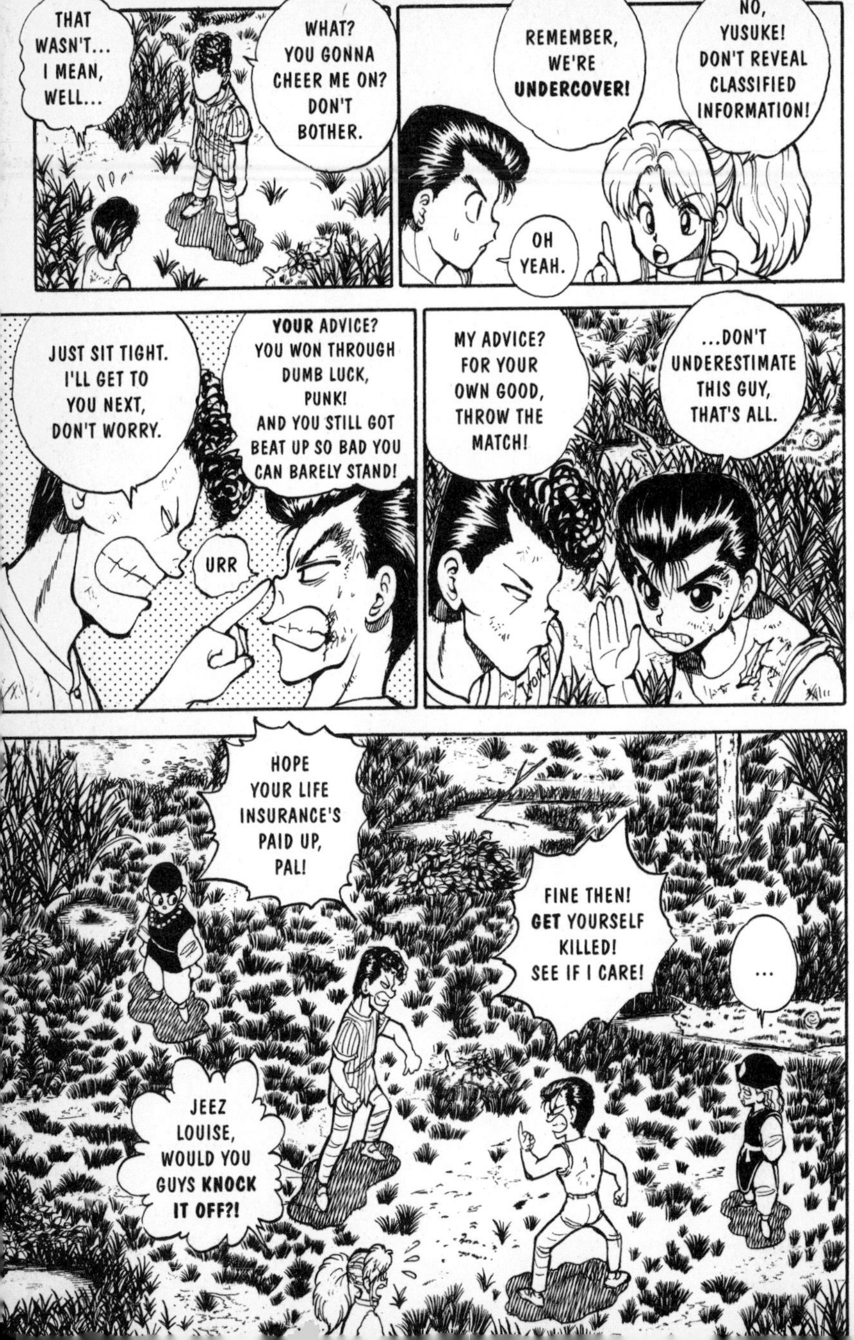
NO, YUSUKE! DON'T REVEAL CLASSIFIED INFORMATION!
REMEMBER, WE'RE **UNDERCOVER!**
OH YEAH.
WHAT? YOU GONNA CHEER ME ON? DON'T BOTHER.
THAT WASN'T... I MEAN, WELL...
...DON'T UNDERESTIMATE THIS GUY, THAT'S ALL.
MY ADVICE? FOR YOUR OWN GOOD, THROW THE MATCH!
YOUR ADVICE? YOU WON THROUGH DUMB LUCK, PUNK! AND YOU STILL GOT BEAT UP SO BAD YOU CAN BARELY STAND!
URR
JUST SIT TIGHT. I'LL GET TO YOU NEXT, DON'T WORRY.
...
FINE THEN! **GET** YOURSELF KILLED! SEE IF I CARE!
HOPE YOUR LIFE INSURANCE'S PAID UP, PAL!
JEEZ LOUISE, WOULD YOU GUYS **KNOCK IT OFF?!**

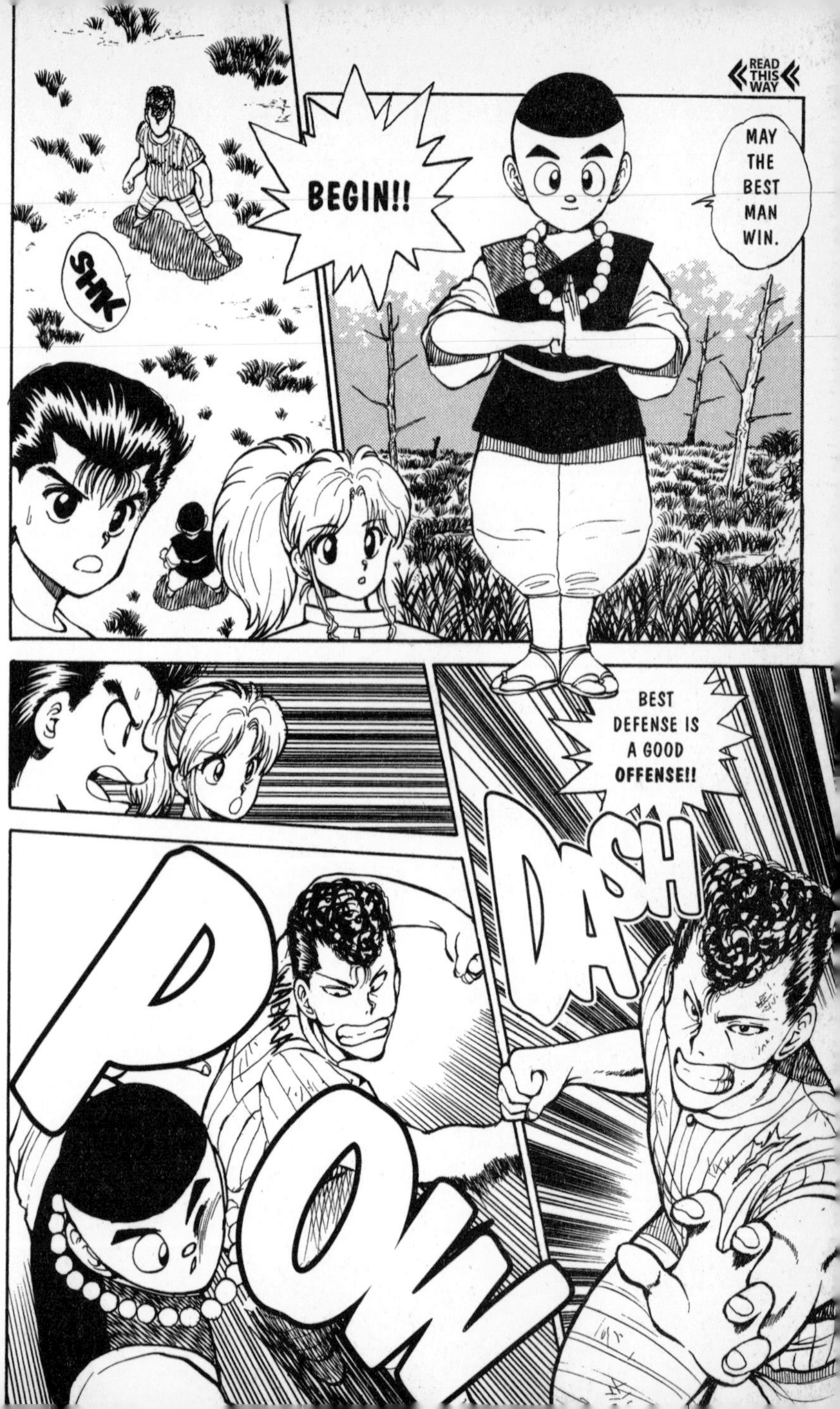
READ THIS WAY
MAY THE BEST MAN WIN.
BEGIN!!
SHINK
BEST DEFENSE IS A GOOD OFFENSE!!
DASH
POW!

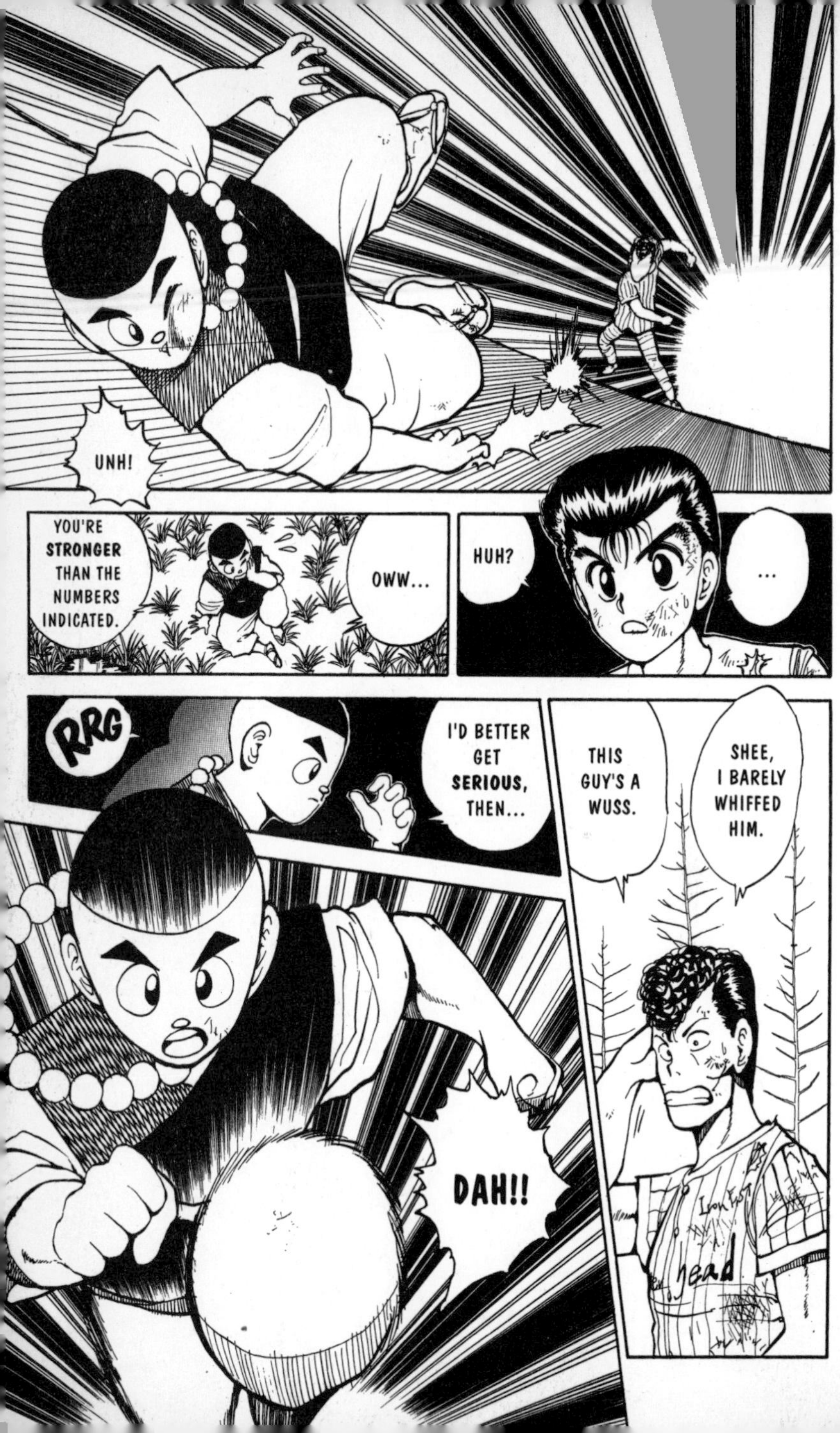

UNH!
...
HUH?
OWW...
YOU'RE **STRONGER** THAN THE NUMBERS INDICATED.
SHEE, I BARELY WHIFFED HIM.
THIS GUY'S A WUSS.
I'D BETTER GET **SERIOUS**, THEN...
RRG
DAH!!

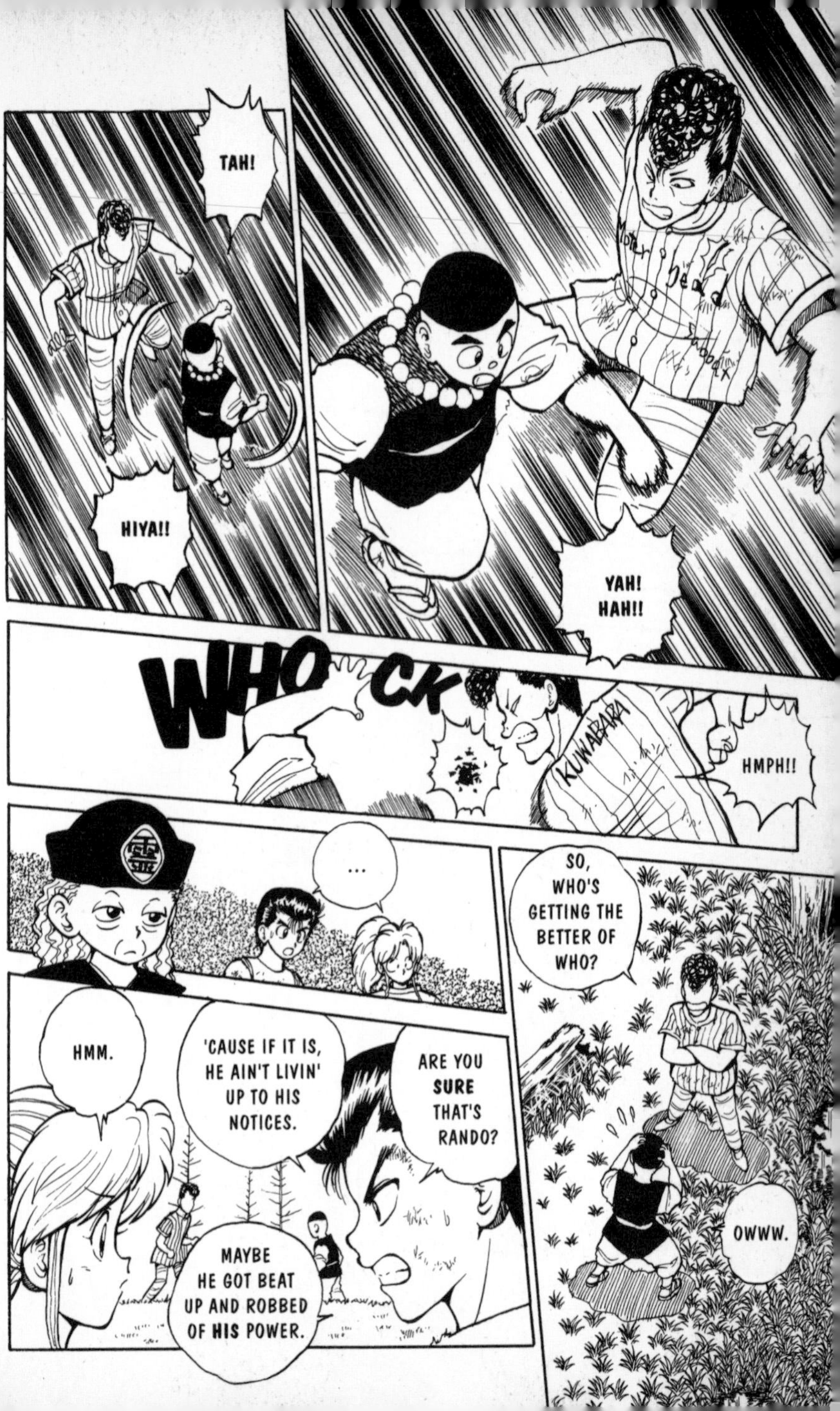
YAH!
HAH!!
TAH!
HIYA!!
HMPH!!
WHOCK
SO, WHO'S GETTING THE BETTER OF WHO?
OWWW.
...
ARE YOU SURE THAT'S RANDO?
'CAUSE IF IT IS, HE AIN'T LIVIN' UP TO HIS NOTICES.
HMM.
MAYBE HE GOT BEAT UP AND ROBBED OF HIS POWER.

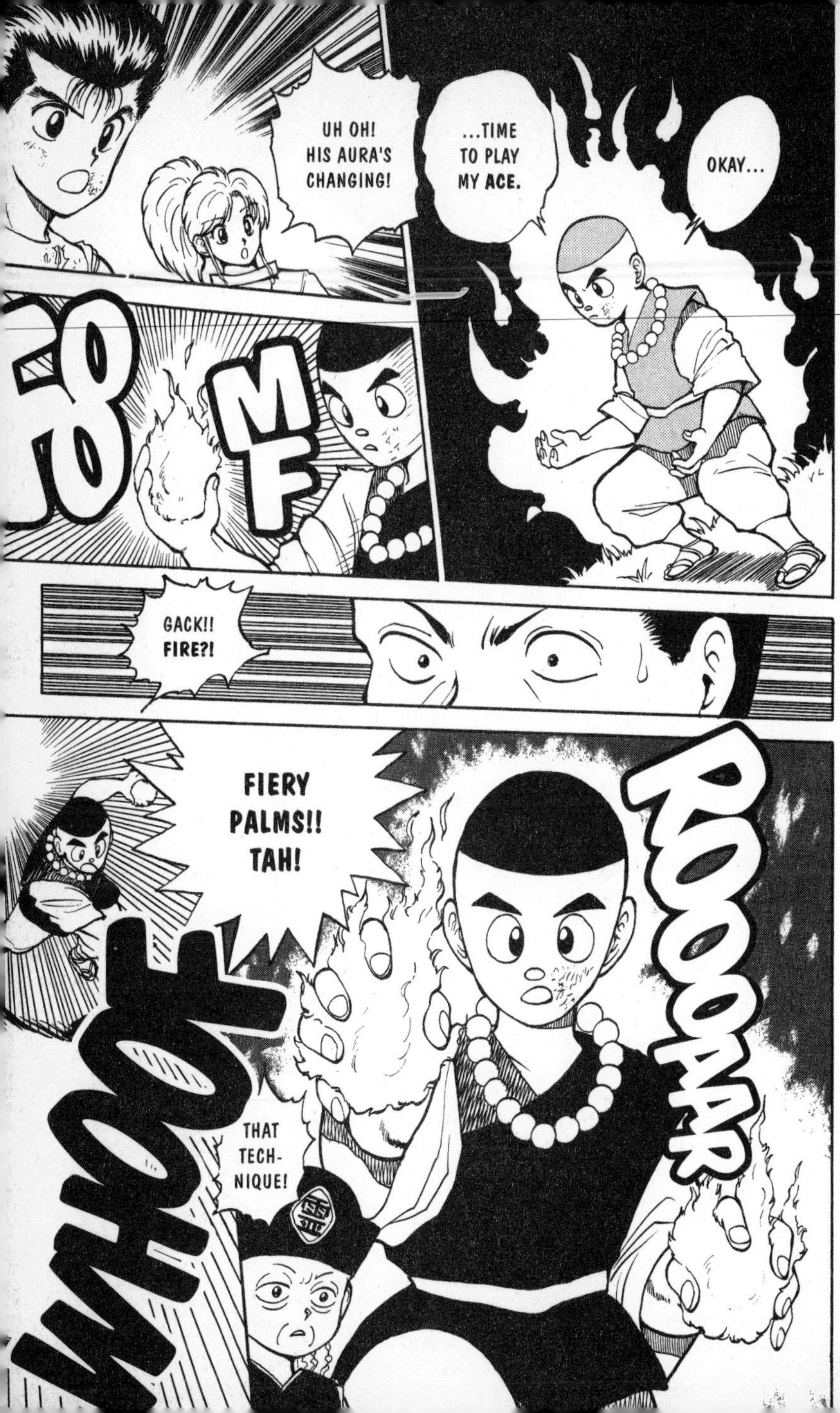
OKAY...
...TIME TO PLAY MY ACE.
UH OH! HIS AURA'S CHANGING!
FOOMF
GACK!! FIRE?!
ROOOAAR
FIERY PALMS!! TAH!
THAT TECH-NIQUE!
WHOOSH

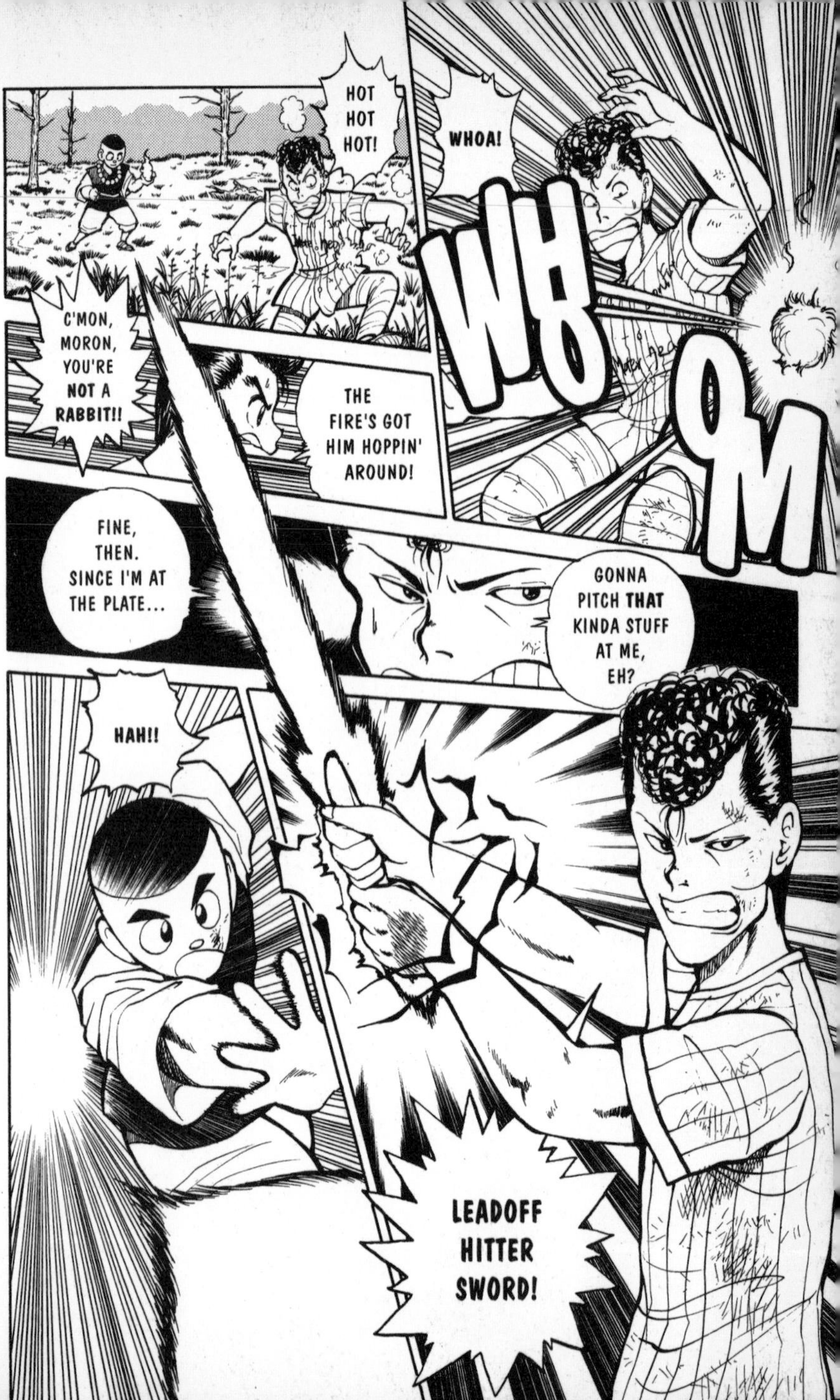
WHOA!
WHOOM
HOT HOT HOT!
THE FIRE'S GOT HIM HOPPIN' AROUND!
C'MON, MORON, YOU'RE **NOT A** RABBIT!!
GONNA PITCH **THAT** KINDA STUFF AT ME, EH?
FINE, THEN. SINCE I'M AT THE PLATE...
LEADOFF HITTER SWORD!
HAH!!

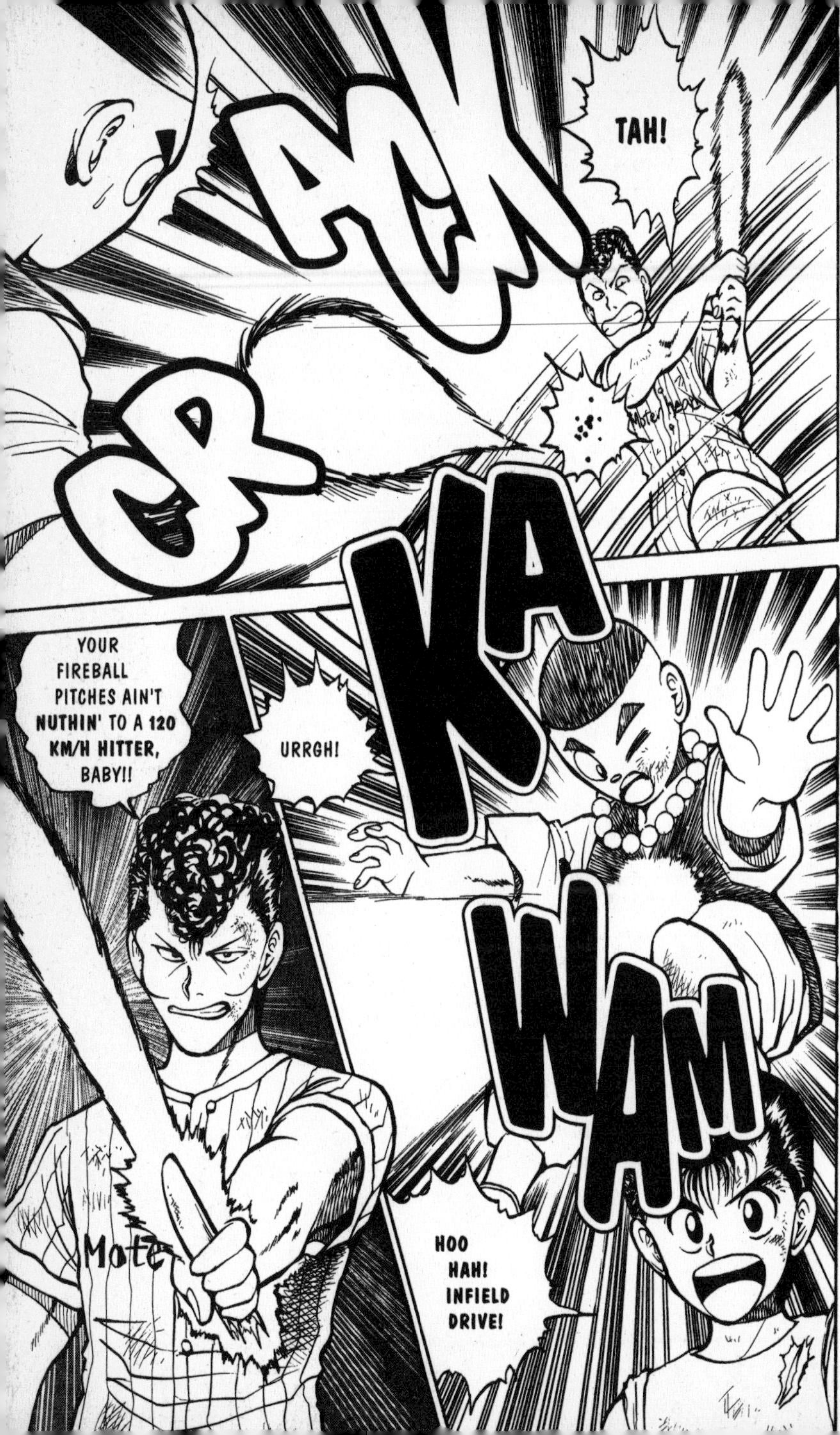
TAH!
CRACK
KA
WAM
URRGH!
HOO HAH! INFIELD DRIVE!
YOUR FIREBALL PITCHES AIN'T NUTHIN' TO A 120 KM/H HITTER, BABY!!
Mote

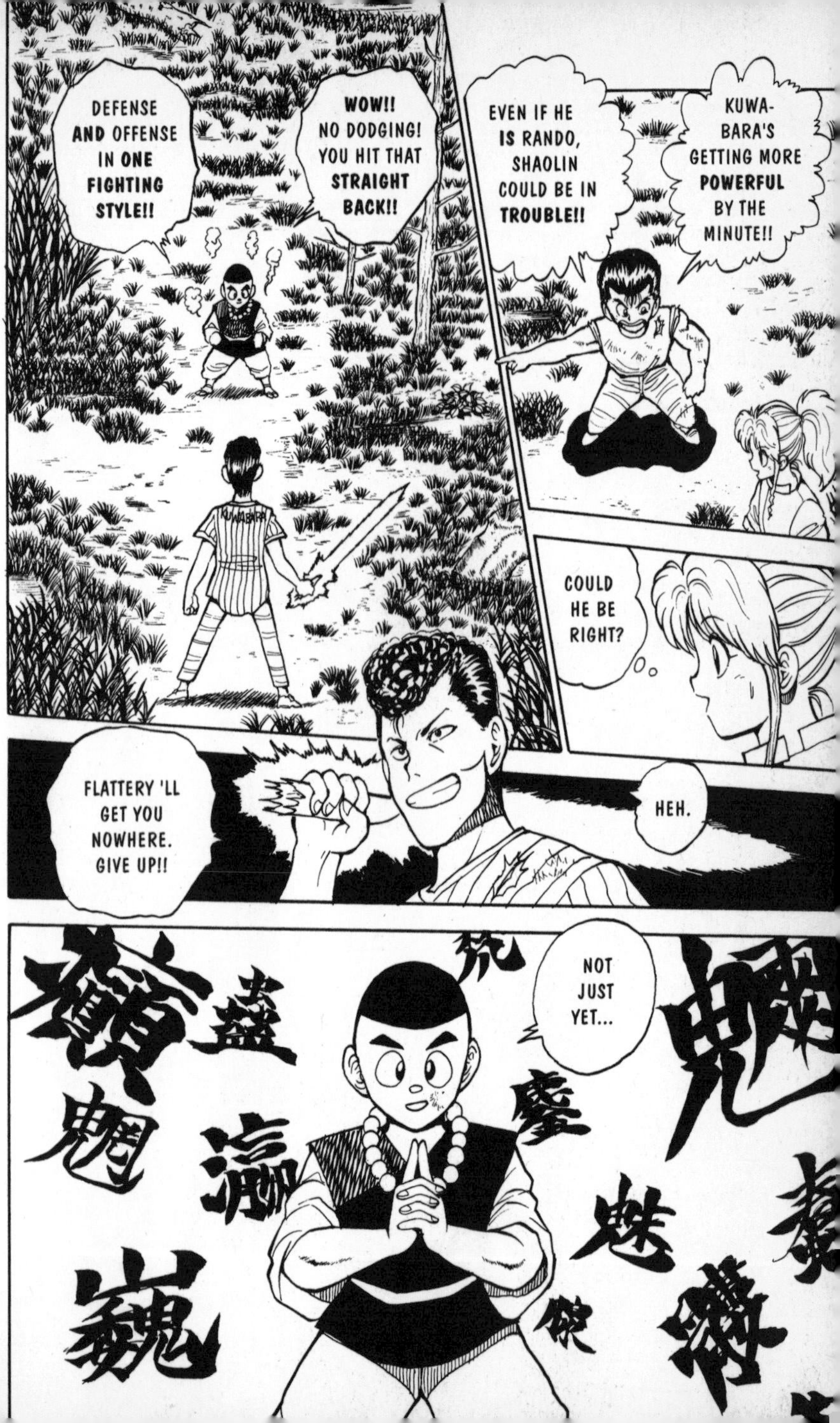
KUWA-BARA'S GETTING MORE POWERFUL BY THE MINUTE!!
EVEN IF HE IS RANDO, SHAOLIN COULD BE IN TROUBLE!!
COULD HE BE RIGHT?
WOW!! NO DODGING! YOU HIT THAT STRAIGHT BACK!!
DEFENSE AND OFFENSE IN ONE FIGHTING STYLE!!
KUWABARA
HEH.
FLATTERY 'LL GET YOU NOWHERE. GIVE UP!!
NOT JUST YET...

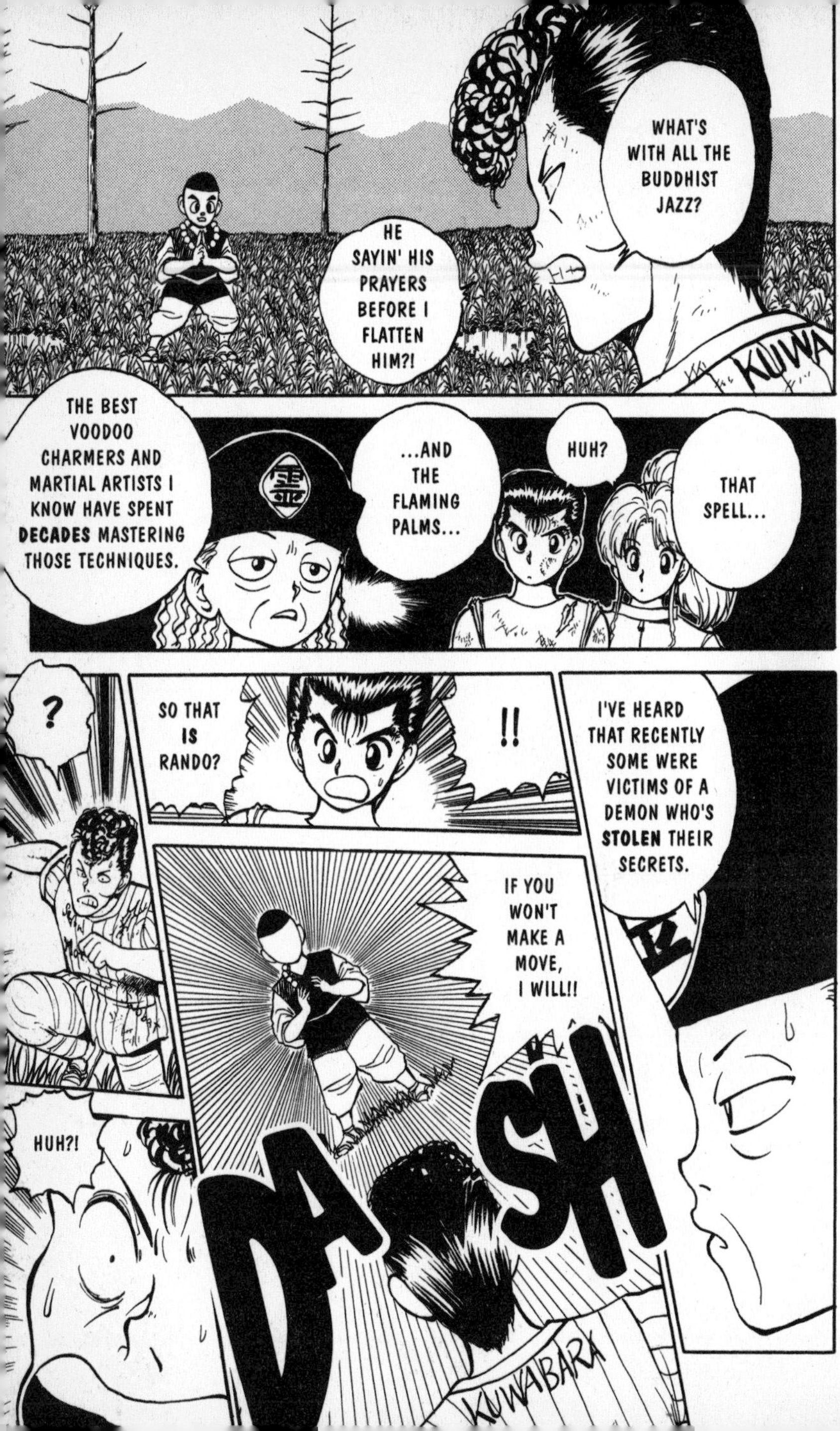
WHAT'S WITH ALL THE BUDDHIST JAZZ?
HE SAYIN' HIS PRAYERS BEFORE I FLATTEN HIM?!
KUWA
THAT SPELL...
HUH?
...AND THE FLAMING PALMS...
THE BEST VOODOO CHARMERS AND MARTIAL ARTISTS I KNOW HAVE SPENT DECADES MASTERING THOSE TECHNIQUES.
I'VE HEARD THAT RECENTLY SOME WERE VICTIMS OF A DEMON WHO'S STOLEN THEIR SECRETS.
!!
SO THAT IS RANDO?
?
IF YOU WON'T MAKE A MOVE, I WILL!!
DASH
HUH?!
KUWABARA

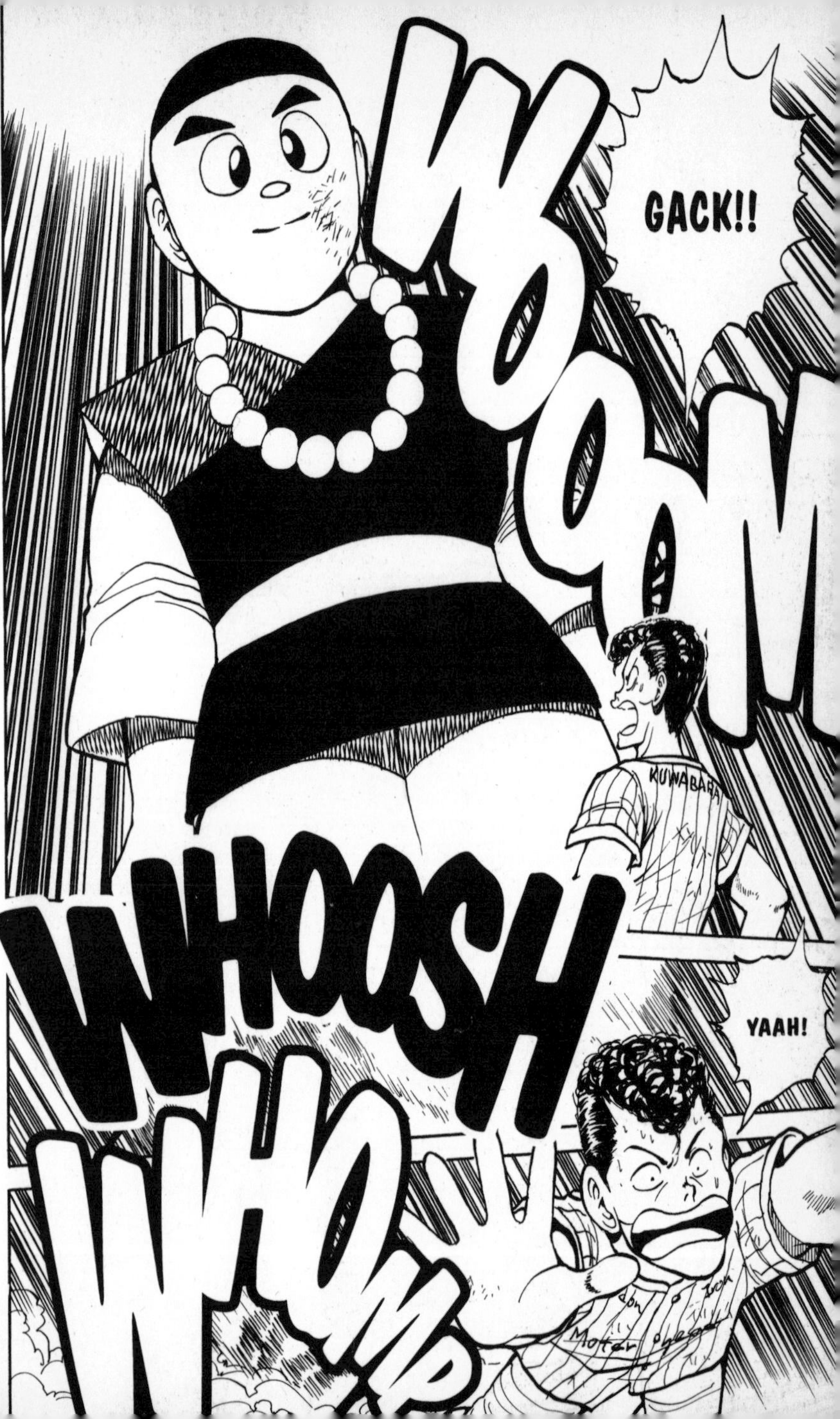
GACK!!
WOOOM
KUWABARA
YAAH!
WHOOSH
WHOMP

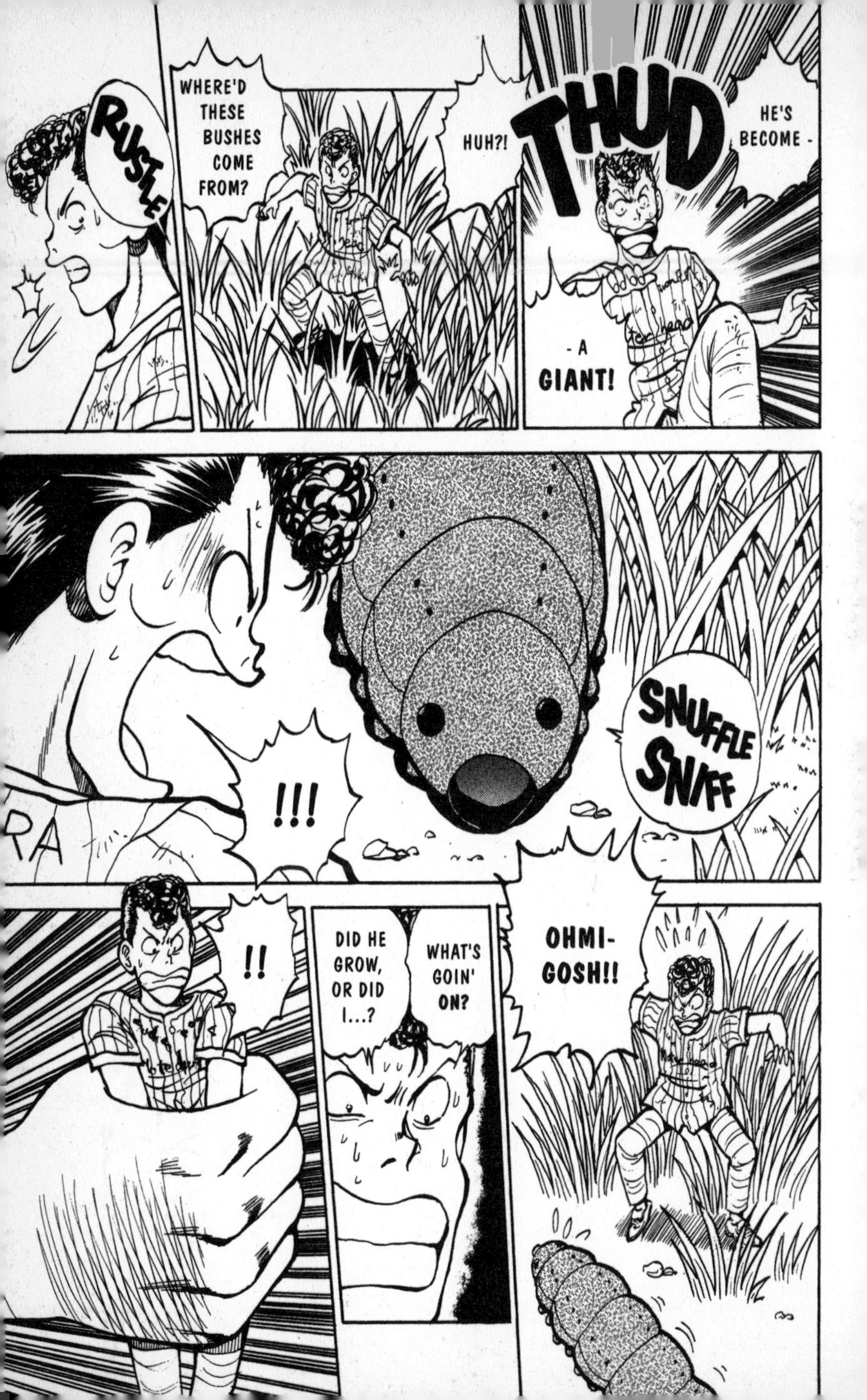
THUD
HE'S BECOME -
- A GIANT!
WHERE'D THESE BUSHES COME FROM?
HUH?!
RUSTLE
SNUFFLE SNIFF
!!!
RA
OHMI-GOSH!!
WHAT'S GOIN' ON?
DID HE GROW, OR DID I...?
!!

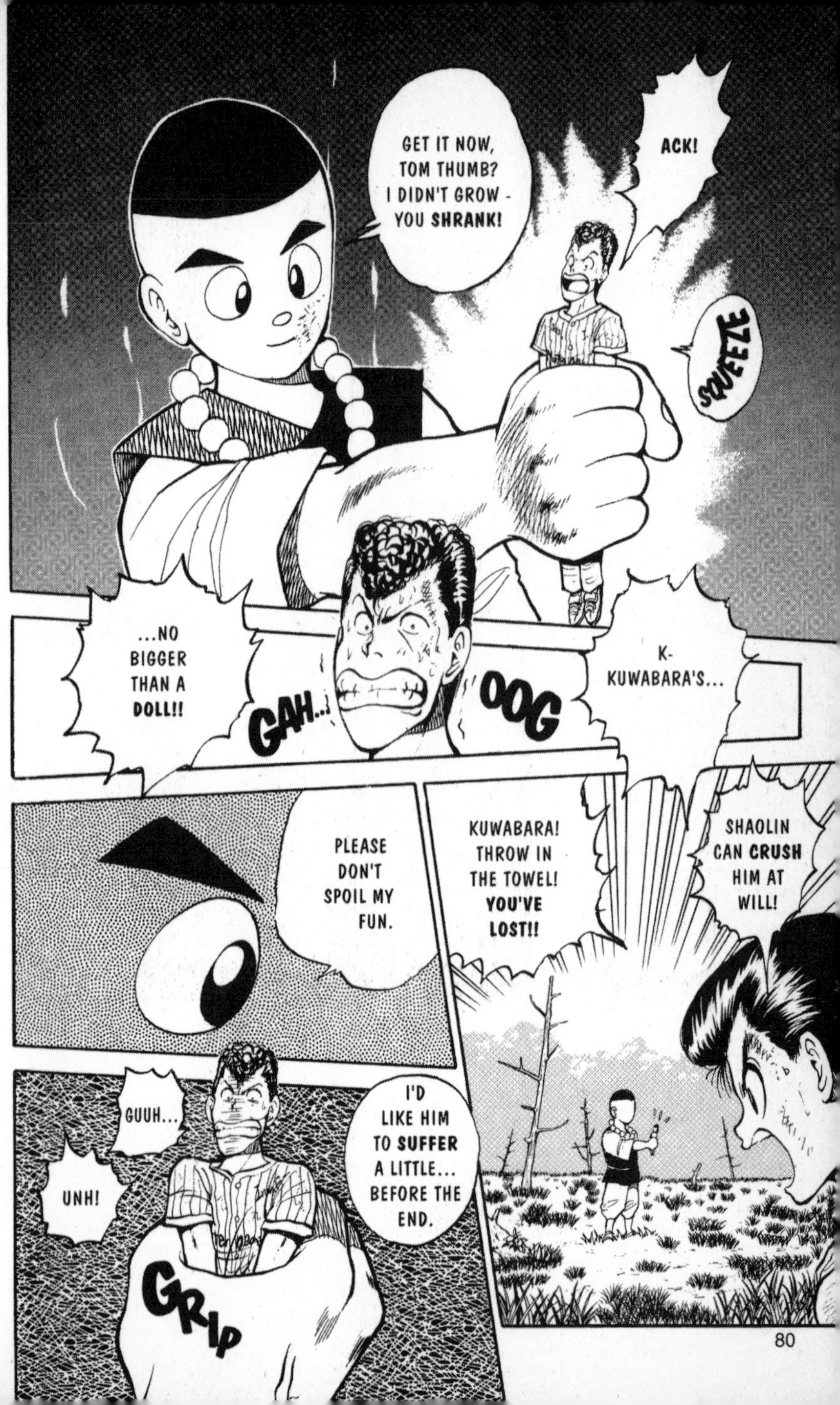
ACK!
GET IT NOW, TOM THUMB? I DIDN'T GROW - YOU SHRANK!
SQUEEZE
K-KUWABARA'S...
OOG
GAH..
...NO BIGGER THAN A DOLL!!
SHAOLIN CAN CRUSH HIM AT WILL!
KUWABARA! THROW IN THE TOWEL! YOU'VE LOST!!
PLEASE DON'T SPOIL MY FUN.
I'D LIKE HIM TO SUFFER A LITTLE... BEFORE THE END.
GUUH...
UNH!
GRIP

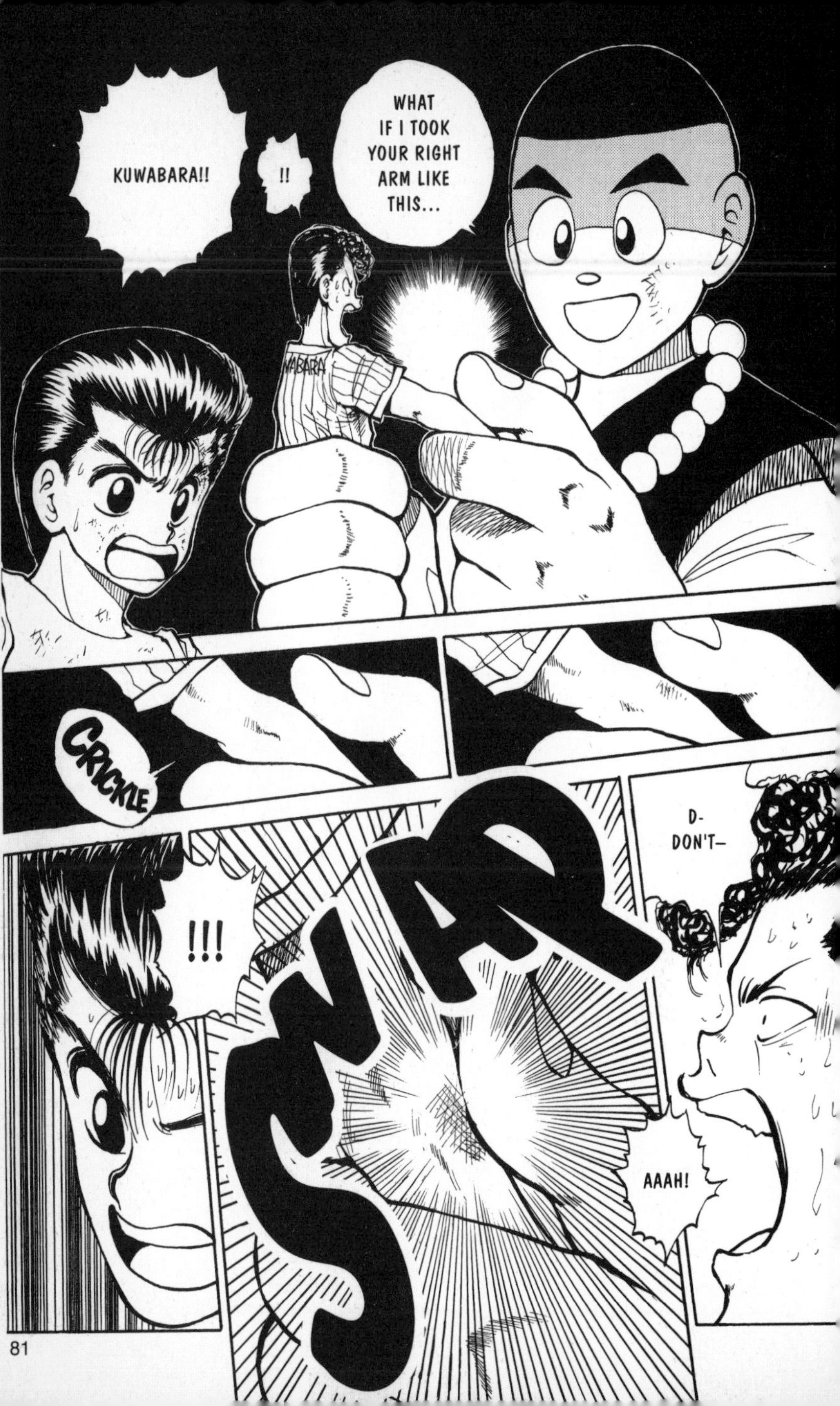
WHAT IF I TOOK YOUR RIGHT ARM LIKE THIS...
!!
KUWABARA!!
CRICKLE
D- DON'T—
AAAH!
SNAP
!!!

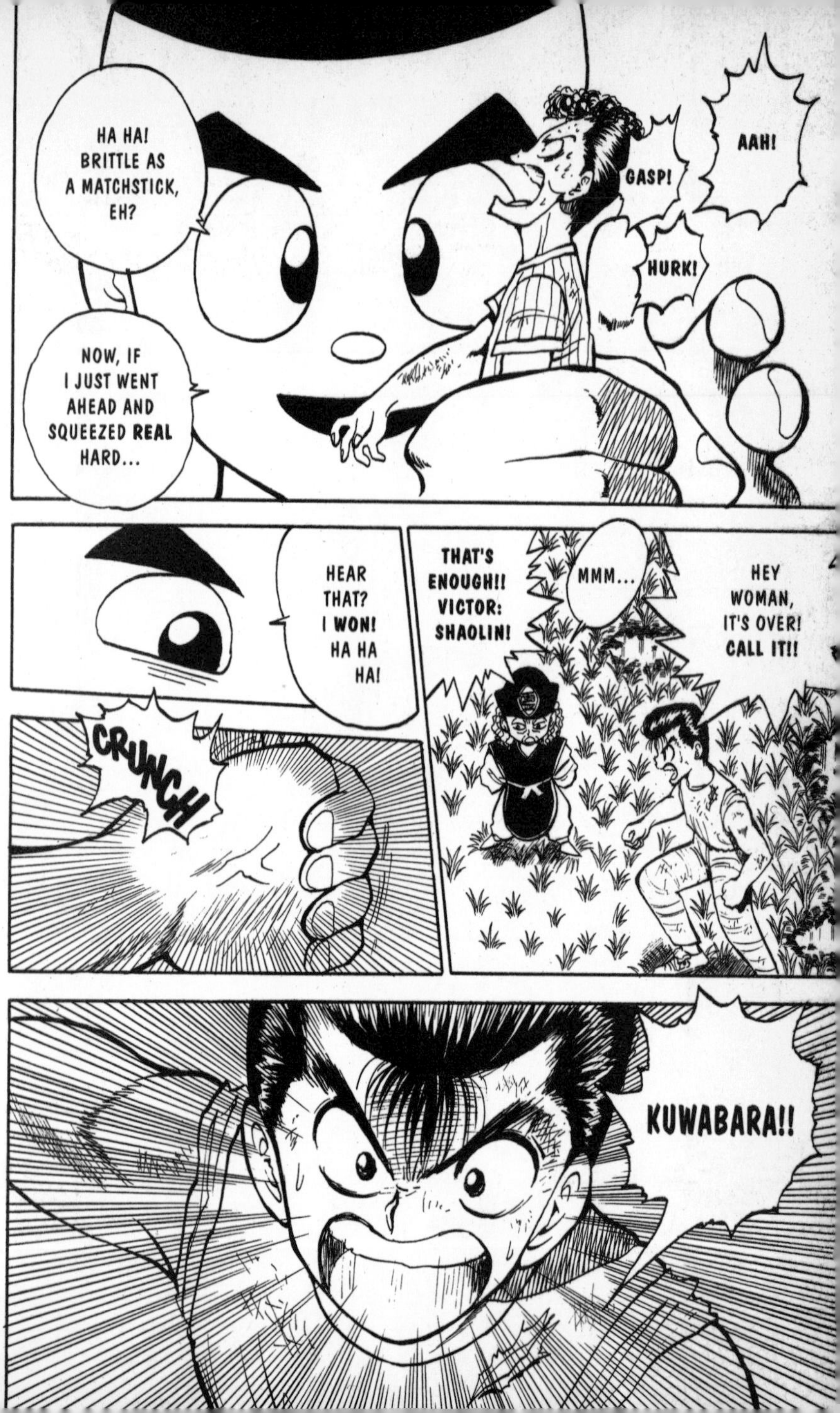
AAH!
GASP!
HURK!
HA HA! BRITTLE AS A MATCHSTICK, EH?
NOW, IF I JUST WENT AHEAD AND SQUEEZED **REAL** HARD...
HEY WOMAN, IT'S OVER! **CALL IT!!**
MMM...
THAT'S ENOUGH!! VICTOR: SHAOLIN!
HEAR THAT? **I WON!** HA HA HA!
CRUNCH
KUWABARA!!

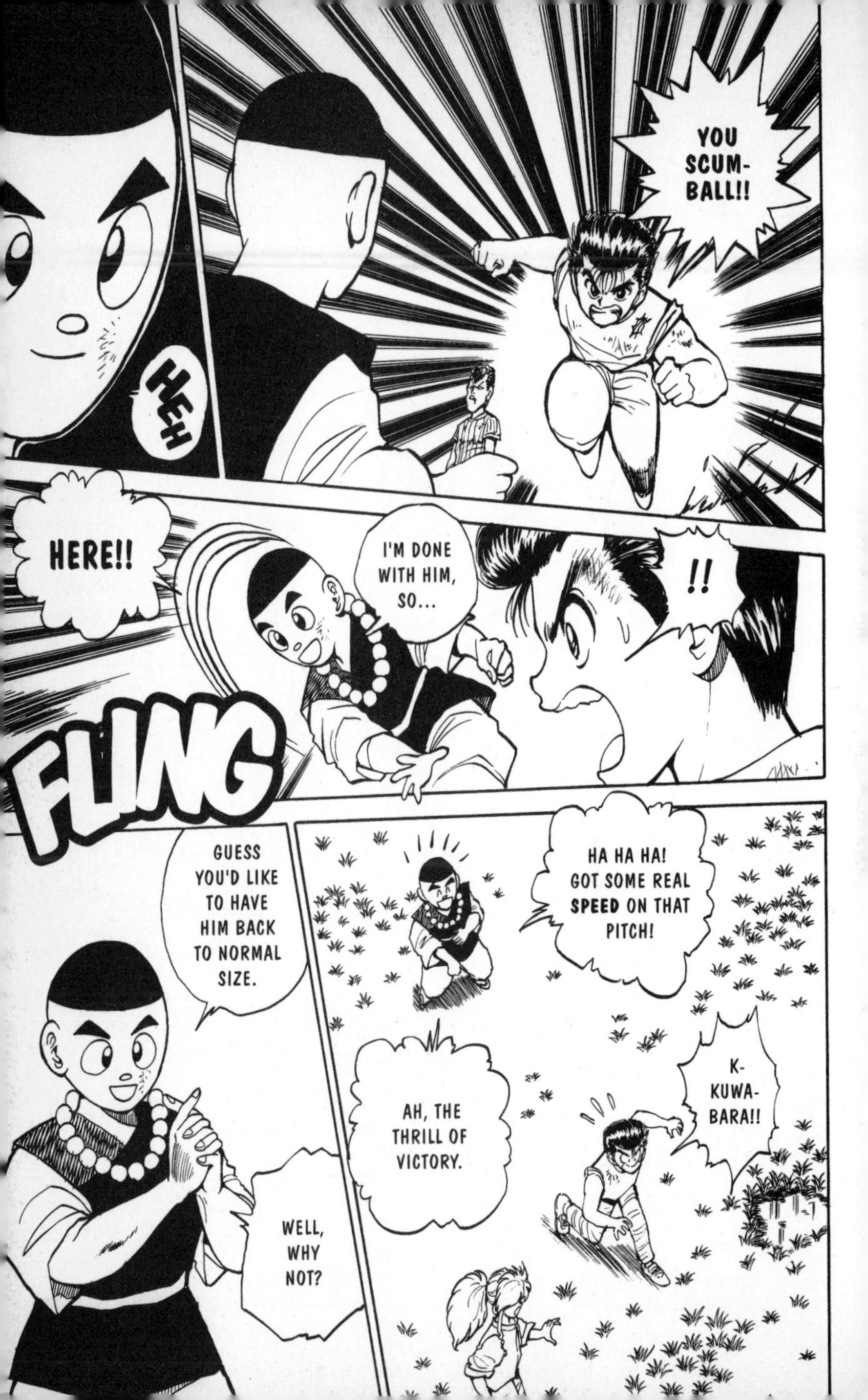
YOU SCUM-BALL!!
HEH
!!
I'M DONE WITH HIM, SO...
HERE!!
FLING
HA HA HA! GOT SOME REAL **SPEED** ON THAT PITCH!
K-KUWA-BARA!!
AH, THE THRILL OF VICTORY.
GUESS YOU'D LIKE TO HAVE HIM BACK TO NORMAL SIZE.
WELL, WHY NOT?

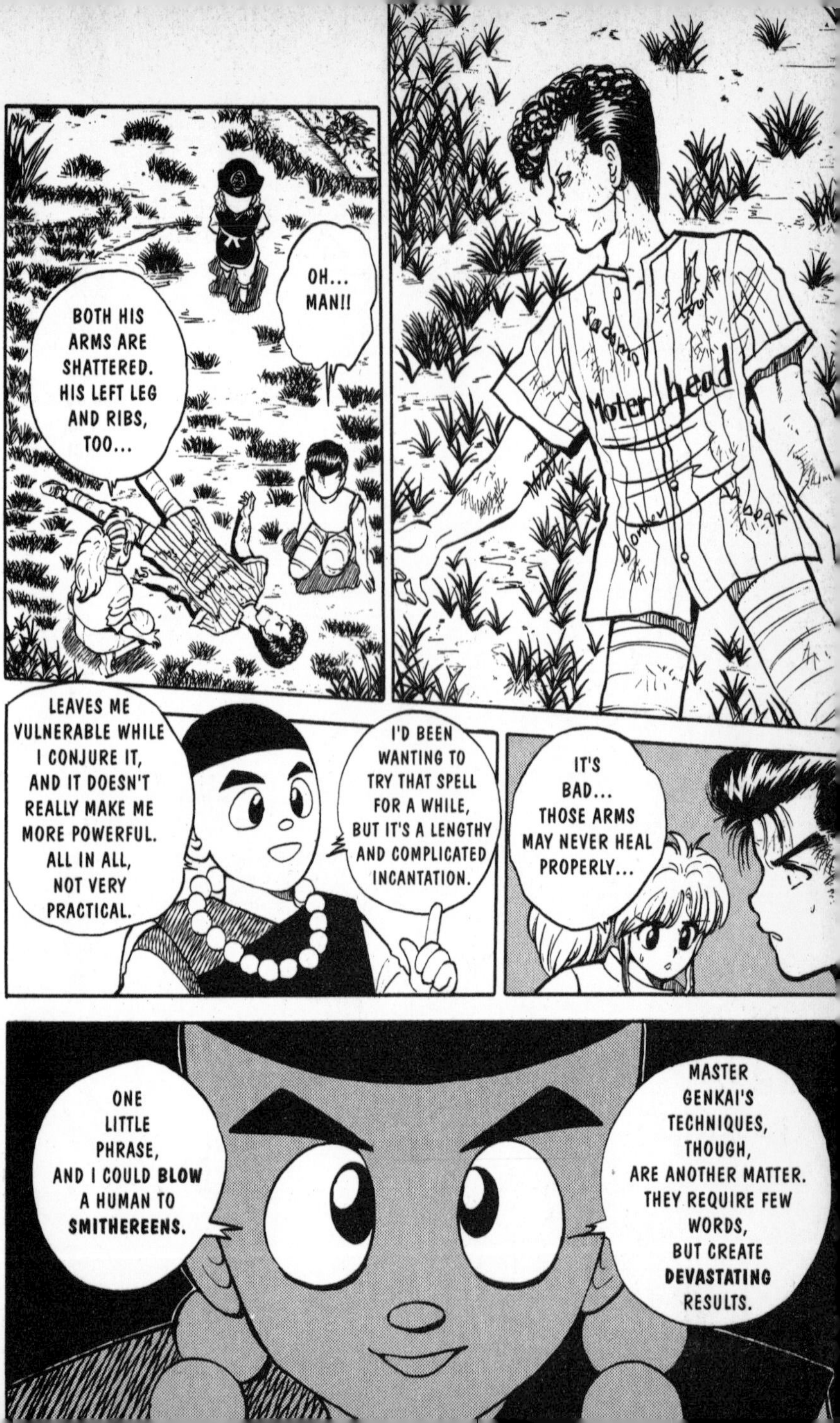
Moter head
OH... MAN!!
BOTH HIS ARMS ARE SHATTERED. HIS LEFT LEG AND RIBS, TOO...
IT'S BAD... THOSE ARMS MAY NEVER HEAL PROPERLY...
I'D BEEN WANTING TO TRY THAT SPELL FOR A WHILE, BUT IT'S A LENGTHY AND COMPLICATED INCANTATION.
LEAVES ME VULNERABLE WHILE I CONJURE IT, AND IT DOESN'T REALLY MAKE ME MORE POWERFUL. ALL IN ALL, NOT VERY PRACTICAL.
MASTER GENKAI'S TECHNIQUES, THOUGH, ARE ANOTHER MATTER. THEY REQUIRE FEW WORDS, BUT CREATE DEVASTATING RESULTS.
ONE LITTLE PHRASE, AND I COULD BLOW A HUMAN TO SMITHEREENS.

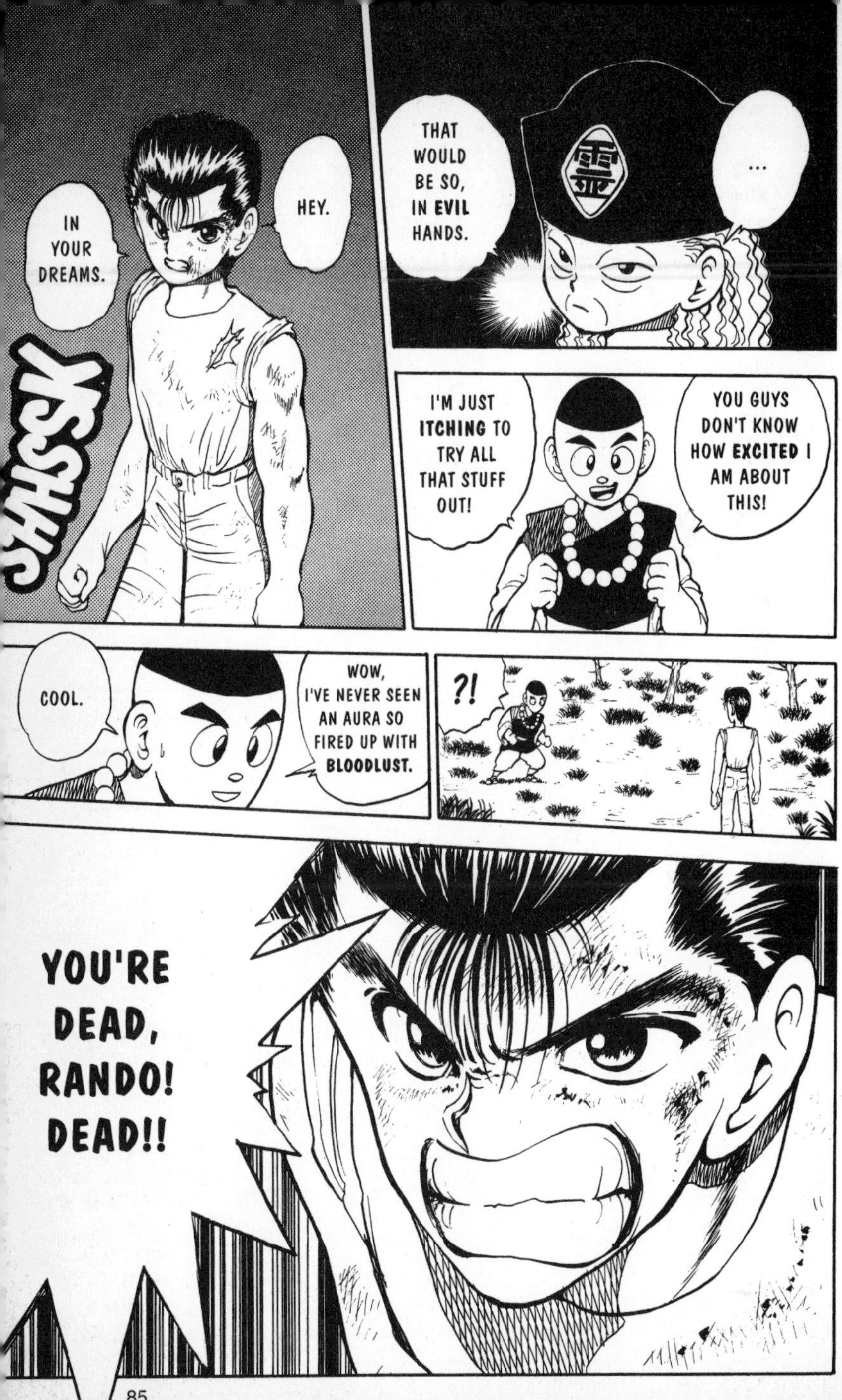
...
THAT WOULD BE SO, IN EVIL HANDS.
YOU GUYS DON'T KNOW HOW EXCITED I AM ABOUT THIS!
I'M JUST ITCHING TO TRY ALL THAT STUFF OUT!
HEY.
IN YOUR DREAMS.
SHSSK
?!
WOW, I'VE NEVER SEEN AN AURA SO FIRED UP WITH BLOODLUST.
COOL.
YOU'RE DEAD, RANDO! DEAD!!

My Rambling Diary, Part 2 ♡ ♭

Hanshin Tigers: 5 Consecutive Wins!!

The pitcher dominated the competition 5 games in a row. This winning streak will probably continue... NO! It will definitely continue!

I want to assert here that if this season goes to a full 200 games, the Tigers will be the champions - 100%.

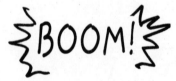

BOOM!

(Following a baseball team with absolute loyalty requires the same kind of brain structure a cartoonist needs to draw a comic every single week. I once witnessed a celebrity fan of the Yomiuri Giants during their disastrous game against the Chunichi Dragons. The celebrity watched with sad and angry eyes all the way to the ninth inning. When your favorite team is losing, that's when you have to look at them with warm and affectionate eyes.)

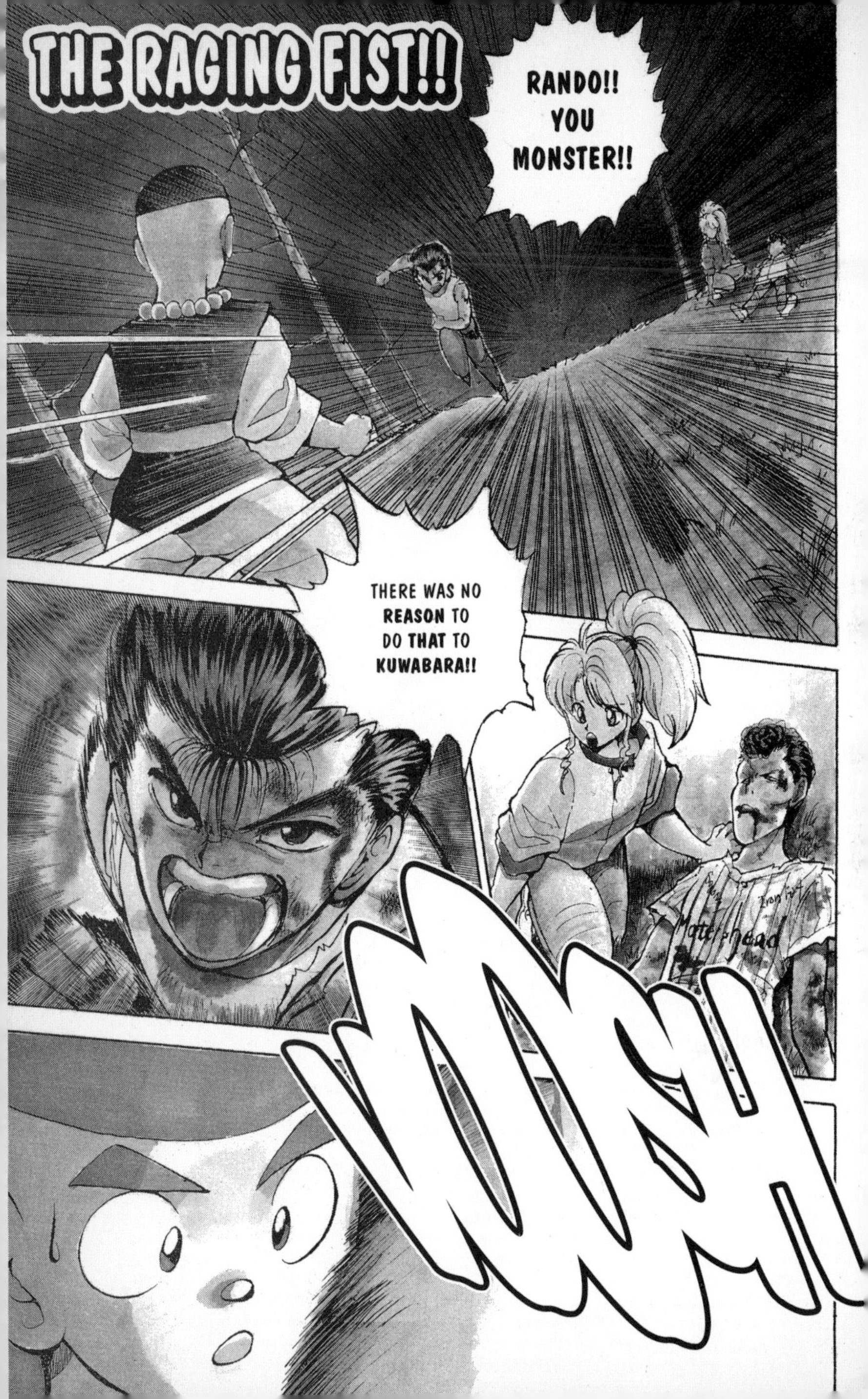
THE RAGING FIST!!
RANDO!! YOU MONSTER!!
THERE WAS NO REASON TO DO THAT TO KUWABARA!!
WOOSH

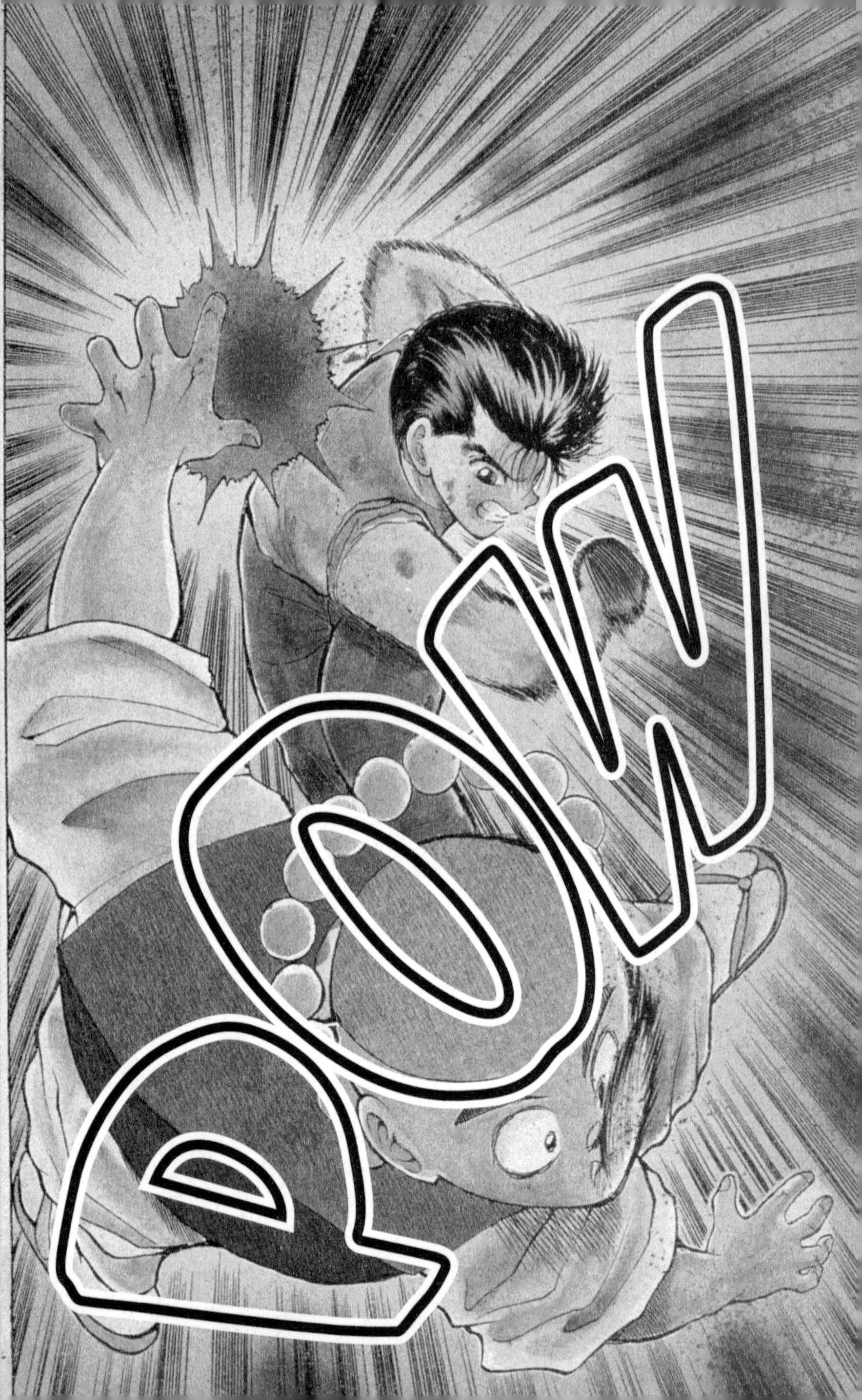
POW

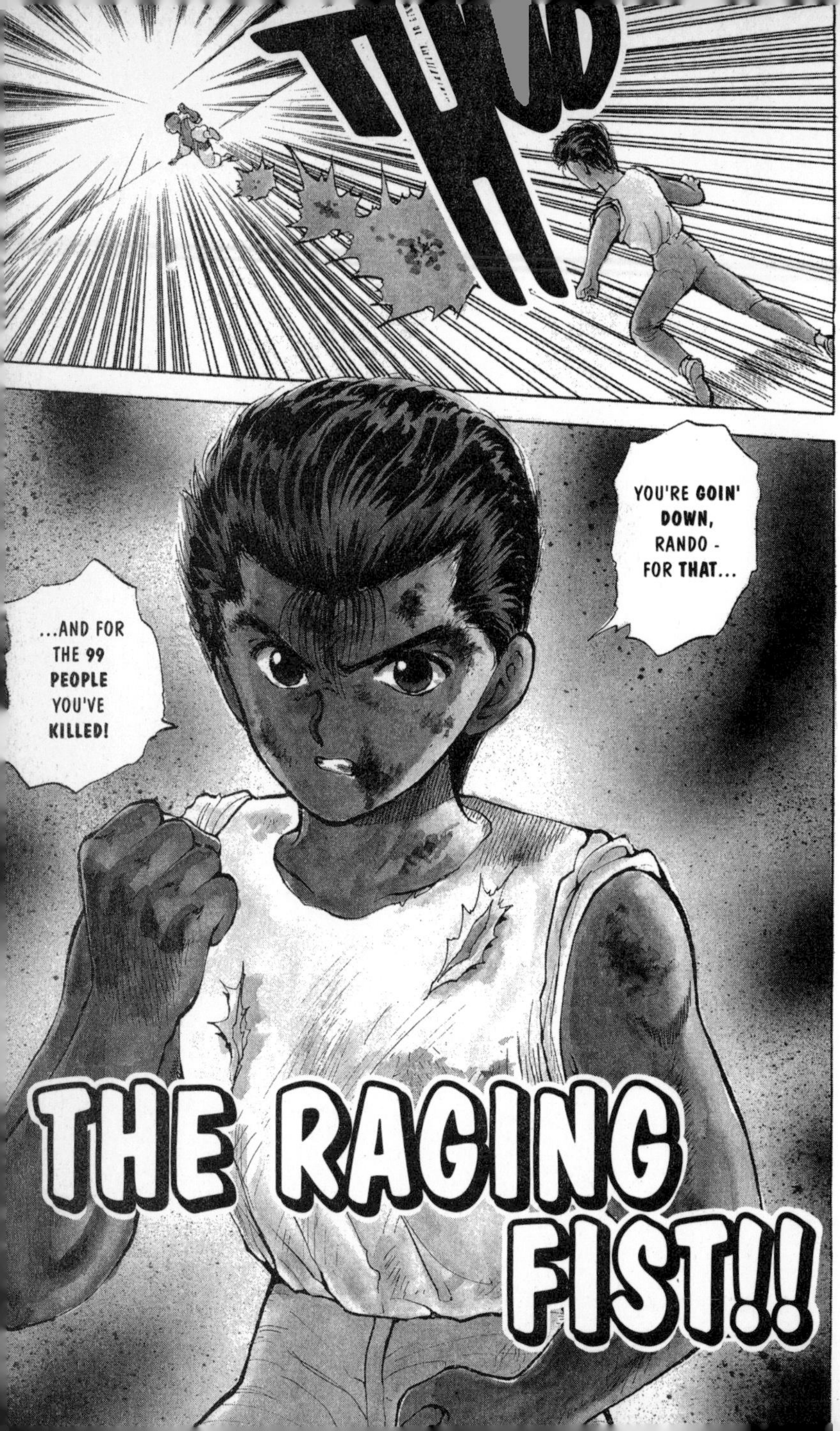
THUD
YOU'RE GOIN' DOWN, RANDO - FOR THAT...
...AND FOR THE 99 PEOPLE YOU'VE KILLED!
THE RAGING FIST!!

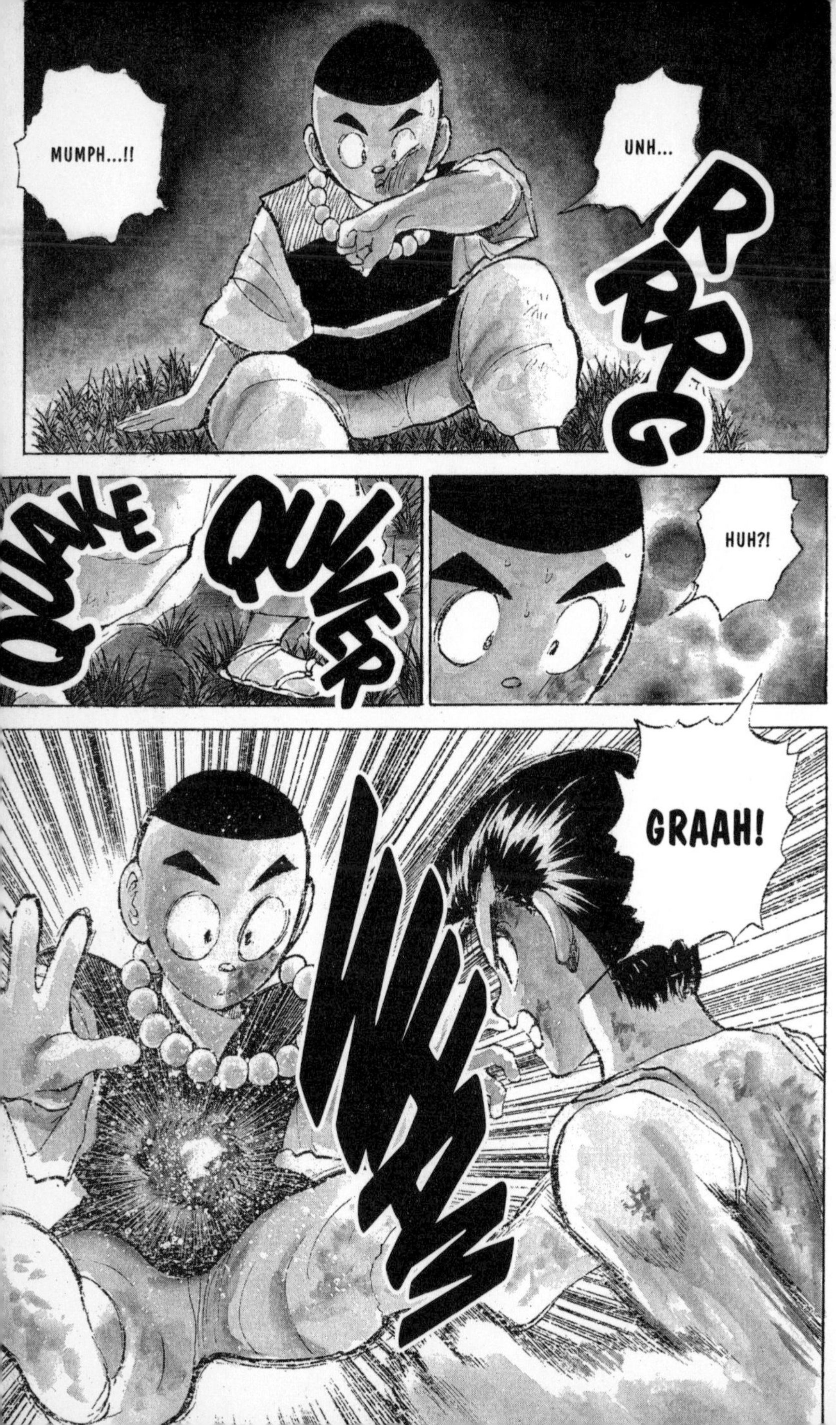
UNH...
RRRG
MUMPH...!!
HUH?!
QUIVER
QUAKE
GRAAH!
WHAM!

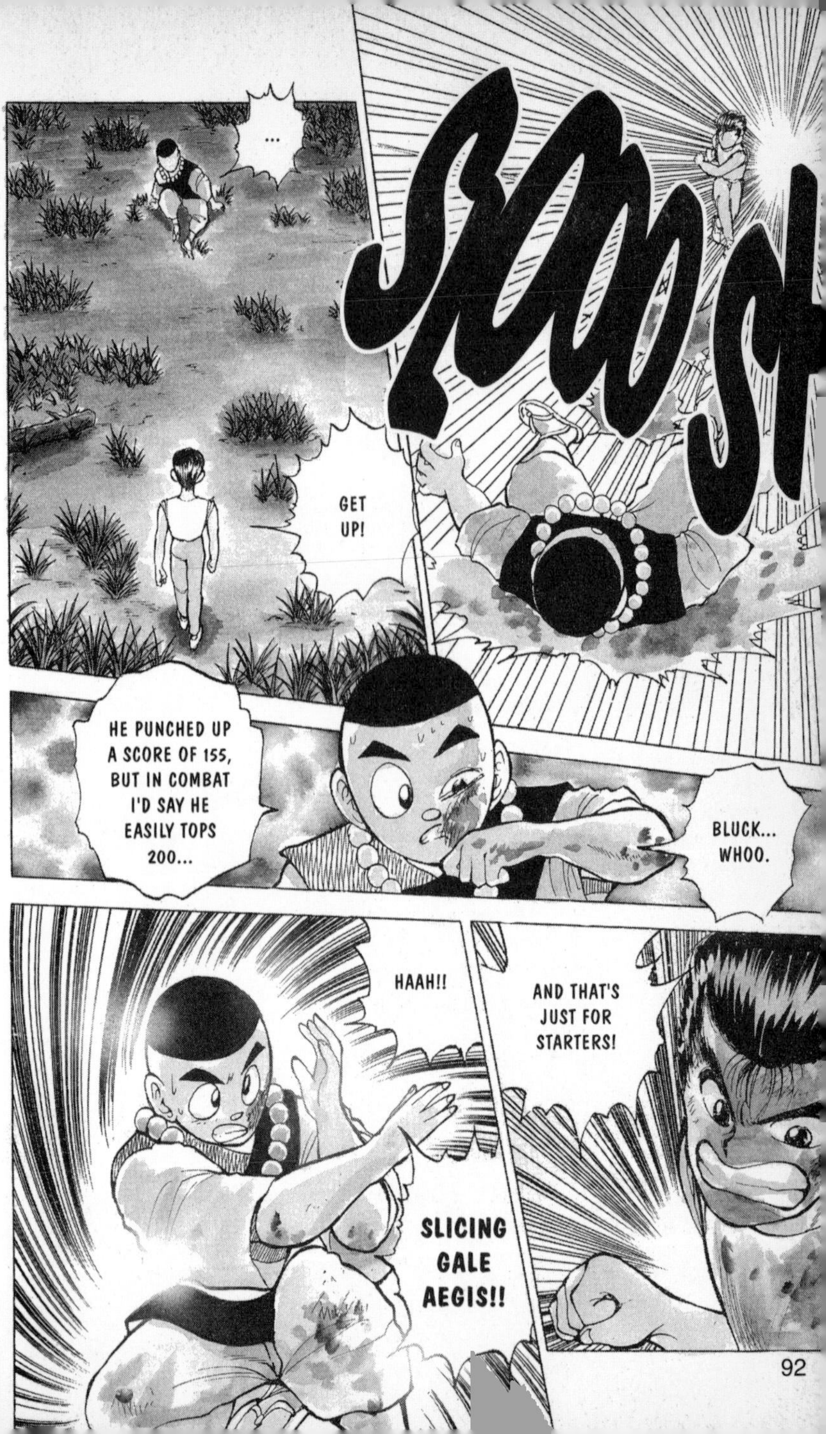
...
GET UP!
BLUCK... WHOO.
HE PUNCHED UP A SCORE OF 155, BUT IN COMBAT I'D SAY HE EASILY TOPS 200...
AND THAT'S JUST FOR STARTERS!
HAAH!!
SLICING GALE AEGIS!!

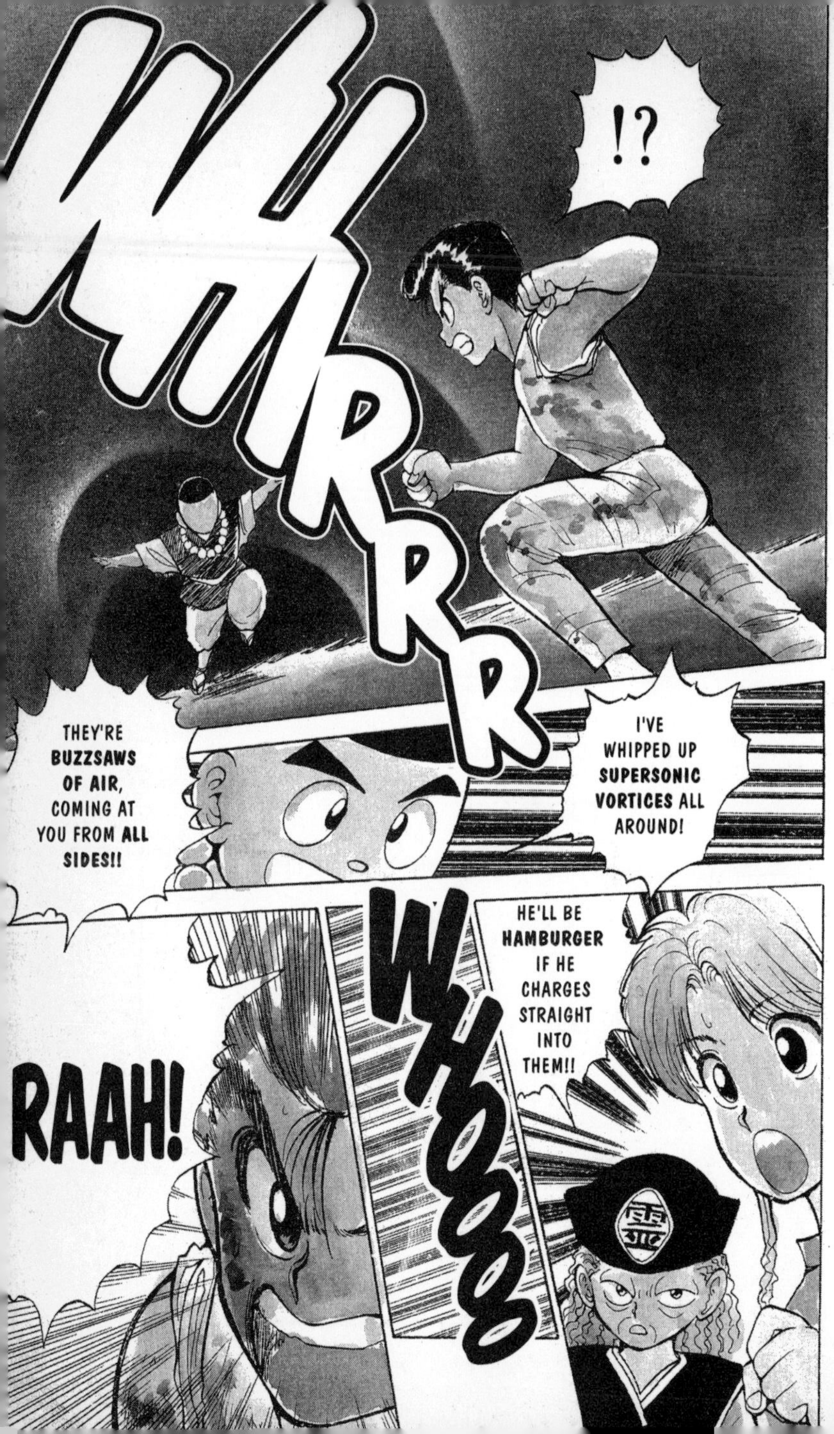
!?
WHIRRRR
I'VE WHIPPED UP SUPERSONIC VORTICES ALL AROUND!
THEY'RE BUZZSAWS OF AIR, COMING AT YOU FROM ALL SIDES!!
HE'LL BE HAMBURGER IF HE CHARGES STRAIGHT INTO THEM!!
WHOOOOO
RAAH!

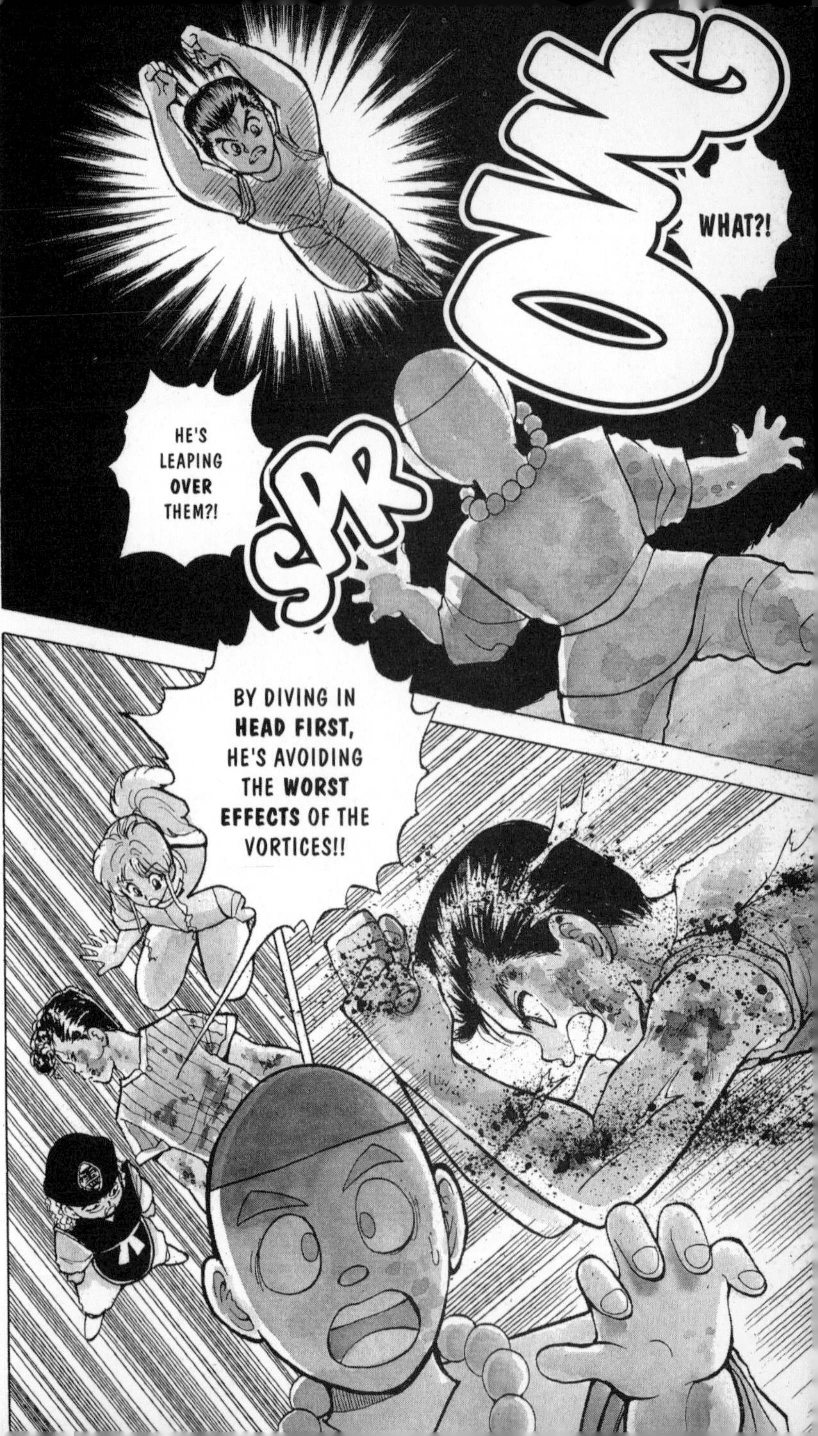
WHAT?!
SPRONG
HE'S LEAPING OVER THEM?!
BY DIVING IN HEAD FIRST, HE'S AVOIDING THE WORST EFFECTS OF THE VORTICES!!

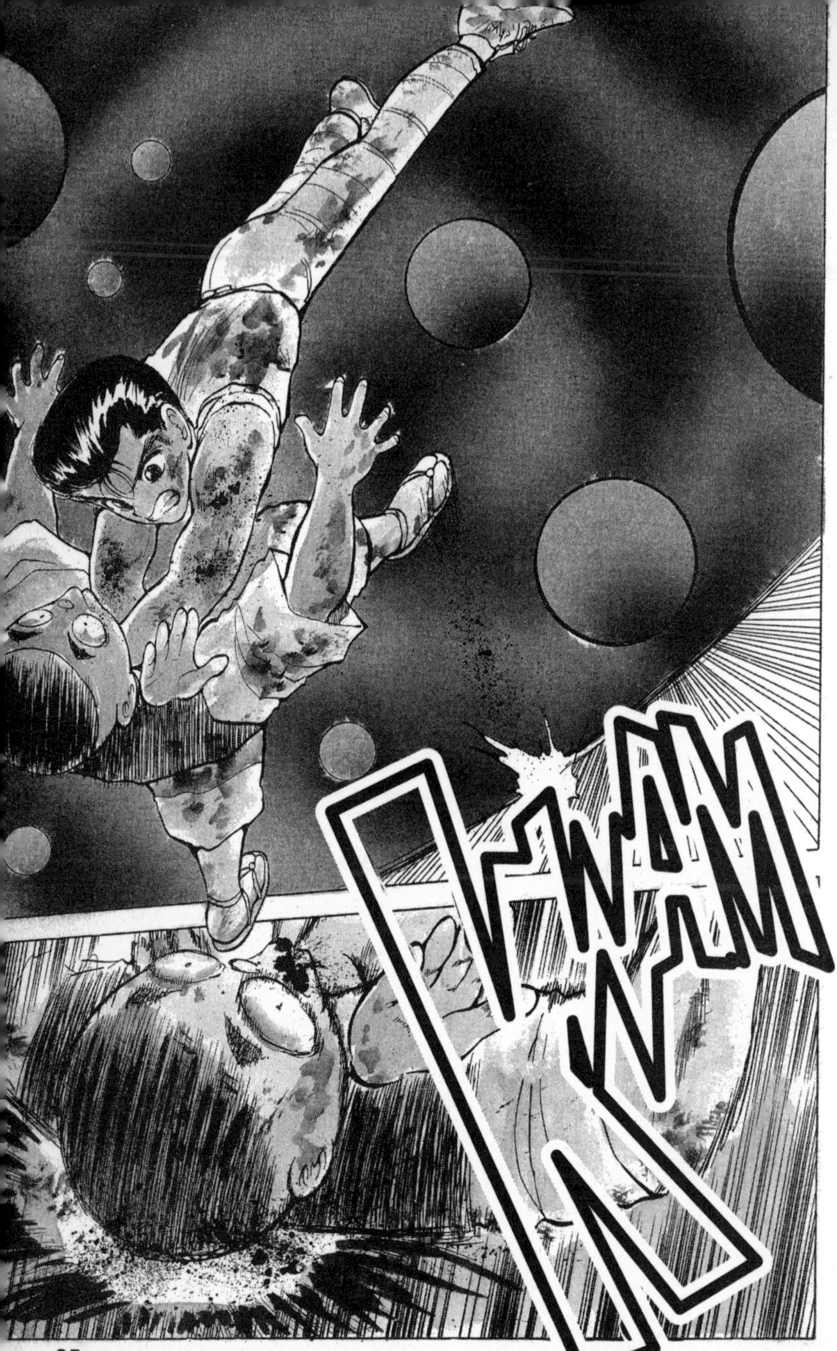
WHAM

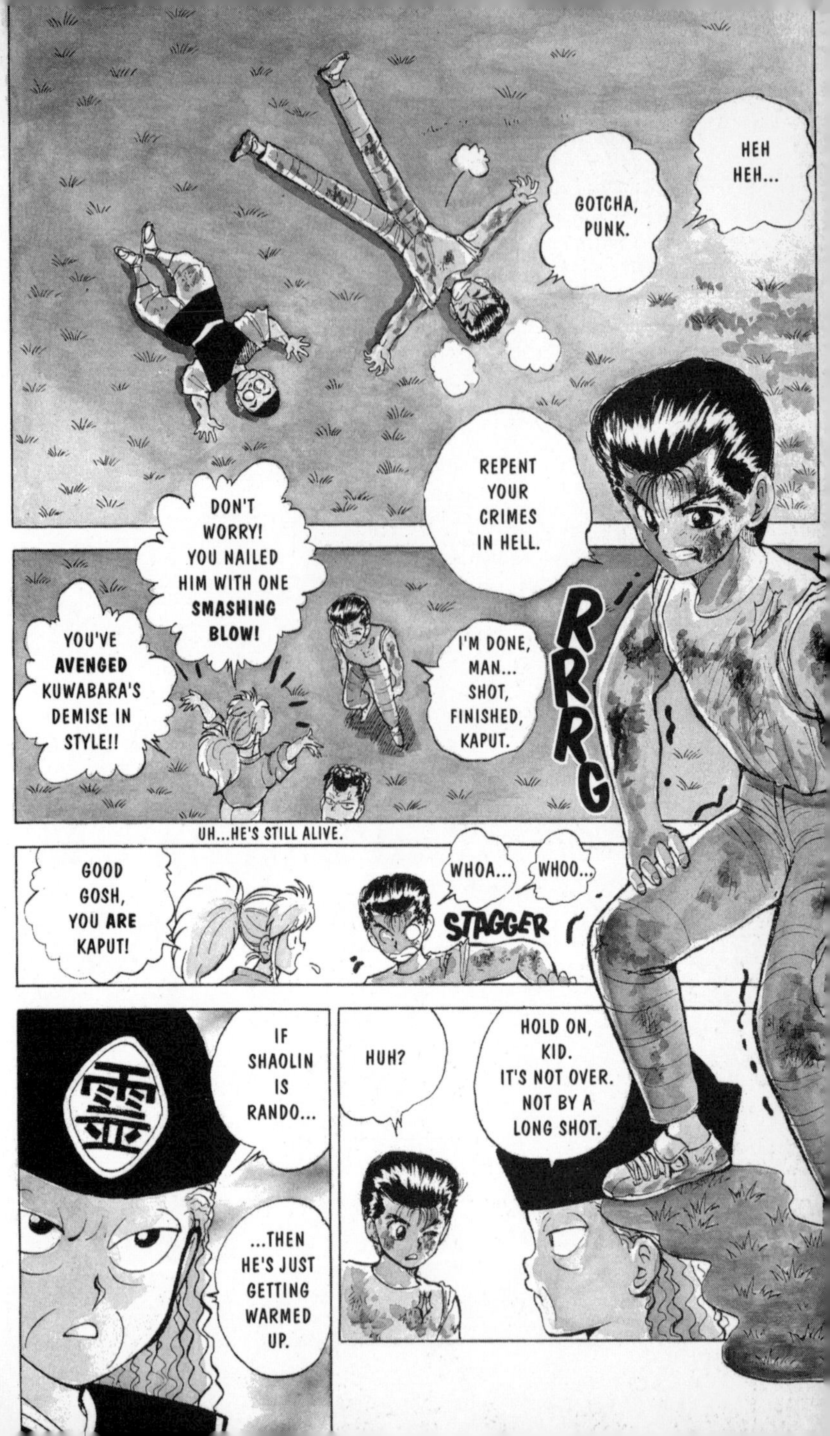
HEH HEH...
GOTCHA, PUNK.
REPENT YOUR CRIMES IN HELL.
RRRG
I'M DONE, MAN... SHOT, FINISHED, KAPUT.
DON'T WORRY! YOU NAILED HIM WITH ONE SMASHING BLOW!
YOU'VE AVENGED KUWABARA'S DEMISE IN STYLE!!
UH...HE'S STILL ALIVE.
WHOO...
WHOA...
STAGGER
GOOD GOSH, YOU ARE KAPUT!
HOLD ON, KID. IT'S NOT OVER. NOT BY A LONG SHOT.
HUH?
IF SHAOLIN IS RANDO...
...THEN HE'S JUST GETTING WARMED UP.

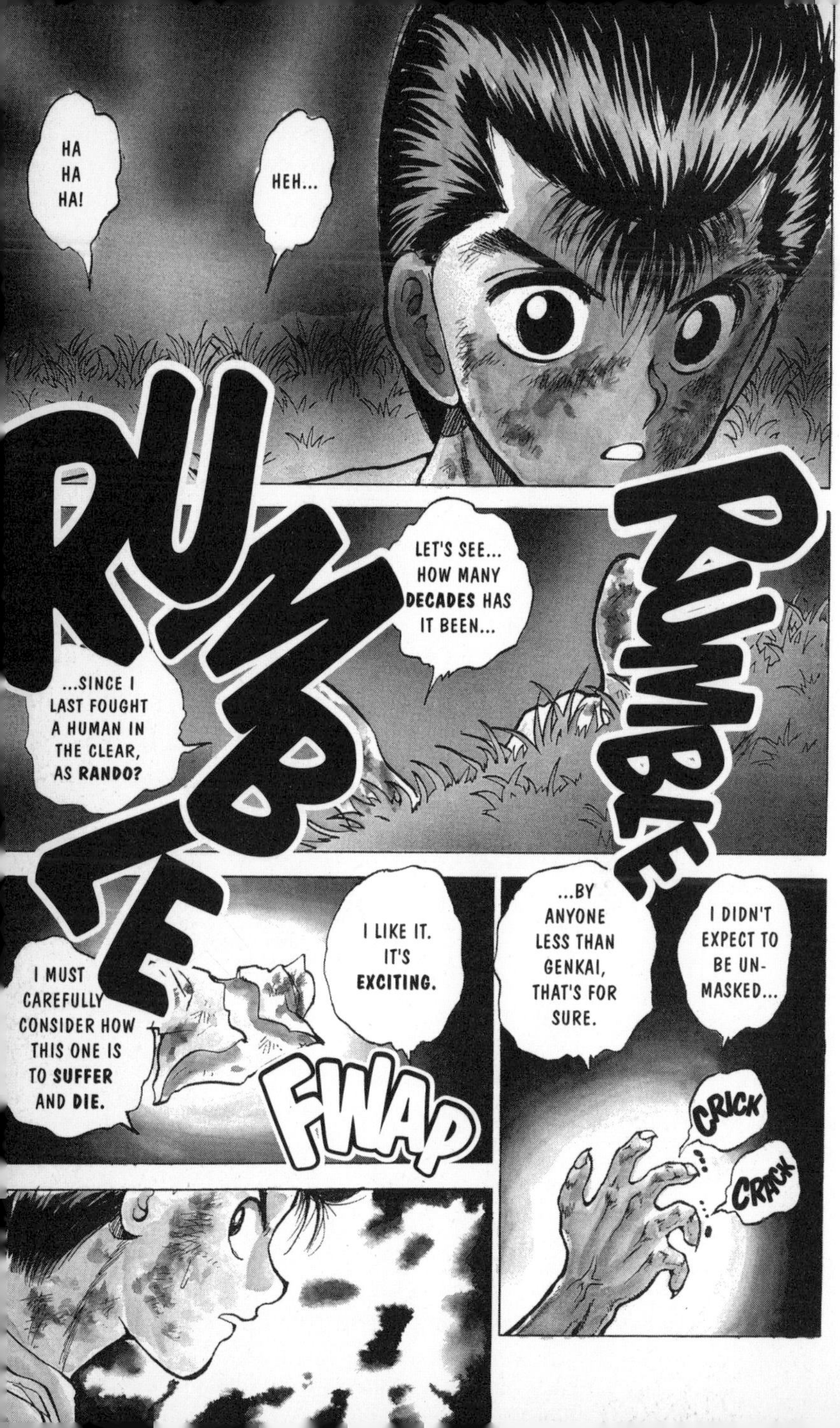
HEH...
HA HA HA!
RUMBLE
RUMBLE
LET'S SEE... HOW MANY DECADES HAS IT BEEN...
...SINCE I LAST FOUGHT A HUMAN IN THE CLEAR, AS RANDO?
I DIDN'T EXPECT TO BE UN-MASKED...
...BY ANYONE LESS THAN GENKAI, THAT'S FOR SURE.
CRICK
CRACK
I LIKE IT. IT'S EXCITING.
FWAP
I MUST CAREFULLY CONSIDER HOW THIS ONE IS TO SUFFER AND DIE.

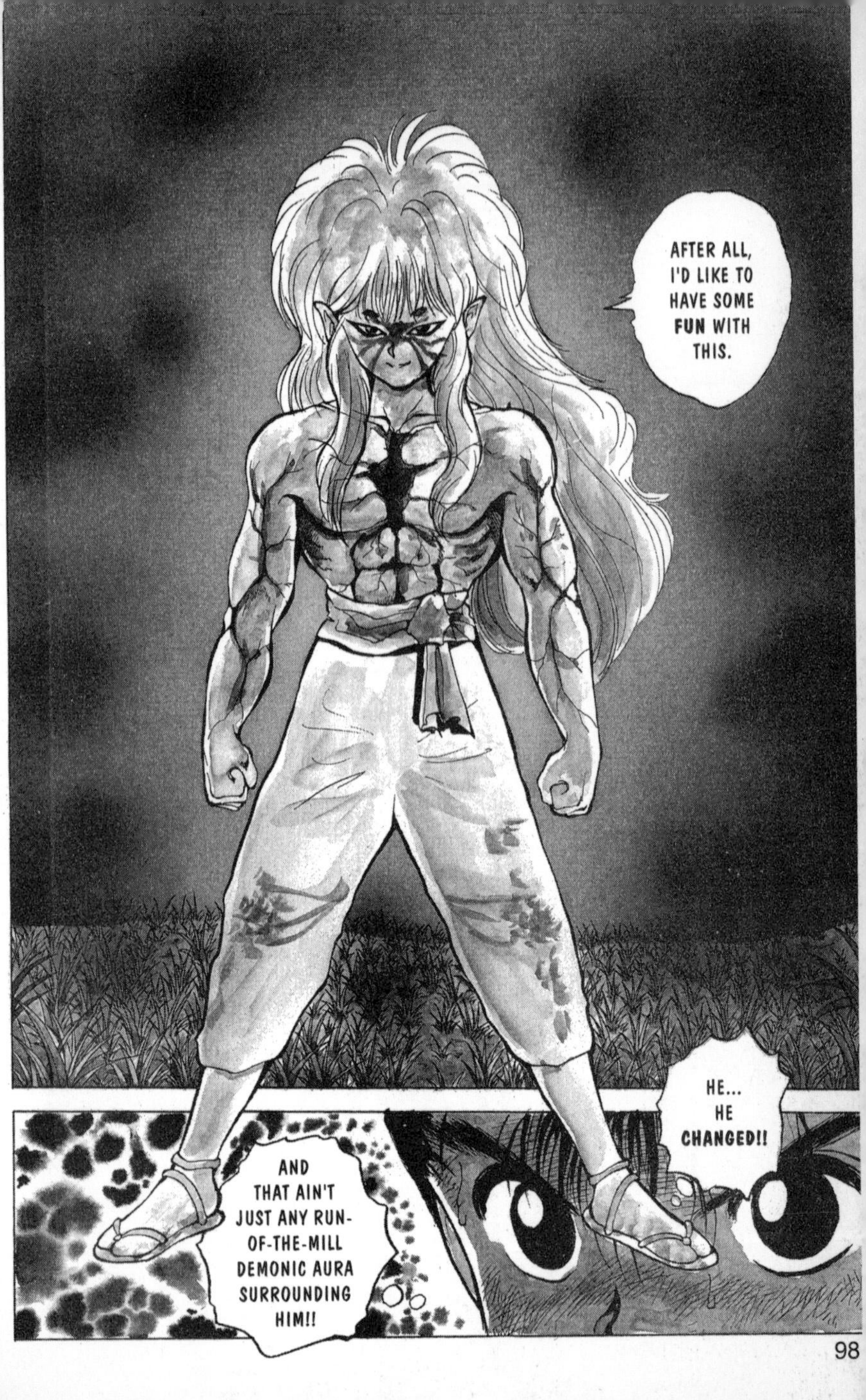

AFTER ALL, I'D LIKE TO HAVE SOME FUN WITH THIS.
HE... HE CHANGED!!
AND THAT AIN'T JUST ANY RUN-OF-THE-MILL DEMONIC AURA SURROUNDING HIM!!

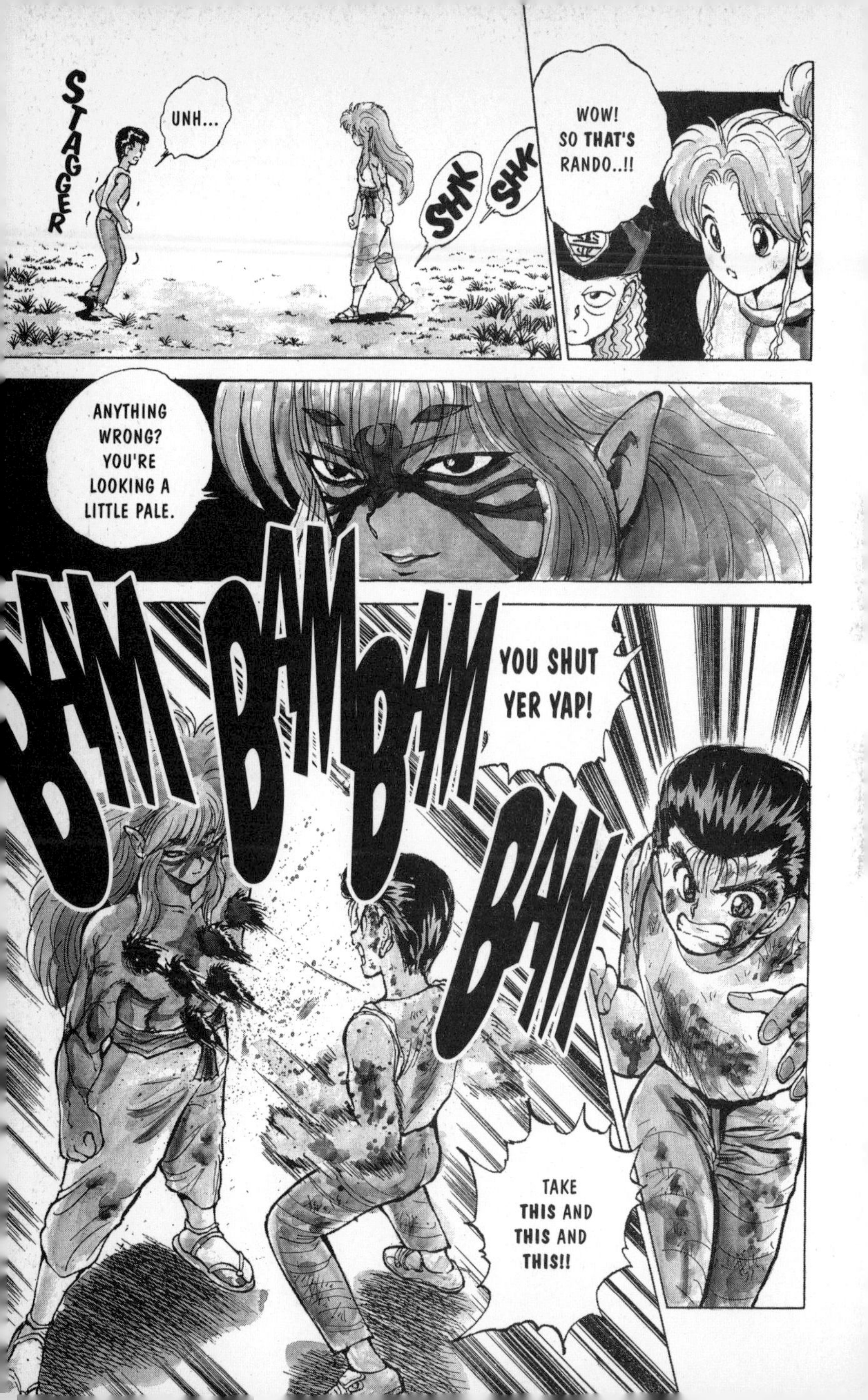
WOW! SO THAT'S RANDO..!!
SHK SHK
UNH...
STAGGER
ANYTHING WRONG? YOU'RE LOOKING A LITTLE PALE.
YOU SHUT YER YAP!
BAM BAM BAM BAM BAM
TAKE THIS AND THIS AND THIS!!

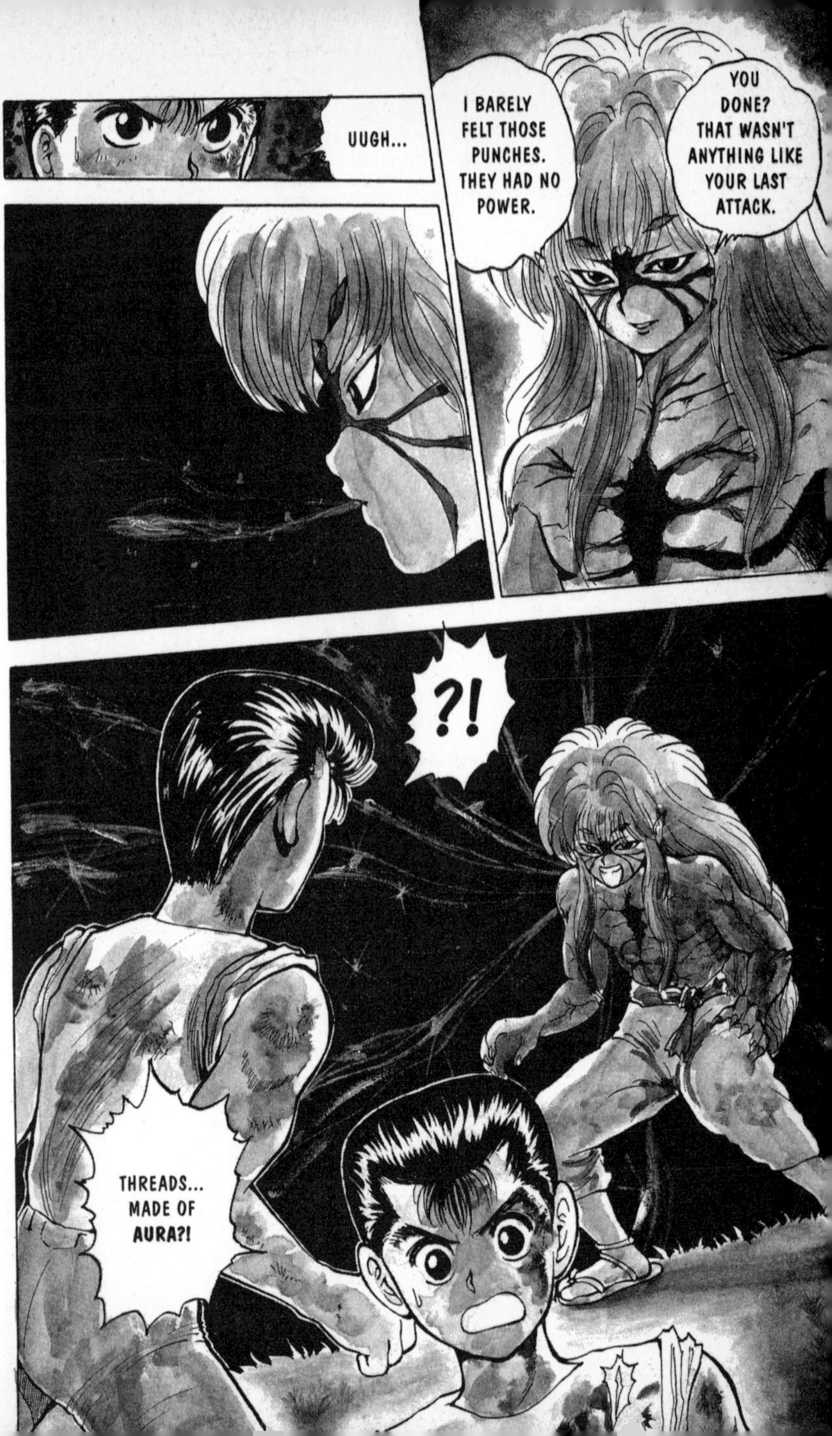
YOU DONE? THAT WASN'T ANYTHING LIKE YOUR LAST ATTACK.
I BARELY FELT THOSE PUNCHES. THEY HAD NO POWER.
UUGH...
?!
THREADS... MADE OF **AURA**?!

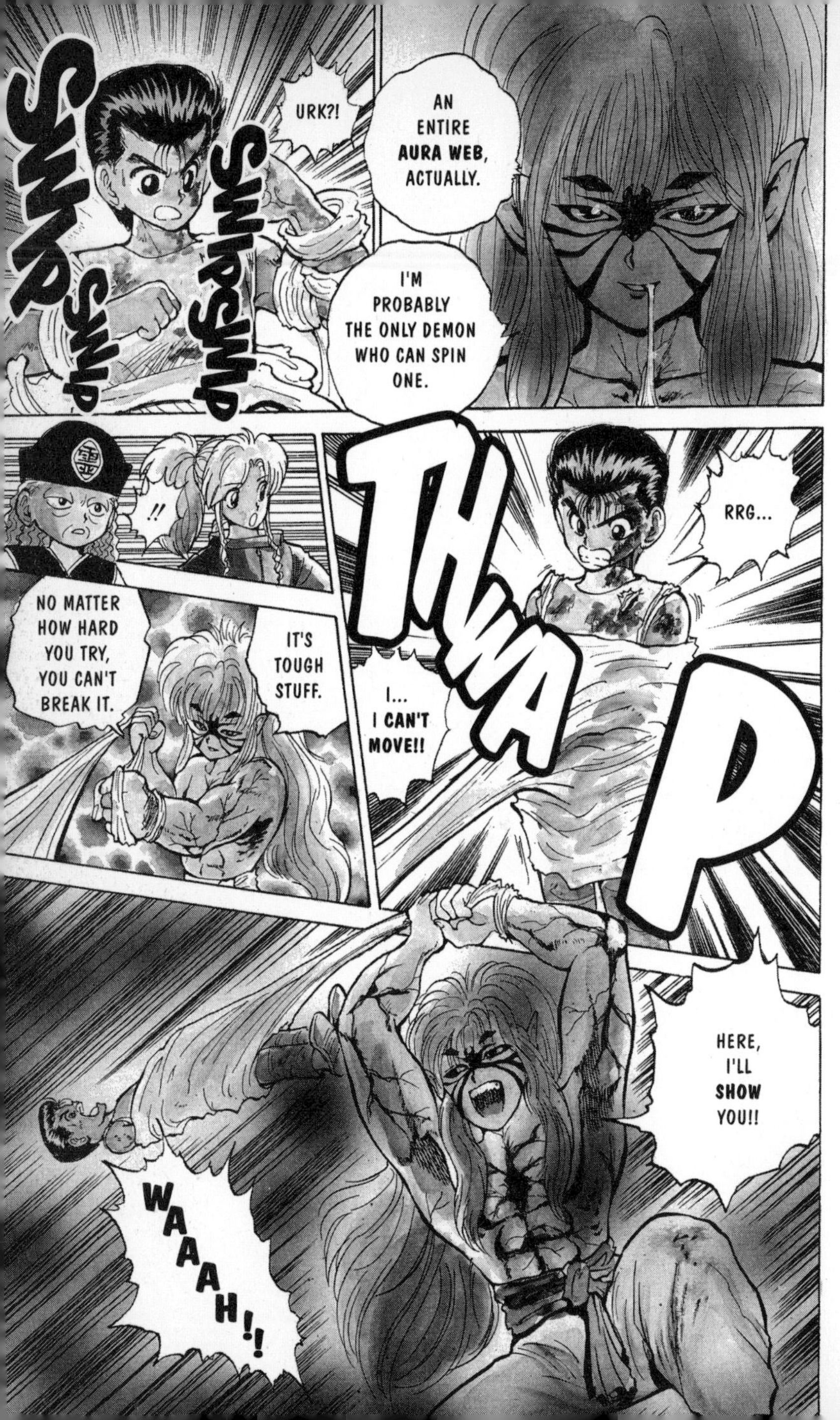
AN ENTIRE AURA WEB, ACTUALLY.
I'M PROBABLY THE ONLY DEMON WHO CAN SPIN ONE.
URK?!
SWIPSWIP
SWIP SWIP
SWIP
THWAP
RRG...
I... I CAN'T MOVE!!
!!
NO MATTER HOW HARD YOU TRY, YOU CAN'T BREAK IT.
IT'S TOUGH STUFF.
HERE, I'LL SHOW YOU!!
WAAAAH!!

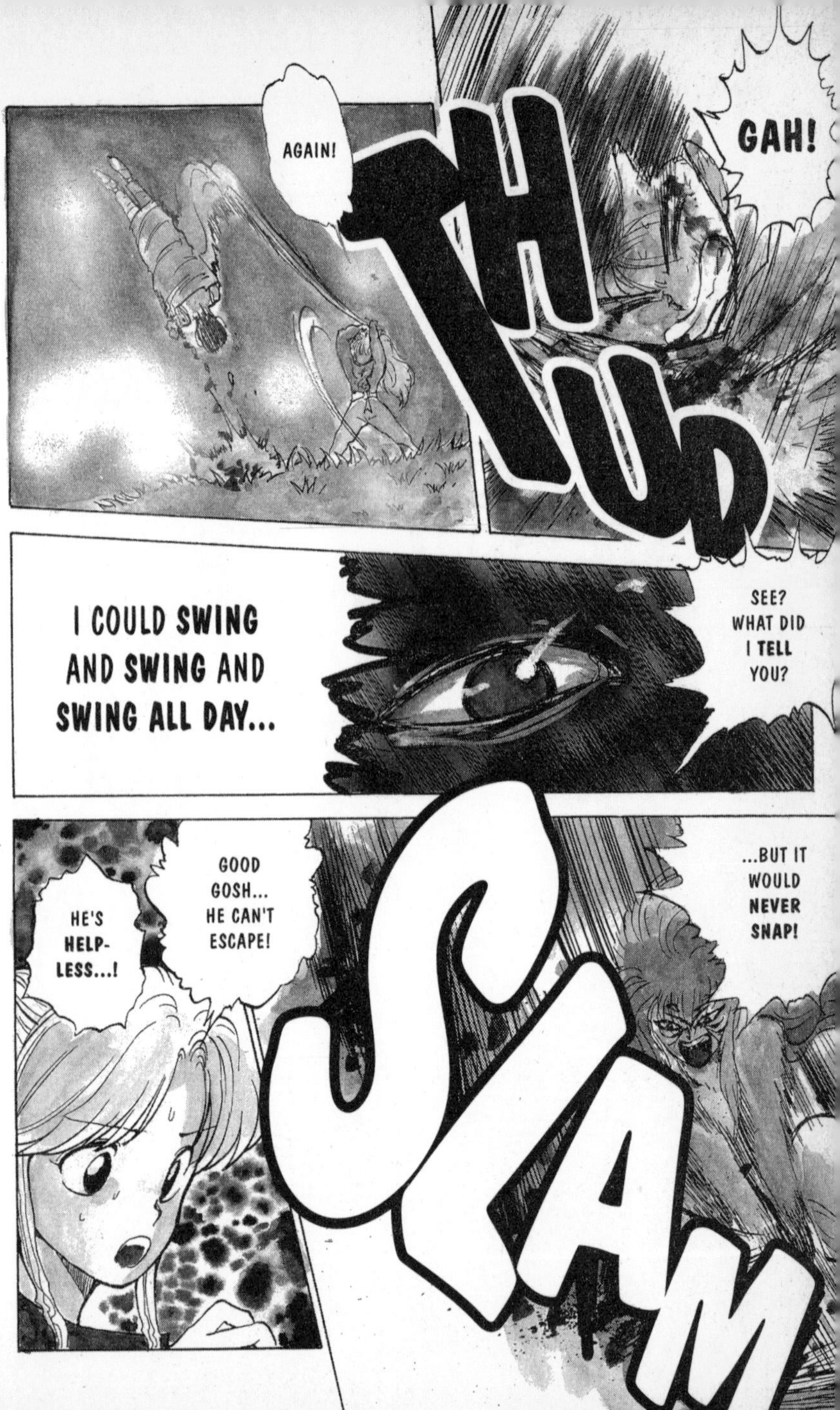
GAH!
THUD
AGAIN!
SEE? WHAT DID I TELL YOU?
I COULD SWING AND SWING AND SWING ALL DAY...
...BUT IT WOULD NEVER SNAP!
SLAM
GOOD GOSH... HE CAN'T ESCAPE!
HE'S HELP-LESS...!

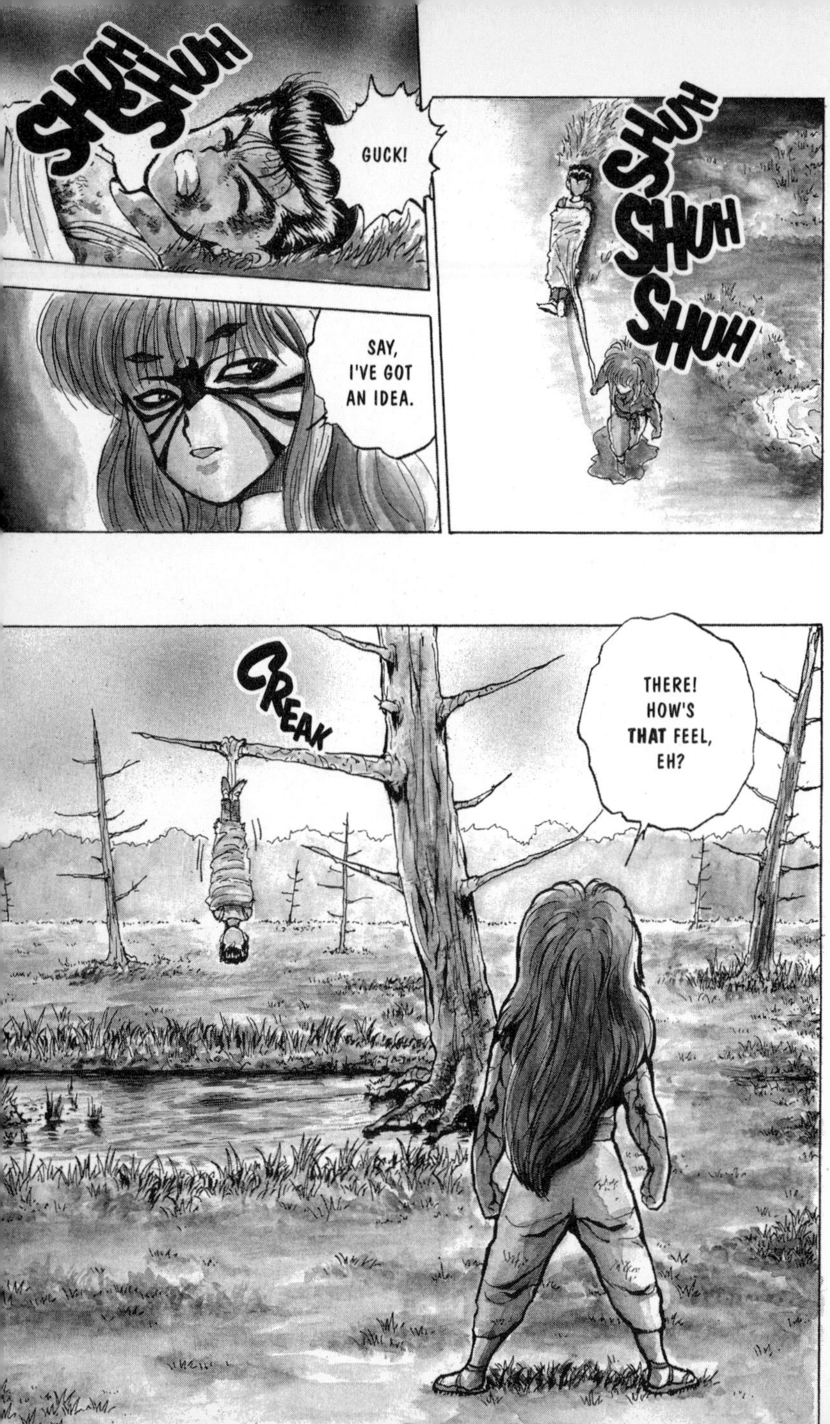
SHUH
SHUH
SHUH
SHUH SHUH
GUCK!
SAY, I'VE GOT AN IDEA.
THERE! HOW'S **THAT** FEEL, EH?
CREAK

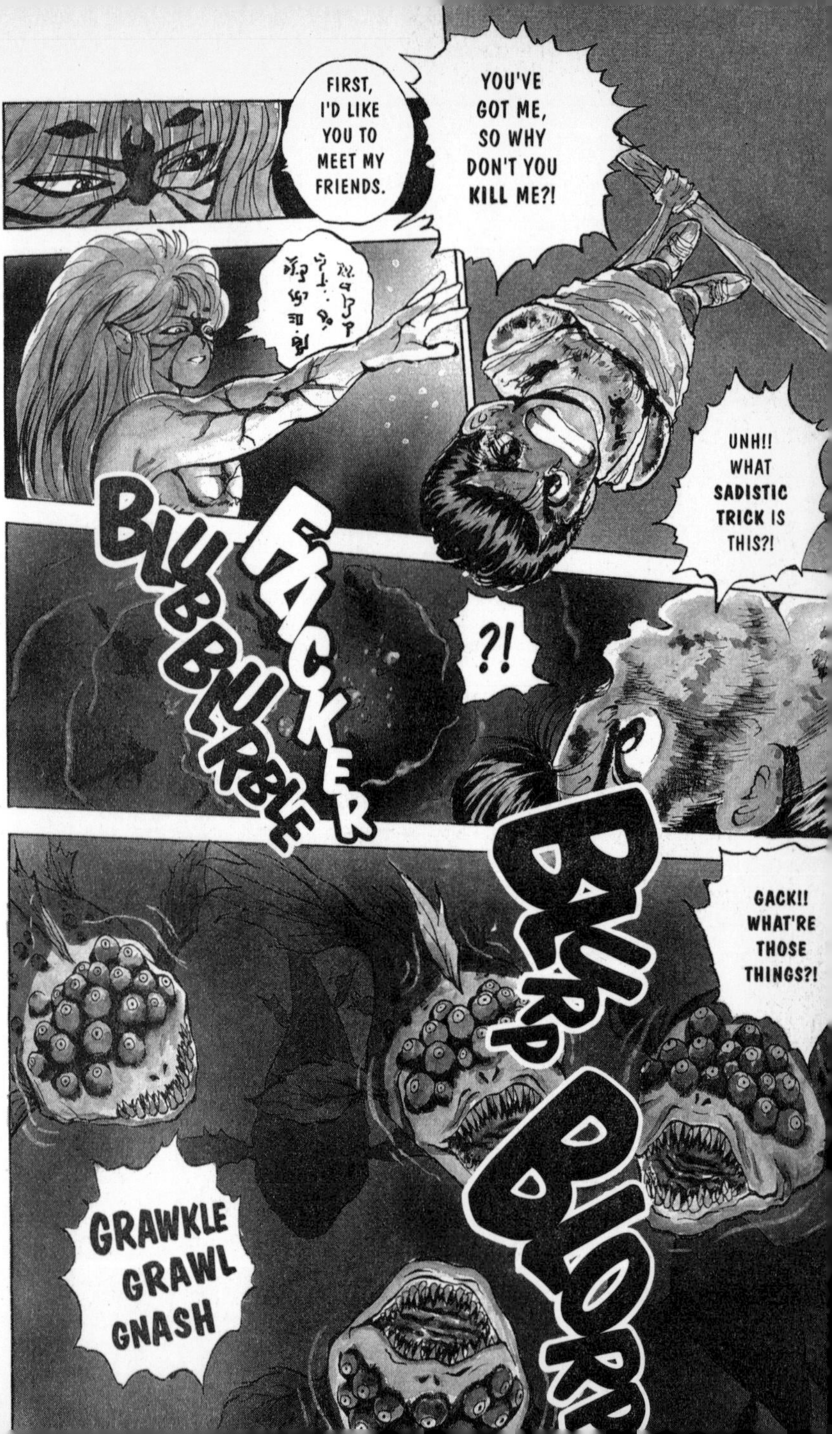

YOU'VE GOT ME, SO WHY DON'T YOU KILL ME?!
FIRST, I'D LIKE YOU TO MEET MY FRIENDS.
UNH!! WHAT SADISTIC TRICK IS THIS?!
?!
FLICKER
BLUBBLUBBLE
GACK!! WHAT'RE THOSE THINGS?!
BURP BLORP
GRAWKLE GRAWL GNASH

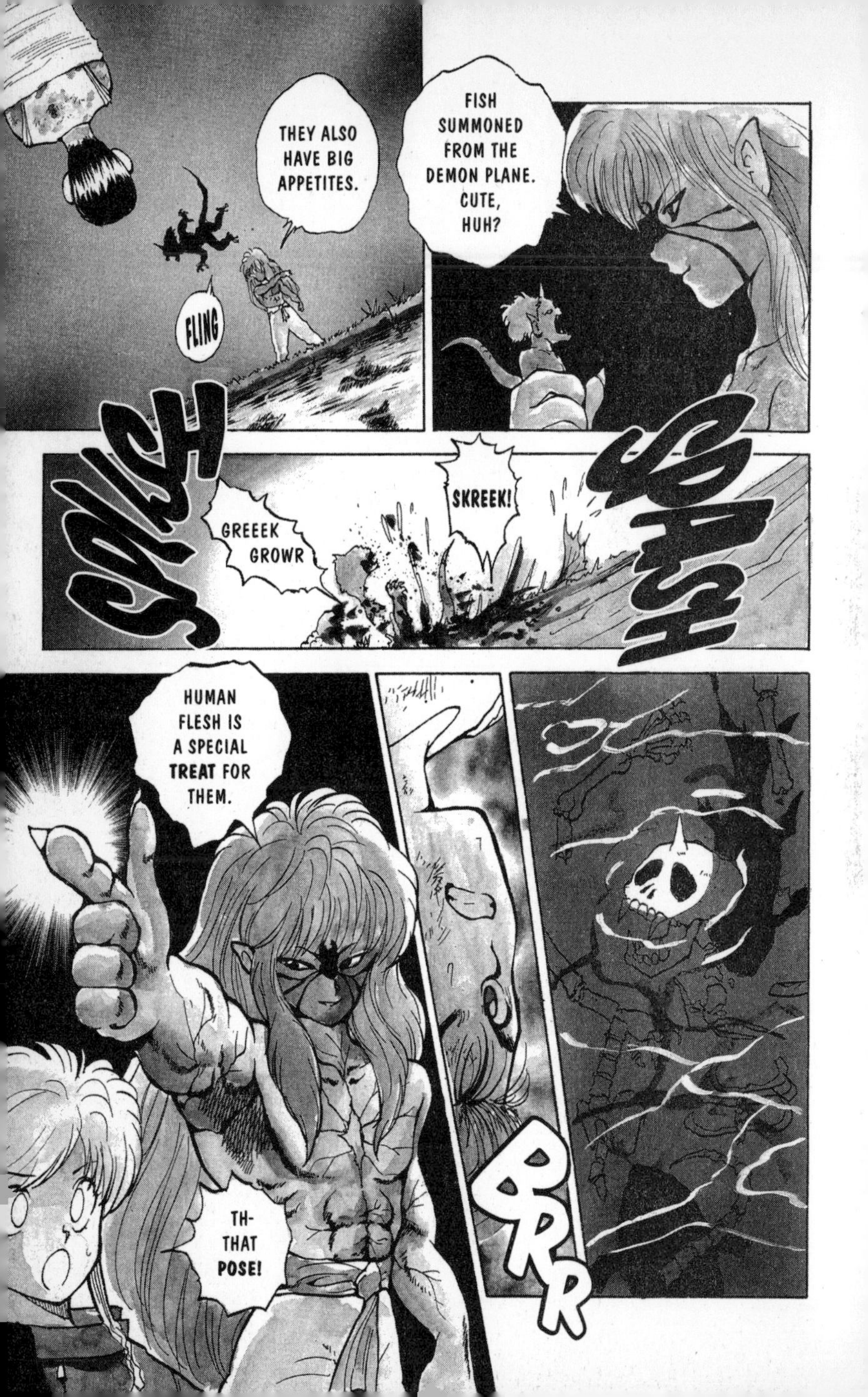
FISH SUMMONED FROM THE DEMON PLANE. CUTE, HUH?
THEY ALSO HAVE BIG APPETITES.
FLING
SPLASH
SKREEK!
GREEEK GROWR
SPLISH
BRRR
HUMAN FLESH IS A SPECIAL **TREAT** FOR THEM.
TH- THAT **POSE!**

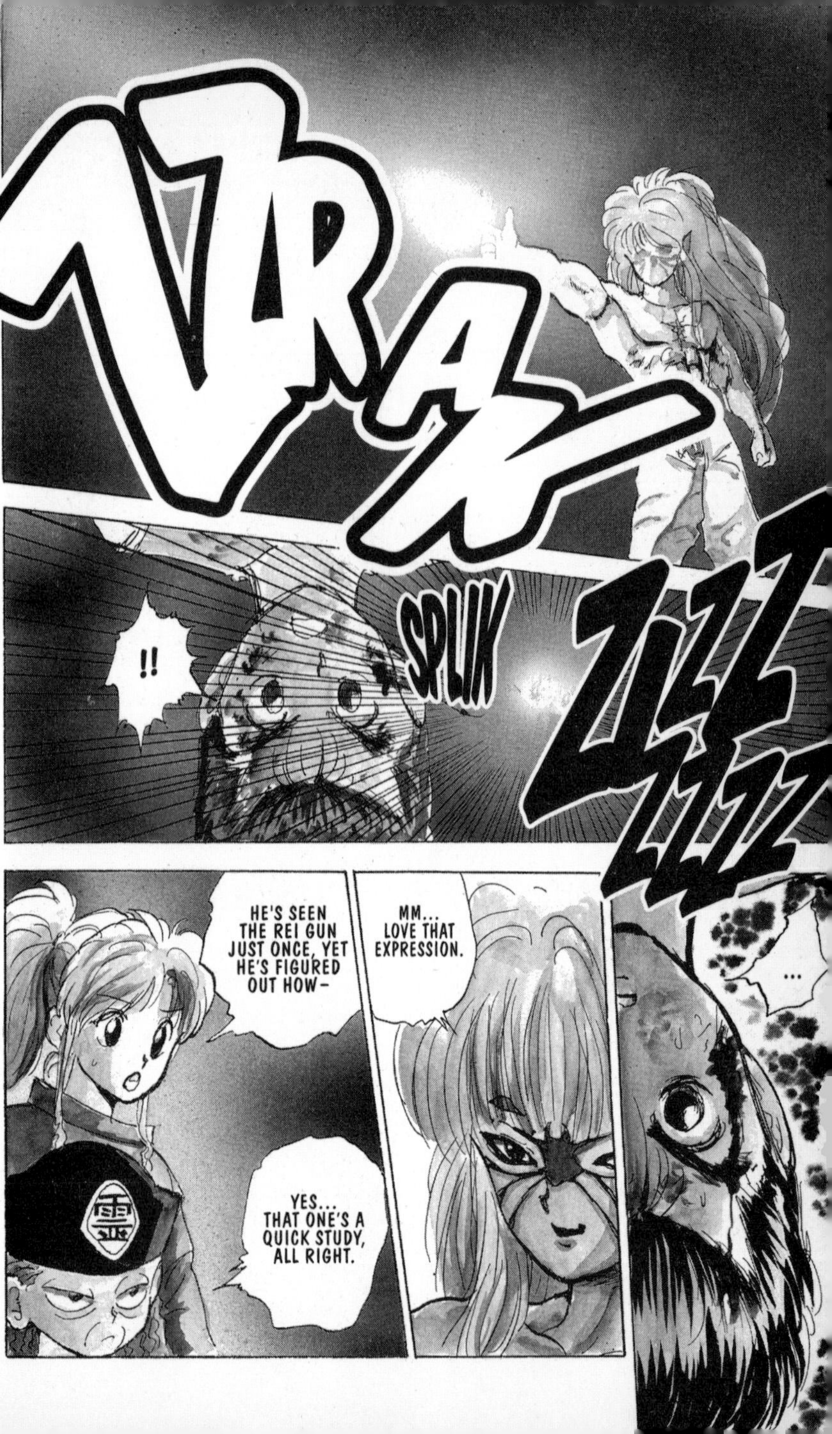
SPLIK
!!
...
MM... LOVE THAT EXPRESSION.
HE'S SEEN THE REI GUN JUST ONCE, YET HE'S FIGURED OUT HOW–
YES... THAT ONE'S A QUICK STUDY, ALL RIGHT.

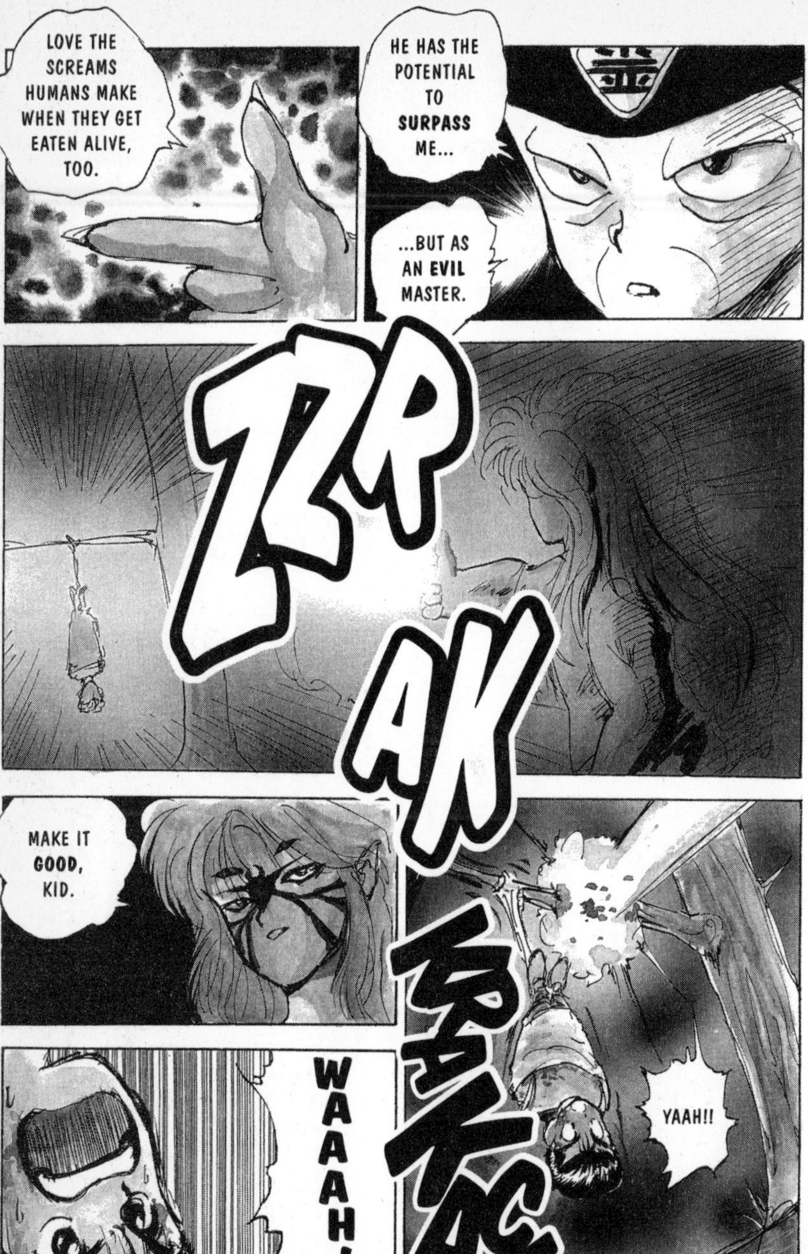
HE HAS THE POTENTIAL TO SURPASS ME...
...BUT AS AN EVIL MASTER.
LOVE THE SCREAMS HUMANS MAKE WHEN THEY GET EATEN ALIVE, TOO.
ZZRAK
KRAKACK
YAAH!!
MAKE IT GOOD, KID.
WAAAAH!

MY RAMBLING DIARY, PART 3

One morning, same as usual, '91

I went out from sheer hunger, exhausted after an all-nighter. I teetered on my bicycle, listening to some random Metallica on my walkman. On the way to Matsuya to grab a bite to eat, I ran into some people who really make me hate myself. They are...

SPARKLE SPARKLE

I'm such a wreck...

URK...

FIGHT FIRE WITH FIRE! BOOM BOOM BOOM BOOM

WOBBLE

WOBBLE

← Bits of Zipatone

They were school girls, neatly groomed and probably on their way to school.

I felt so empty, covered in tobacco stains and scraps of zipatone, looking at their faces brimming with dreams and hopes (look at me, I'm already talking like an old man).

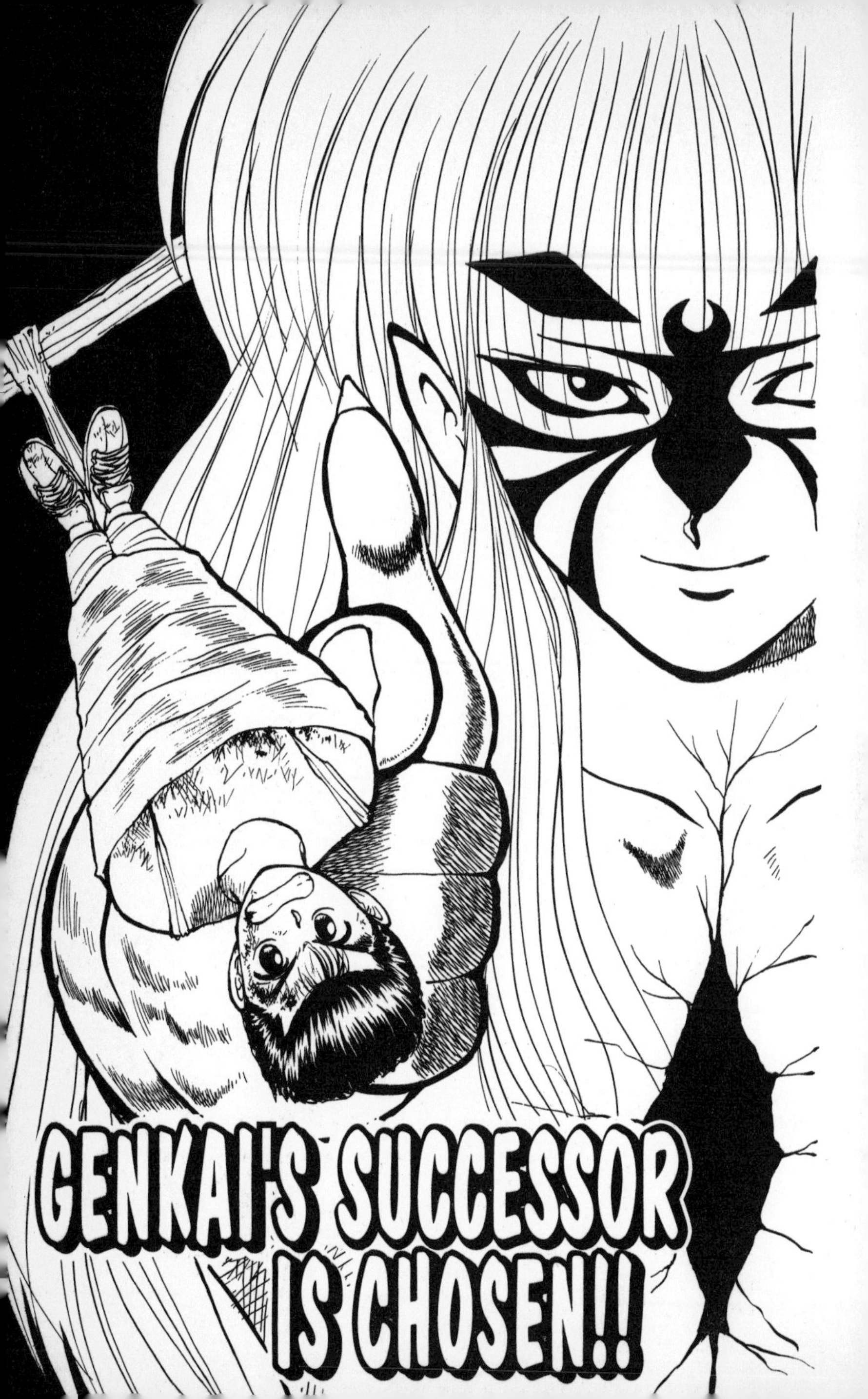
GENKAI'S SUCCESSOR IS CHOSEN!!

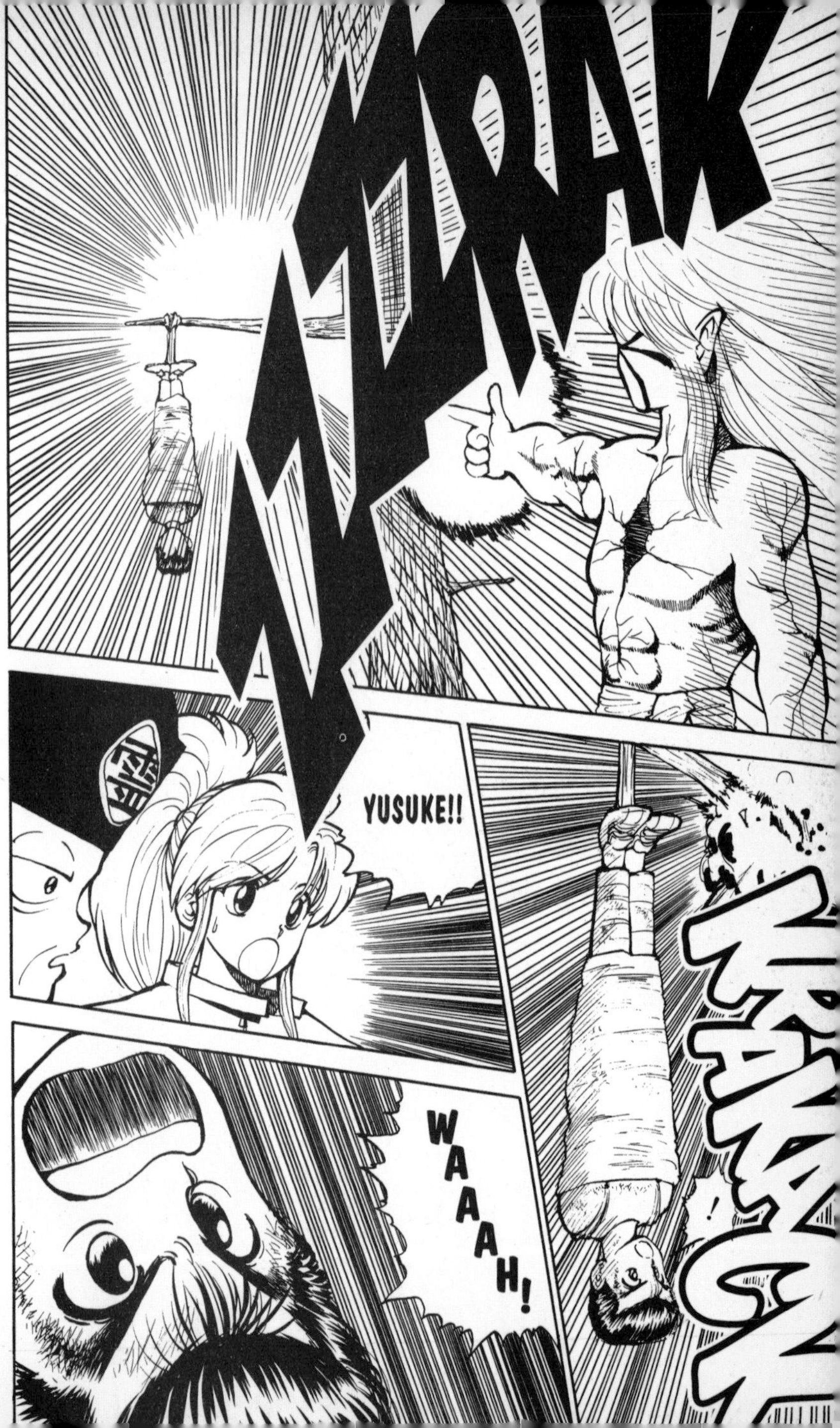
YUSUKE!!
WAAAAH!

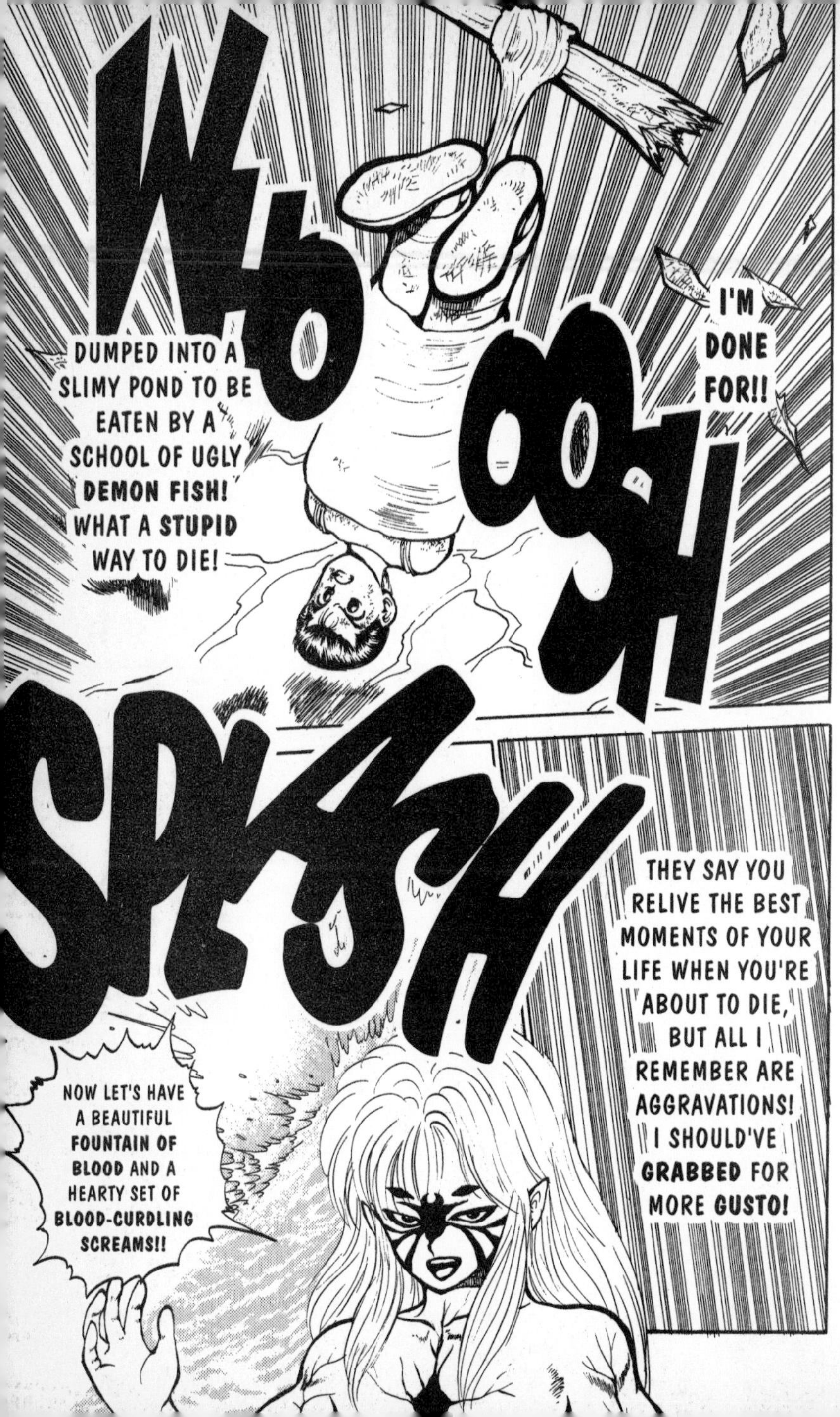
I'M DONE FOR!!
WHOOOSH
DUMPED INTO A SLIMY POND TO BE EATEN BY A SCHOOL OF UGLY DEMON FISH! WHAT A STUPID WAY TO DIE!
SPLASH
THEY SAY YOU RELIVE THE BEST MOMENTS OF YOUR LIFE WHEN YOU'RE ABOUT TO DIE, BUT ALL I REMEMBER ARE AGGRAVATIONS! I SHOULD'VE GRABBED FOR MORE GUSTO!
NOW LET'S HAVE A BEAUTIFUL FOUNTAIN OF BLOOD AND A HEARTY SET OF BLOOD-CURDLING SCREAMS!!

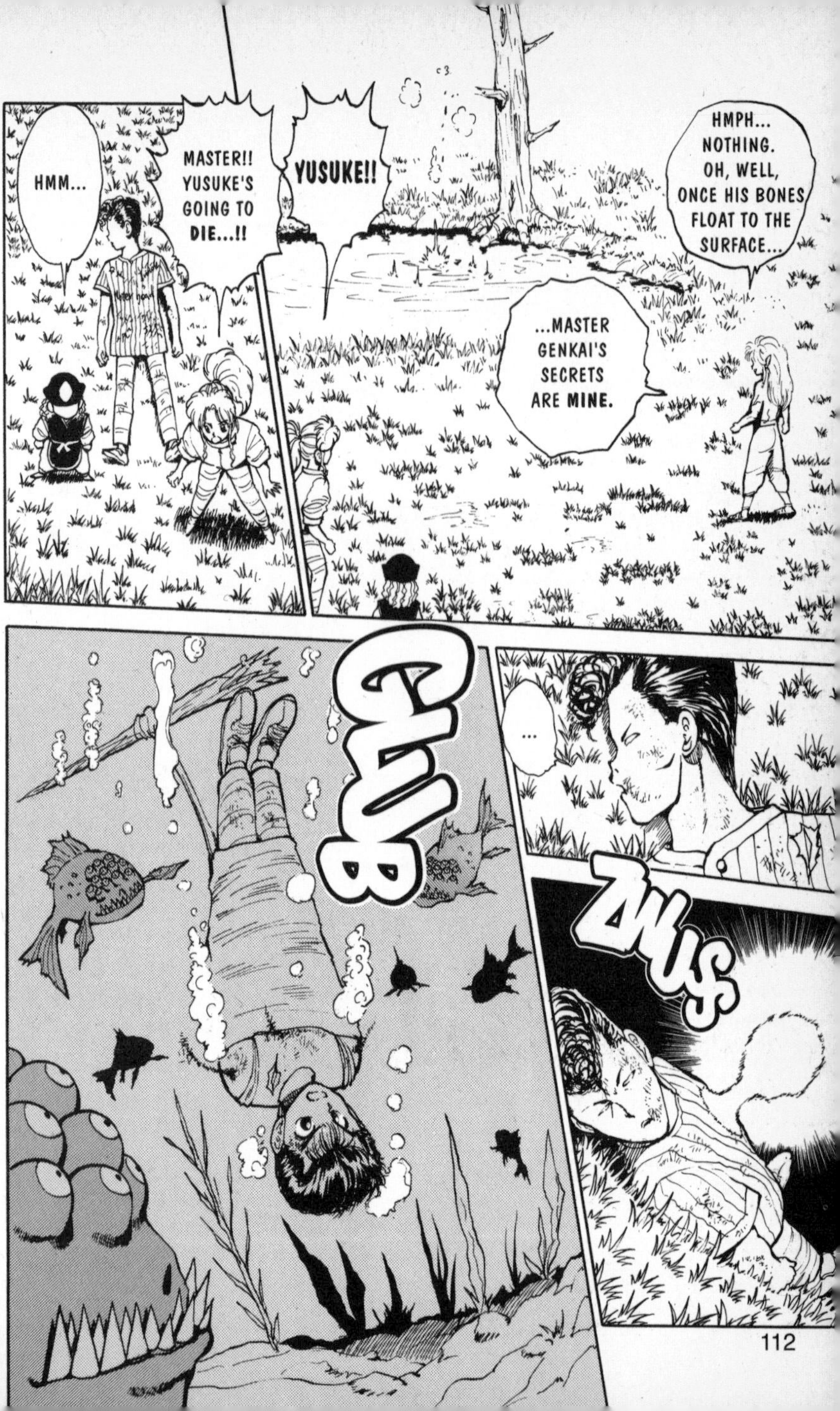
HMPH... NOTHING. OH, WELL, ONCE HIS BONES FLOAT TO THE SURFACE...
YUSUKE!!
...MASTER GENKAI'S SECRETS ARE MINE.
MASTER!! YUSUKE'S GOING TO DIE...!!
HMM...
...
ZWUS
GLUB

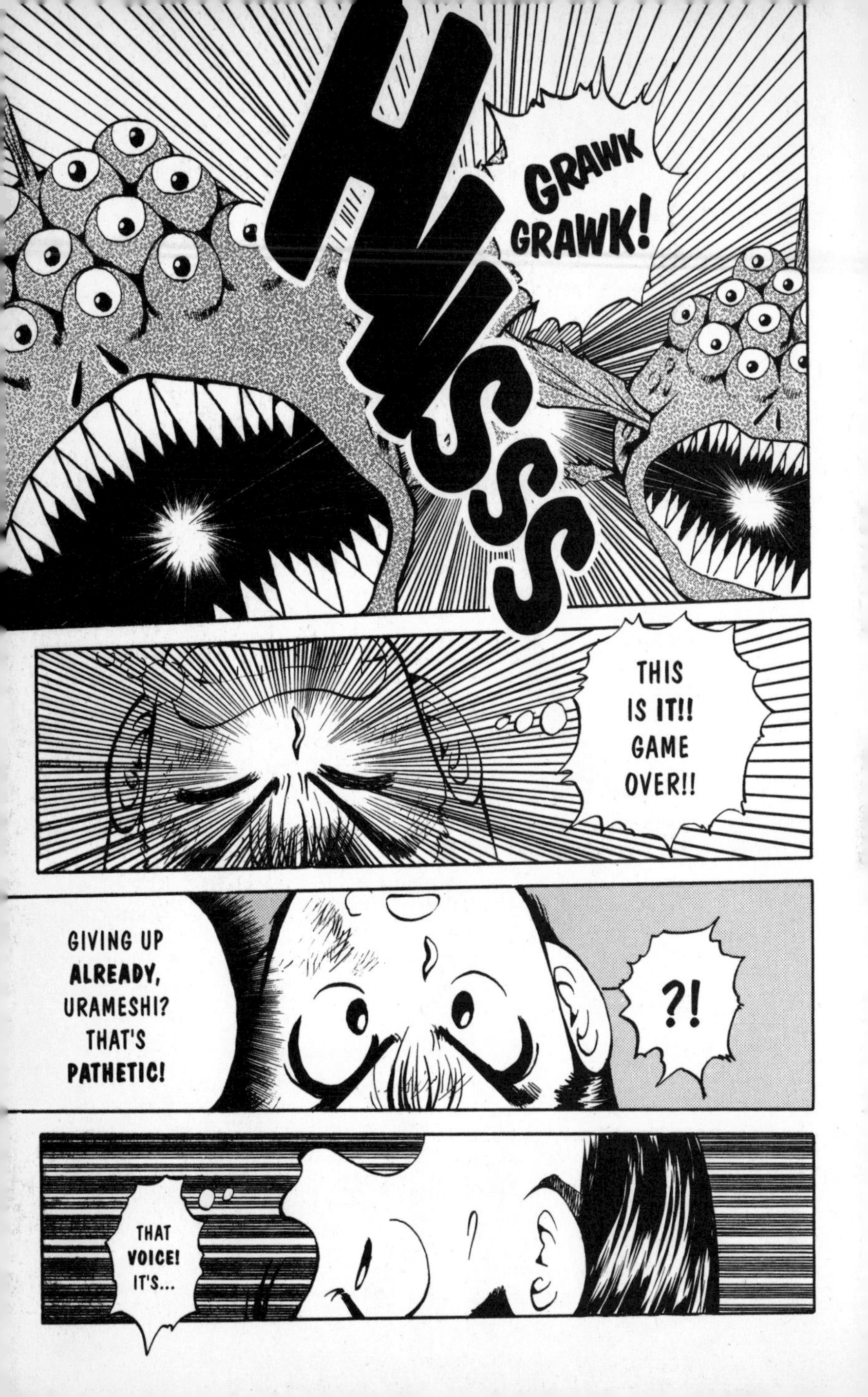
GRAWK GRAWK!
HISSS
THIS IS IT!! GAME OVER!!
?!
GIVING UP ALREADY, URAMESHI? THAT'S PATHETIC!
THAT VOICE! IT'S...

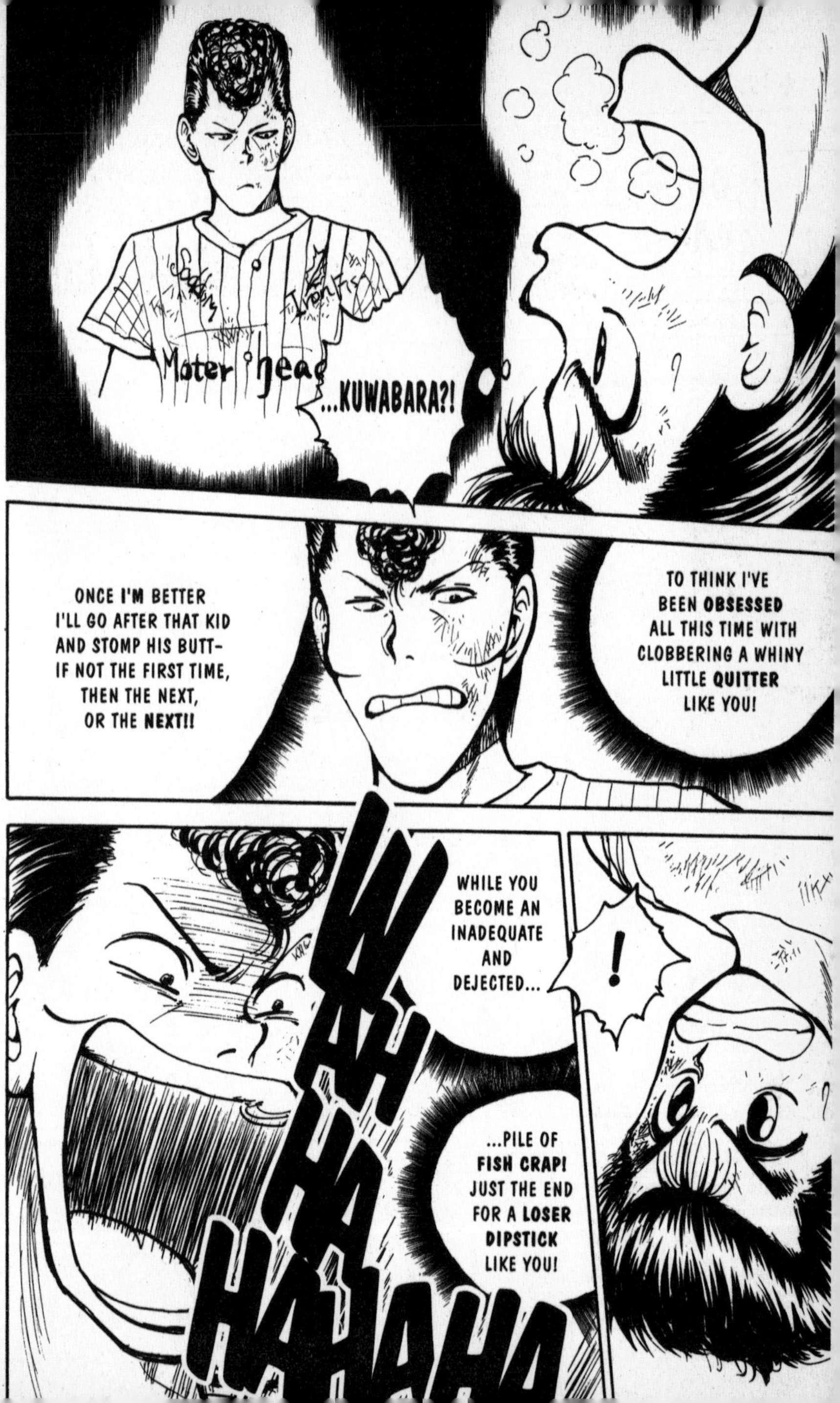
...KUWABARA?!
TO THINK I'VE BEEN **OBSESSED** ALL THIS TIME WITH CLOBBERING A WHINY LITTLE **QUITTER** LIKE YOU!
ONCE **I'M** BETTER I'LL GO AFTER THAT KID AND STOMP HIS BUTT– IF NOT THE FIRST TIME, THEN THE NEXT, OR THE **NEXT!!**
!
WHILE YOU BECOME AN INADEQUATE AND DEJECTED...
...PILE OF **FISH CRAP!** JUST THE END FOR A **LOSER DIPSTICK** LIKE YOU!
WAH HA HA HAHAHA

READ THIS WAY

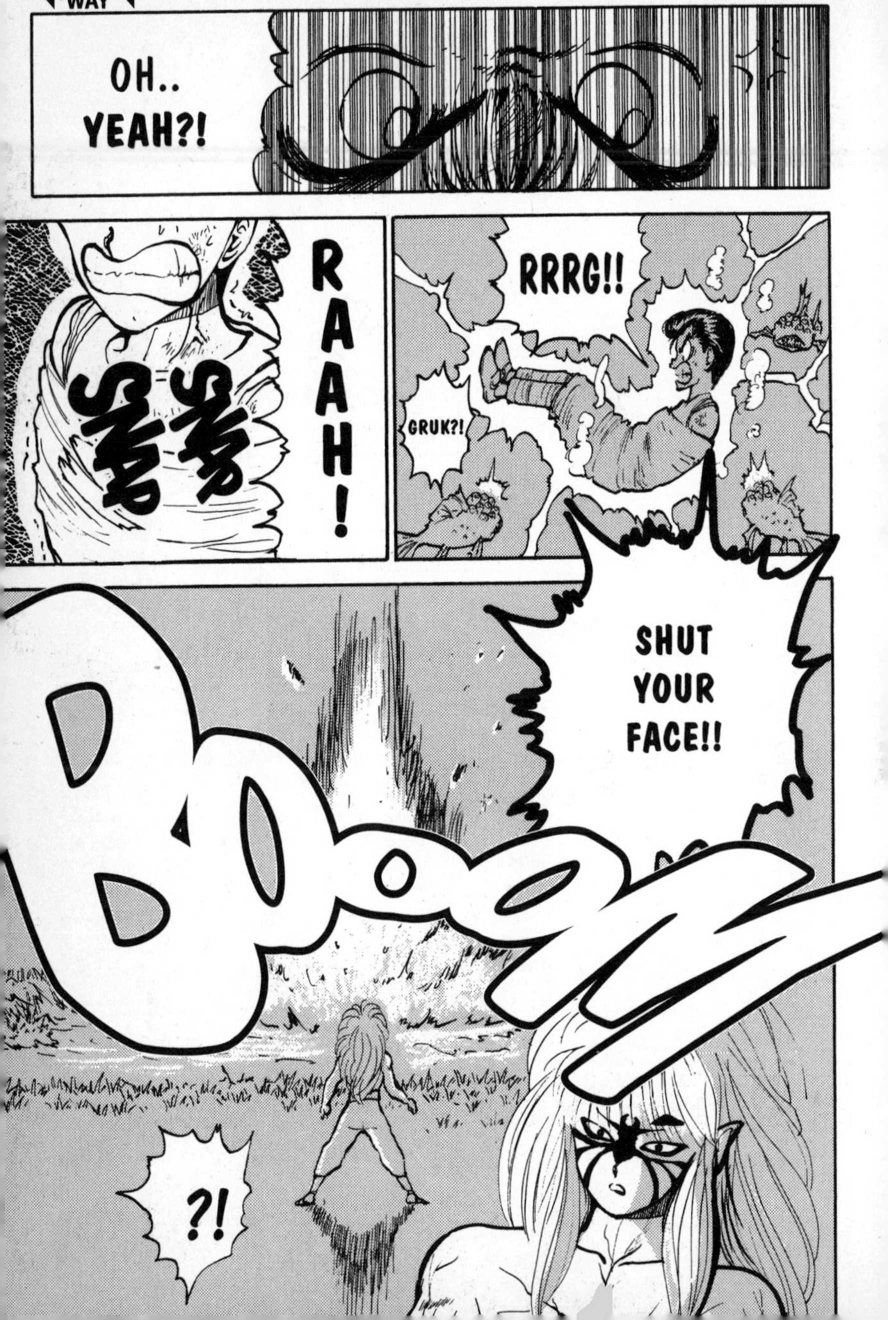
OH.. YEAH?!
RRRG!!
GRUK?!
RAAH!
SNAP SNAP
SHUT YOUR FACE!!
?!

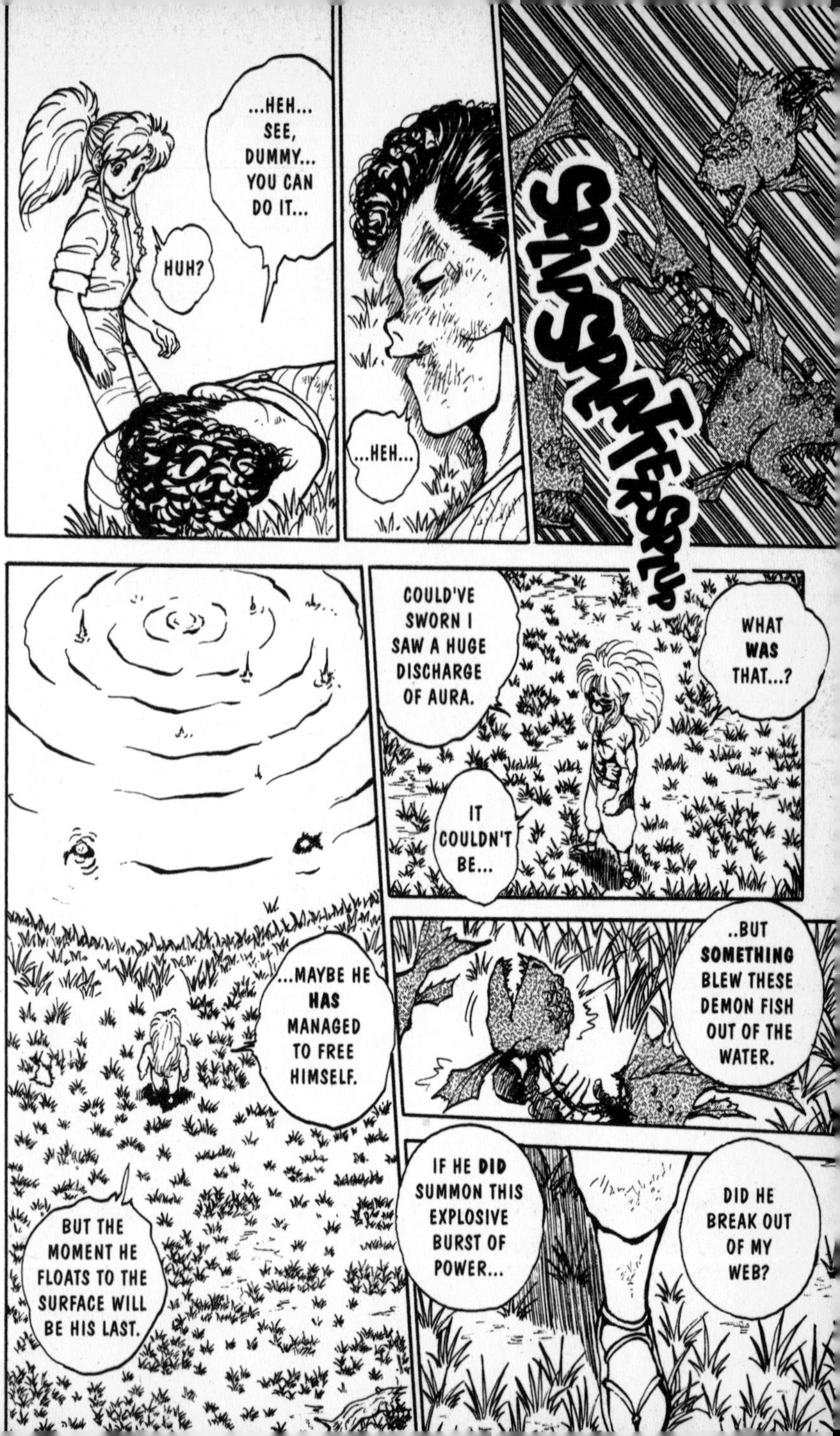
SPLASPLATTERSPLUP
...HEH...
...HEH... SEE, DUMMY... YOU CAN DO IT...
HUH?
WHAT WAS THAT...?
COULD'VE SWORN I SAW A HUGE DISCHARGE OF AURA.
IT COULDN'T BE...
..BUT SOMETHING BLEW THESE DEMON FISH OUT OF THE WATER.
DID HE BREAK OUT OF MY WEB?
IF HE DID SUMMON THIS EXPLOSIVE BURST OF POWER...
...MAYBE HE HAS MANAGED TO FREE HIMSELF.
BUT THE MOMENT HE FLOATS TO THE SURFACE WILL BE HIS LAST.

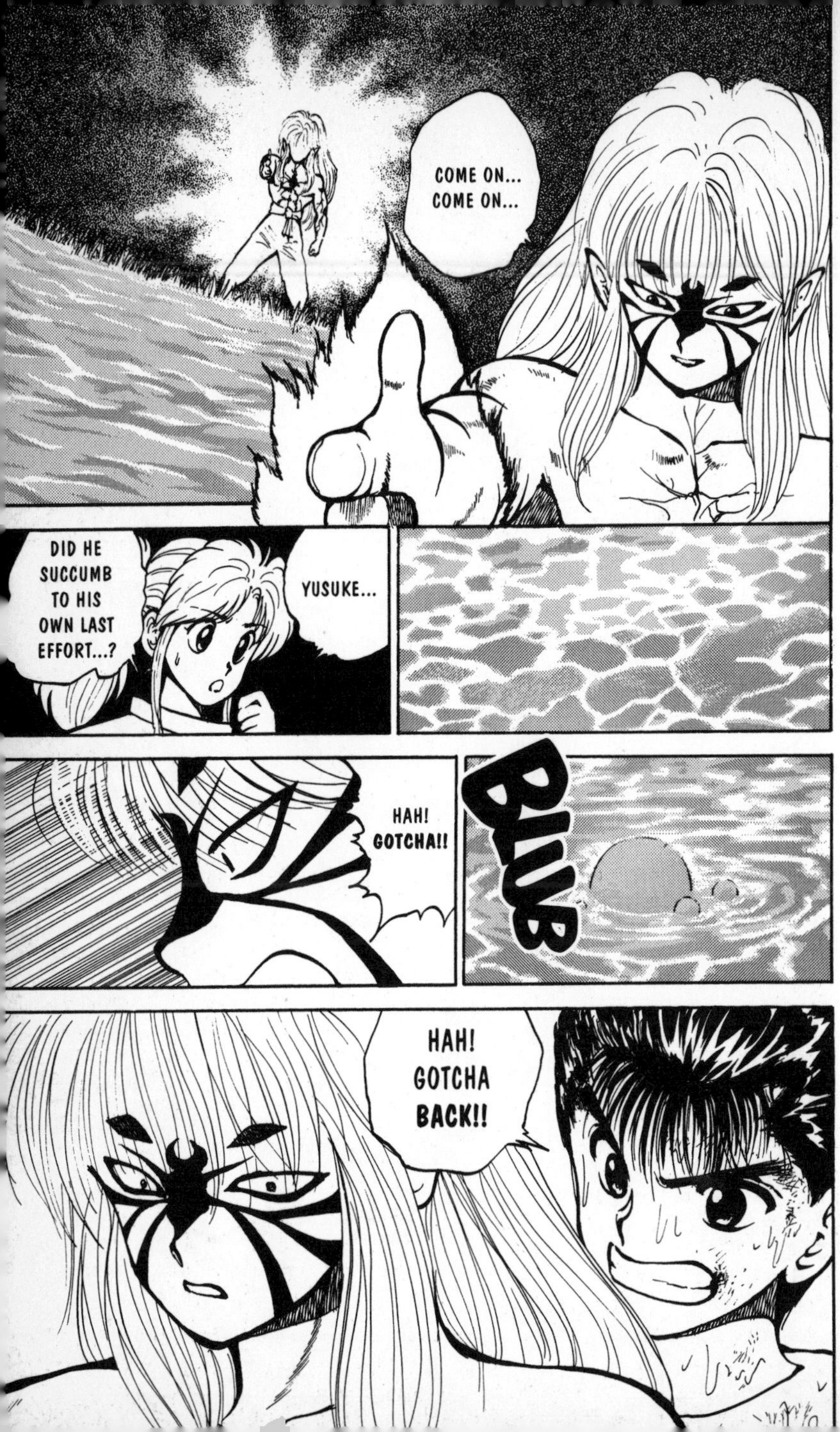
COME ON... COME ON...
YUSUKE...
DID HE SUCCUMB TO HIS OWN LAST EFFORT...?
BLUB
HAH! GOTCHA!!
HAH! GOTCHA BACK!!

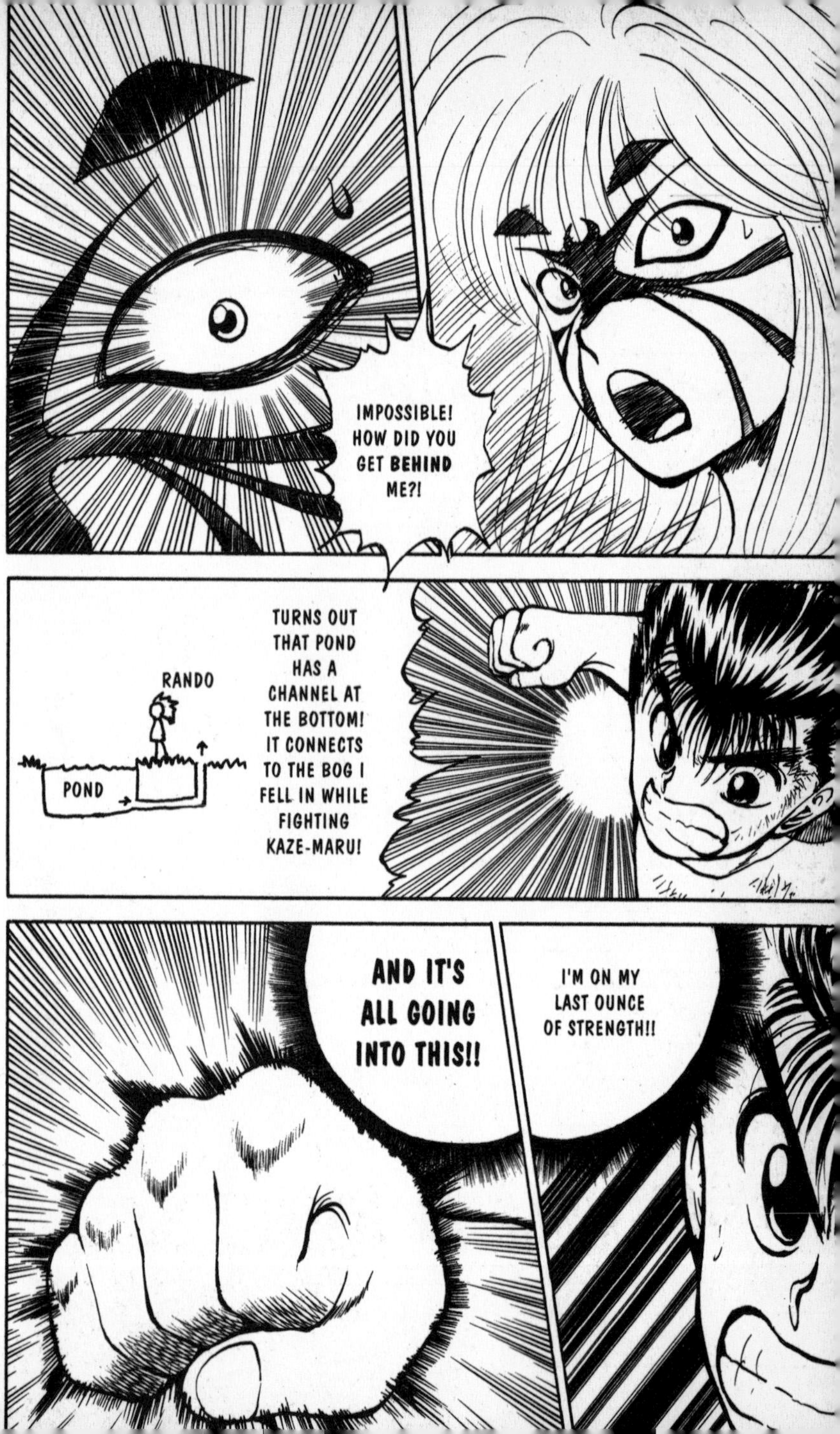
IMPOSSIBLE! HOW DID YOU GET BEHIND ME?!
TURNS OUT THAT POND HAS A CHANNEL AT THE BOTTOM! IT CONNECTS TO THE BOG I FELL IN WHILE FIGHTING KAZE-MARU!
RANDO
POND
I'M ON MY LAST OUNCE OF STRENGTH!!
AND IT'S ALL GOING INTO THIS!!

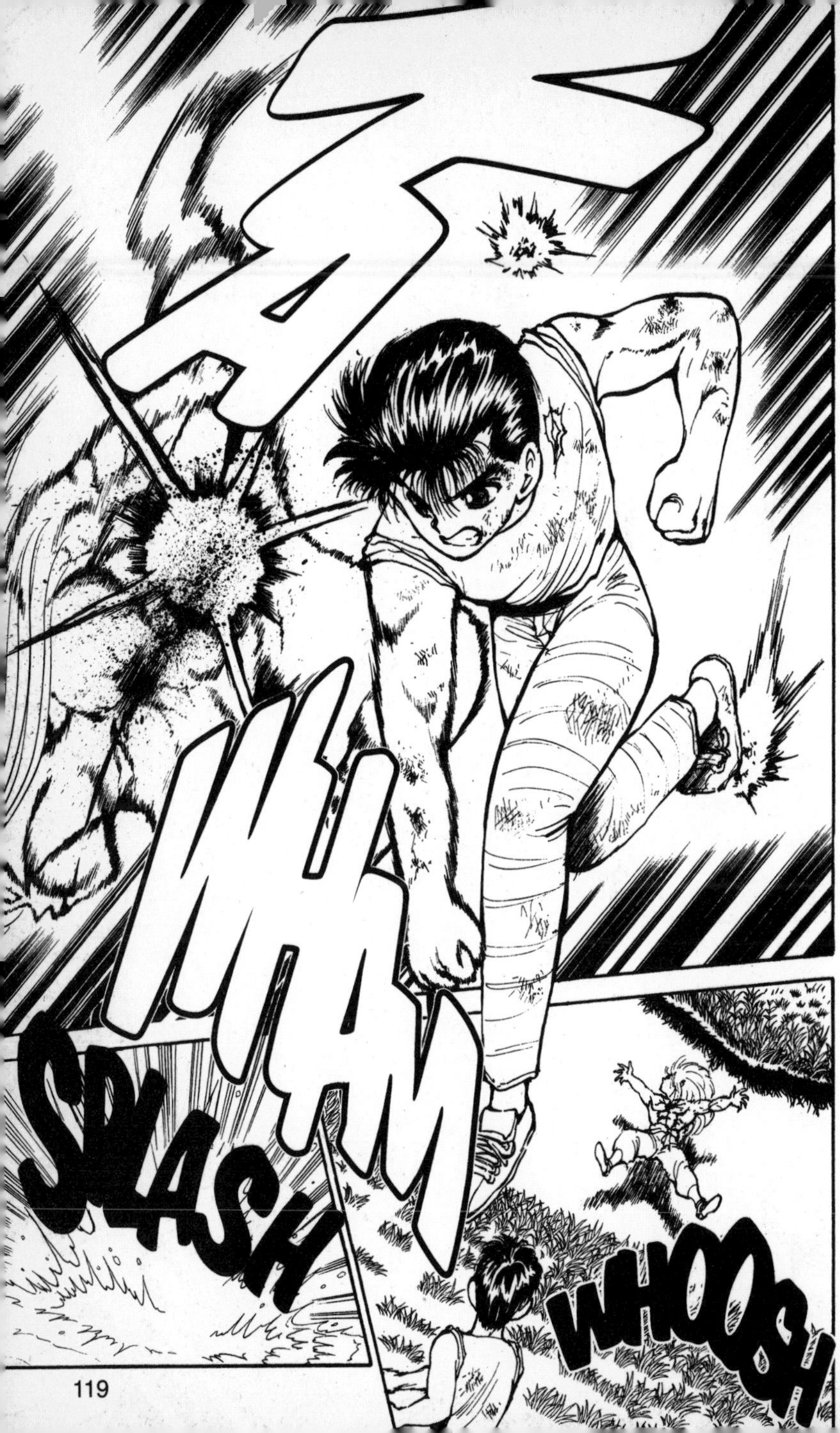
WHAM
WHOOSH
SPLASH

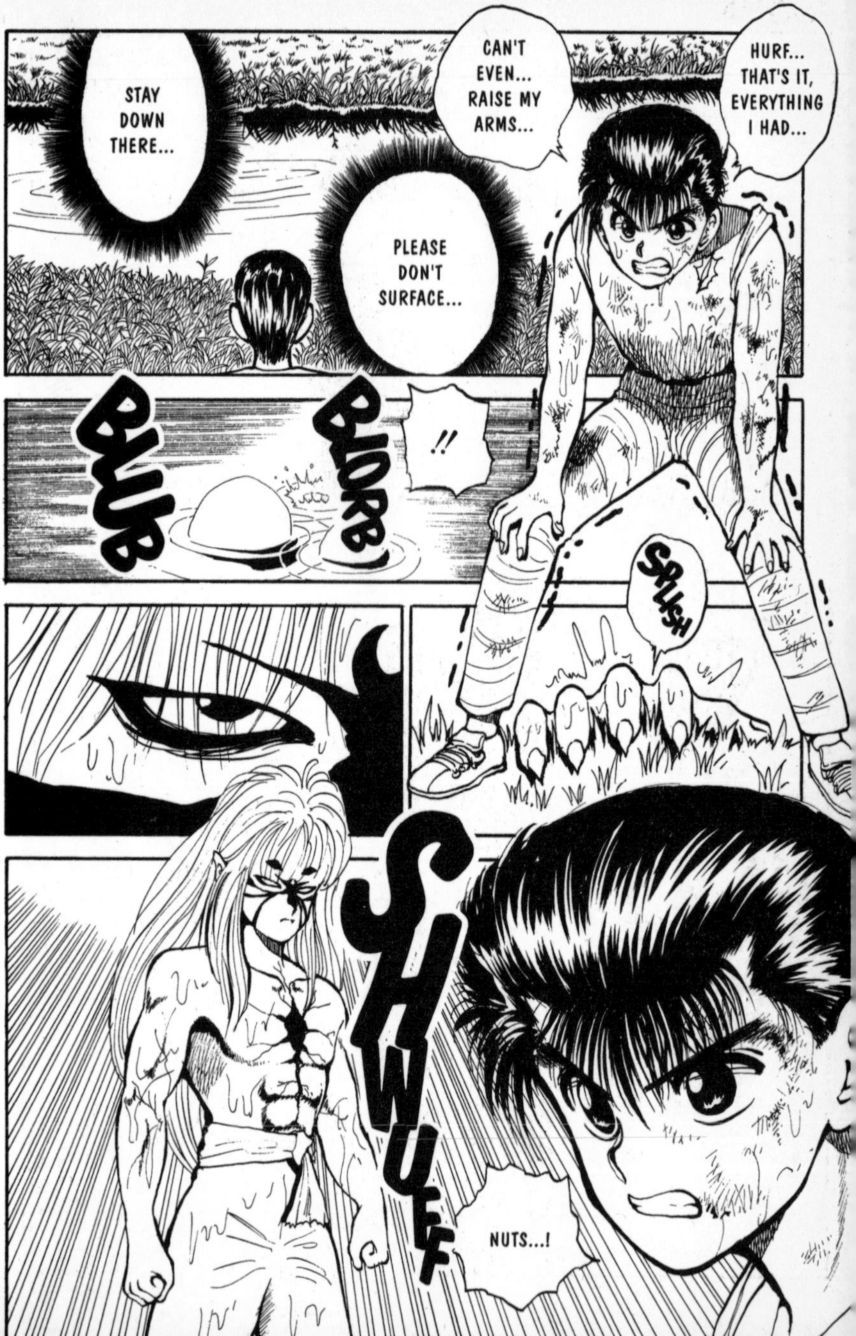
HURF... THAT'S IT, EVERYTHING I HAD...
CAN'T EVEN... RAISE MY ARMS...
STAY DOWN THERE...
PLEASE DON'T SURFACE...
!!
BLORB
BLUB
SPLISH
SHWUFF
NUTS...!

READ THIS WAY

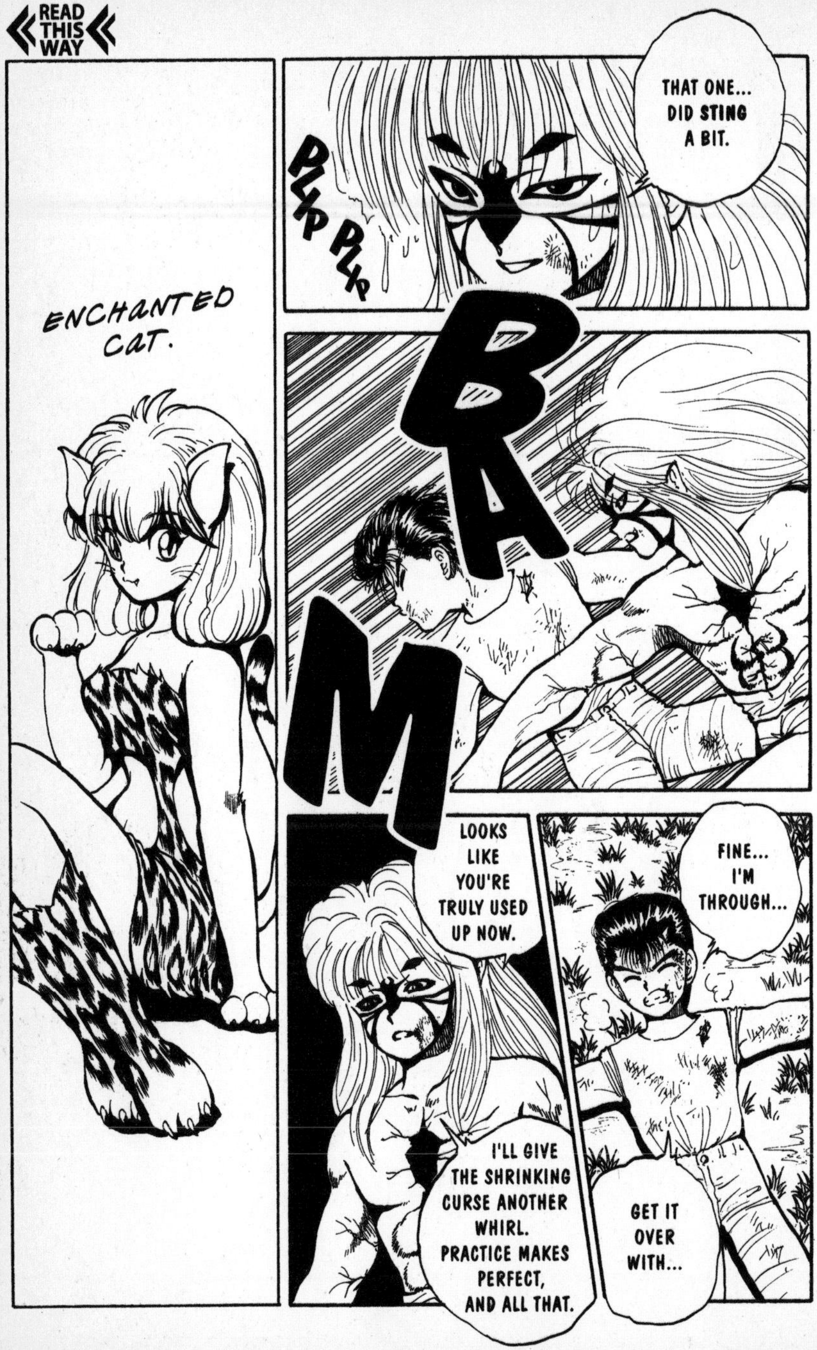
THAT ONE... DID STING A BIT.
PLIP PLIP
BAM
FINE... I'M THROUGH...
GET IT OVER WITH...
LOOKS LIKE YOU'RE TRULY USED UP NOW.
I'LL GIVE THE SHRINKING CURSE ANOTHER WHIRL. PRACTICE MAKES PERFECT, AND ALL THAT.
ENCHANTED CAT.

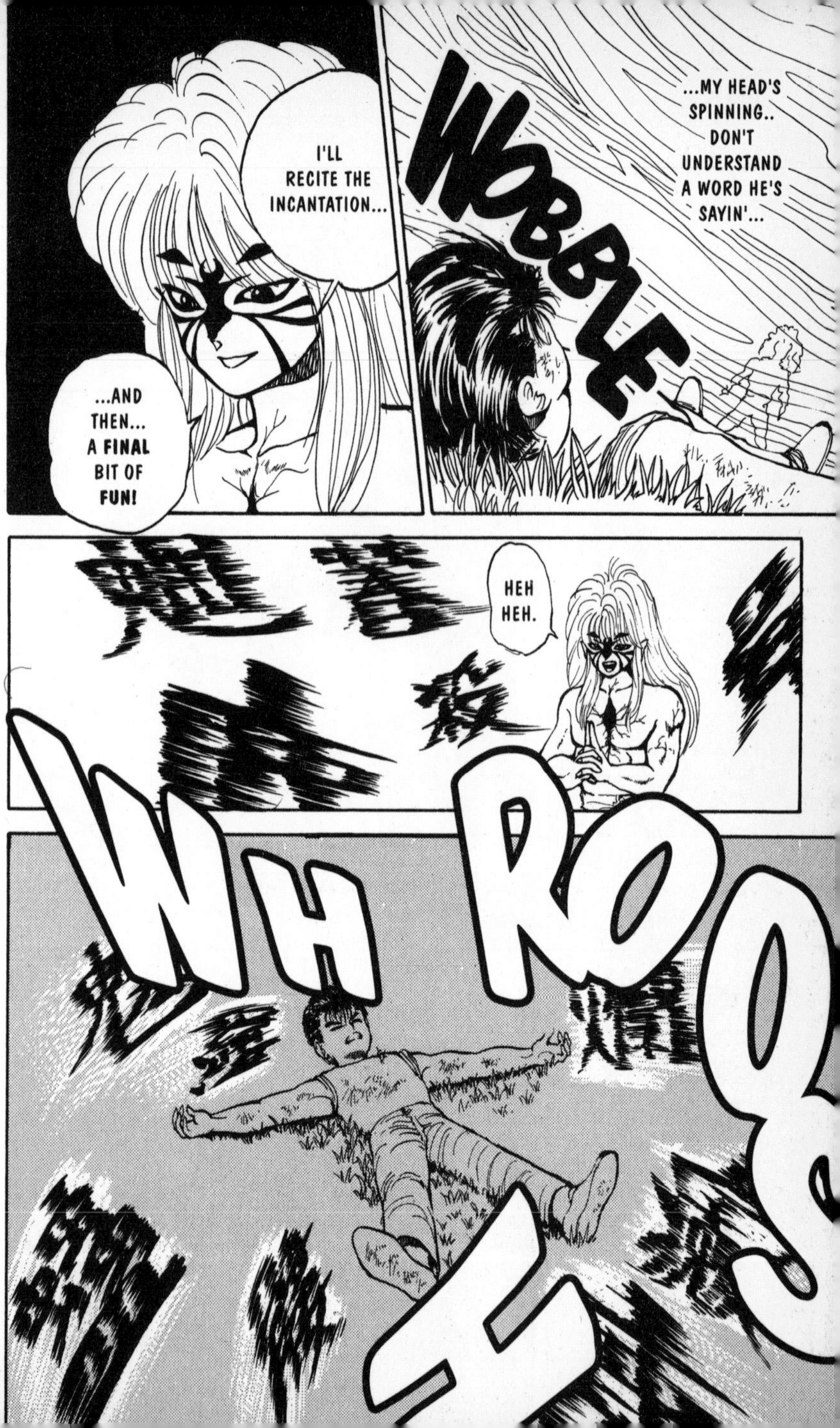
WOBBLE
...MY HEAD'S SPINNING.. DON'T UNDERSTAND A WORD HE'S SAYIN'...
I'LL RECITE THE INCANTATION...
...AND THEN... A **FINAL** BIT OF **FUN!**
HEH HEH.
WHROOSH

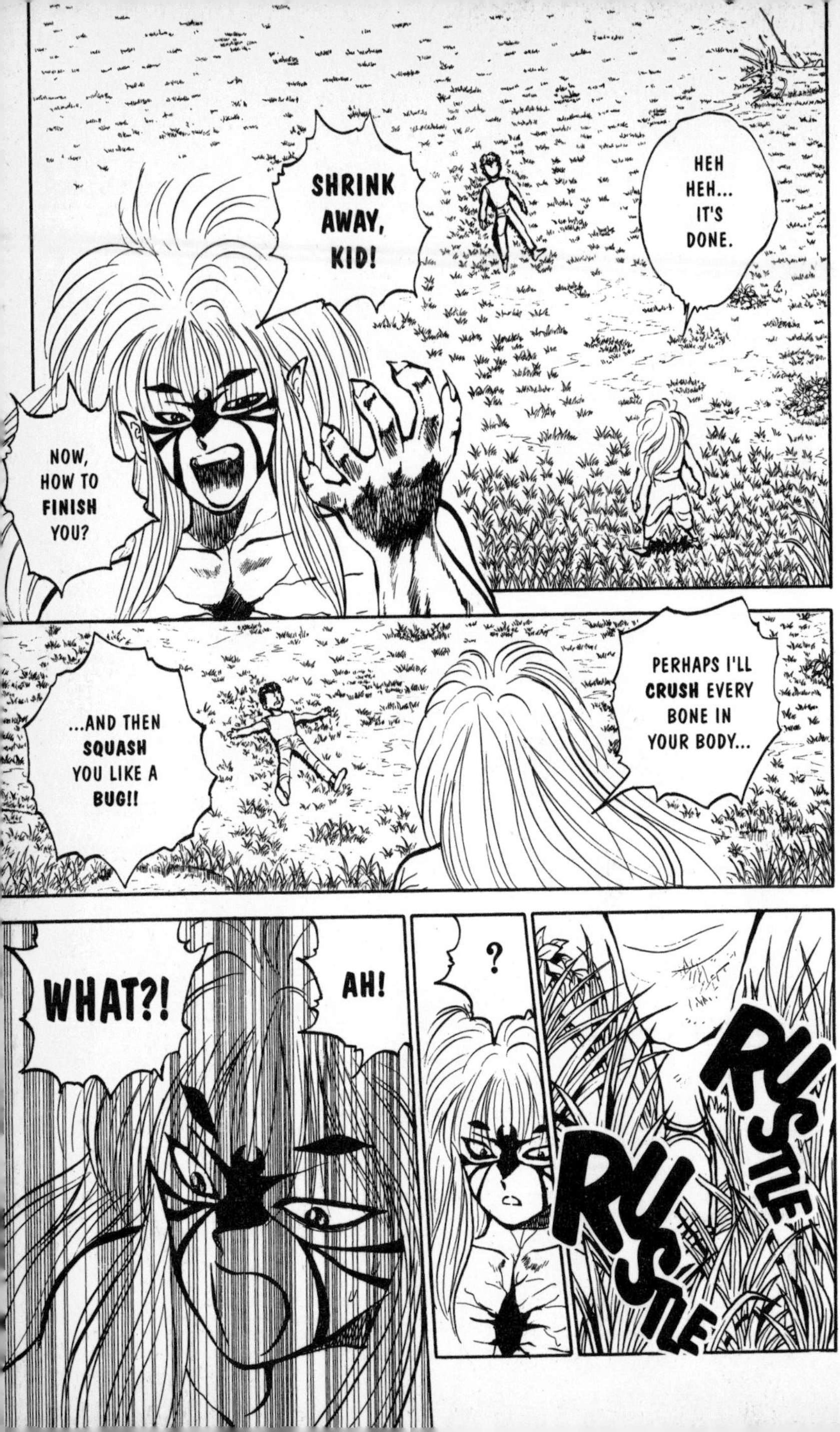
HEH HEH... IT'S DONE.
SHRINK AWAY, KID!
NOW, HOW TO FINISH YOU?
PERHAPS I'LL CRUSH EVERY BONE IN YOUR BODY...
...AND THEN SQUASH YOU LIKE A BUG!!
RUSTLE
RUSTLE
?
AH!
WHAT?!

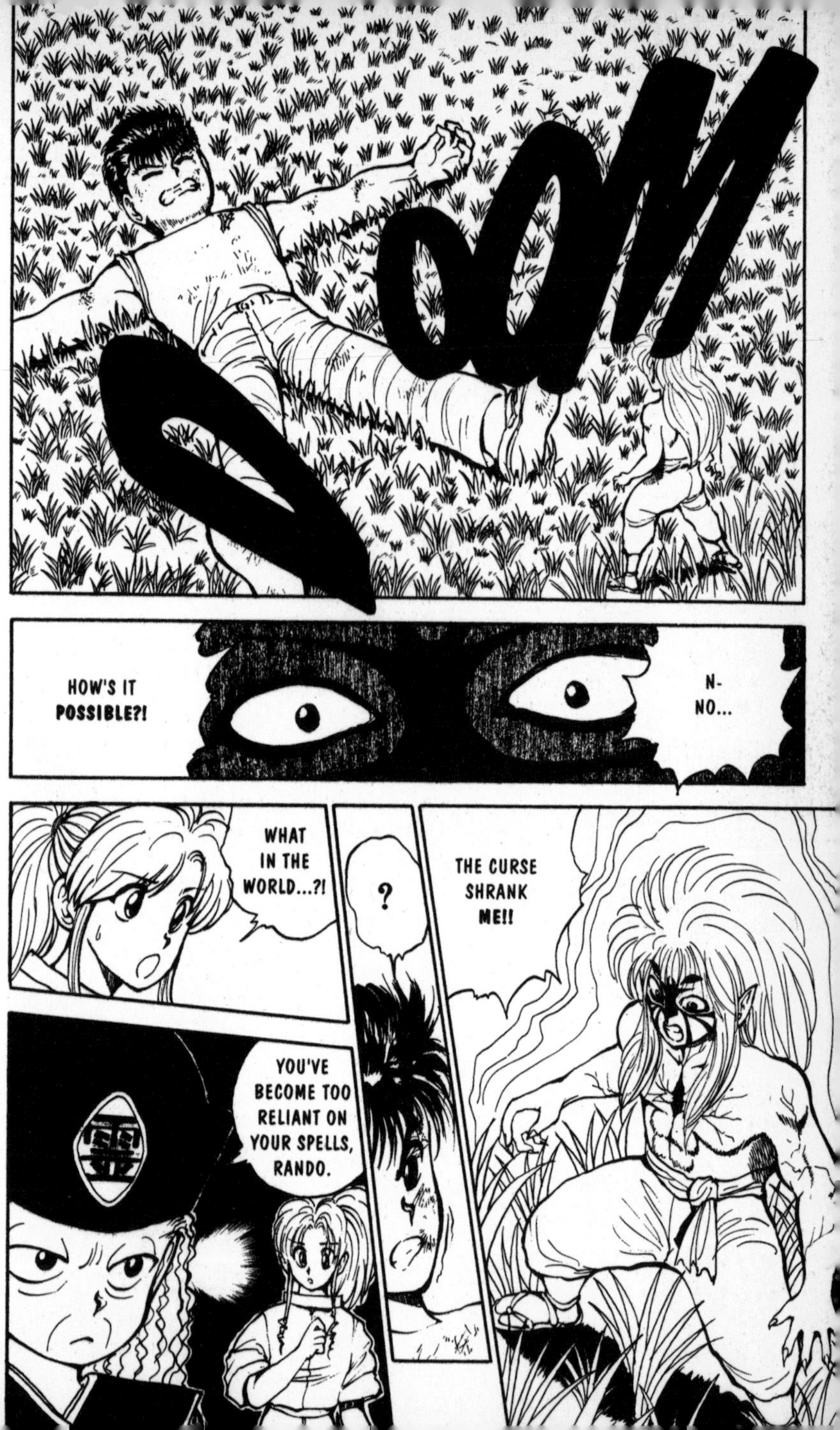
DOOM
N- NO...
HOW'S IT POSSIBLE?!
THE CURSE SHRANK ME!!
?
WHAT IN THE WORLD...?!
YOU'VE BECOME TOO RELIANT ON YOUR SPELLS, RANDO.

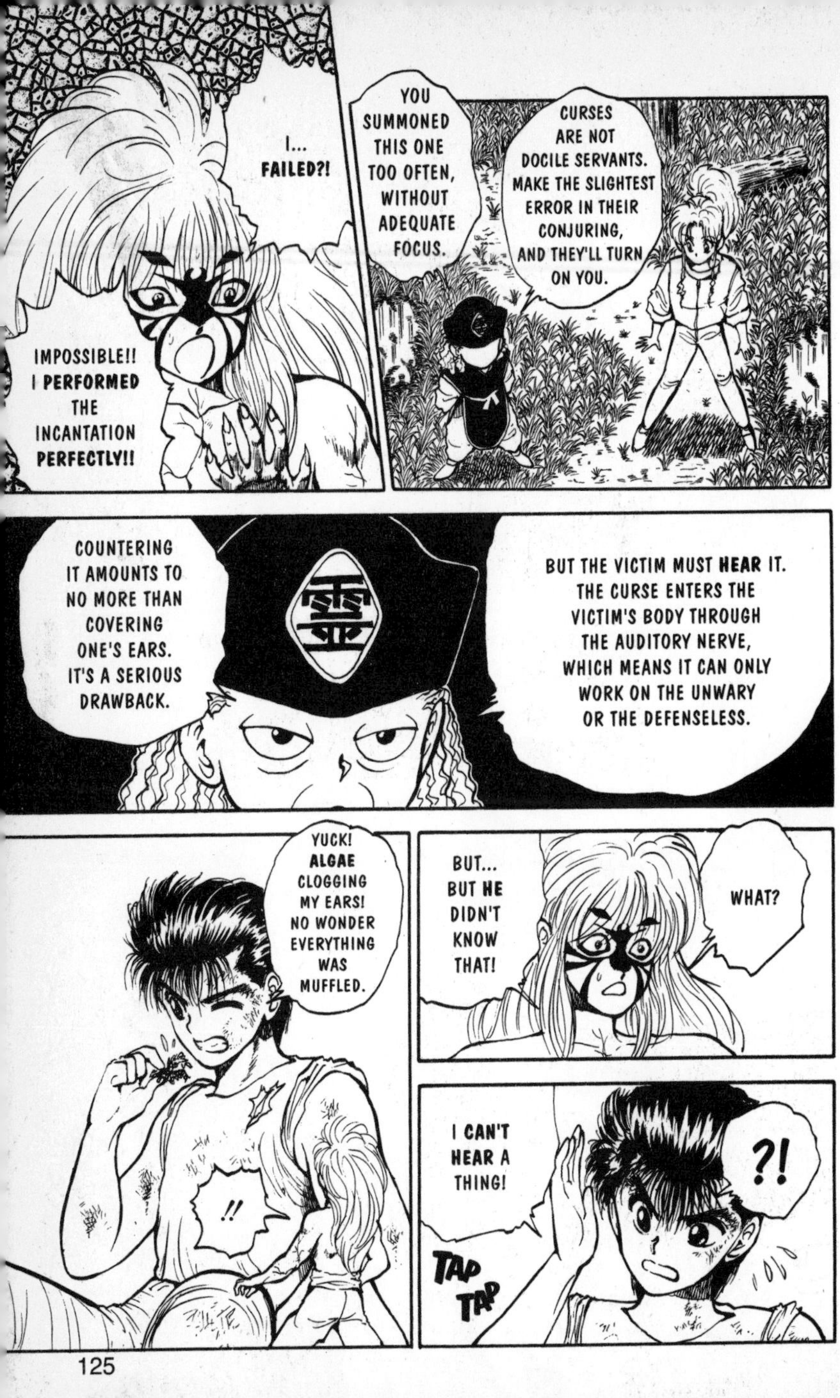
CURSES ARE NOT DOCILE SERVANTS. MAKE THE SLIGHTEST ERROR IN THEIR CONJURING, AND THEY'LL TURN ON YOU.
YOU SUMMONED THIS ONE TOO OFTEN, WITHOUT ADEQUATE FOCUS.
I... **FAILED?!**
IMPOSSIBLE!! I **PERFORMED** THE INCANTATION **PERFECTLY!!**
BUT THE VICTIM MUST **HEAR** IT. THE CURSE ENTERS THE VICTIM'S BODY THROUGH THE AUDITORY NERVE, WHICH MEANS IT CAN ONLY WORK ON THE UNWARY OR THE DEFENSELESS.
COUNTERING IT AMOUNTS TO NO MORE THAN COVERING ONE'S EARS. IT'S A SERIOUS DRAWBACK.
WHAT?
BUT... BUT **HE** DIDN'T KNOW THAT!
?!
I CAN'T HEAR A THING!
TAP TAP
YUCK! **ALGAE** CLOGGING MY EARS! NO WONDER EVERYTHING WAS MUFFLED.
!!

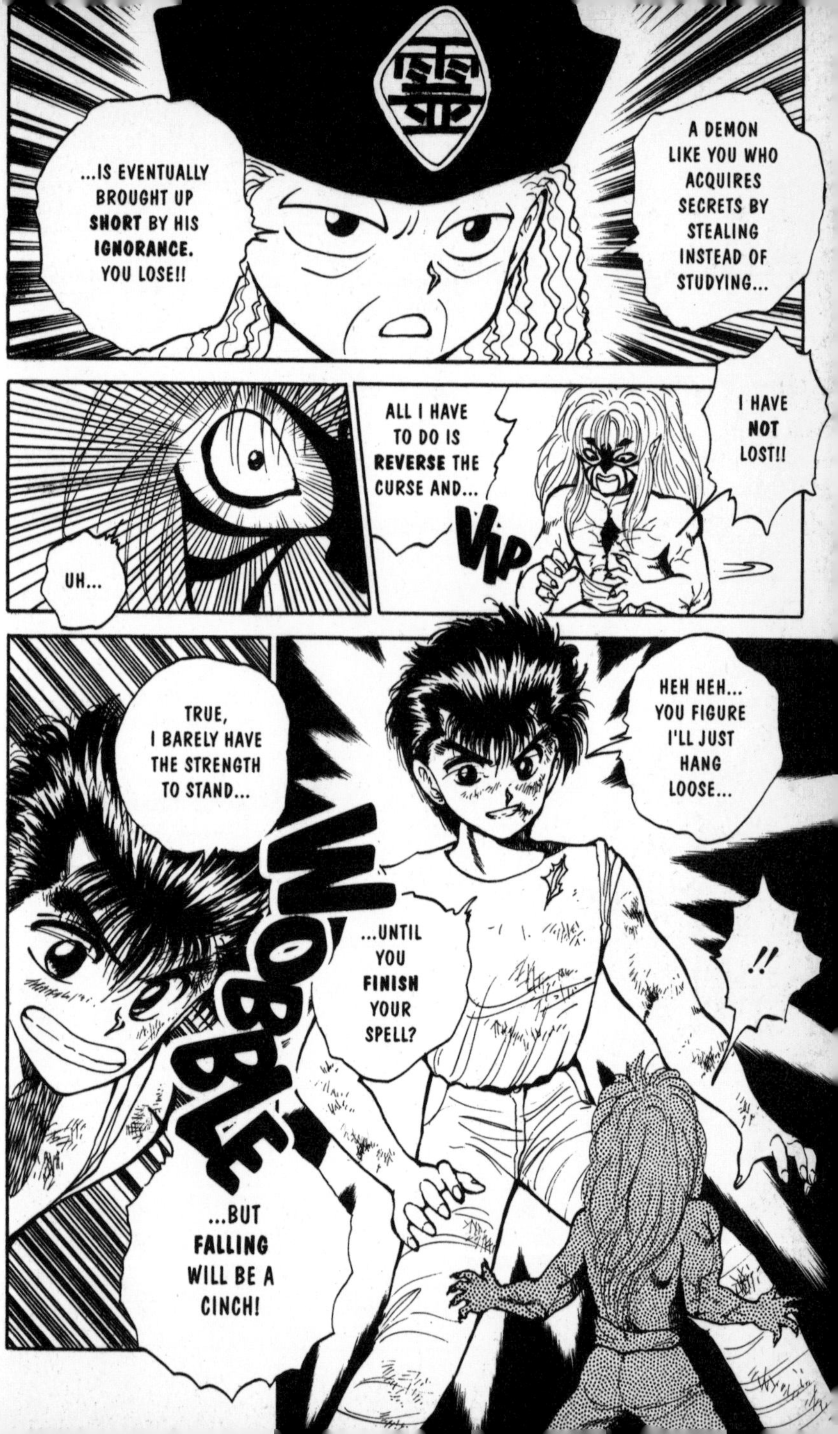
A DEMON LIKE YOU WHO ACQUIRES SECRETS BY STEALING INSTEAD OF STUDYING...
...IS EVENTUALLY BROUGHT UP SHORT BY HIS IGNORANCE. YOU LOSE!!
I HAVE NOT LOST!!
ALL I HAVE TO DO IS REVERSE THE CURSE AND...
VIP
UH...
HEH HEH... YOU FIGURE I'LL JUST HANG LOOSE...
...UNTIL YOU FINISH YOUR SPELL?
!!
TRUE, I BARELY HAVE THE STRENGTH TO STAND...
WOBBLE
...BUT FALLING WILL BE A CINCH!

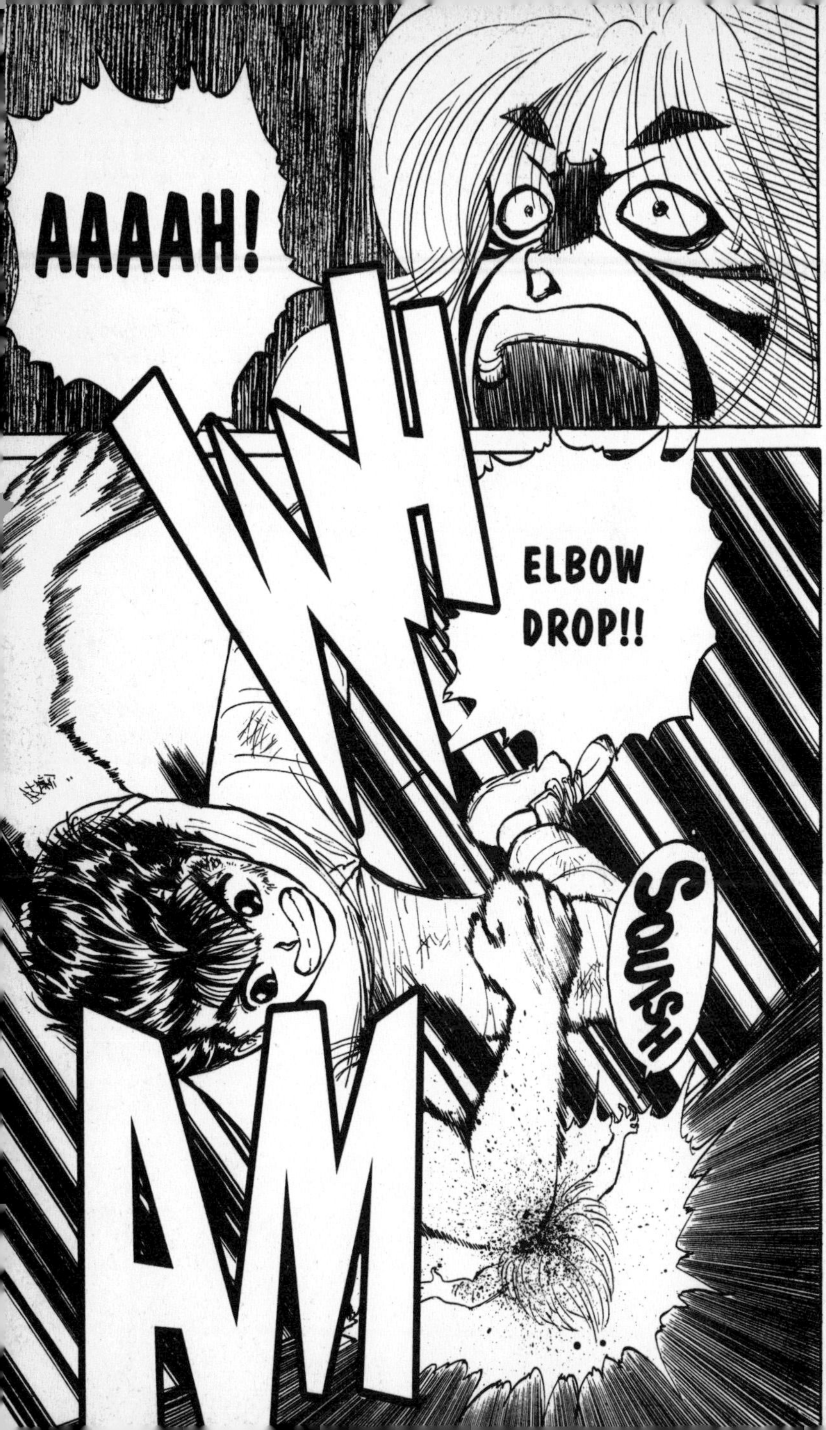
AAAAH!
WHAM
ELBOW DROP!!
SQUISH

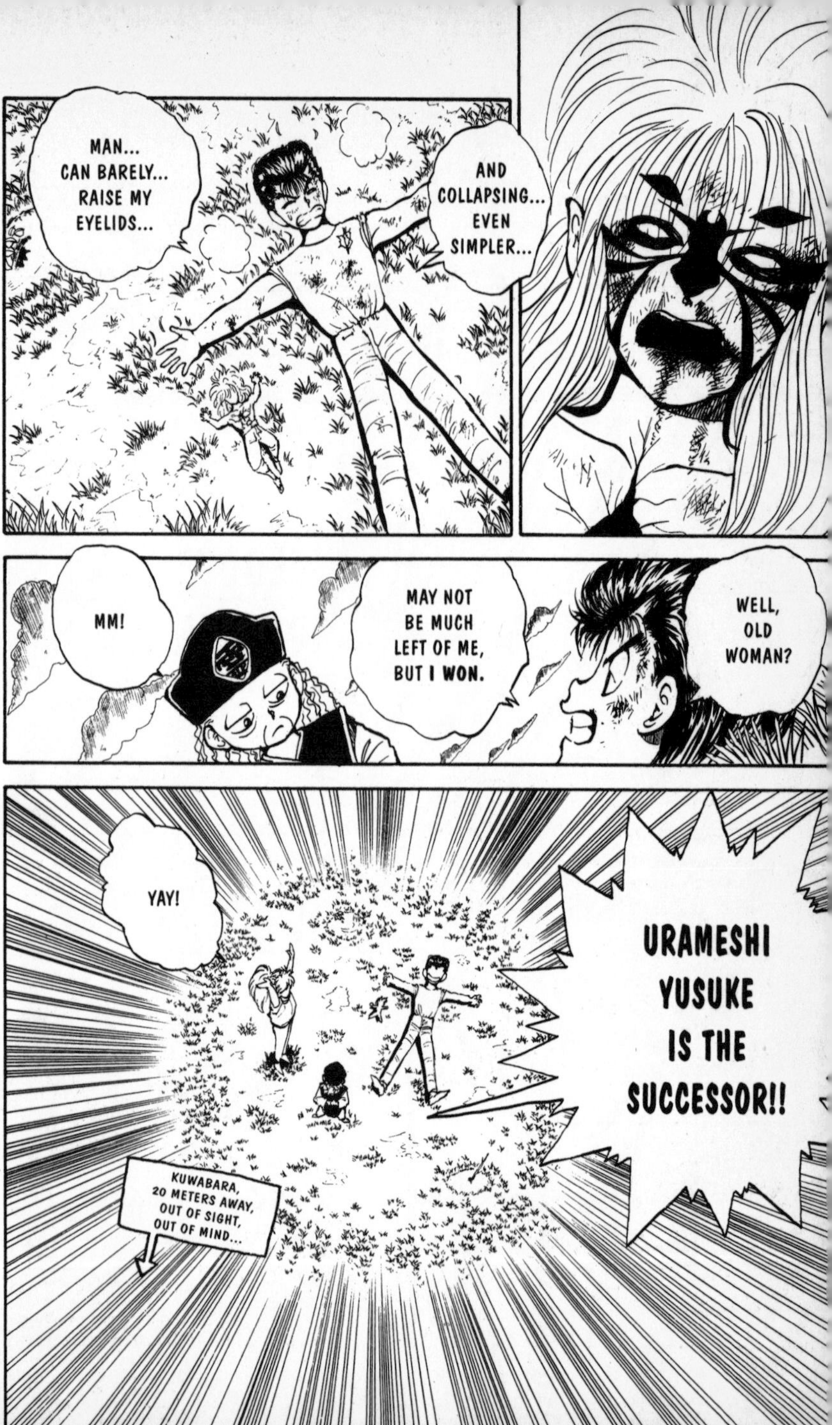
AND COLLAPSING... EVEN SIMPLER...
MAN... CAN BARELY... RAISE MY EYELIDS...
WELL, OLD WOMAN?
MAY NOT BE MUCH LEFT OF ME, BUT I WON.
MM!
URAMESHI YUSUKE IS THE SUCCESSOR!!
YAY!
KUWABARA, 20 METERS AWAY, OUT OF SIGHT, OUT OF MIND...

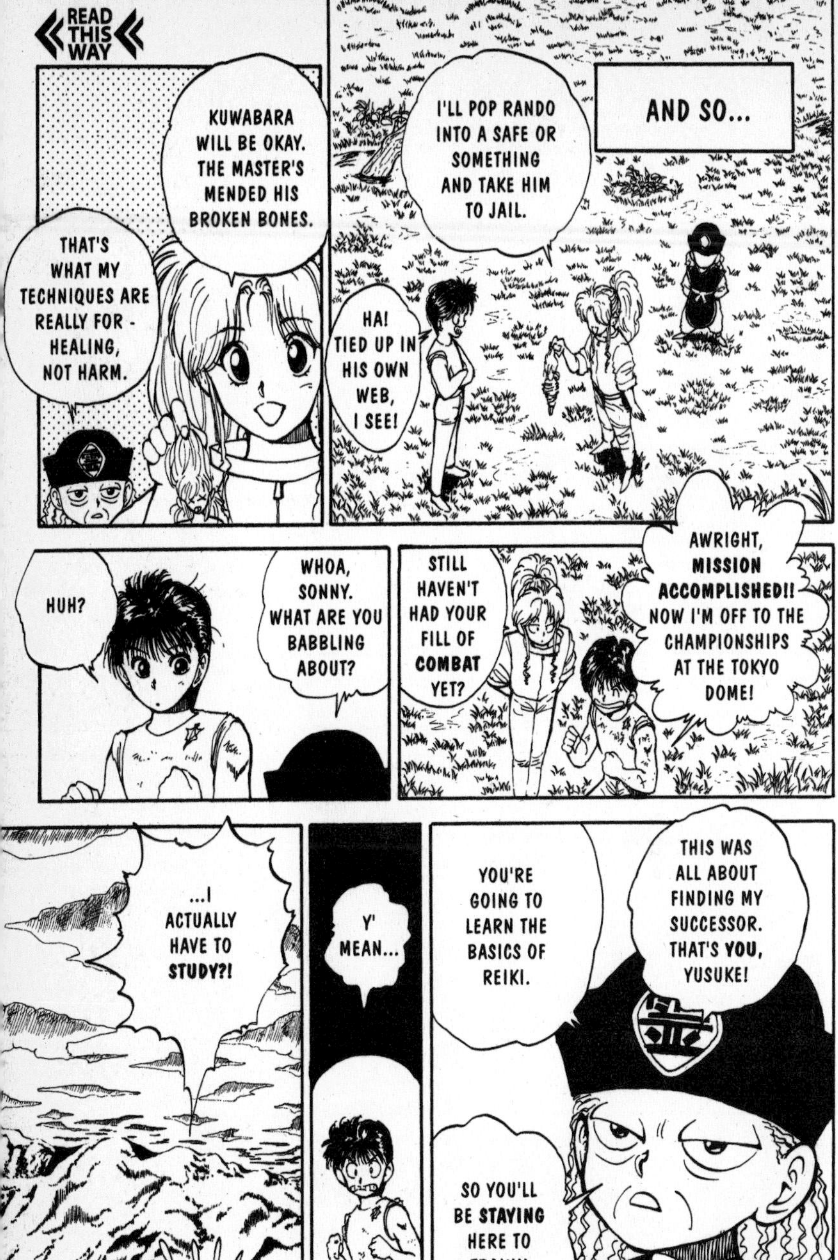
READ THIS WAY
AND SO...
I'LL POP RANDO INTO A SAFE OR SOMETHING AND TAKE HIM TO JAIL.
HA! TIED UP IN HIS OWN WEB, I SEE!
KUWABARA WILL BE OKAY. THE MASTER'S MENDED HIS BROKEN BONES.
THAT'S WHAT MY TECHNIQUES ARE REALLY FOR - HEALING, NOT HARM.
AWRIGHT, **MISSION ACCOMPLISHED!!** NOW I'M OFF TO THE CHAMPIONSHIPS AT THE TOKYO DOME!
STILL HAVEN'T HAD YOUR FILL OF **COMBAT** YET?
WHOA, SONNY. WHAT ARE YOU BABBLING ABOUT?
HUH?
THIS WAS ALL ABOUT FINDING MY SUCCESSOR. THAT'S **YOU**, YUSUKE!
YOU'RE GOING TO LEARN THE BASICS OF REIKI.
SO YOU'LL BE **STAYING** HERE TO TRAIN!!
Y' MEAN...
...I ACTUALLY HAVE TO **STUDY?!**

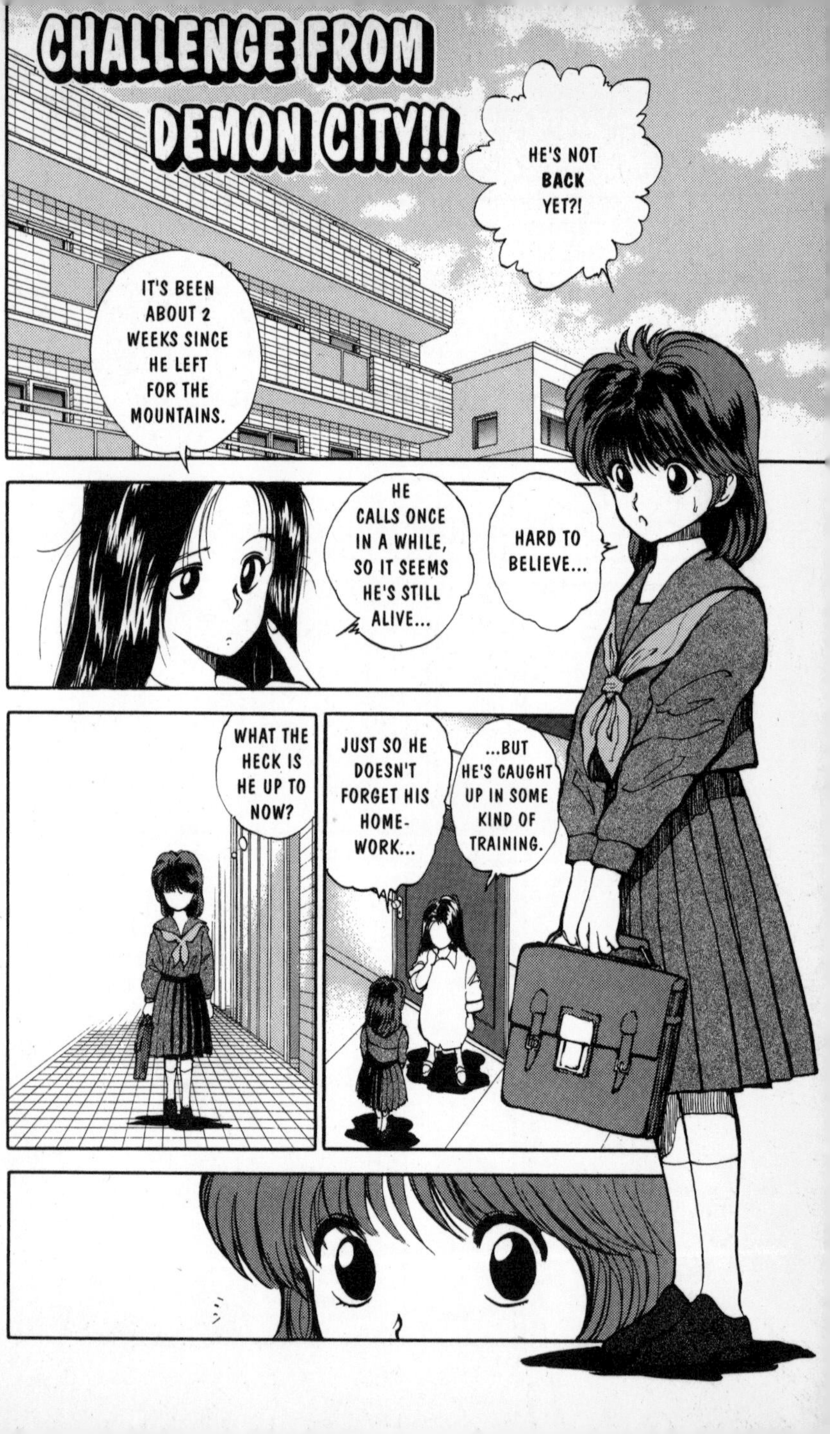
CHALLENGE FROM DEMON CITY!!
IT'S BEEN ABOUT 2 WEEKS SINCE HE LEFT FOR THE MOUNTAINS.
HE'S NOT BACK YET?!
HE CALLS ONCE IN A WHILE, SO IT SEEMS HE'S STILL ALIVE...
HARD TO BELIEVE...
WHAT THE HECK IS HE UP TO NOW?
JUST SO HE DOESN'T FORGET HIS HOME-WORK...
...BUT HE'S CAUGHT UP IN SOME KIND OF TRAINING.

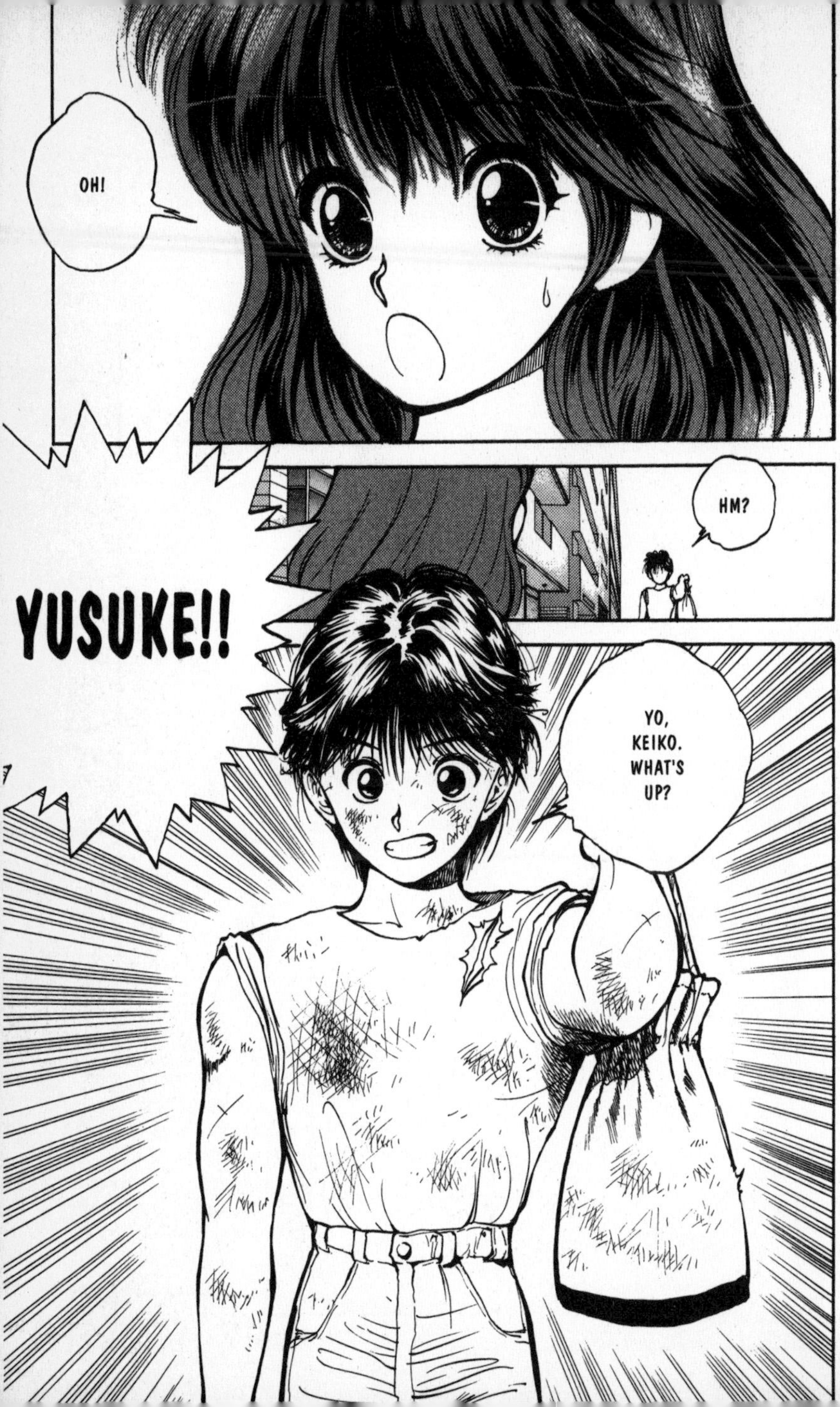
OH!
YUSUKE!!
HM?
YO, KEIKO. WHAT'S UP?

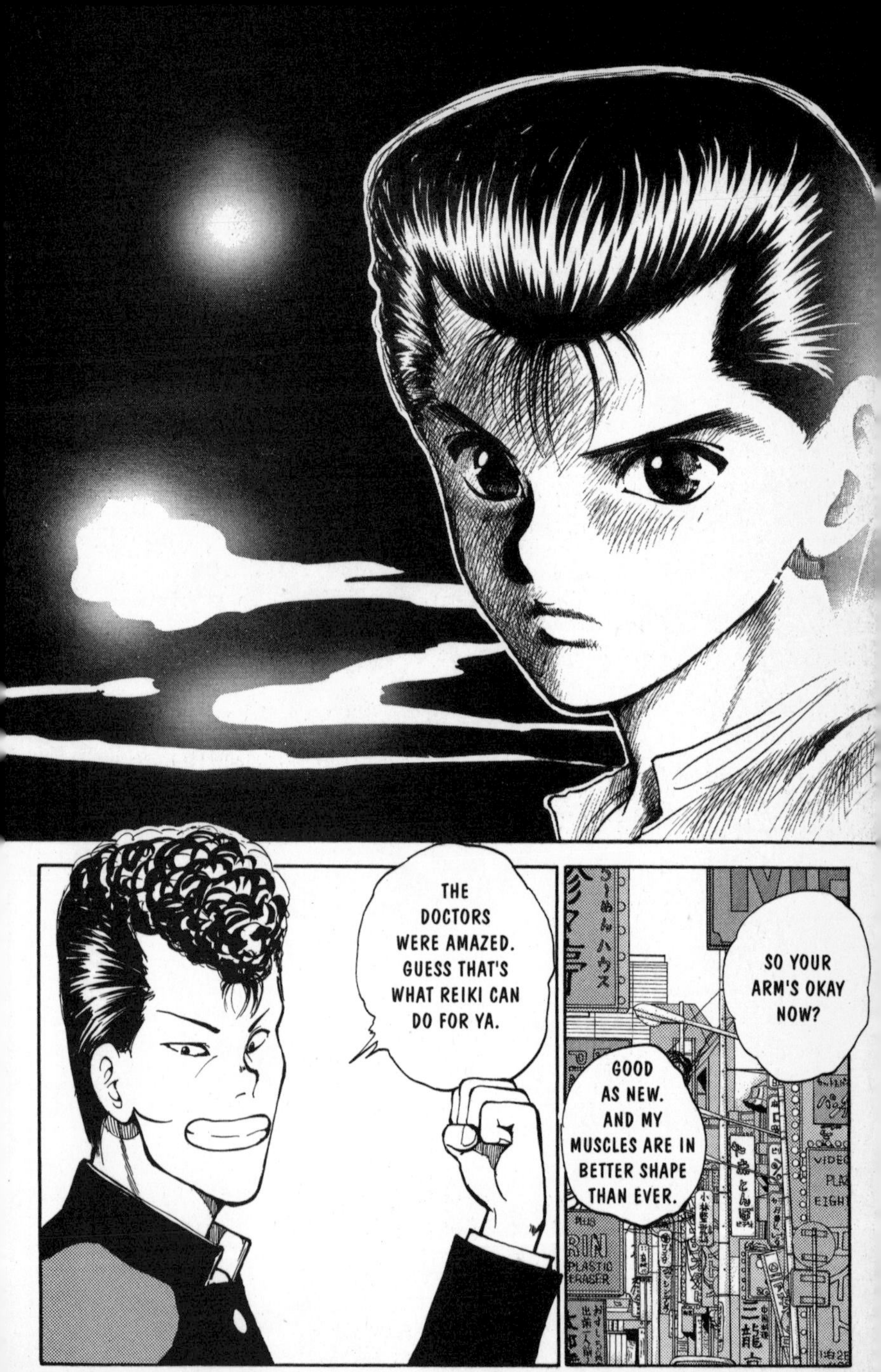
SO YOUR ARM'S OKAY NOW?
GOOD AS NEW. AND MY MUSCLES ARE IN BETTER SHAPE THAN EVER.
THE DOCTORS WERE AMAZED. GUESS THAT'S WHAT REIKI CAN DO FOR YA.

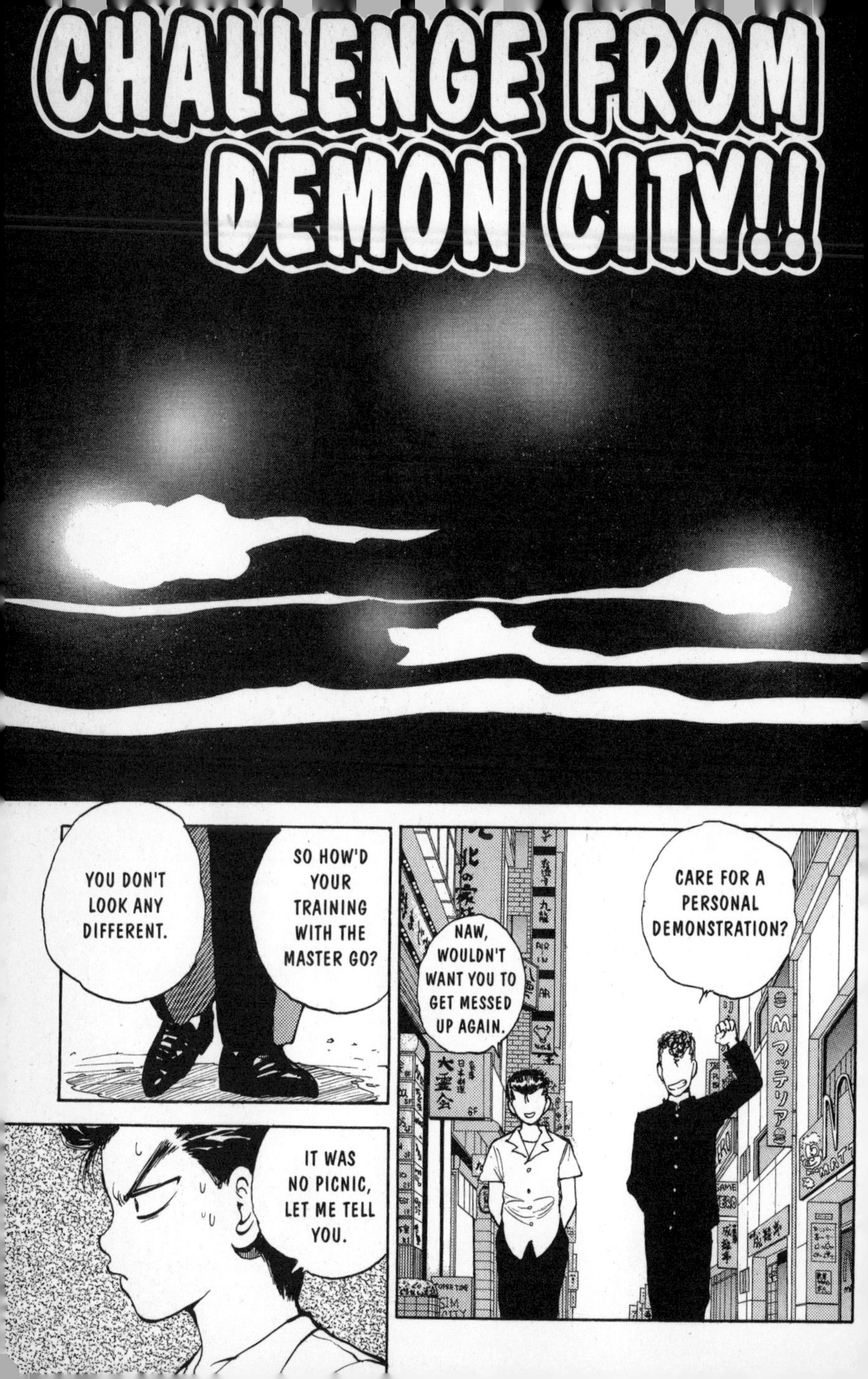
CHALLENGE FROM DEMON CITY!!!
CARE FOR A PERSONAL DEMONSTRATION?
NAW, WOULDN'T WANT YOU TO GET MESSED UP AGAIN.
SO HOW'D YOUR TRAINING WITH THE MASTER GO?
YOU DON'T LOOK ANY DIFFERENT.
IT WAS NO PICNIC, LET ME TELL YOU.

READ THIS WAY

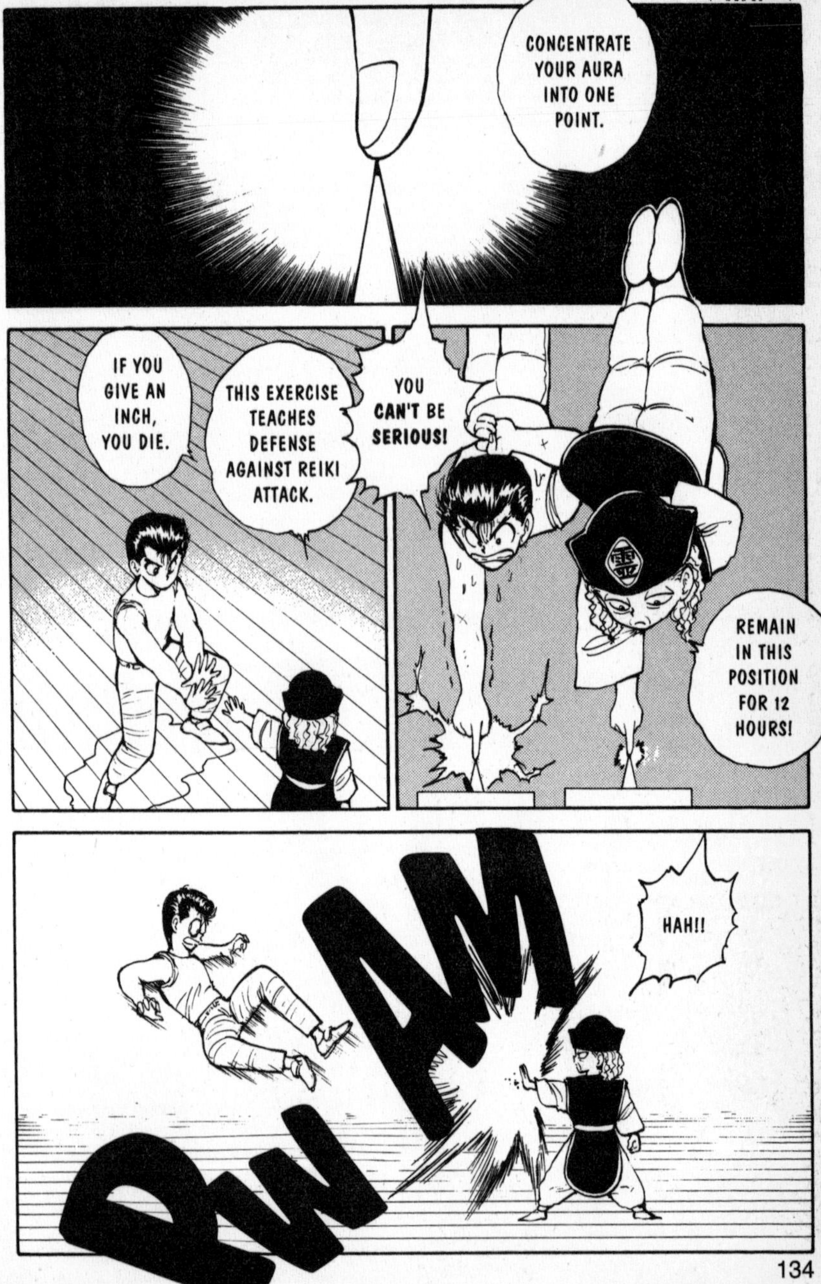
CONCENTRATE YOUR AURA INTO ONE POINT.
REMAIN IN THIS POSITION FOR 12 HOURS!
YOU CAN'T BE SERIOUS!
THIS EXERCISE TEACHES DEFENSE AGAINST REIKI ATTACK.
IF YOU GIVE AN INCH, YOU DIE.
HAH!!
PWAM

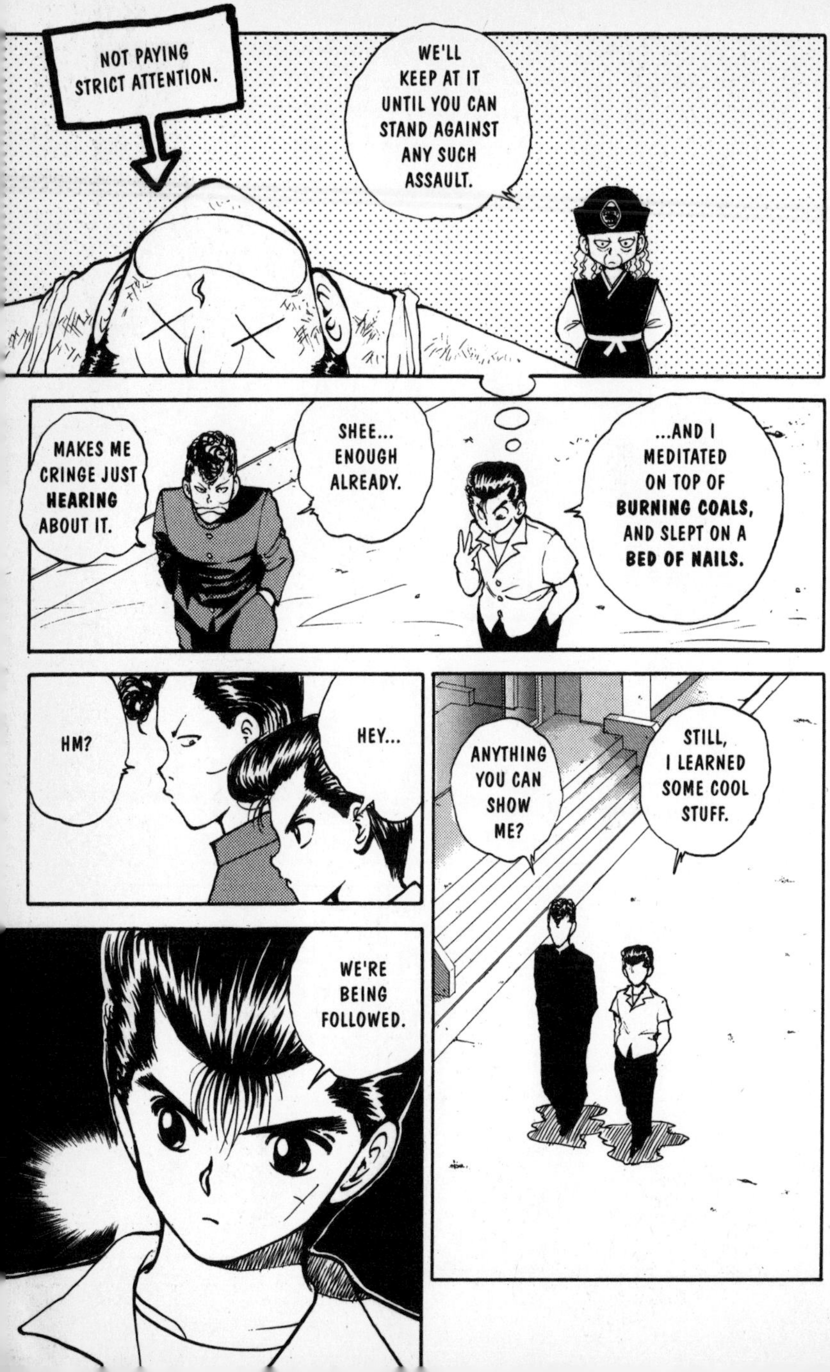
WE'LL KEEP AT IT UNTIL YOU CAN STAND AGAINST ANY SUCH ASSAULT.
NOT PAYING STRICT ATTENTION.
...AND I MEDITATED ON TOP OF **BURNING COALS,** AND SLEPT ON A **BED OF NAILS.**
SHEE... ENOUGH ALREADY.
MAKES ME CRINGE JUST **HEARING** ABOUT IT.
STILL, I LEARNED SOME COOL STUFF.
ANYTHING YOU CAN SHOW ME?
HEY...
HM?
WE'RE BEING FOLLOWED.

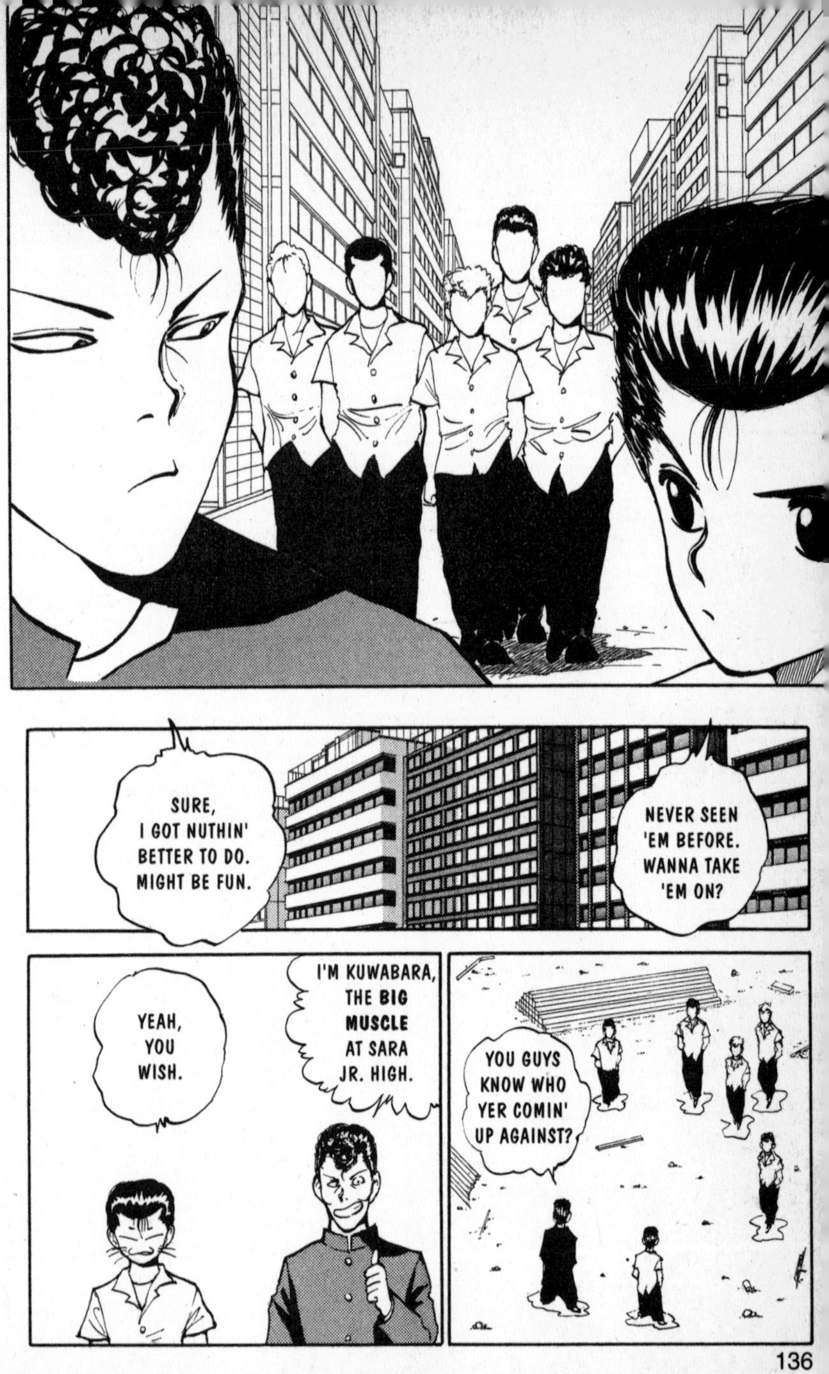
NEVER SEEN 'EM BEFORE. WANNA TAKE 'EM ON?
SURE, I GOT NUTHIN' BETTER TO DO. MIGHT BE FUN.
YOU GUYS KNOW WHO YER COMIN' UP AGAINST?
I'M KUWABARA, THE **BIG MUSCLE** AT SARA JR. HIGH.
YEAH, YOU WISH.

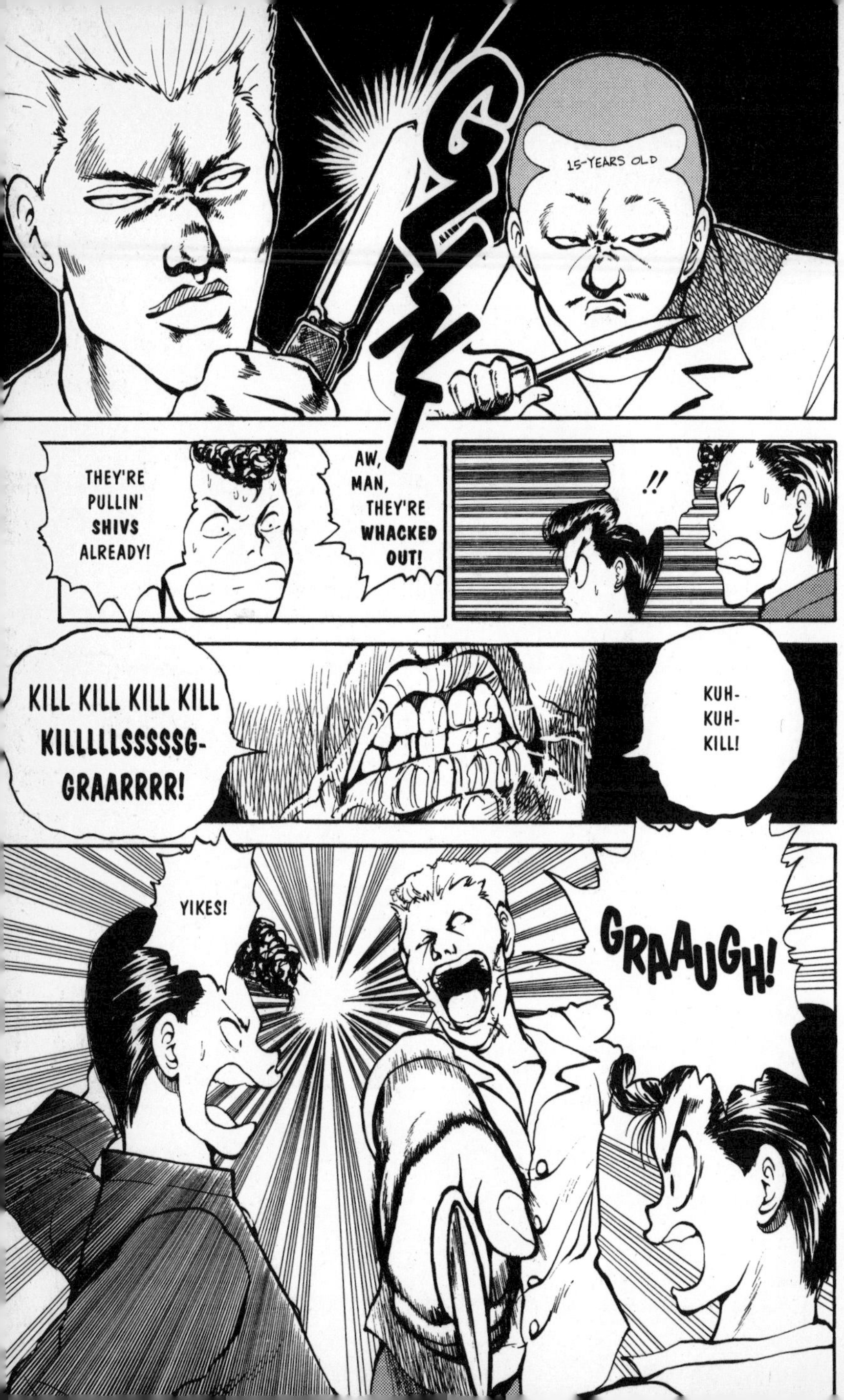
GLINT
15-YEARS OLD
!!
AW, MAN, THEY'RE WHACKED OUT!
THEY'RE PULLIN' SHIVS ALREADY!
KUH-KUH-KILL!
KILL KILL KILL KILL KILLLLLLSSSSSG-GRAARRRR!
GRAAUGH!
YIKES!

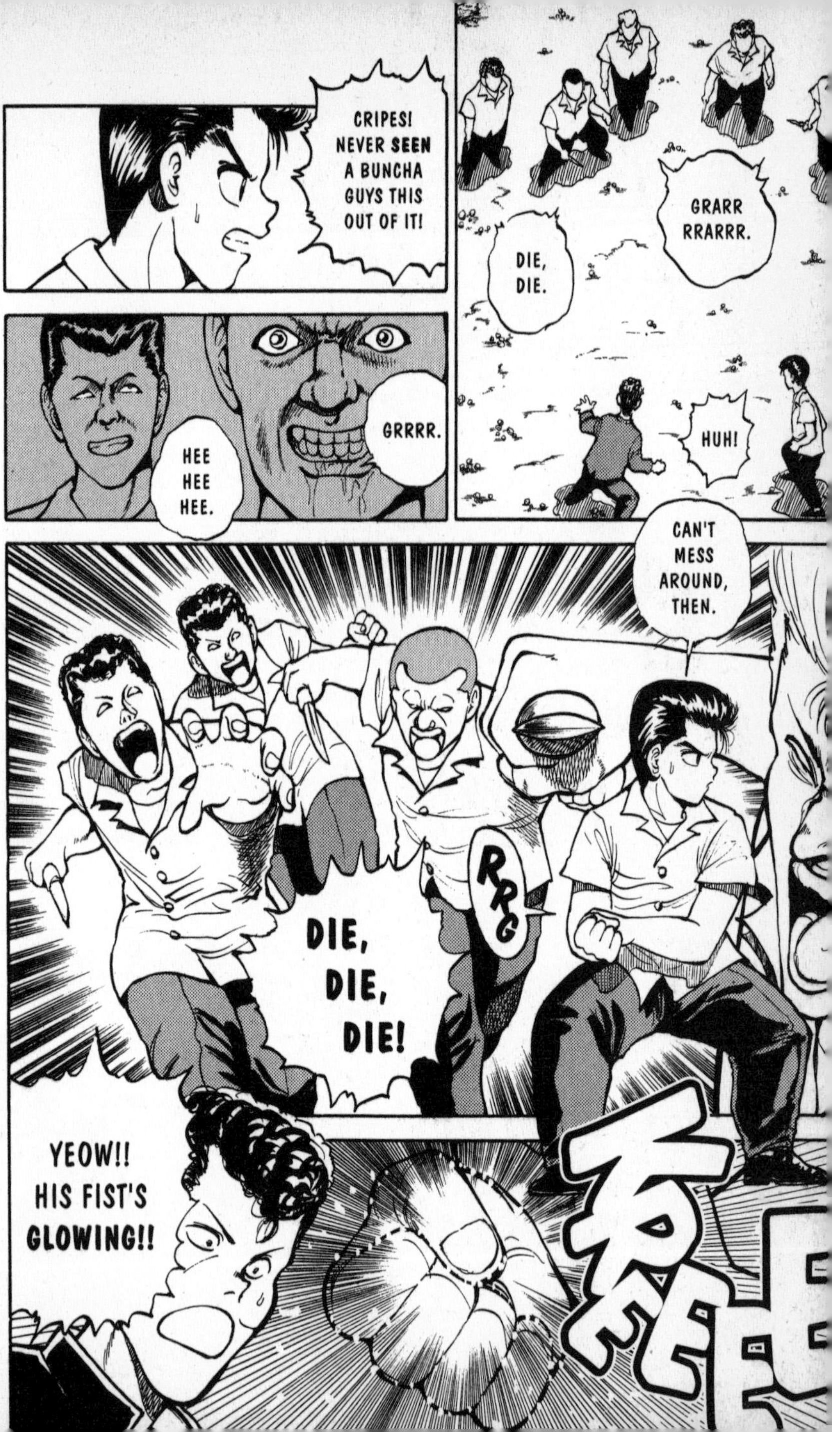
GRARR RRARRR.
DIE, DIE.
HUH!
CRIPES! NEVER SEEN A BUNCHA GUYS THIS OUT OF IT!
GRRRR.
HEE HEE HEE.
CAN'T MESS AROUND, THEN.
RRG
DIE, DIE, DIE!
YEOW!! HIS FIST'S GLOWING!!

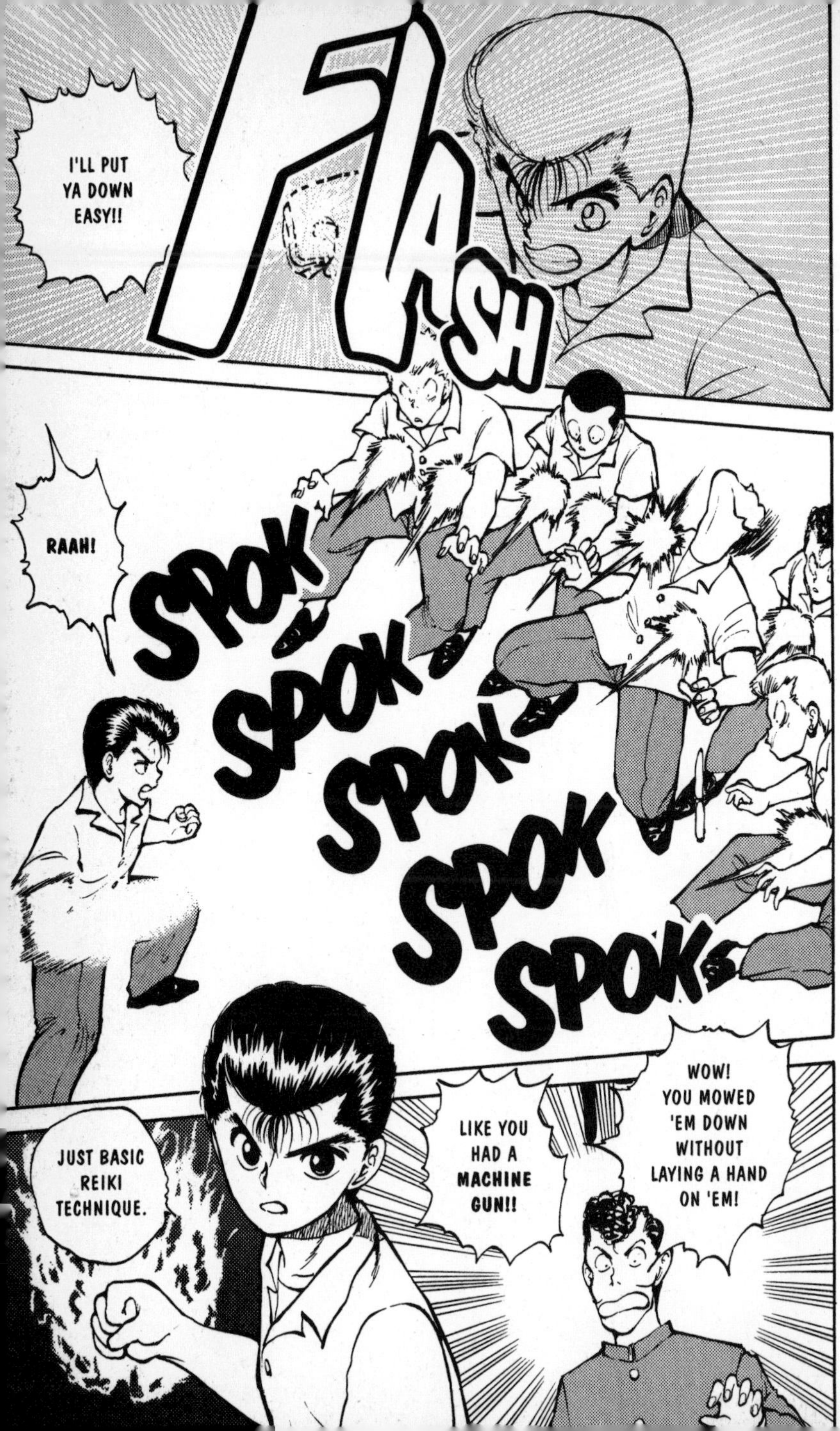
FLASH
I'LL PUT YA DOWN EASY!!
RAAH!
SPOK SPOK SPOK SPOK SPOKS
WOW! YOU MOWED 'EM DOWN WITHOUT LAYING A HAND ON 'EM!
LIKE YOU HAD A MACHINE GUN!!
JUST BASIC REIKI TECHNIQUE.

READ THIS WAY

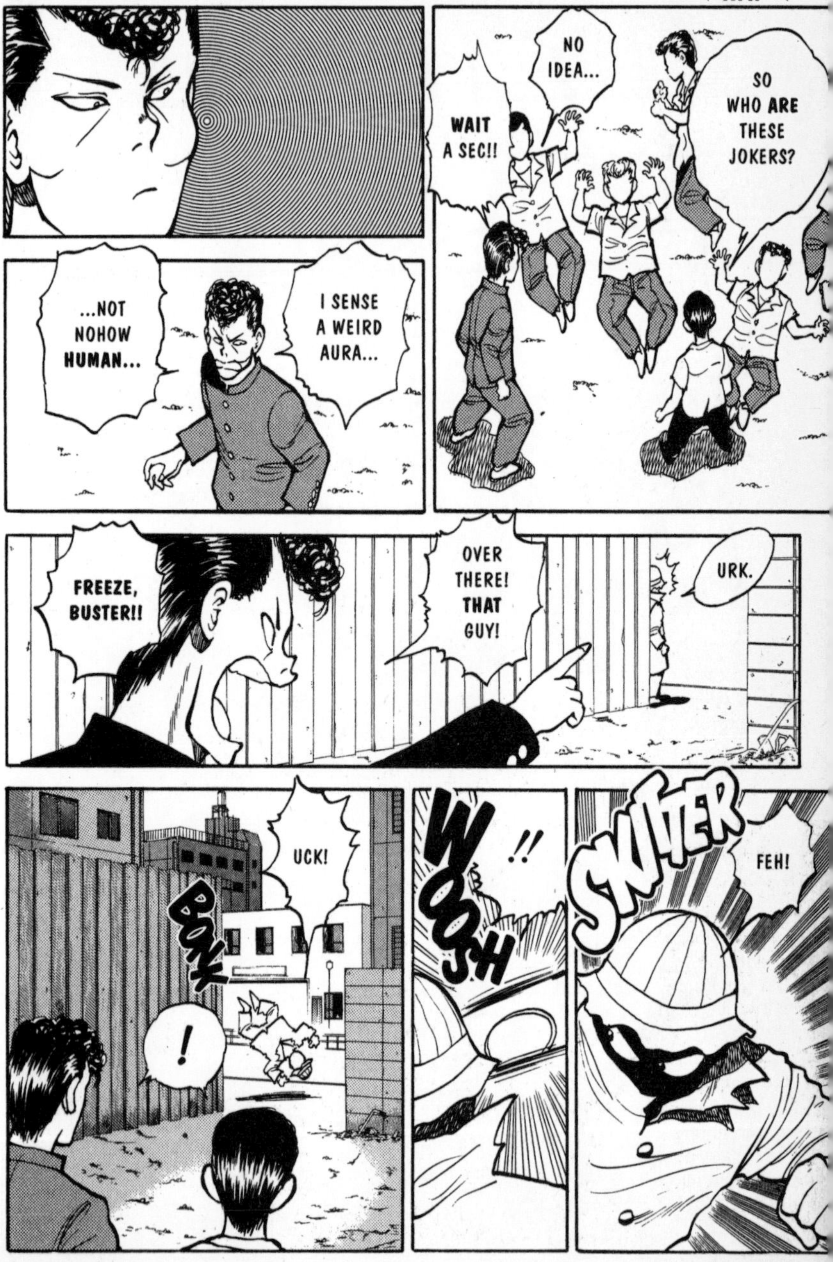

SO WHO ARE THESE JOKERS?
NO IDEA...
WAIT A SEC!!
I SENSE A WEIRD AURA...
...NOT NOHOW HUMAN...
URK.
OVER THERE! THAT GUY!
FREEZE, BUSTER!!
FEH!
SKITTER
!!
WOOSH
UCK!
BONK
!

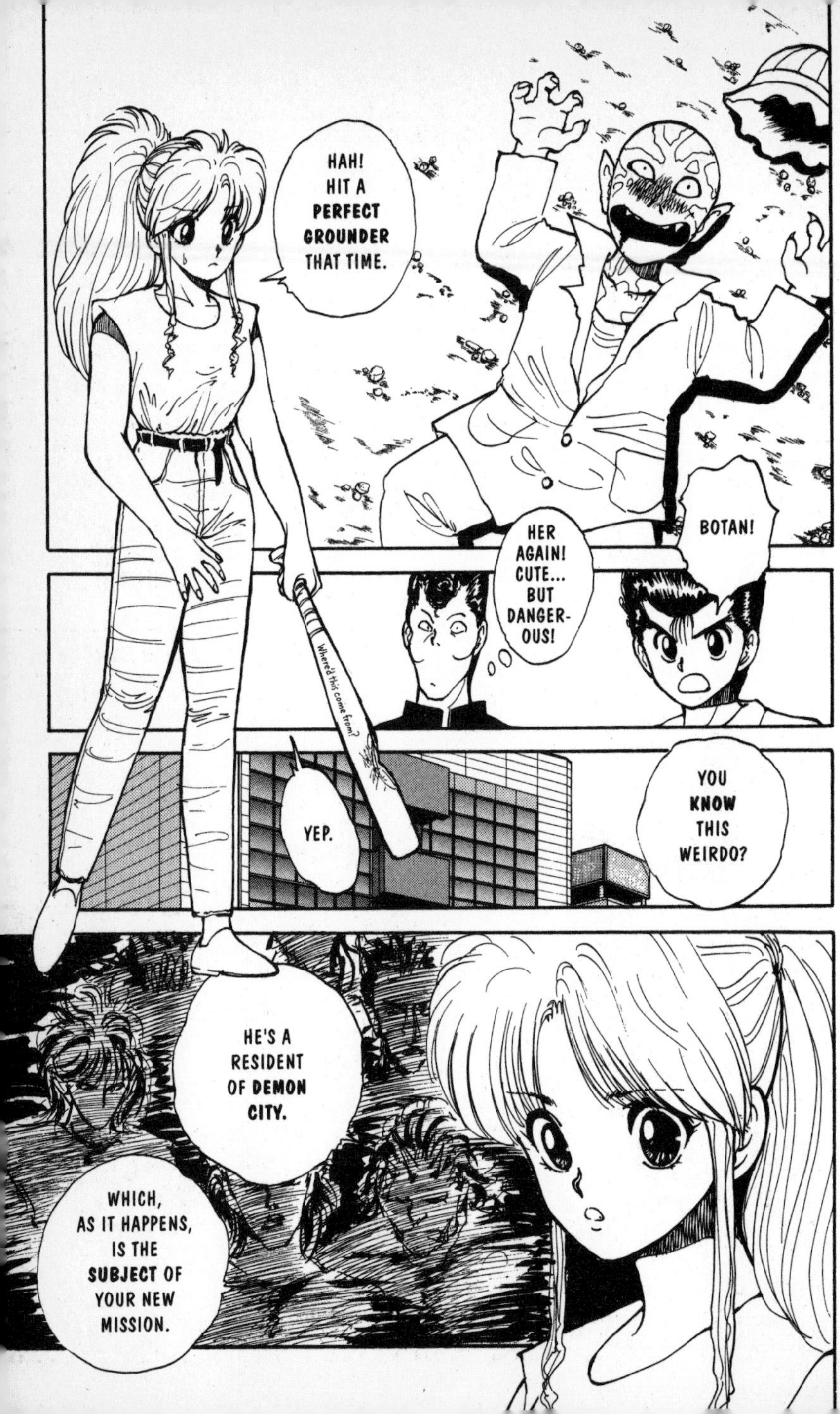
HAH! HIT A PERFECT GROUNDER THAT TIME.
BOTAN!
HER AGAIN! CUTE... BUT DANGER-OUS!
Where'd this come from?
YOU KNOW THIS WEIRDO?
YEP.
HE'S A RESIDENT OF DEMON CITY.
WHICH, AS IT HAPPENS, IS THE SUBJECT OF YOUR NEW MISSION.

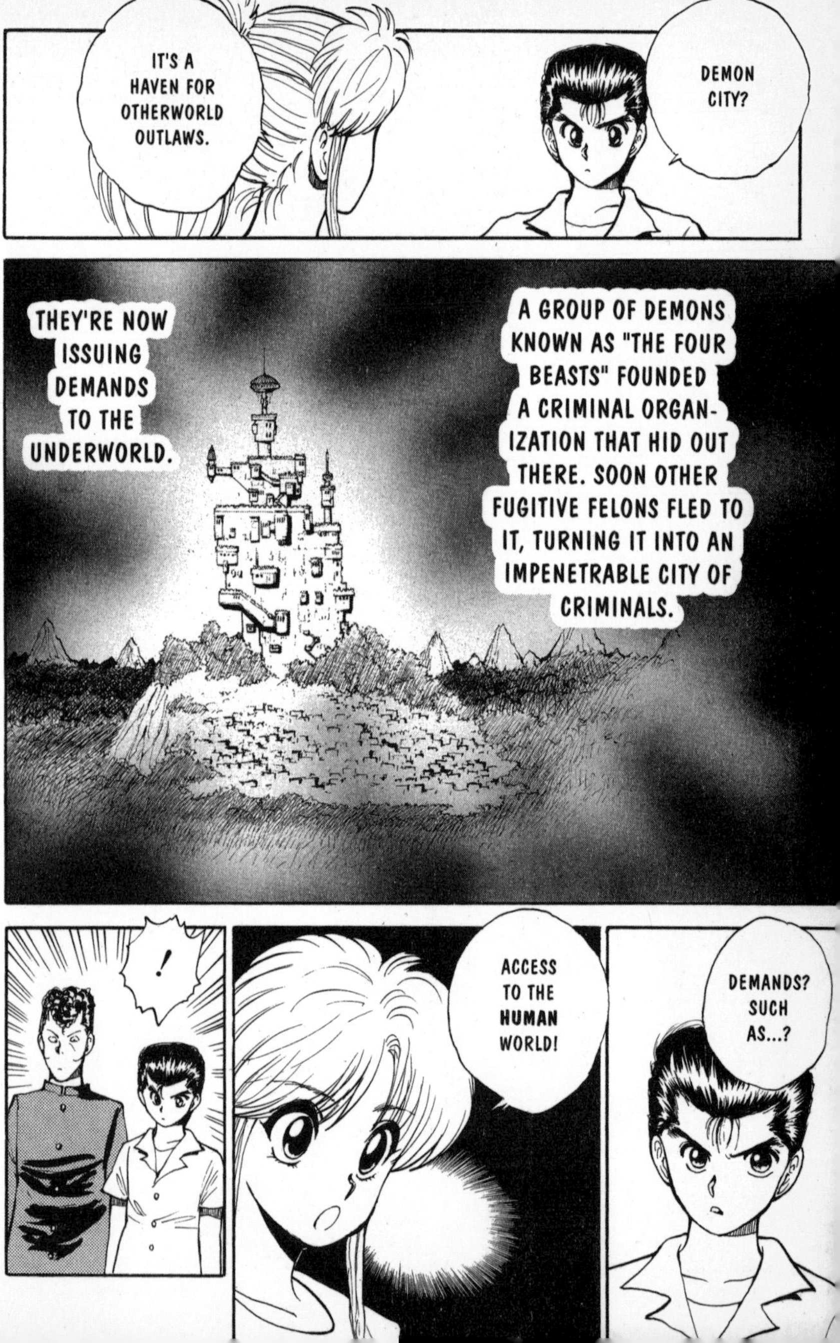
DEMON CITY?
IT'S A HAVEN FOR OTHERWORLD OUTLAWS.
A GROUP OF DEMONS KNOWN AS "THE FOUR BEASTS" FOUNDED A CRIMINAL ORGAN-IZATION THAT HID OUT THERE. SOON OTHER FUGITIVE FELONS FLED TO IT, TURNING IT INTO AN IMPENETRABLE CITY OF CRIMINALS.
THEY'RE NOW ISSUING DEMANDS TO THE UNDERWORLD.
DEMANDS? SUCH AS...?
ACCESS TO THE **HUMAN** WORLD!
!

READ THIS WAY

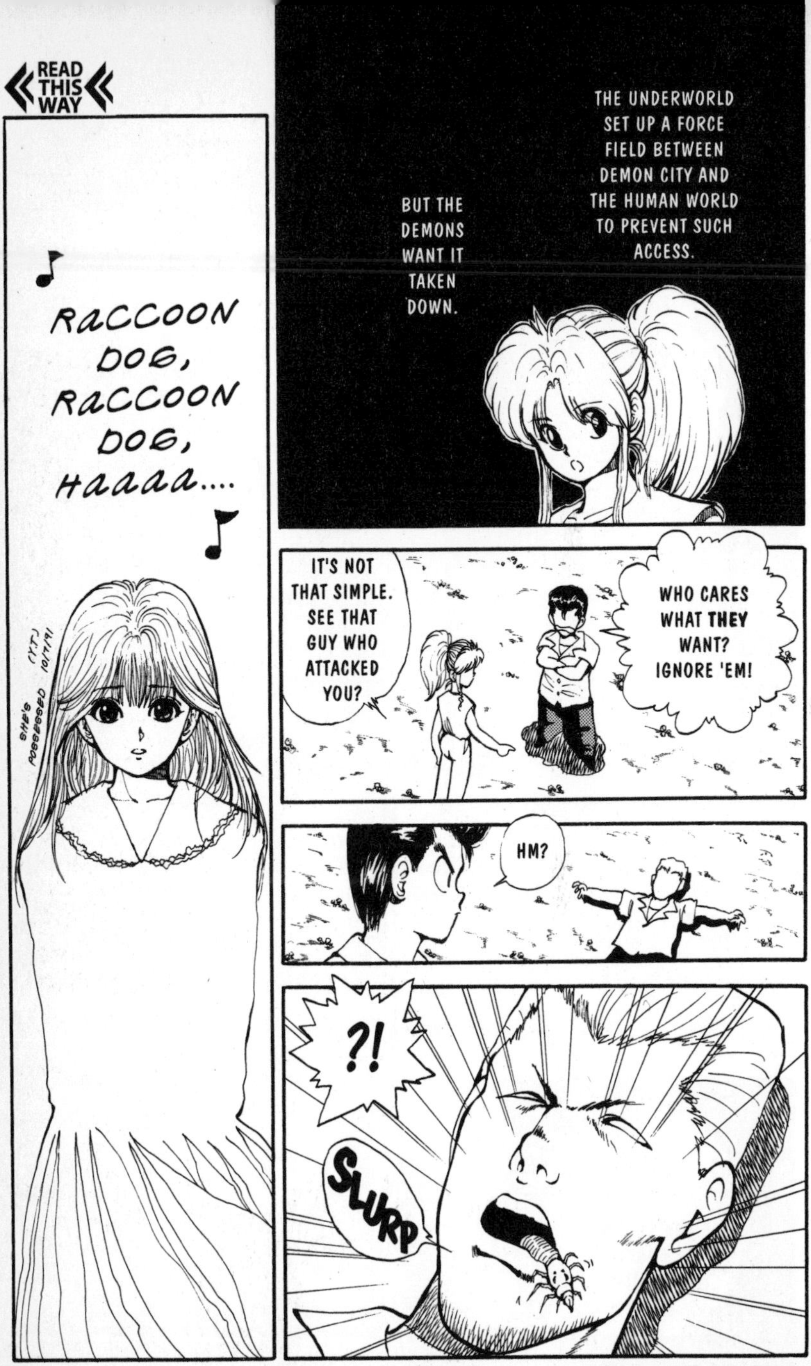
THE UNDERWORLD SET UP A FORCE FIELD BETWEEN DEMON CITY AND THE HUMAN WORLD TO PREVENT SUCH ACCESS.
BUT THE DEMONS WANT IT TAKEN DOWN.
WHO CARES WHAT **THEY** WANT? IGNORE 'EM!
IT'S NOT THAT SIMPLE. SEE THAT GUY WHO ATTACKED YOU?
HM?
?!
SLURP
RACCOON DOG, RACCOON DOG, HAAAA....
(Y.T.) 10/7/91
SHE'S POSSESSED

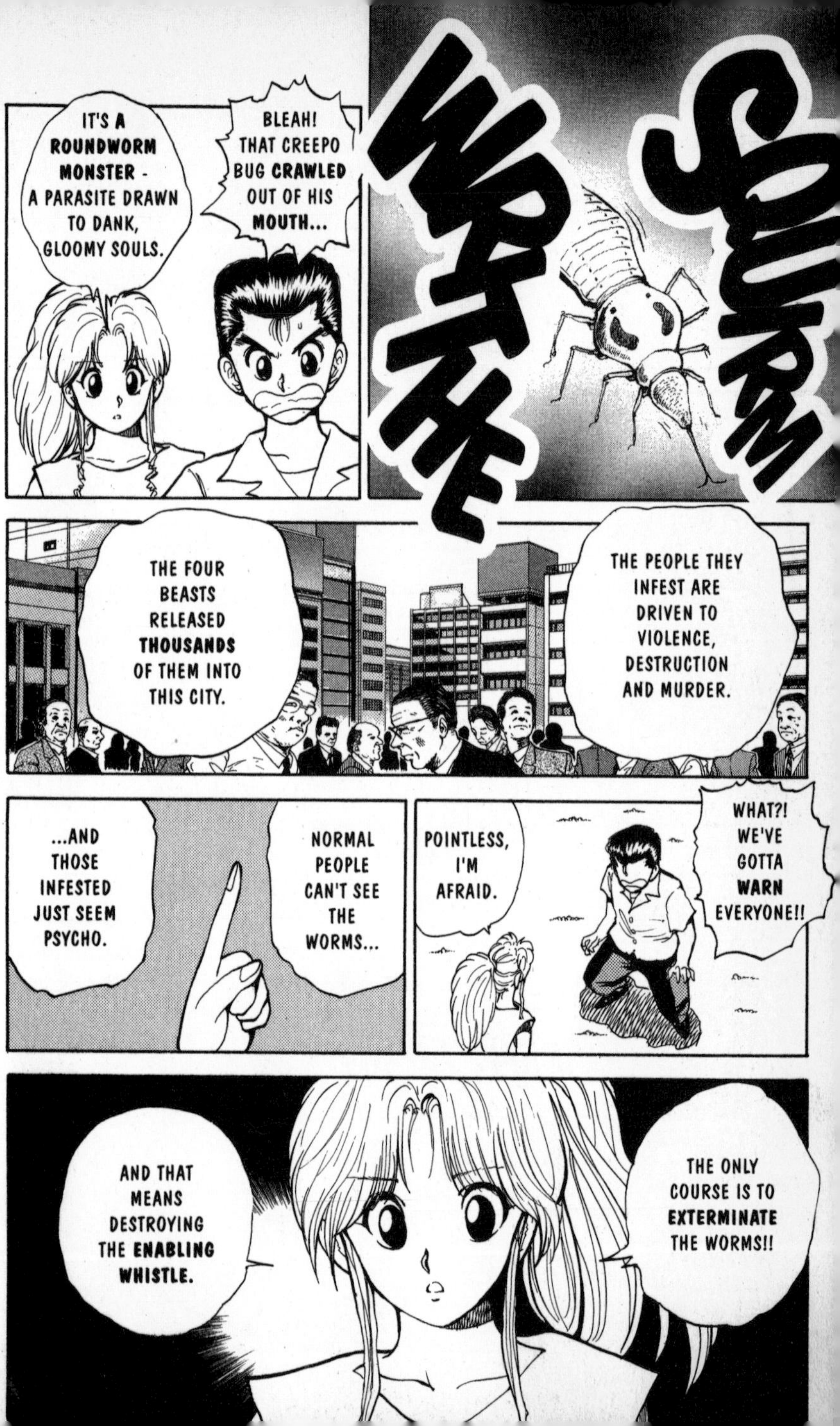
SQUIRM
WRITHE
BLEAH! THAT CREEPO BUG CRAWLED OUT OF HIS MOUTH...
IT'S A ROUNDWORM MONSTER - A PARASITE DRAWN TO DANK, GLOOMY SOULS.
THE PEOPLE THEY INFEST ARE DRIVEN TO VIOLENCE, DESTRUCTION AND MURDER.
THE FOUR BEASTS RELEASED THOUSANDS OF THEM INTO THIS CITY.
WHAT?! WE'VE GOTTA WARN EVERYONE!!
POINTLESS, I'M AFRAID.
NORMAL PEOPLE CAN'T SEE THE WORMS...
...AND THOSE INFESTED JUST SEEM PSYCHO.
THE ONLY COURSE IS TO EXTERMINATE THE WORMS!!
AND THAT MEANS DESTROYING THE ENABLING WHISTLE.

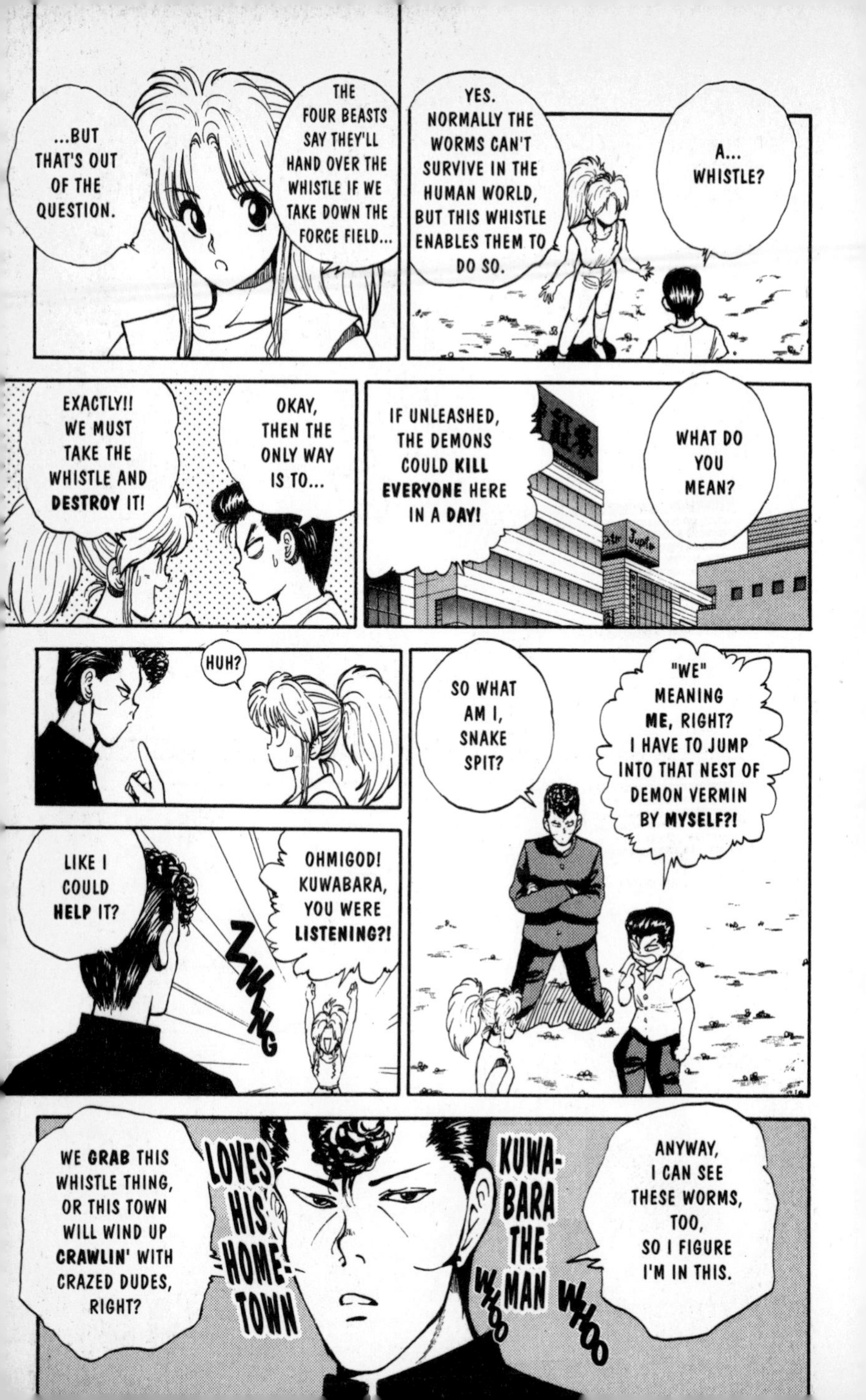
A... WHISTLE?
YES. NORMALLY THE WORMS CAN'T SURVIVE IN THE HUMAN WORLD, BUT THIS WHISTLE ENABLES THEM TO DO SO.
THE FOUR BEASTS SAY THEY'LL HAND OVER THE WHISTLE IF WE TAKE DOWN THE FORCE FIELD...
...BUT THAT'S OUT OF THE QUESTION.
WHAT DO YOU MEAN?
IF UNLEASHED, THE DEMONS COULD **KILL EVERYONE** HERE IN A **DAY!**
OKAY, THEN THE ONLY WAY IS TO...
EXACTLY!! WE MUST TAKE THE WHISTLE AND **DESTROY** IT!
"WE" MEANING **ME,** RIGHT? I HAVE TO JUMP INTO THAT NEST OF DEMON VERMIN BY **MYSELF?!**
SO WHAT AM I, SNAKE SPIT?
HUH?
OHMIGOD! KUWABARA, YOU WERE **LISTENING?!**
ZWANG
LIKE I COULD **HELP** IT?
ANYWAY, I CAN SEE THESE WORMS, TOO, SO I FIGURE I'M IN THIS.
WHOO
KUWA-BARA THE MAN
WHOO
LOVES HIS HOME-TOWN
WE **GRAB** THIS WHISTLE THING, OR THIS TOWN WILL WIND UP **CRAWLIN'** WITH CRAZED DUDES, RIGHT?

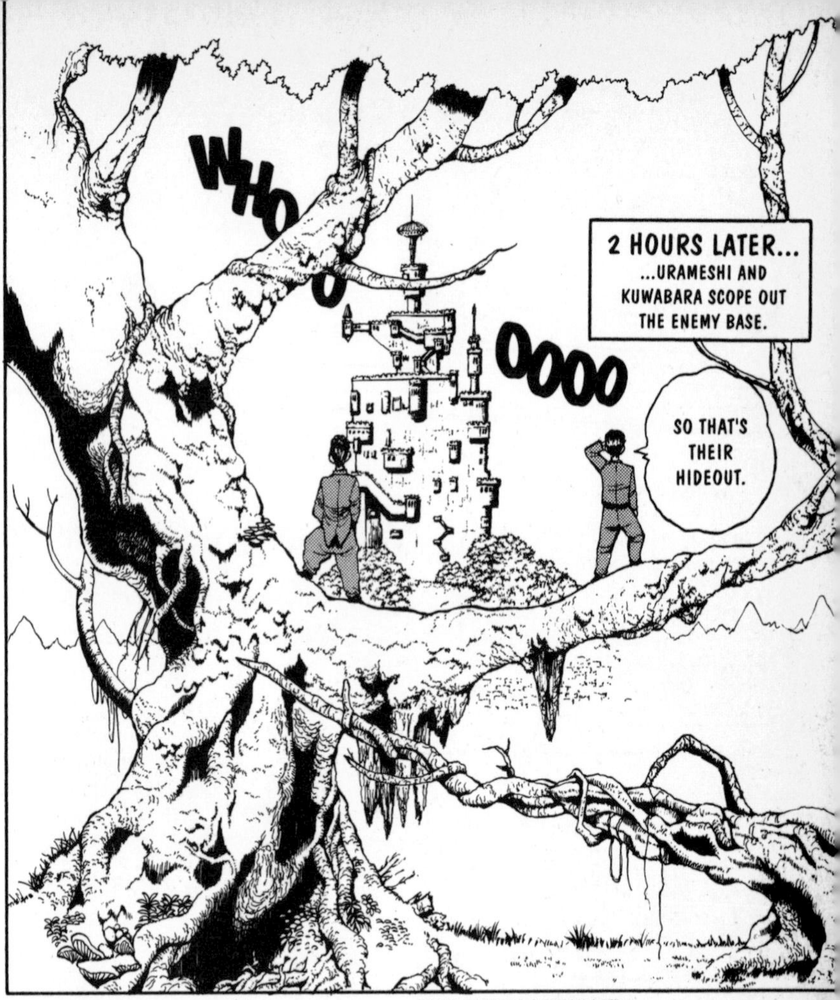
2 HOURS LATER...
...URAMESHI AND KUWABARA SCOPE OUT THE ENEMY BASE.
WHOOOOOO
SO THAT'S THEIR HIDEOUT.

HOW'S THAT FOR A QUICK CUT?

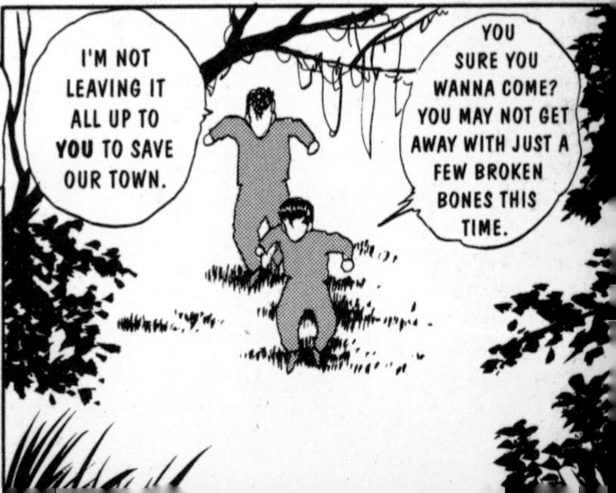
YOU SURE YOU WANNA COME? YOU MAY NOT GET AWAY WITH JUST A FEW BROKEN BONES THIS TIME.
I'M NOT LEAVING IT ALL UP TO **YOU** TO SAVE OUR TOWN.

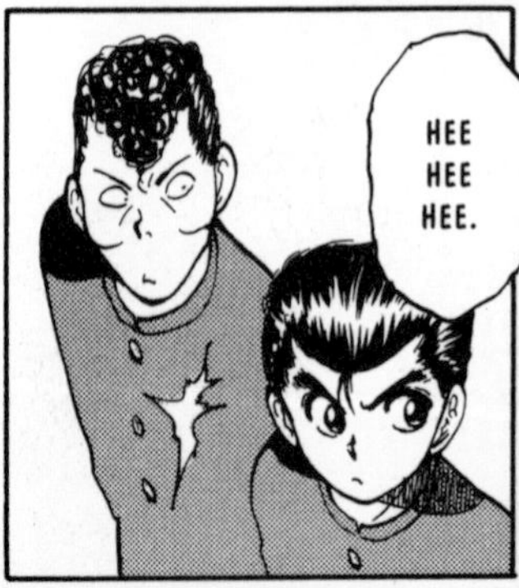
HEE HEE HEE.

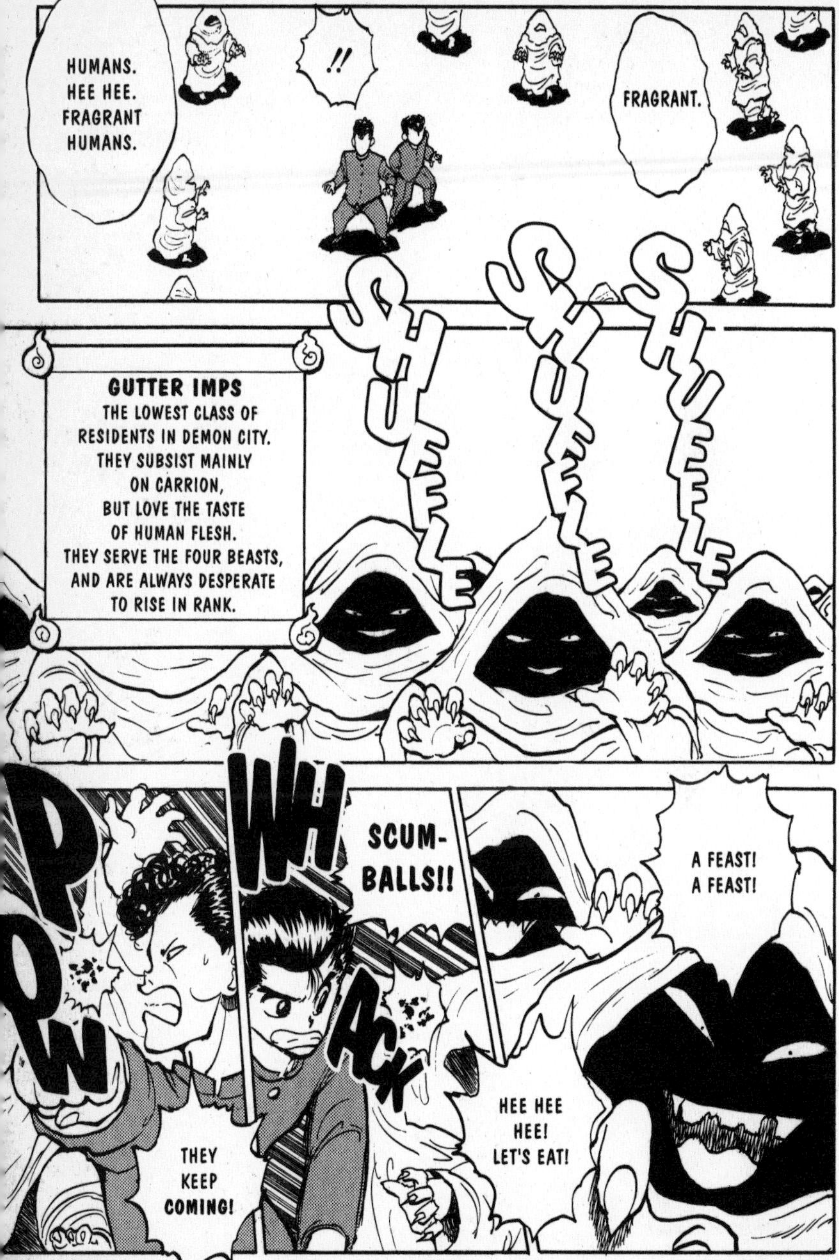
FRAGRANT.
!!
HUMANS. HEE HEE. FRAGRANT HUMANS.
SHUFFLE
SHUFFLE
SHUFFLE
GUTTER IMPS
THE LOWEST CLASS OF RESIDENTS IN DEMON CITY. THEY SUBSIST MAINLY ON CARRION, BUT LOVE THE TASTE OF HUMAN FLESH. THEY SERVE THE FOUR BEASTS, AND ARE ALWAYS DESPERATE TO RISE IN RANK.
A FEAST! A FEAST!
HEE HEE HEE! LET'S EAT!
SCUM-BALLS!!
WHACK
POW
THEY KEEP COMING!

READ THIS WAY

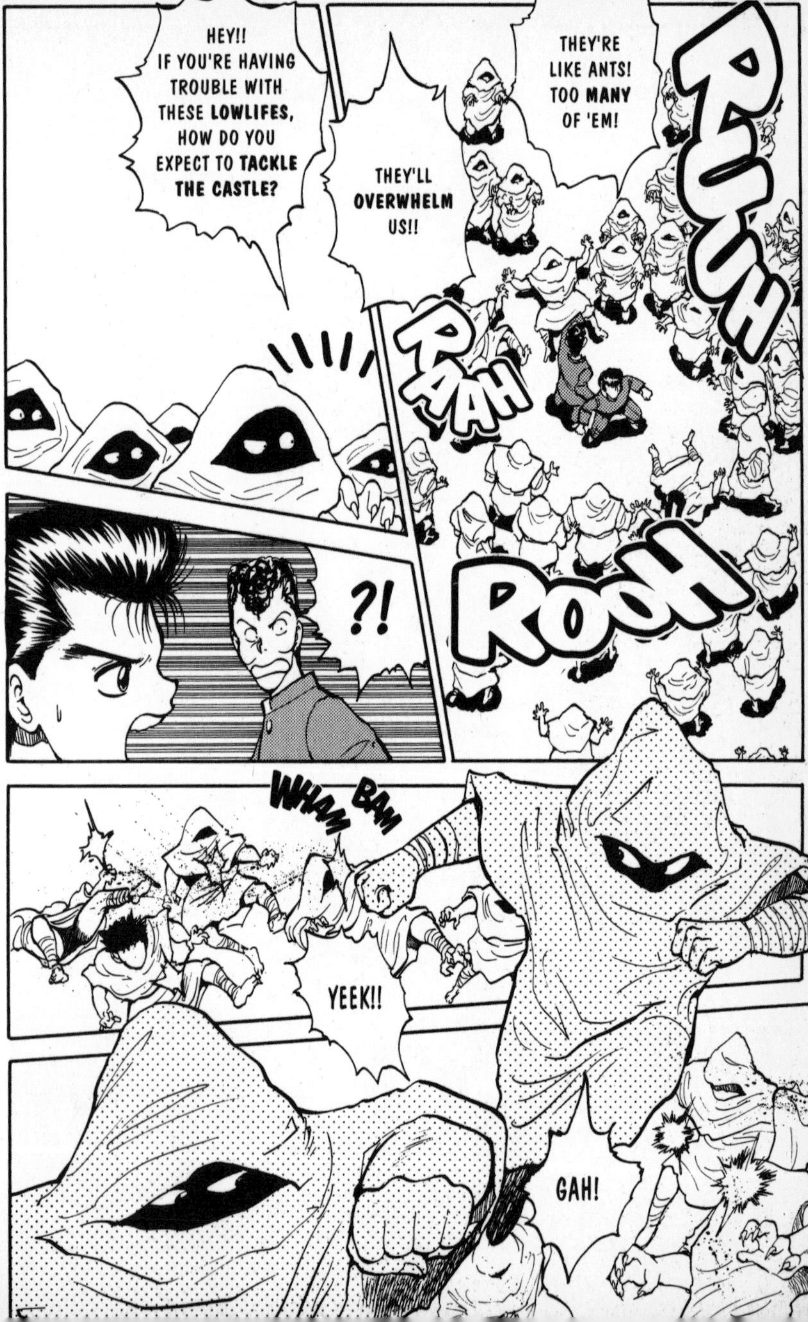
THEY'RE LIKE ANTS! TOO MANY OF 'EM!
RUUSH
THEY'LL OVERWHELM US!!
RAAH
ROOH
HEY!! IF YOU'RE HAVING TROUBLE WITH THESE LOWLIFES, HOW DO YOU EXPECT TO TACKLE THE CASTLE?
?!
WHAM BAM
YEEK!!
GAH!

READ THIS WAY

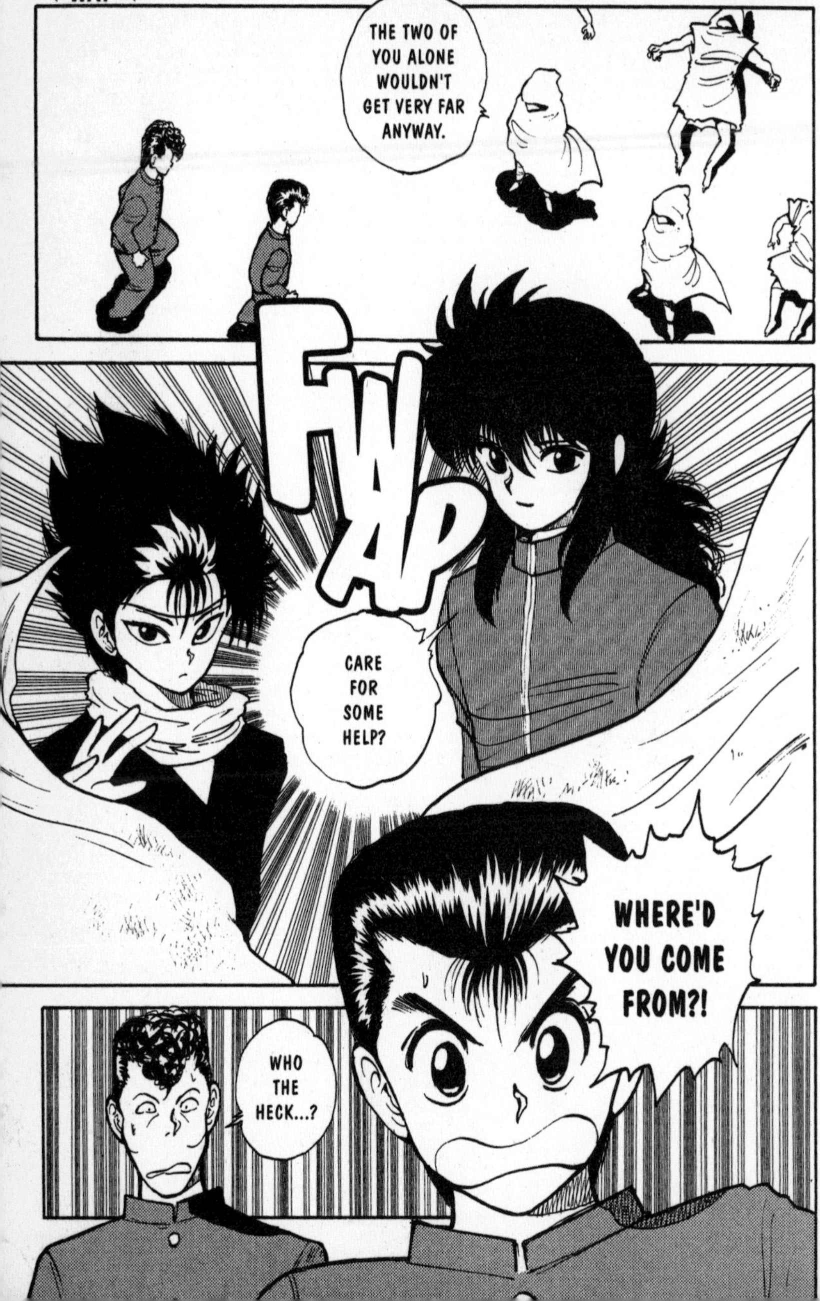
THE TWO OF YOU ALONE WOULDN'T GET VERY FAR ANYWAY.
FWAP
CARE FOR SOME HELP?
WHERE'D YOU COME FROM?!
WHO THE HECK...?

My Rambling Diary, Part 4

Some day in September, '91

1) I saw a kid in a department store who clearly looked like he was lacking in gray matter. (As a fellow man, I could sort of understand - on second thought, I would probably do the same.)

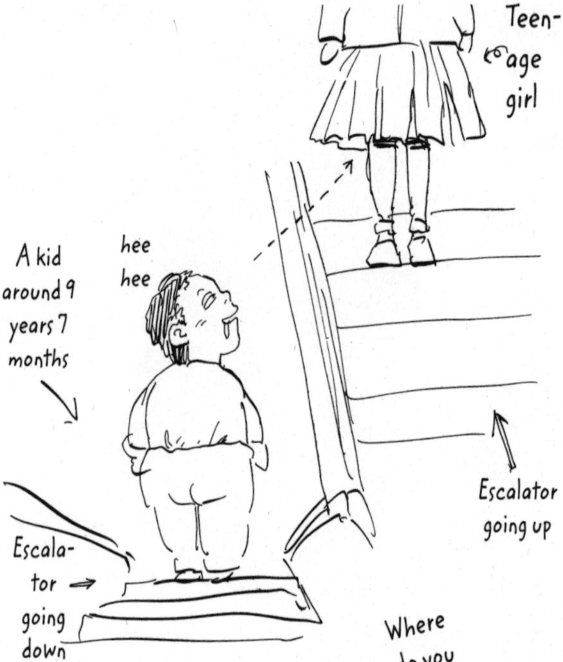
Teen-age girl
hee hee
A kid around 9 years 7 months
Escalator going up
Escala-tor going down

2) Then the gorgeous woman ahead of him turned out to be his mother!

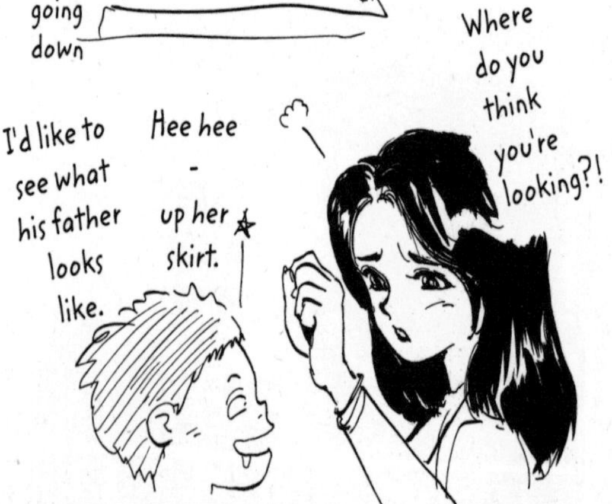
Where do you think you're looking?!
Hee hee - up her skirt.
I'd like to see what his father looks like.

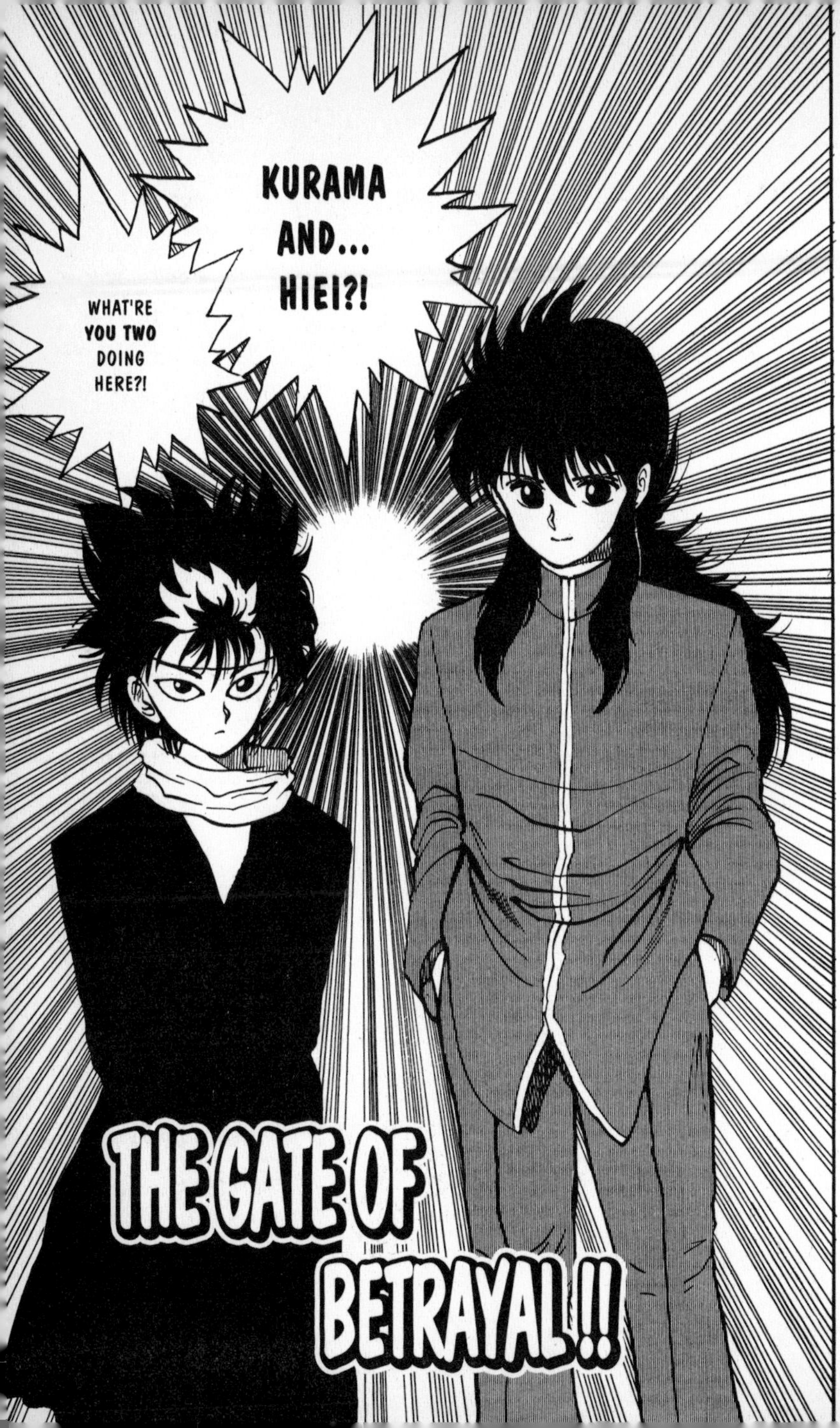
KURAMA AND... HIEI?!
WHAT'RE YOU TWO DOING HERE?!
THE GATE OF BETRAYAL!!

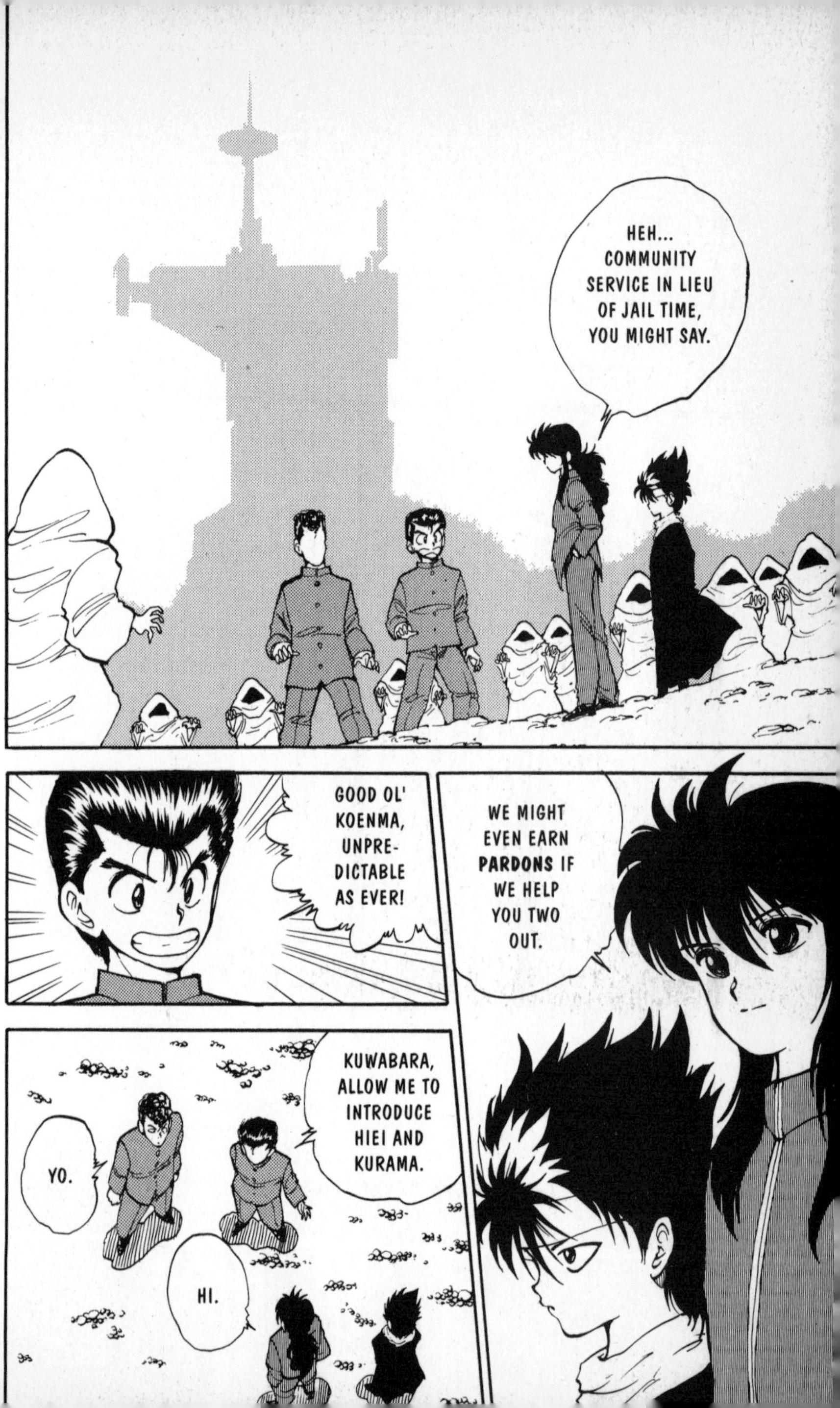
HEH... COMMUNITY SERVICE IN LIEU OF JAIL TIME, YOU MIGHT SAY.
WE MIGHT EVEN EARN **PARDONS** IF WE HELP YOU TWO OUT.
GOOD OL' KOENMA, UNPRE-DICTABLE AS EVER!
KUWABARA, ALLOW ME TO INTRODUCE HIEI AND KURAMA.
YO.
HI.

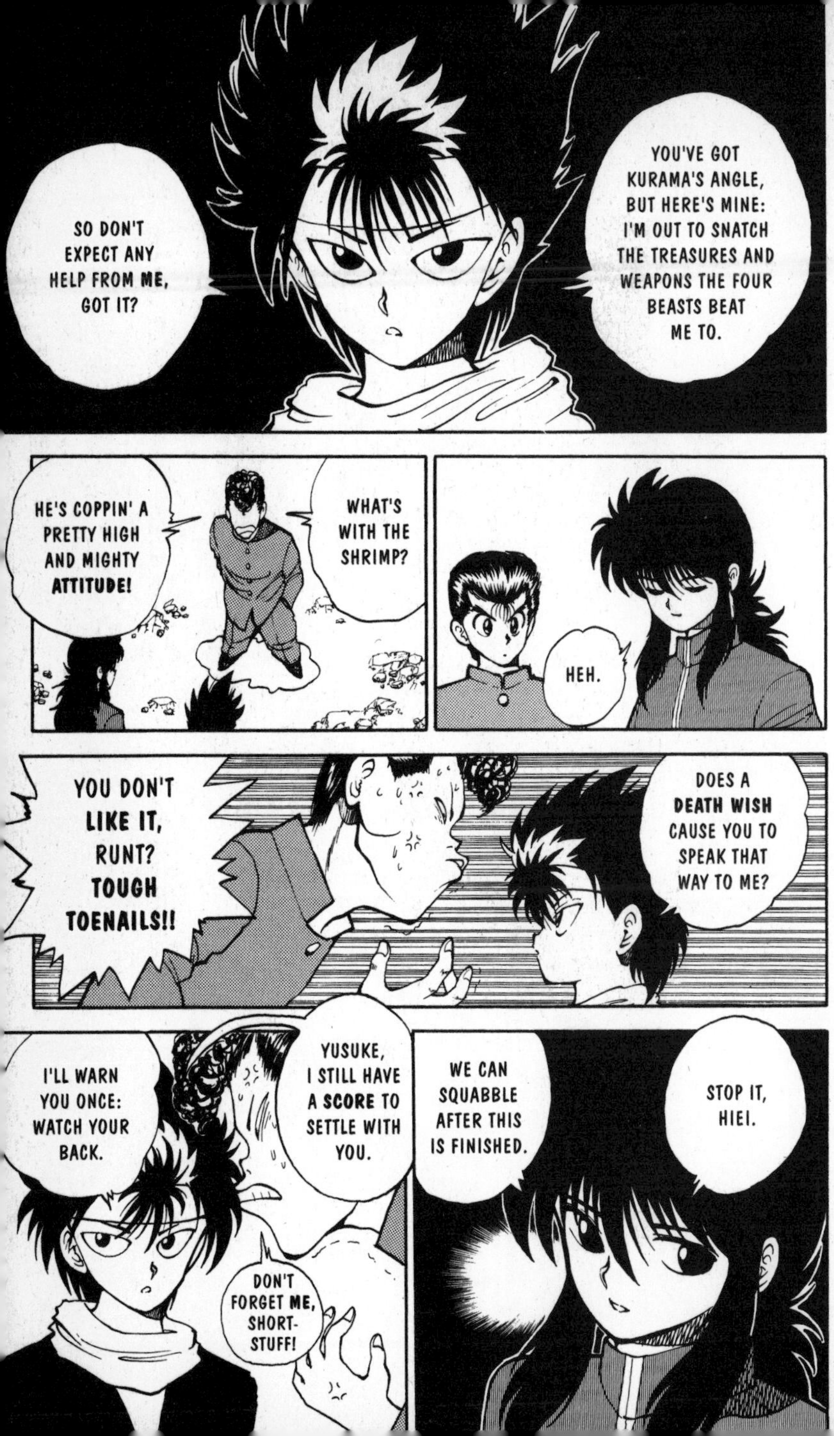
YOU'VE GOT KURAMA'S ANGLE, BUT HERE'S MINE: I'M OUT TO SNATCH THE TREASURES AND WEAPONS THE FOUR BEASTS BEAT ME TO.
SO DON'T EXPECT ANY HELP FROM ME, GOT IT?
HEH.
WHAT'S WITH THE SHRIMP?
HE'S COPPIN' A PRETTY HIGH AND MIGHTY ATTITUDE!
DOES A DEATH WISH CAUSE YOU TO SPEAK THAT WAY TO ME?
YOU DON'T LIKE IT, RUNT? TOUGH TOENAILS!!
STOP IT, HIEI.
WE CAN SQUABBLE AFTER THIS IS FINISHED.
YUSUKE, I STILL HAVE A SCORE TO SETTLE WITH YOU.
I'LL WARN YOU ONCE: WATCH YOUR BACK.
DON'T FORGET ME, SHORT-STUFF!

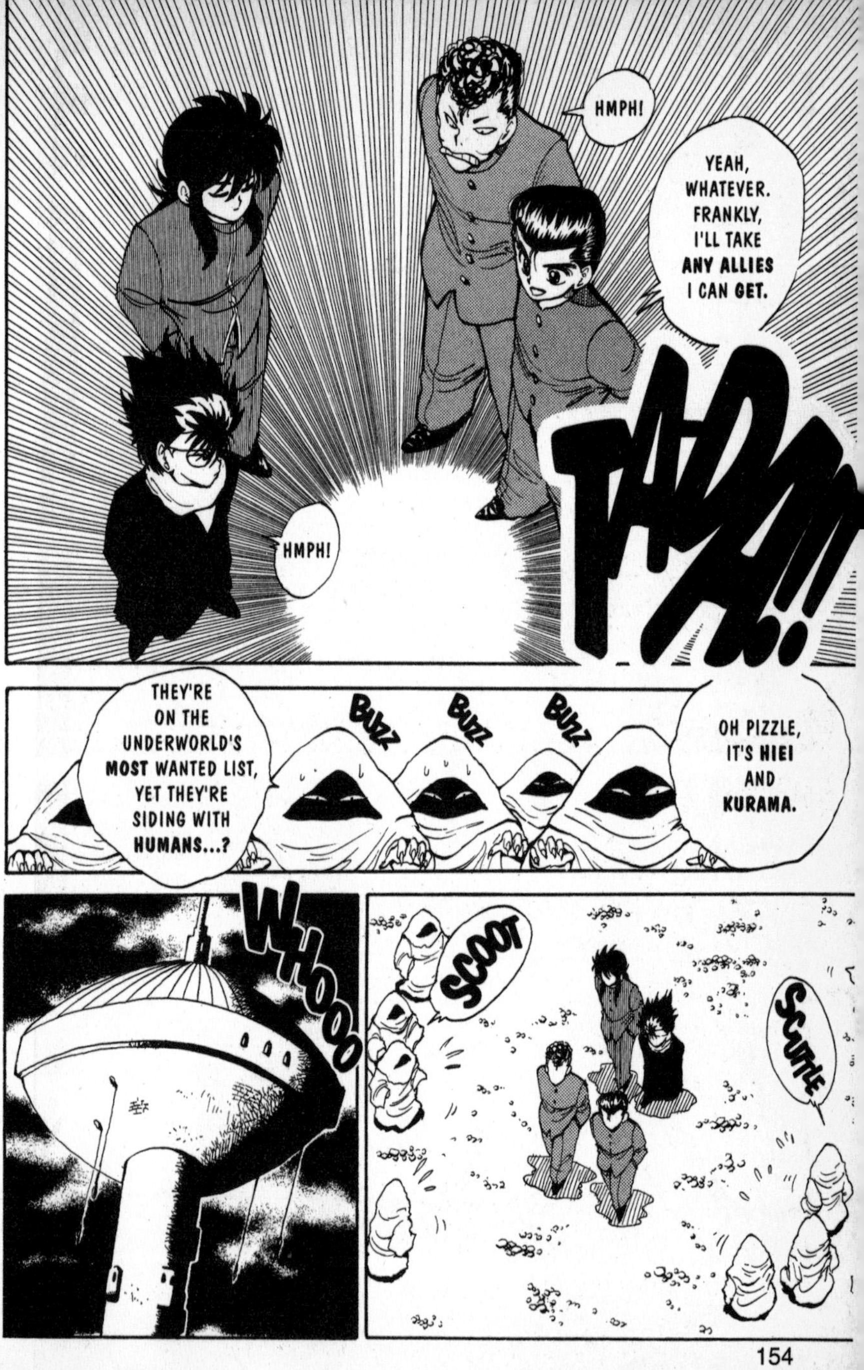
HMPH!
YEAH, WHATEVER. FRANKLY, I'LL TAKE ANY ALLIES I CAN GET.
TADA!!
HMPH!
OH PIZZLE, IT'S HIEI AND KURAMA.
BUZZ
BUZZ
BUZZ
THEY'RE ON THE UNDERWORLD'S MOST WANTED LIST, YET THEY'RE SIDING WITH HUMANS...?
SCUTTLE
SCOOT
WHOOOO

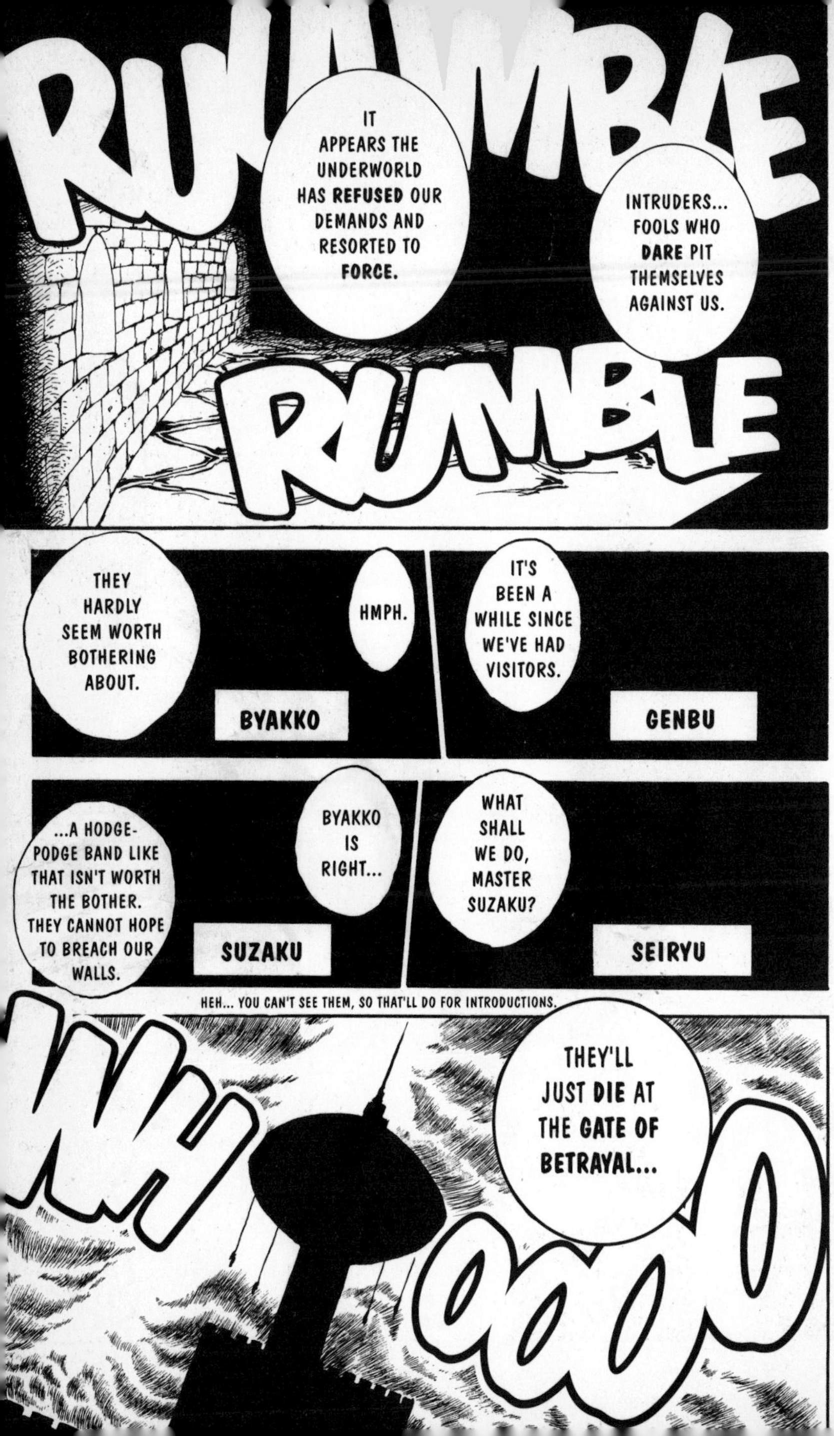
RUMMMBLE
IT APPEARS THE UNDERWORLD HAS REFUSED OUR DEMANDS AND RESORTED TO FORCE.
INTRUDERS... FOOLS WHO DARE PIT THEMSELVES AGAINST US.
RUMBLE
IT'S BEEN A WHILE SINCE WE'VE HAD VISITORS.
GENBU
HMPH.
THEY HARDLY SEEM WORTH BOTHERING ABOUT.
BYAKKO
WHAT SHALL WE DO, MASTER SUZAKU?
SEIRYU
BYAKKO IS RIGHT...
...A HODGE-PODGE BAND LIKE THAT ISN'T WORTH THE BOTHER. THEY CANNOT HOPE TO BREACH OUR WALLS.
SUZAKU
HEH... YOU CAN'T SEE THEM, SO THAT'LL DO FOR INTRODUCTIONS.
THEY'LL JUST DIE AT THE GATE OF BETRAYAL...
WHOOOOO

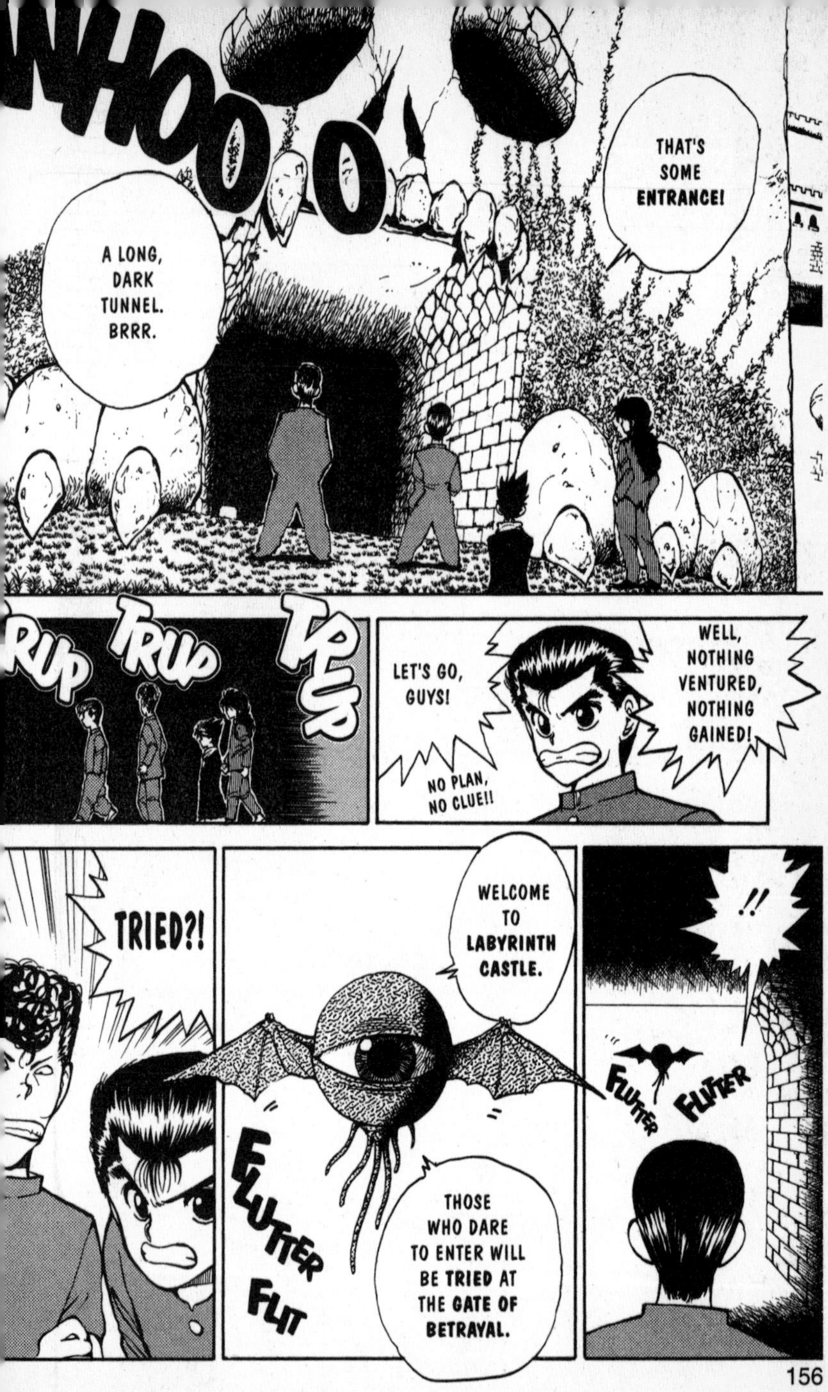
THAT'S SOME ENTRANCE!
WHOOOO
A LONG, DARK TUNNEL. BRRR.
WELL, NOTHING VENTURED, NOTHING GAINED!
LET'S GO, GUYS!
NO PLAN, NO CLUE!!
TRUP
TRUD
RUP
!!
FLUTTER FLUTTER
WELCOME TO LABYRINTH CASTLE.
FLUTTER FLIT
THOSE WHO DARE TO ENTER WILL BE TRIED AT THE GATE OF BETRAYAL.
TRIED?!

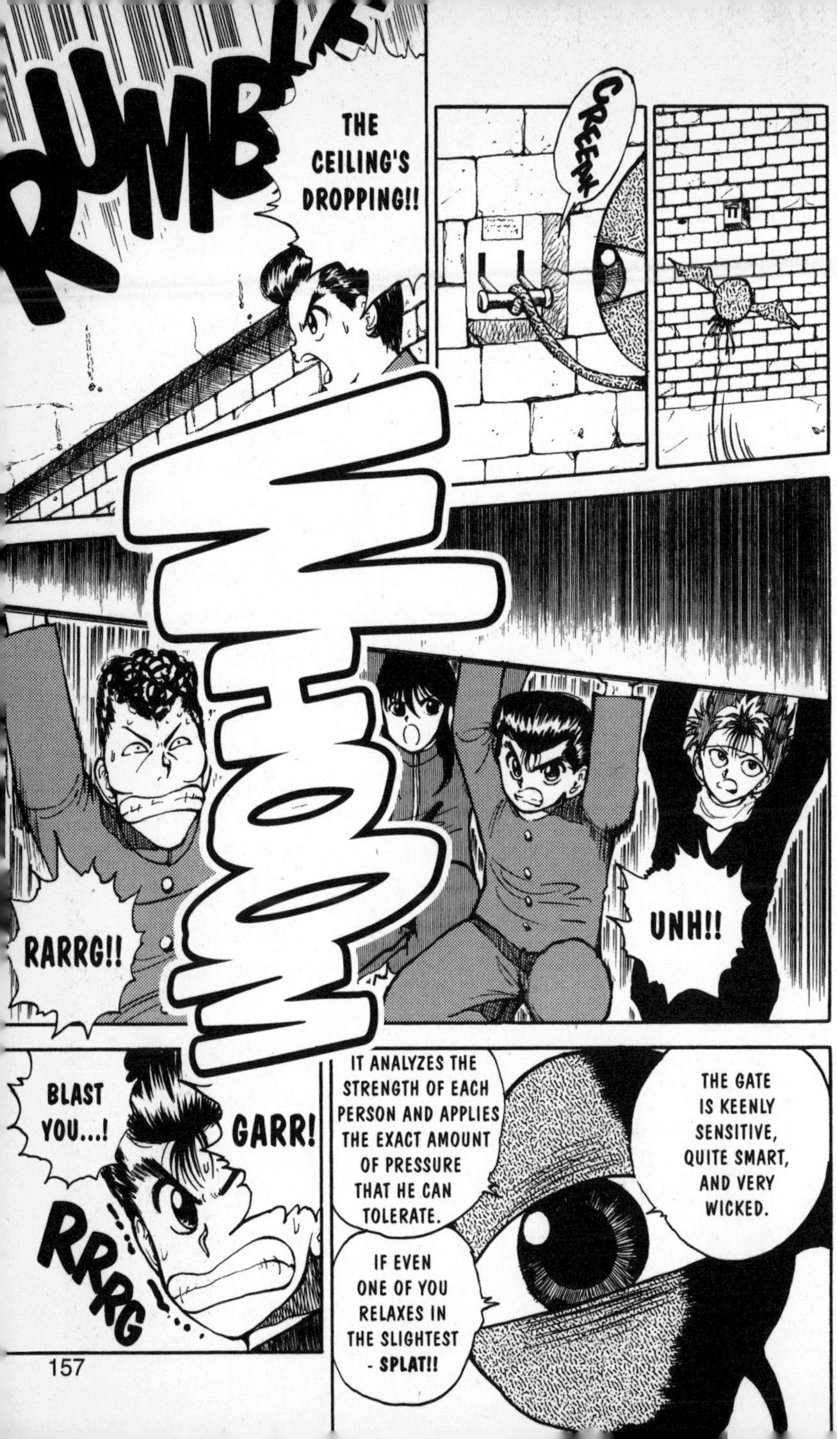
CREEAK
RUMBLE
THE CEILING'S DROPPING!!
WHOOM
UNH!!
RARRG!!
THE GATE IS KEENLY SENSITIVE, QUITE SMART, AND VERY WICKED.
IT ANALYZES THE STRENGTH OF EACH PERSON AND APPLIES THE EXACT AMOUNT OF PRESSURE THAT HE CAN TOLERATE.
IF EVEN ONE OF YOU RELAXES IN THE SLIGHTEST - SPLAT!!
GARR!
BLAST YOU...!
RRRG

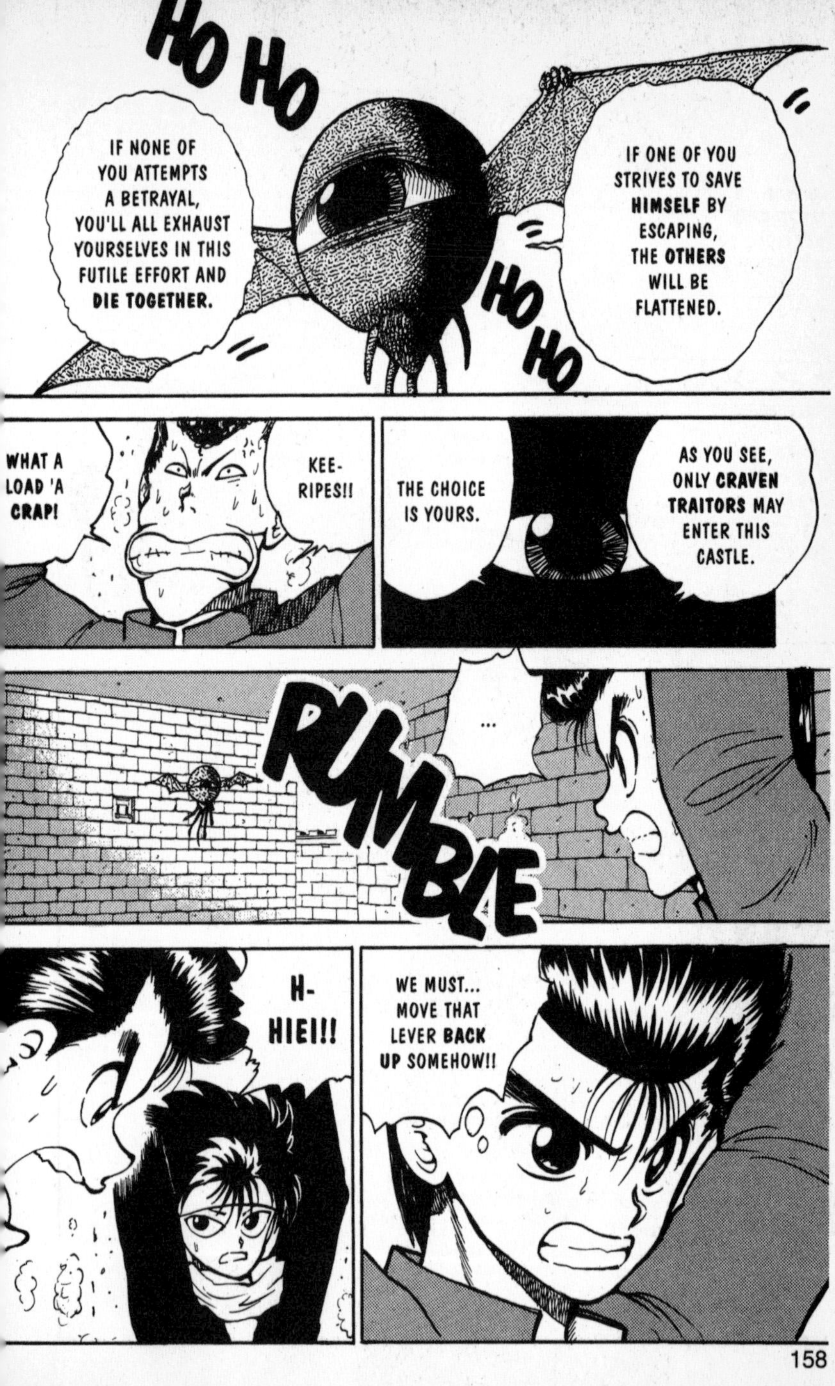
IF ONE OF YOU STRIVES TO SAVE HIMSELF BY ESCAPING, THE OTHERS WILL BE FLATTENED.
HO HO
IF NONE OF YOU ATTEMPTS A BETRAYAL, YOU'LL ALL EXHAUST YOURSELVES IN THIS FUTILE EFFORT AND DIE TOGETHER.
HO HO
AS YOU SEE, ONLY CRAVEN TRAITORS MAY ENTER THIS CASTLE.
THE CHOICE IS YOURS.
KEE-RIPES!!
WHAT A LOAD 'A CRAP!
...
RUMBLE
WE MUST... MOVE THAT LEVER BACK UP SOMEHOW!!
H-HIEI!!

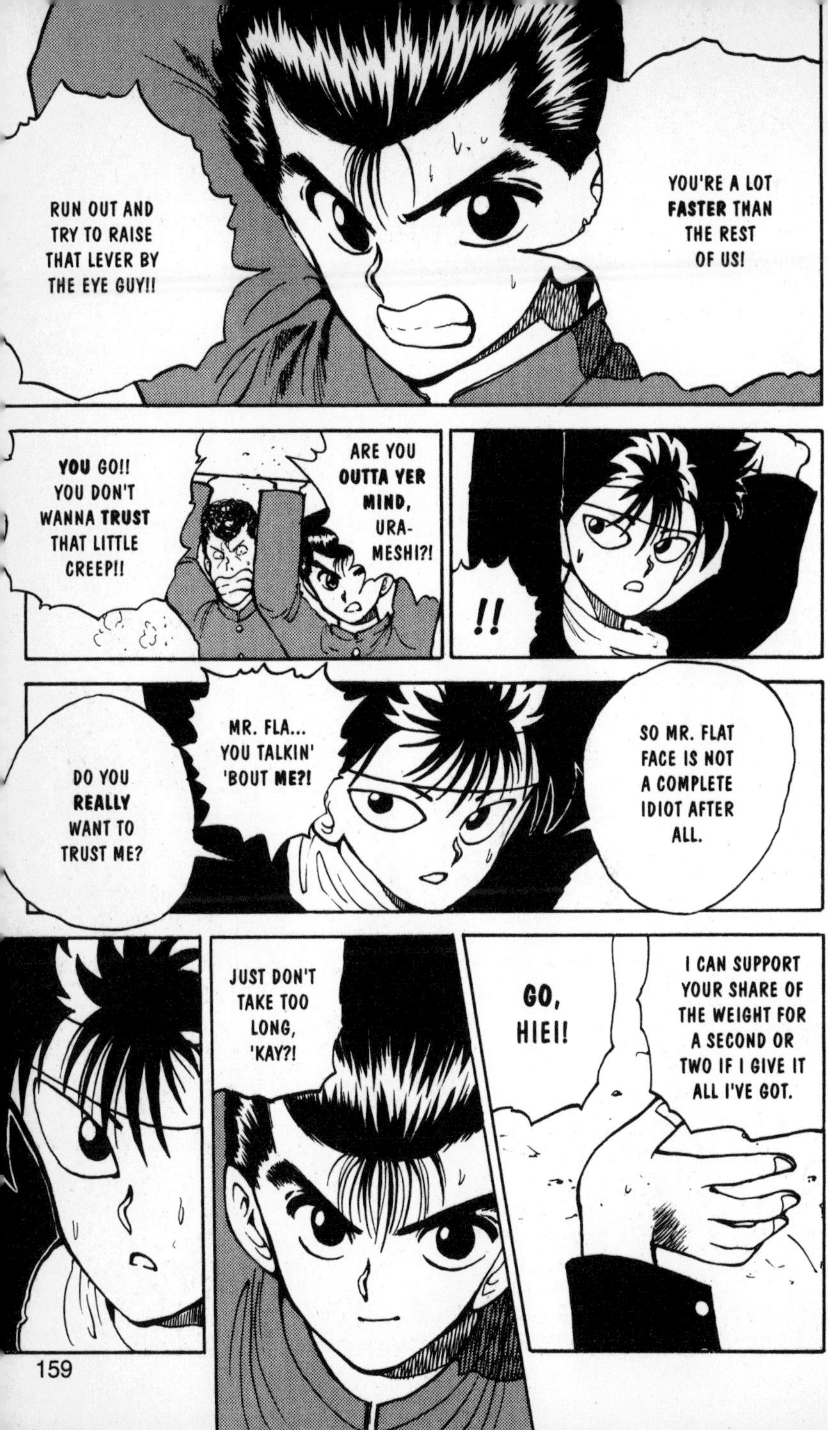
YOU'RE A LOT FASTER THAN THE REST OF US!
RUN OUT AND TRY TO RAISE THAT LEVER BY THE EYE GUY!!
!!
ARE YOU OUTTA YER MIND, URA-MESHI?!
YOU GO!! YOU DON'T WANNA TRUST THAT LITTLE CREEP!!
SO MR. FLAT FACE IS NOT A COMPLETE IDIOT AFTER ALL.
MR. FLA... YOU TALKIN' 'BOUT ME?!
DO YOU REALLY WANT TO TRUST ME?
I CAN SUPPORT YOUR SHARE OF THE WEIGHT FOR A SECOND OR TWO IF I GIVE IT ALL I'VE GOT.
GO, HIEI!
JUST DON'T TAKE TOO LONG, 'KAY?!

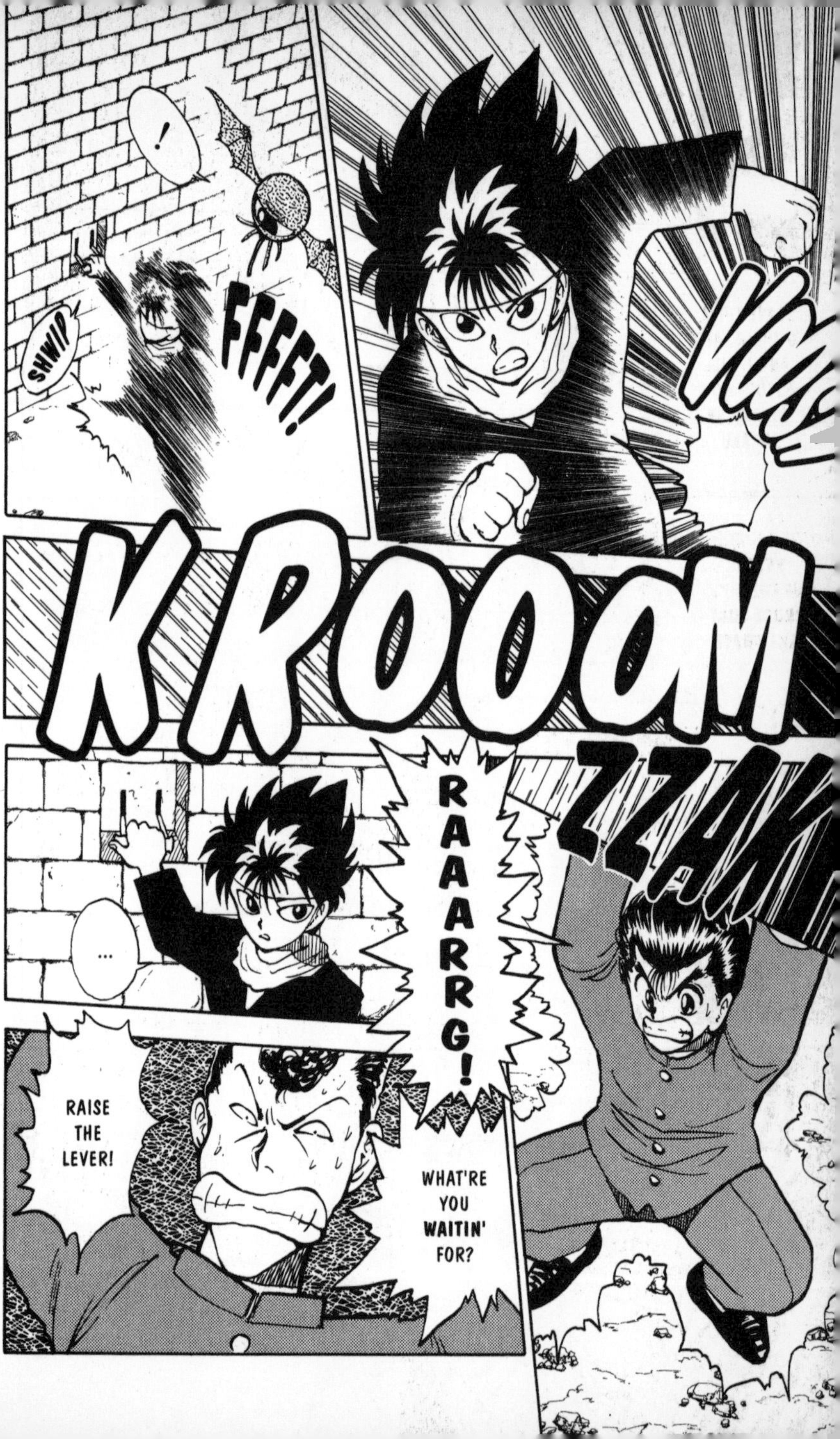
VOOSH!
!
FFFFT!!
SHWIP
KROOOM
ZZAK
RAAAARRG!
...
RAISE THE LEVER!
WHAT'RE YOU WAITIN' FOR?

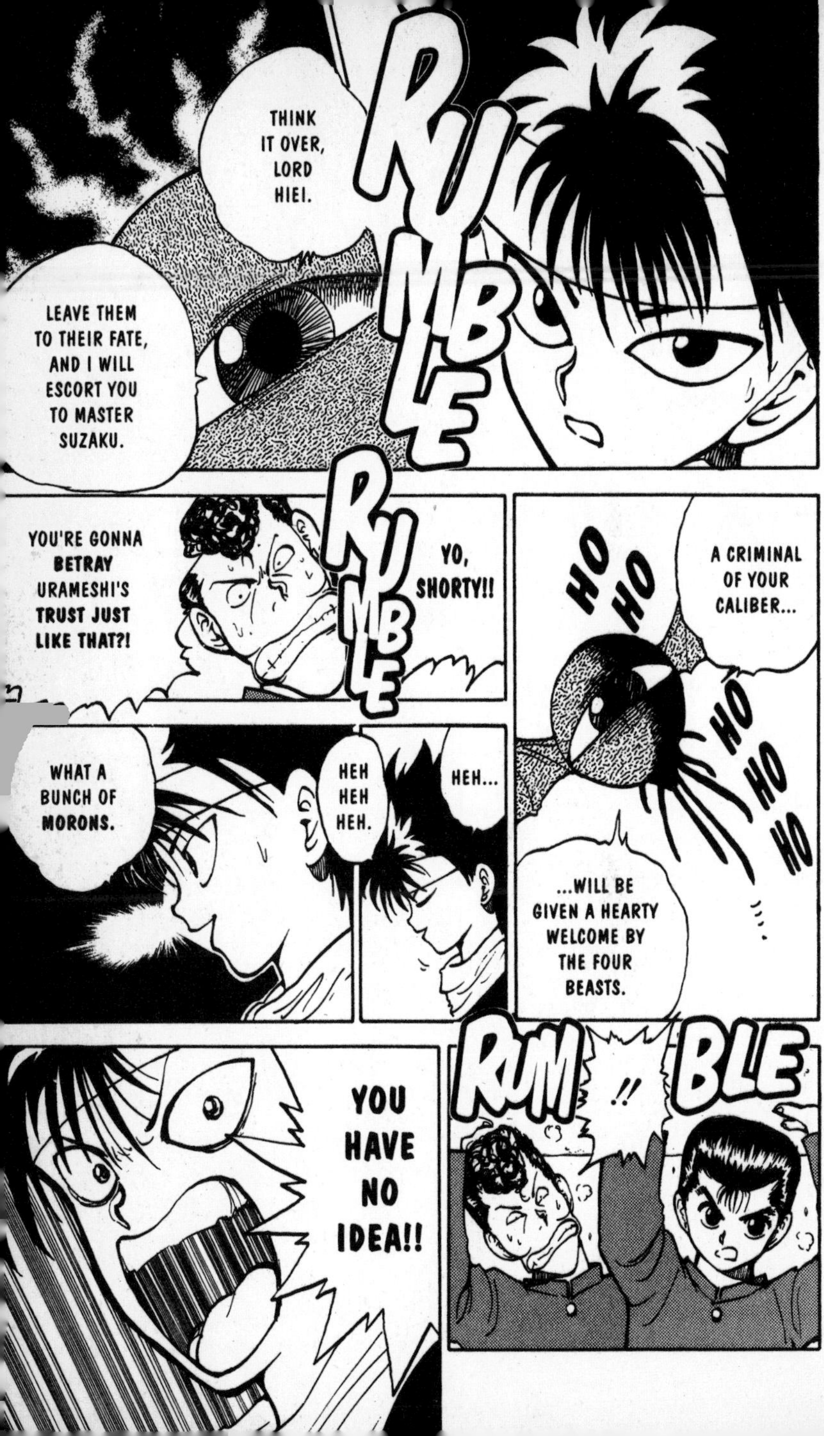
THINK IT OVER, LORD HIEI.
LEAVE THEM TO THEIR FATE, AND I WILL ESCORT YOU TO MASTER SUZAKU.
RUMBLE
RUMBLE
HO HO
A CRIMINAL OF YOUR CALIBER...
HO HO HO
...WILL BE GIVEN A HEARTY WELCOME BY THE FOUR BEASTS.
YO, SHORTY!!
YOU'RE GONNA BETRAY URAMESHI'S TRUST JUST LIKE THAT?!
HEH...
HEH HEH HEH.
WHAT A BUNCH OF MORONS.
RUMBLE
!!
YOU HAVE NO IDEA!!

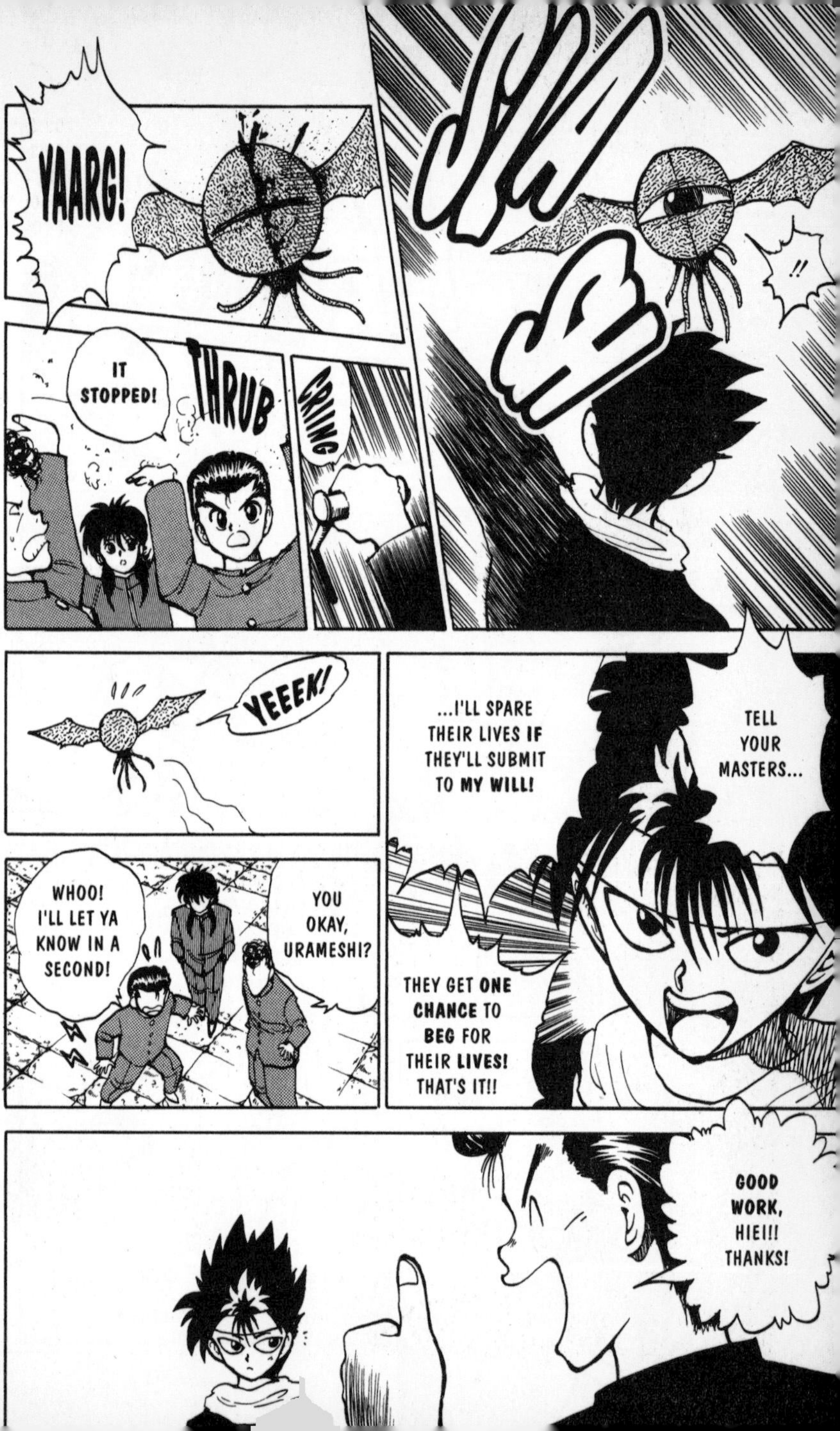
!!
YAARG!
CRING
THRUB
IT STOPPED!
TELL YOUR MASTERS...
...I'LL SPARE THEIR LIVES IF THEY'LL SUBMIT TO MY WILL!
THEY GET ONE CHANCE TO BEG FOR THEIR LIVES! THAT'S IT!!
YEEEK!
YOU OKAY, URAMESHI?
WHOO! I'LL LET YA KNOW IN A SECOND!
GOOD WORK, HIEI!!! THANKS!

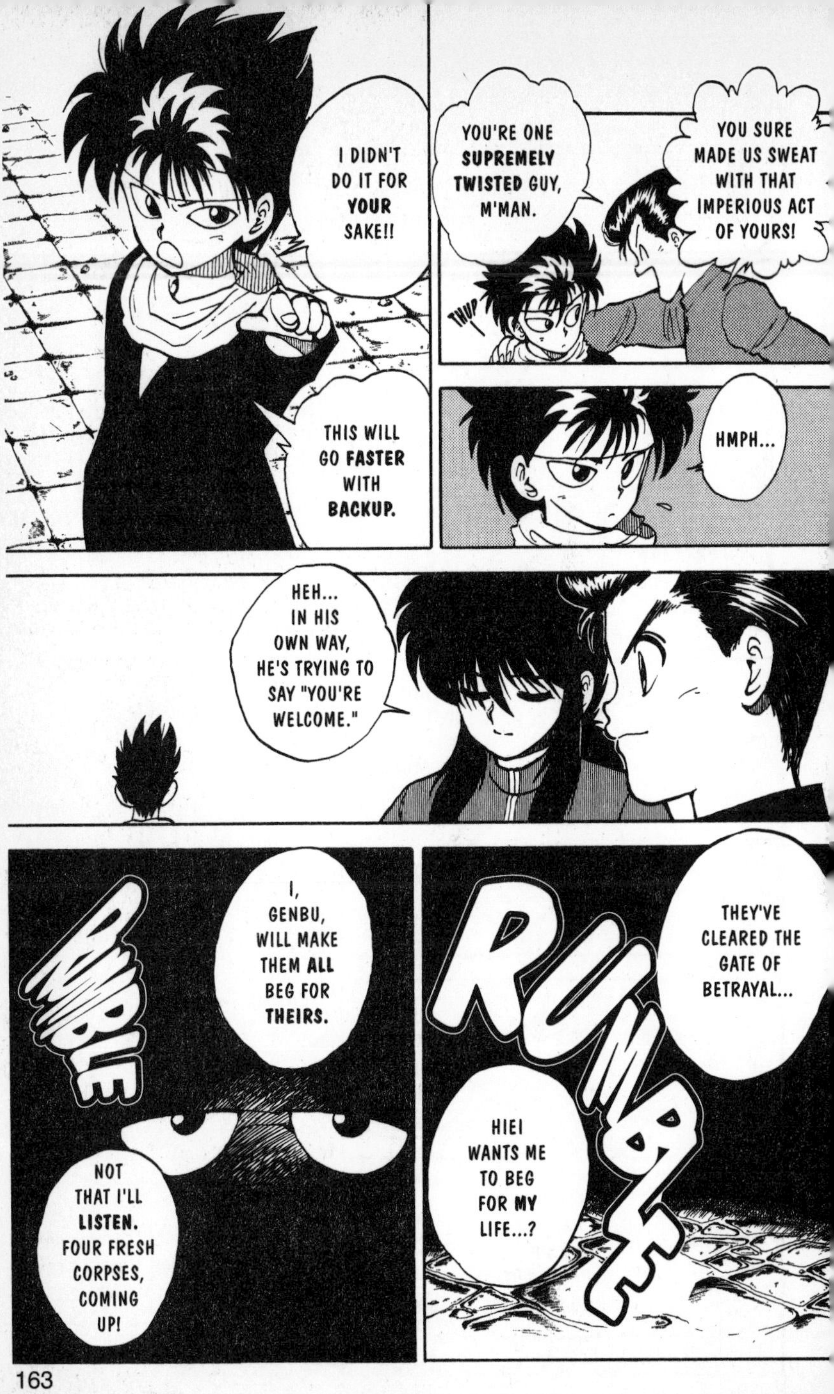
YOU SURE MADE US SWEAT WITH THAT IMPERIOUS ACT OF YOURS!
YOU'RE ONE SUPREMELY TWISTED GUY, M'MAN.
THUP
HMPH...
I DIDN'T DO IT FOR YOUR SAKE!!
THIS WILL GO FASTER WITH BACKUP.
HEH... IN HIS OWN WAY, HE'S TRYING TO SAY "YOU'RE WELCOME."
THEY'VE CLEARED THE GATE OF BETRAYAL...
RUMBLE
HIEI WANTS ME TO BEG FOR MY LIFE...?
RUMBLE
I, GENBU, WILL MAKE THEM ALL BEG FOR THEIRS.
NOT THAT I'LL LISTEN. FOUR FRESH CORPSES, COMING UP!

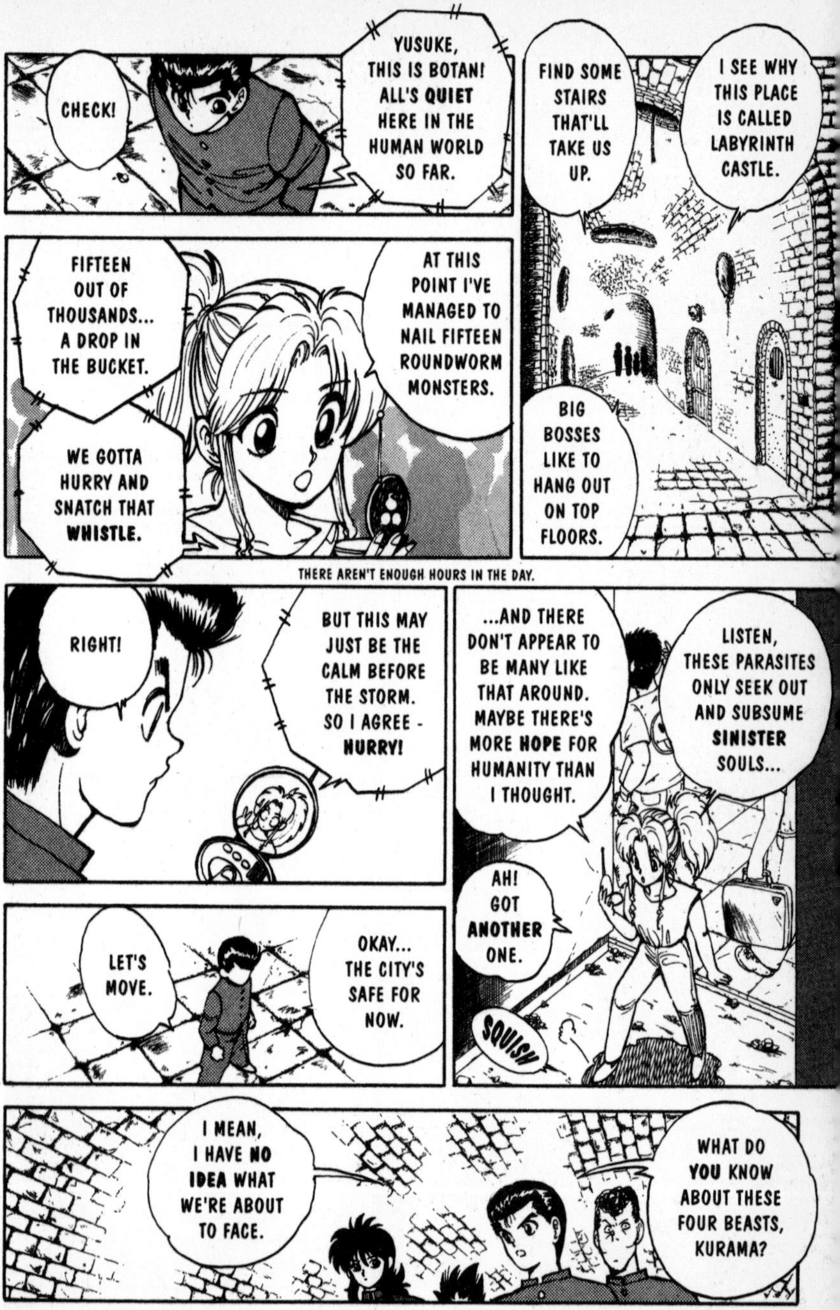
I SEE WHY THIS PLACE IS CALLED LABYRINTH CASTLE.
FIND SOME STAIRS THAT'LL TAKE US UP.
BIG BOSSES LIKE TO HANG OUT ON TOP FLOORS.
YUSUKE, THIS IS BOTAN! ALL'S QUIET HERE IN THE HUMAN WORLD SO FAR.
CHECK!
AT THIS POINT I'VE MANAGED TO NAIL FIFTEEN ROUNDWORM MONSTERS.
FIFTEEN OUT OF THOUSANDS... A DROP IN THE BUCKET.
WE GOTTA HURRY AND SNATCH THAT WHISTLE.
THERE AREN'T ENOUGH HOURS IN THE DAY.
LISTEN, THESE PARASITES ONLY SEEK OUT AND SUBSUME SINISTER SOULS...
...AND THERE DON'T APPEAR TO BE MANY LIKE THAT AROUND. MAYBE THERE'S MORE HOPE FOR HUMANITY THAN I THOUGHT.
AH! GOT ANOTHER ONE.
SQUISH
BUT THIS MAY JUST BE THE CALM BEFORE THE STORM. SO I AGREE - HURRY!
RIGHT!
OKAY... THE CITY'S SAFE FOR NOW.
LET'S MOVE.
WHAT DO YOU KNOW ABOUT THESE FOUR BEASTS, KURAMA?
I MEAN, I HAVE NO IDEA WHAT WE'RE ABOUT TO FACE.

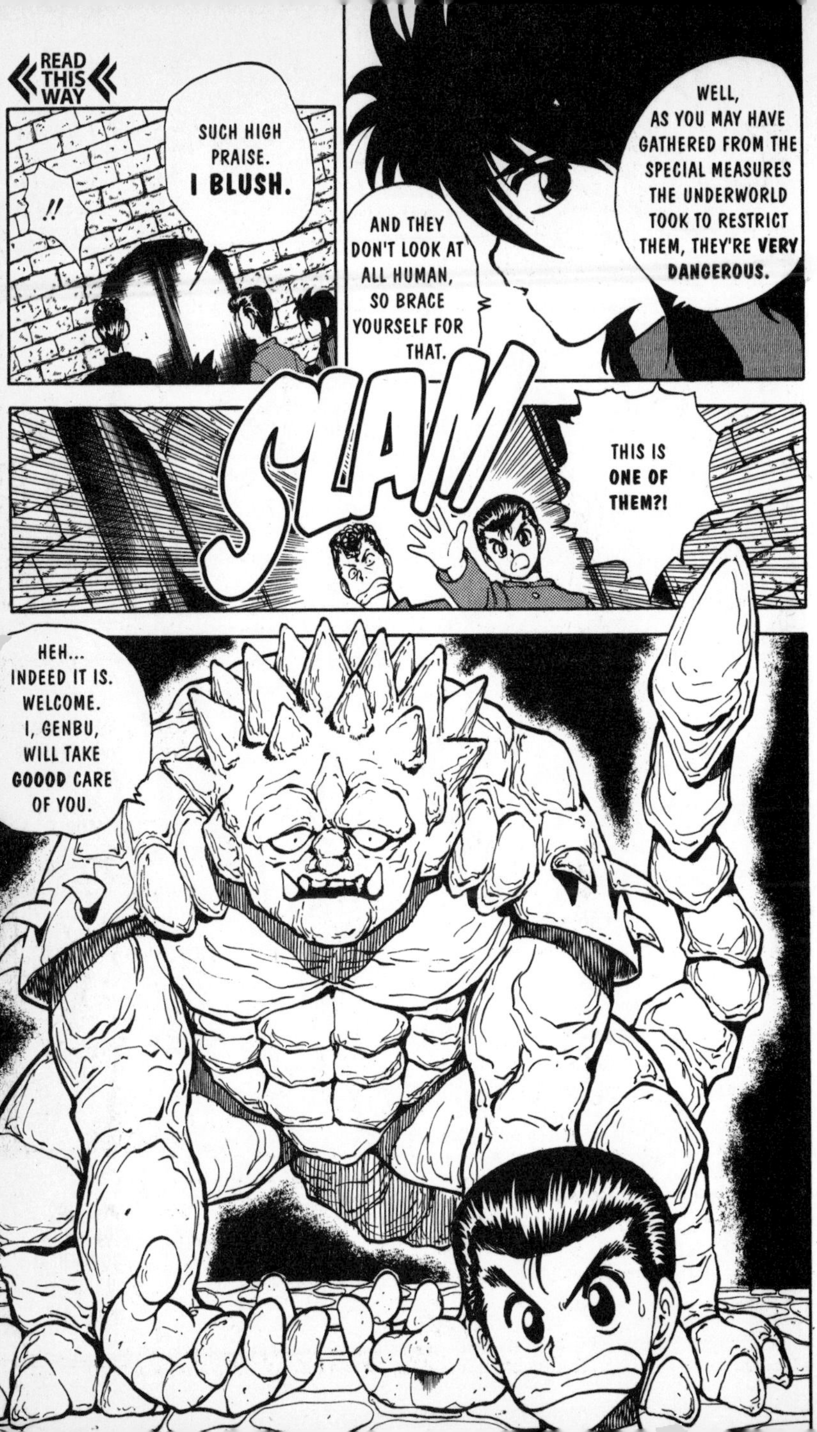
READ THIS WAY
WELL, AS YOU MAY HAVE GATHERED FROM THE SPECIAL MEASURES THE UNDERWORLD TOOK TO RESTRICT THEM, THEY'RE **VERY DANGEROUS.**
AND THEY DON'T LOOK AT ALL HUMAN, SO BRACE YOURSELF FOR THAT.
SUCH HIGH PRAISE. **I BLUSH.**
!!
SLAM
THIS IS **ONE OF THEM?!**
HEH... INDEED IT IS. WELCOME. I, GENBU, WILL TAKE **GOOOD** CARE OF YOU.

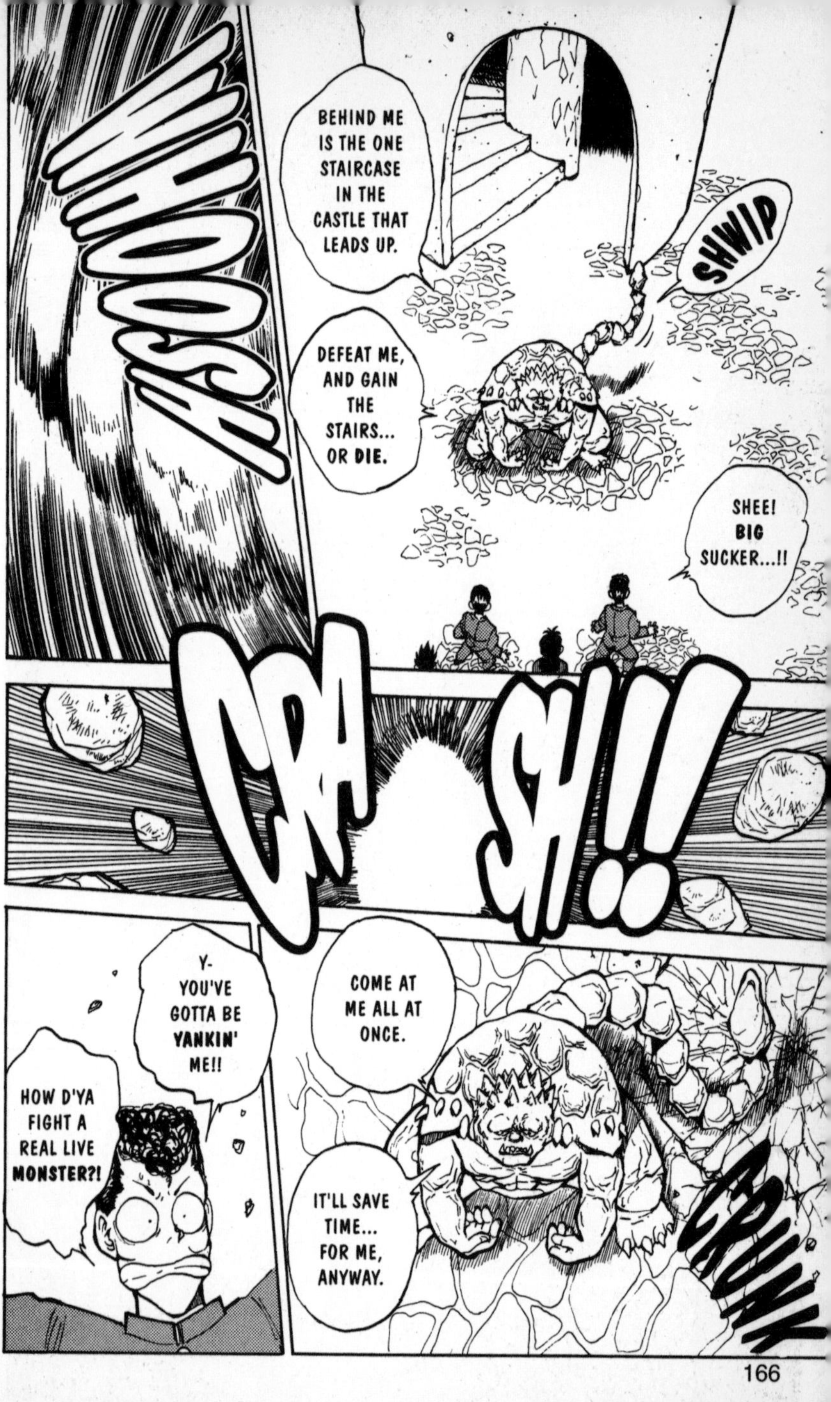
SHWIP
BEHIND ME IS THE ONE STAIRCASE IN THE CASTLE THAT LEADS UP.
DEFEAT ME, AND GAIN THE STAIRS... OR **DIE.**
SHEE! **BIG** SUCKER...!!
WHOOSH
CRASH!!
COME AT ME ALL AT ONCE.
IT'LL SAVE TIME... FOR ME, ANYWAY.
CRUNK
Y- YOU'VE GOTTA BE **YANKIN'** ME!!
HOW D'YA FIGHT A REAL LIVE **MONSTER?!**

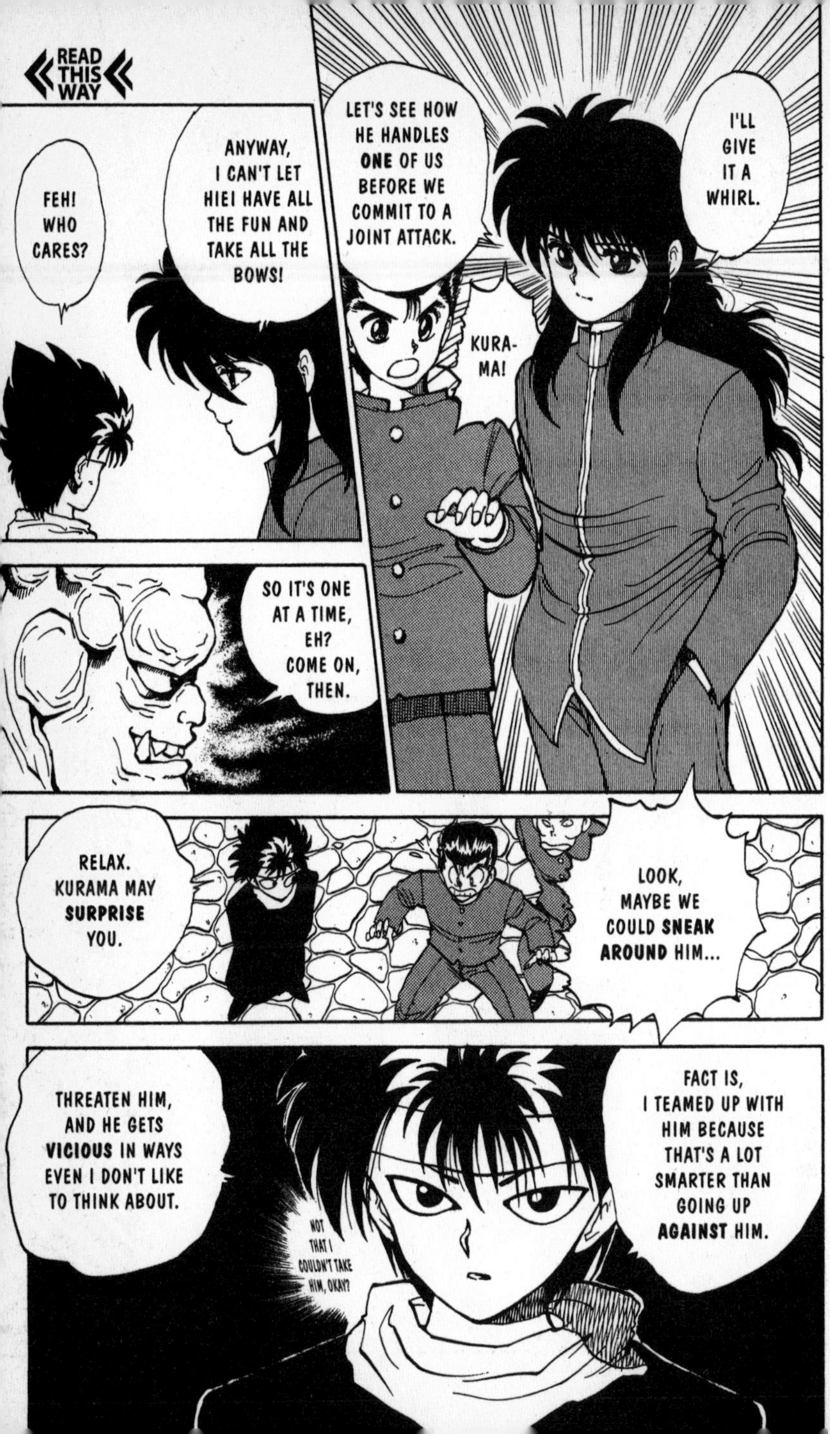
READ THIS WAY
I'LL GIVE IT A WHIRL.
LET'S SEE HOW HE HANDLES **ONE** OF US BEFORE WE COMMIT TO A JOINT ATTACK.
KURAMA!
ANYWAY, I CAN'T LET HIEI HAVE ALL THE FUN AND TAKE ALL THE BOWS!
FEH! WHO CARES?
SO IT'S ONE AT A TIME, EH? COME ON, THEN.
LOOK, MAYBE WE COULD **SNEAK AROUND** HIM...
RELAX. KURAMA MAY **SURPRISE** YOU.
FACT IS, I TEAMED UP WITH HIM BECAUSE THAT'S A LOT SMARTER THAN GOING UP **AGAINST** HIM.
NOT THAT I COULDN'T TAKE HIM, OKAY?
THREATEN HIM, AND HE GETS **VICIOUS** IN WAYS EVEN I DON'T LIKE TO THINK ABOUT.

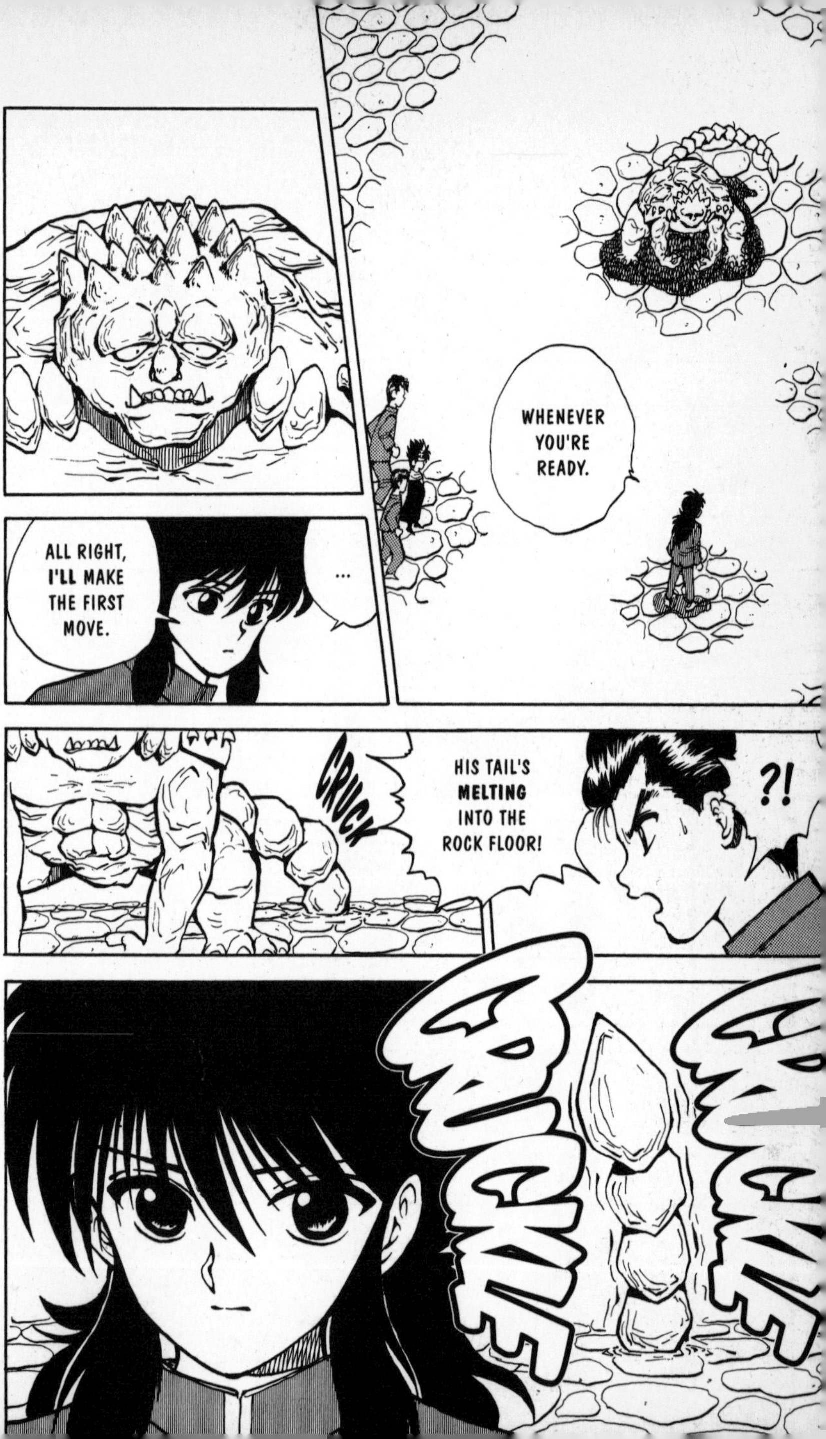
WHENEVER YOU'RE READY.
...
ALL RIGHT, I'LL MAKE THE FIRST MOVE.
?!
HIS TAIL'S MELTING INTO THE ROCK FLOOR!
CRUCK
CRACKLE
CRACKLE

READ THIS WAY

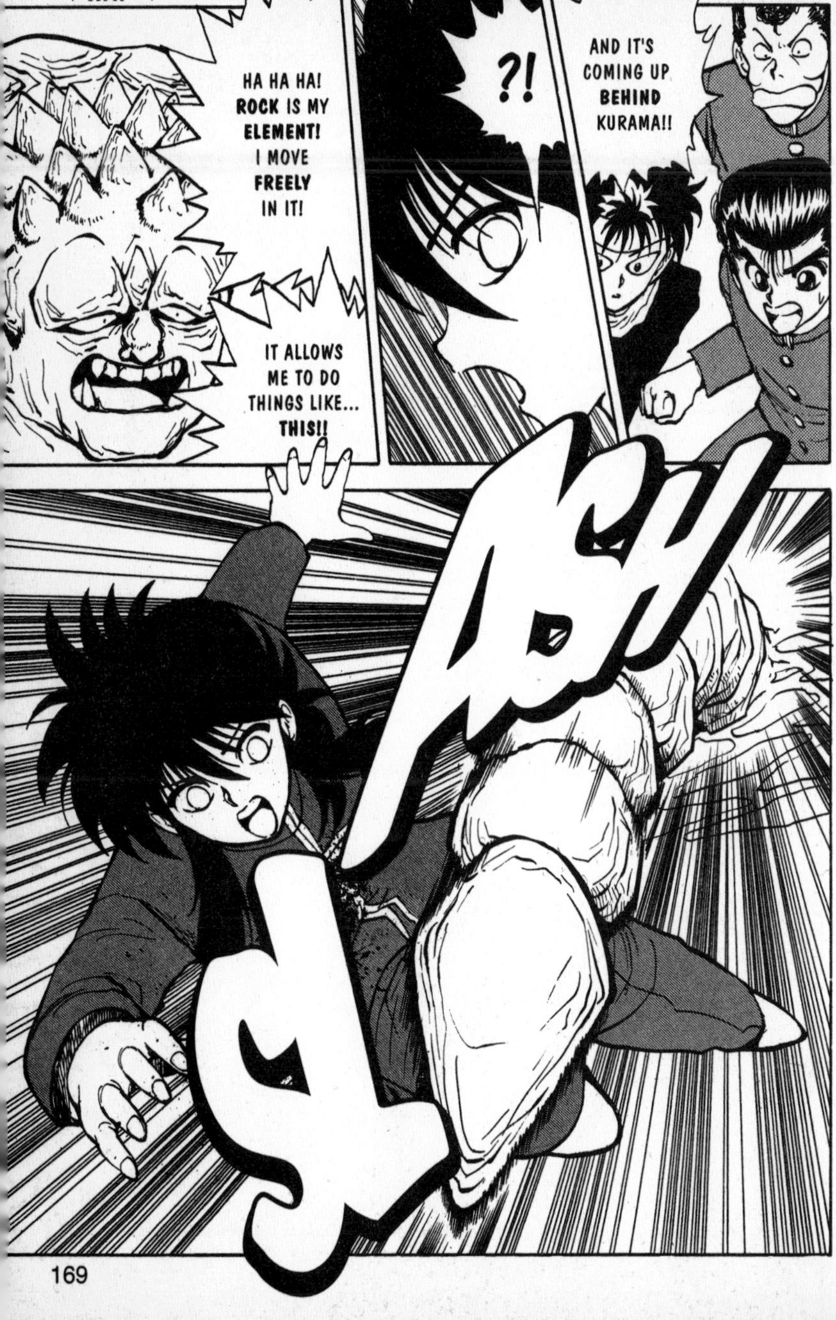

AND IT'S COMING UP BEHIND KURAMA!!
?!
HA HA HA! ROCK IS MY ELEMENT! I MOVE FREELY IN IT!
IT ALLOWS ME TO DO THINGS LIKE... THIS!!

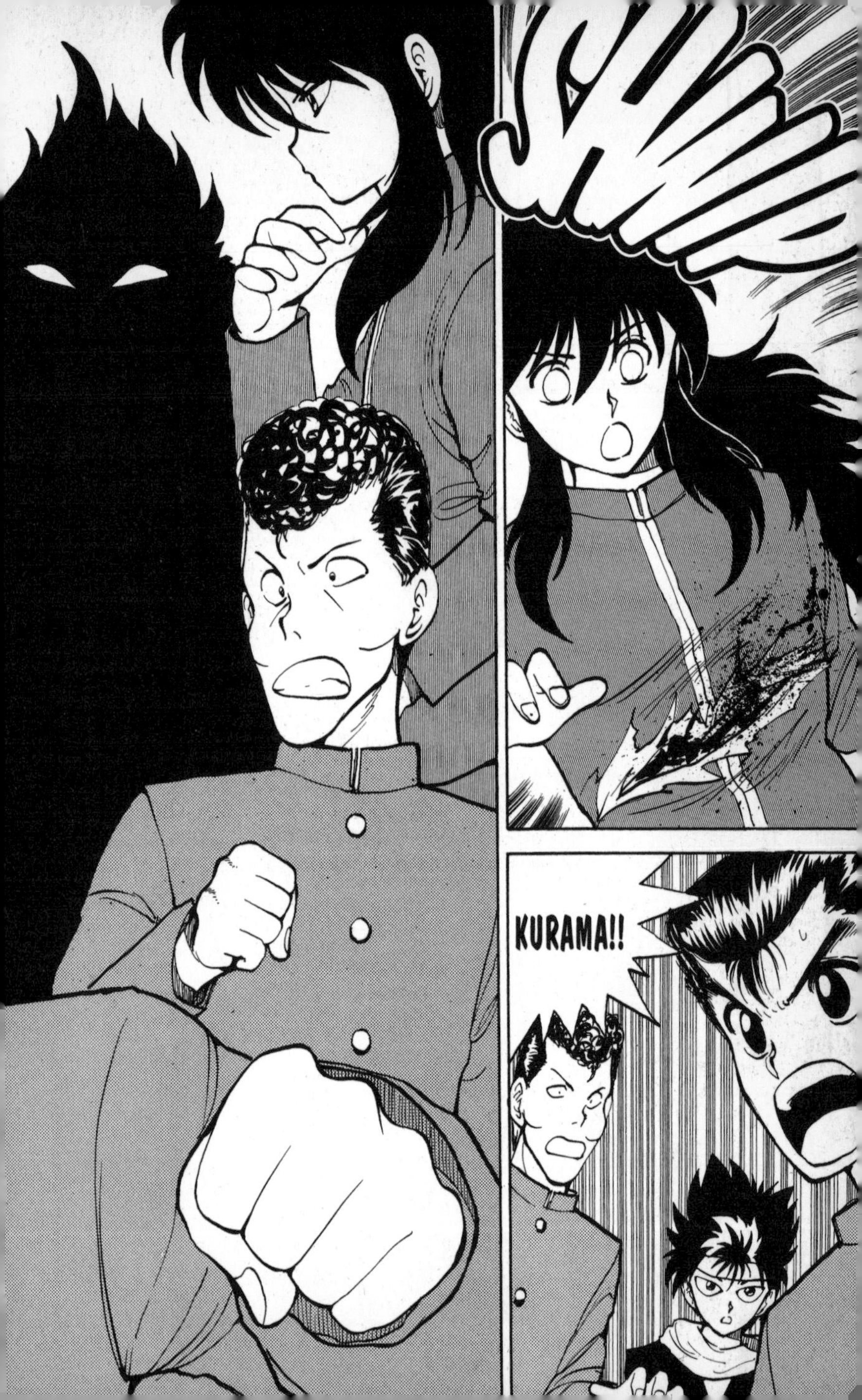
KURAMA!!

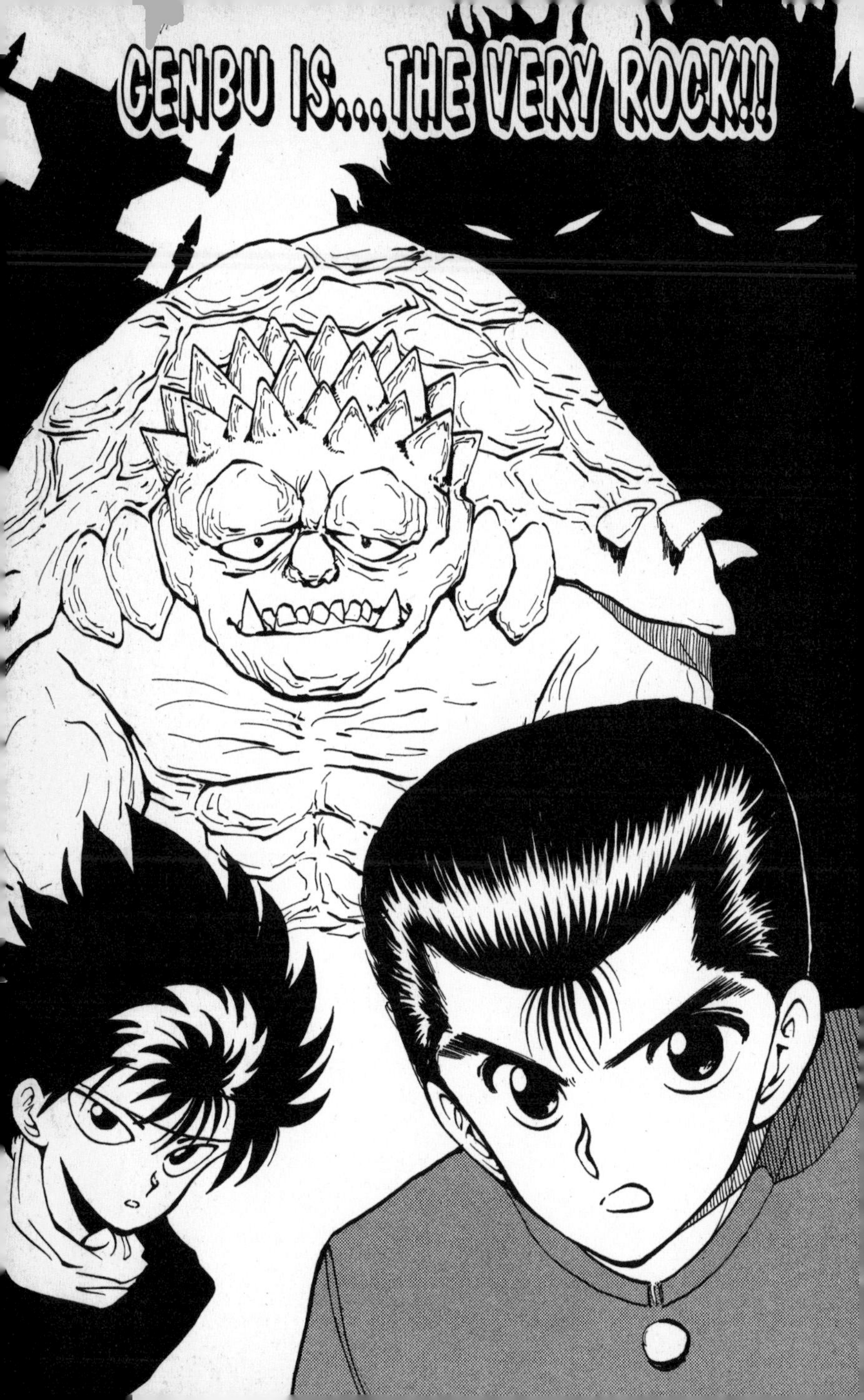
GENBU IS...THE VERY ROCK!!

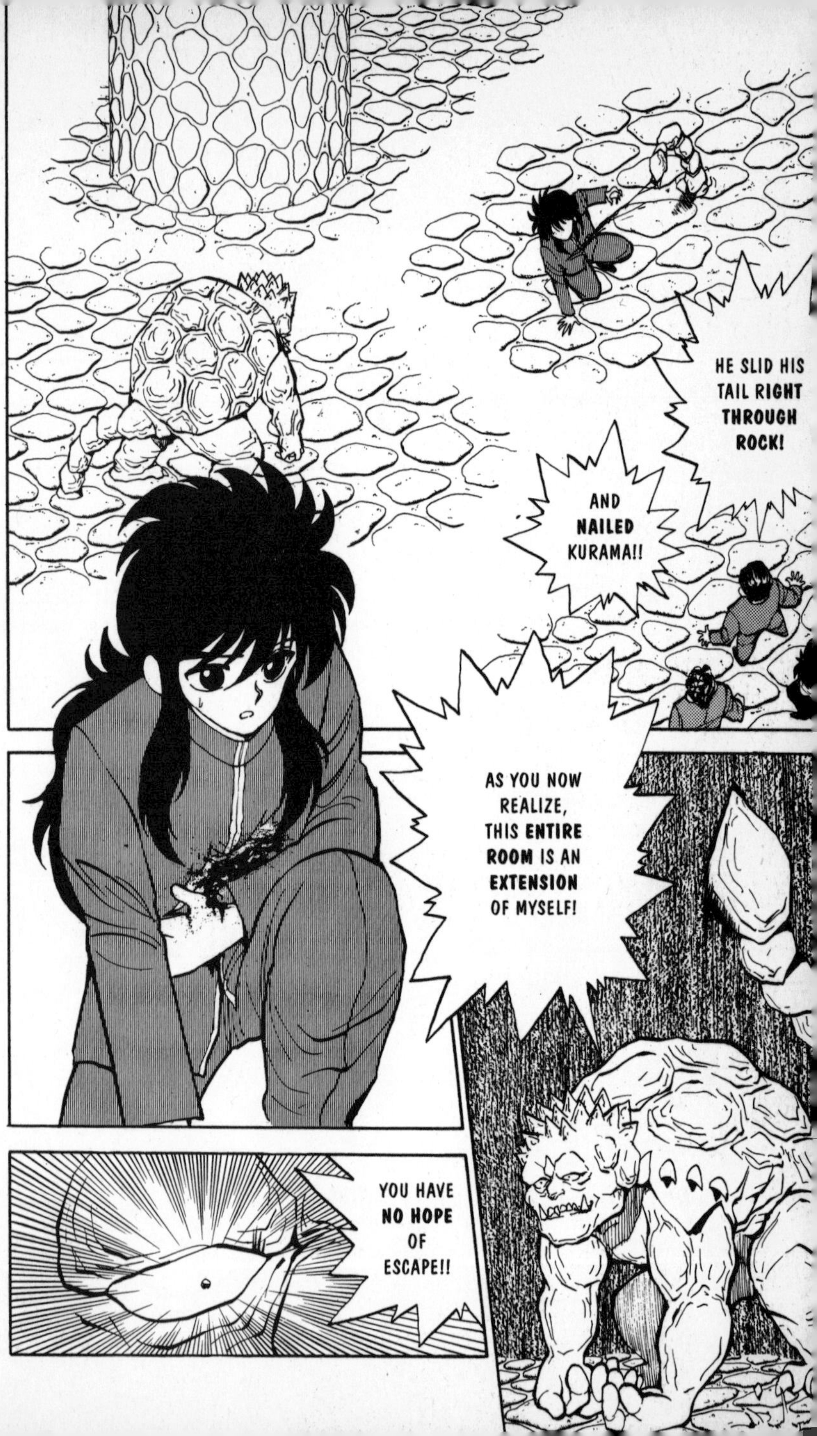
HE SLID HIS TAIL RIGHT THROUGH ROCK!
AND NAILED KURAMA!!
AS YOU NOW REALIZE, THIS ENTIRE ROOM IS AN EXTENSION OF MYSELF!
YOU HAVE NO HOPE OF ESCAPE!!

READ THIS WAY

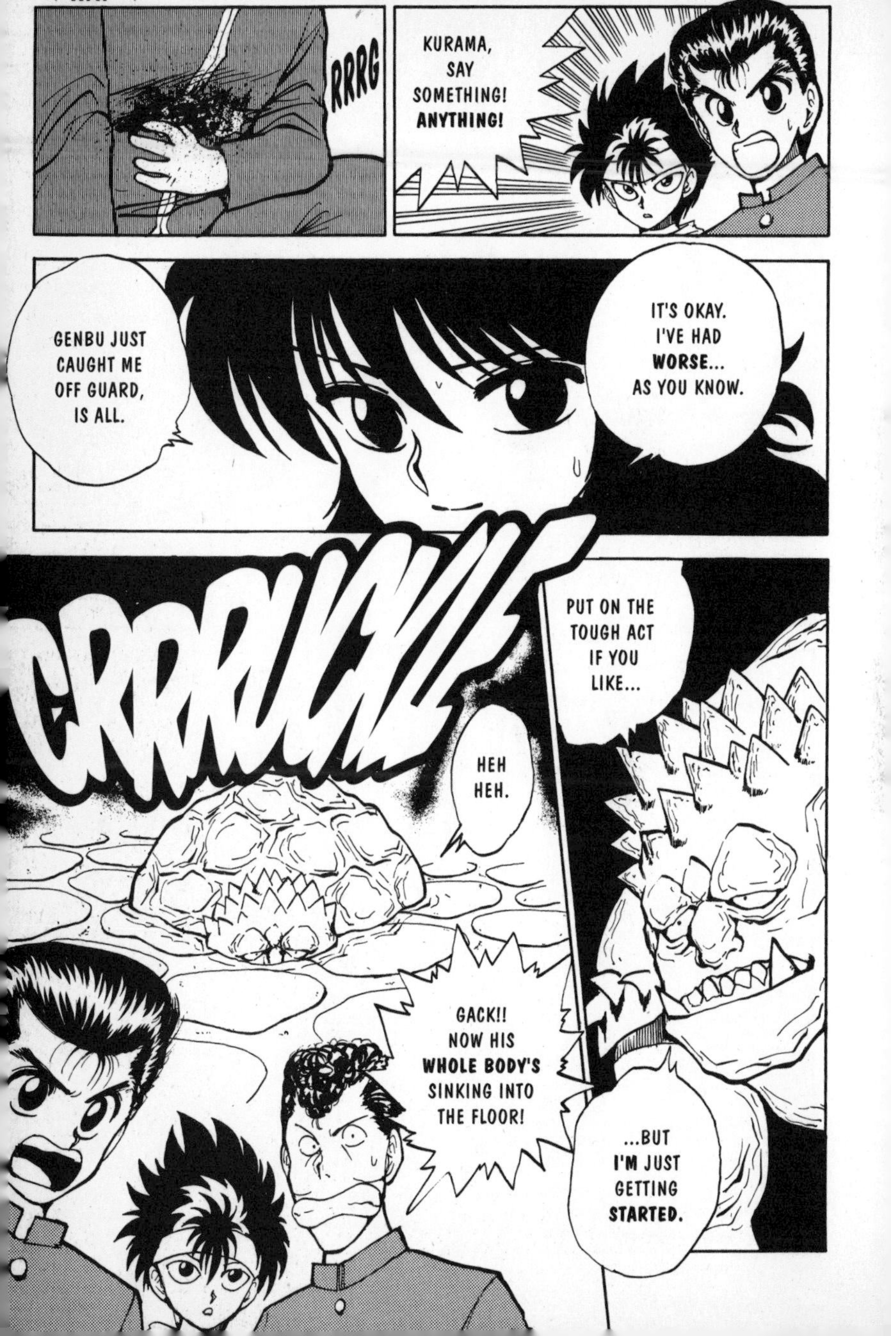
KURAMA, SAY SOMETHING! **ANYTHING!**
RRRG
IT'S OKAY. I'VE HAD **WORSE...** AS YOU KNOW.
GENBU JUST CAUGHT ME OFF GUARD, IS ALL.
PUT ON THE TOUGH ACT IF YOU LIKE...
...BUT **I'M JUST** GETTING **STARTED.**
CRRUNCH
HEH HEH.
GACK!! NOW HIS **WHOLE BODY'S** SINKING INTO THE FLOOR!

READ THIS WAY

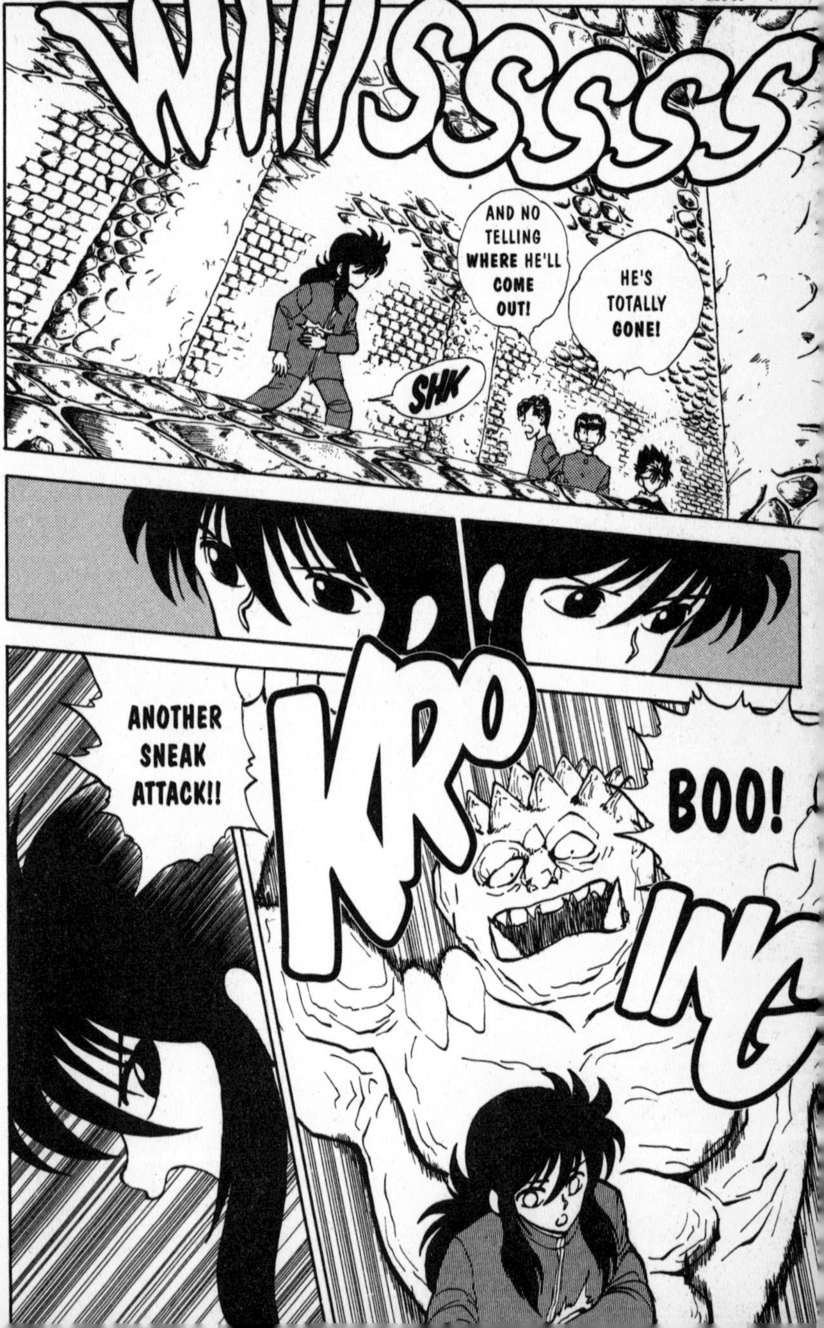
WHSSSSS
HE'S TOTALLY GONE!
AND NO TELLING WHERE HE'LL COME OUT!
SHK
BOO!
KRO
ING
ANOTHER SNEAK ATTACK!!

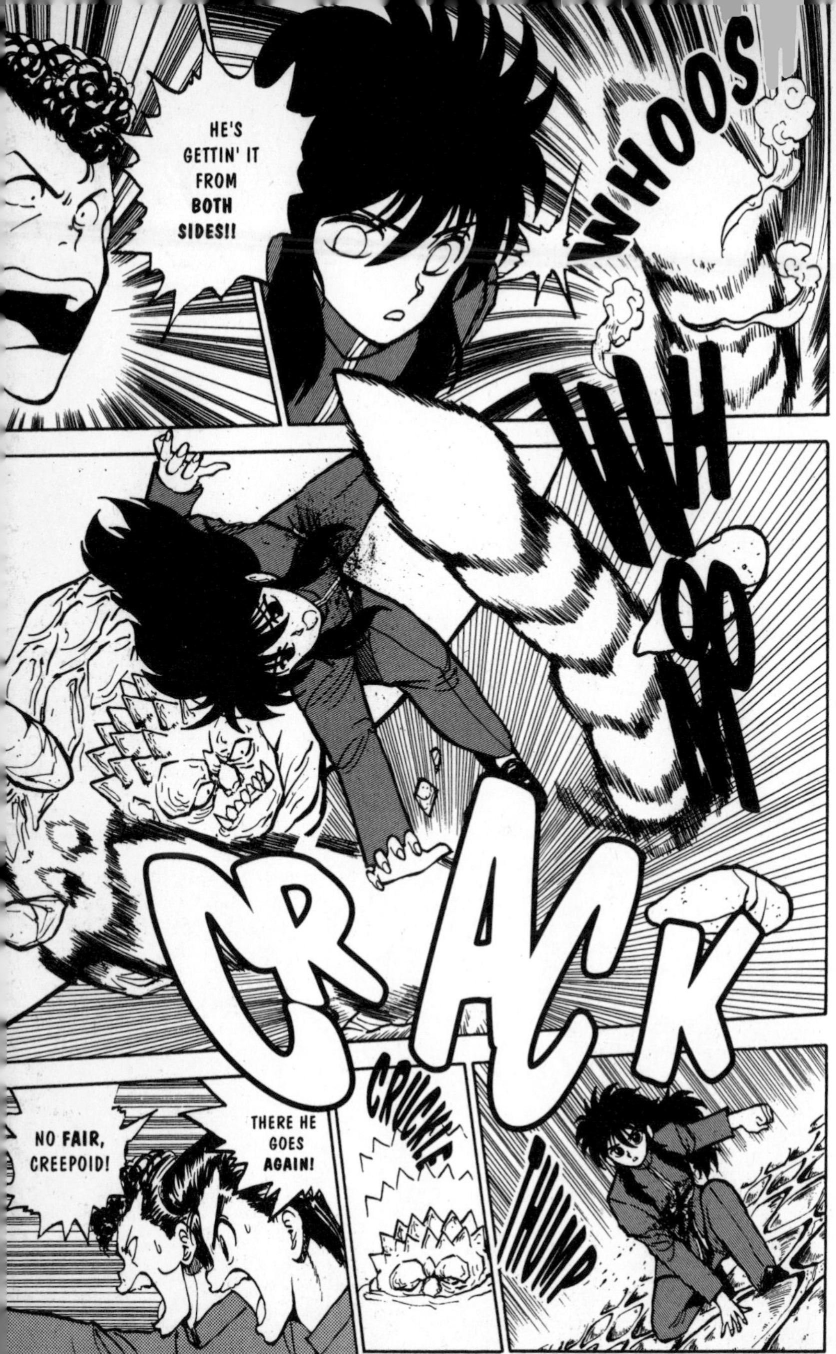
WHOOS
HE'S GETTIN' IT FROM BOTH SIDES!!
WHOOMP
CRACK
THUMP
CRUNKLE
THERE HE GOES AGAIN!
NO FAIR, CREEPOID!

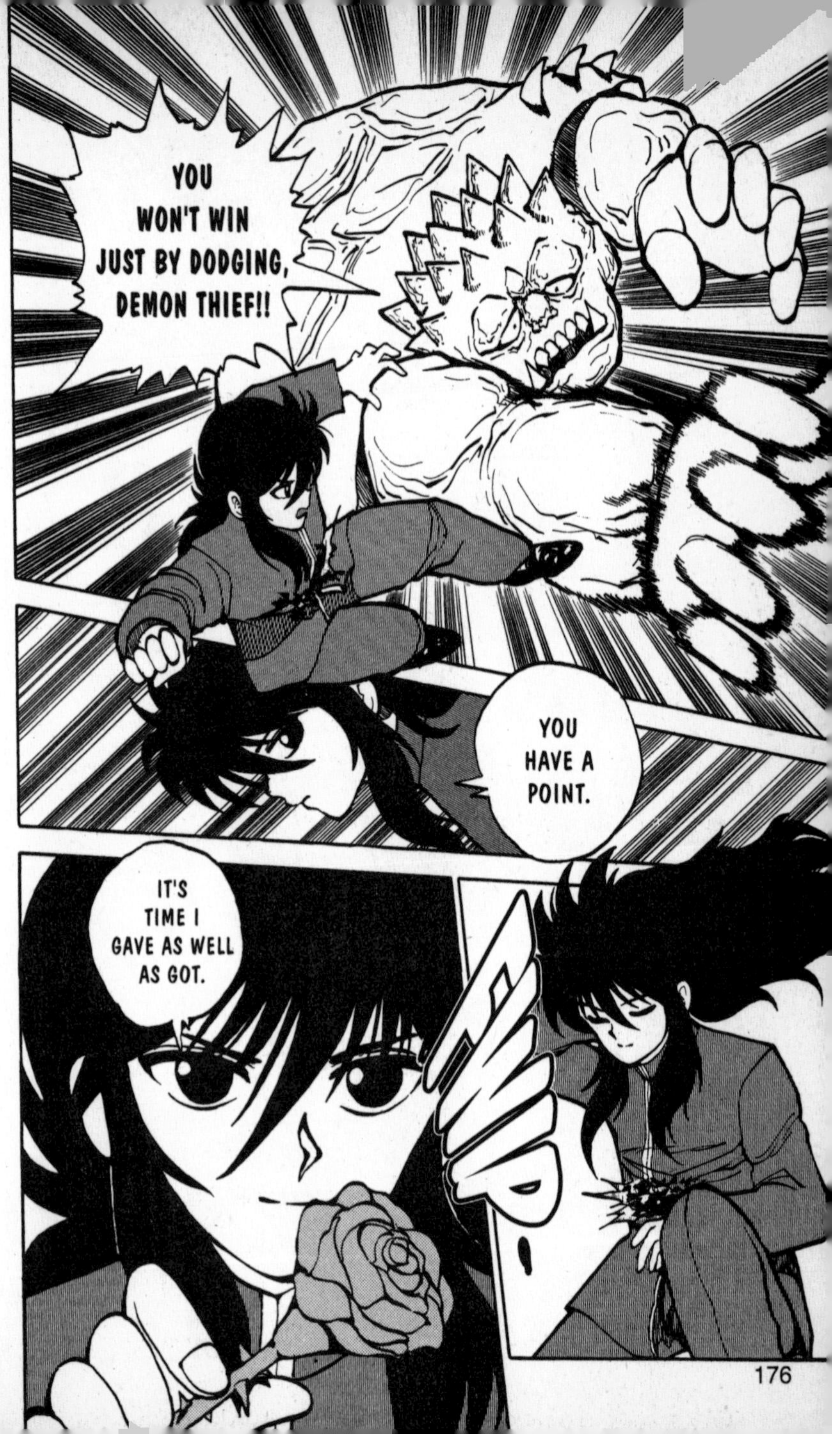
YOU WON'T WIN JUST BY DODGING, DEMON THIEF!!
YOU HAVE A POINT.
IT'S TIME I GAVE AS WELL AS GOT.

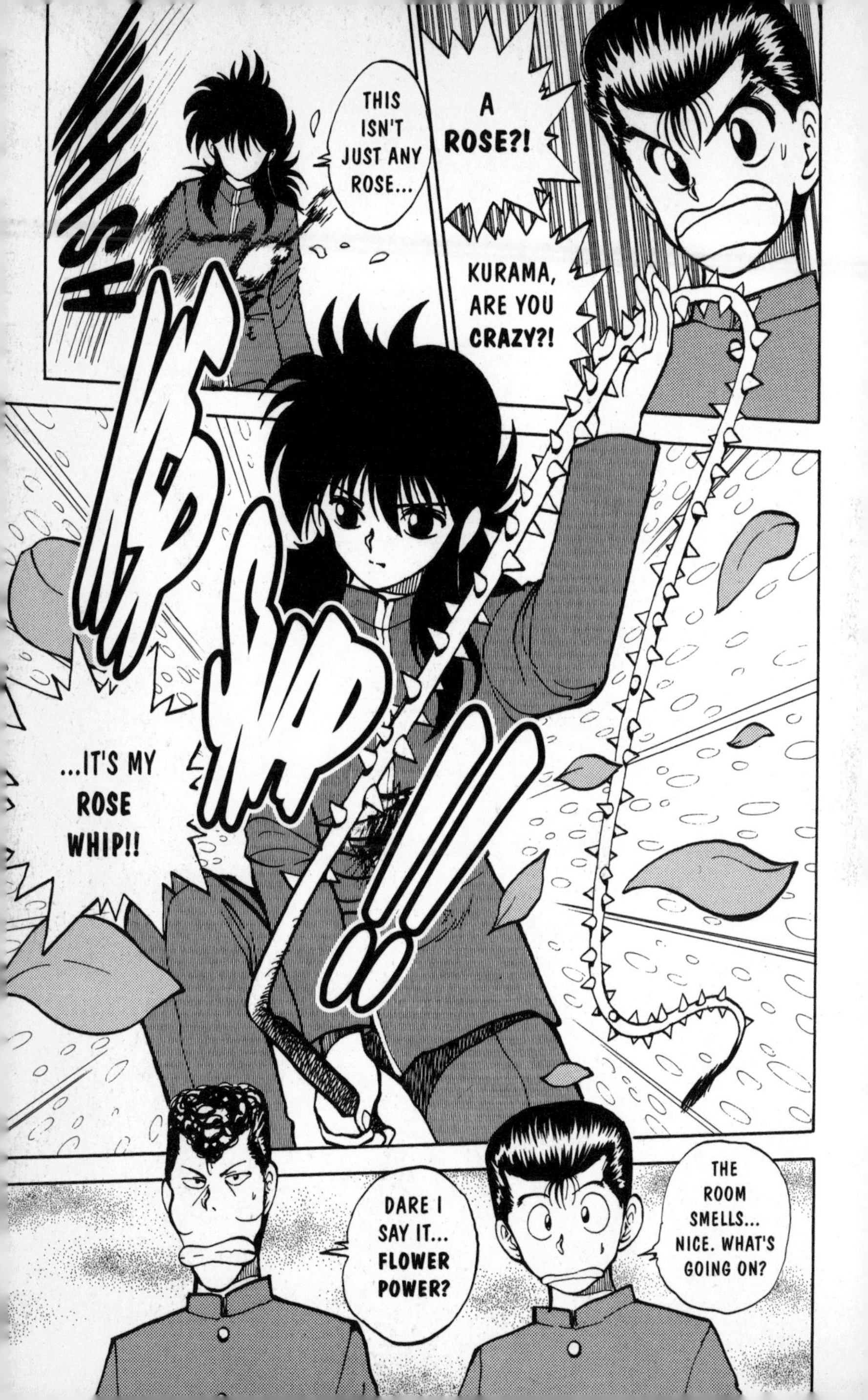
A ROSE?!
KURAMA, ARE YOU CRAZY?!
THIS ISN'T JUST ANY ROSE...
...IT'S MY ROSE WHIP!!
THE ROOM SMELLS... NICE. WHAT'S GOING ON?
DARE I SAY IT... FLOWER POWER?

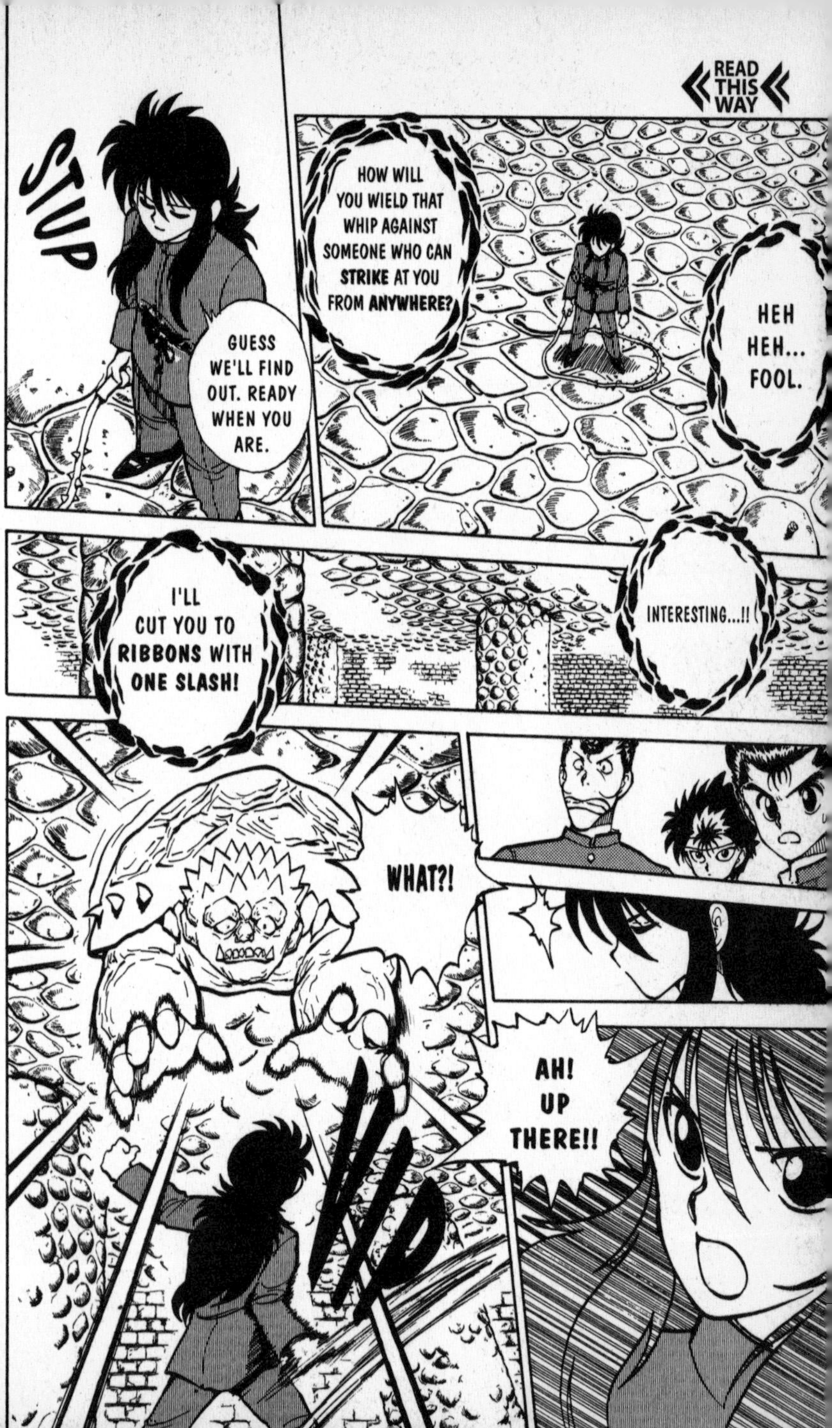
READ THIS WAY
HEH HEH... FOOL.
HOW WILL YOU WIELD THAT WHIP AGAINST SOMEONE WHO CAN STRIKE AT YOU FROM ANYWHERE?
STUP
GUESS WE'LL FIND OUT. READY WHEN YOU ARE.
INTERESTING...!!
I'LL CUT YOU TO RIBBONS WITH ONE SLASH!
WHAT?!
AH! UP THERE!!

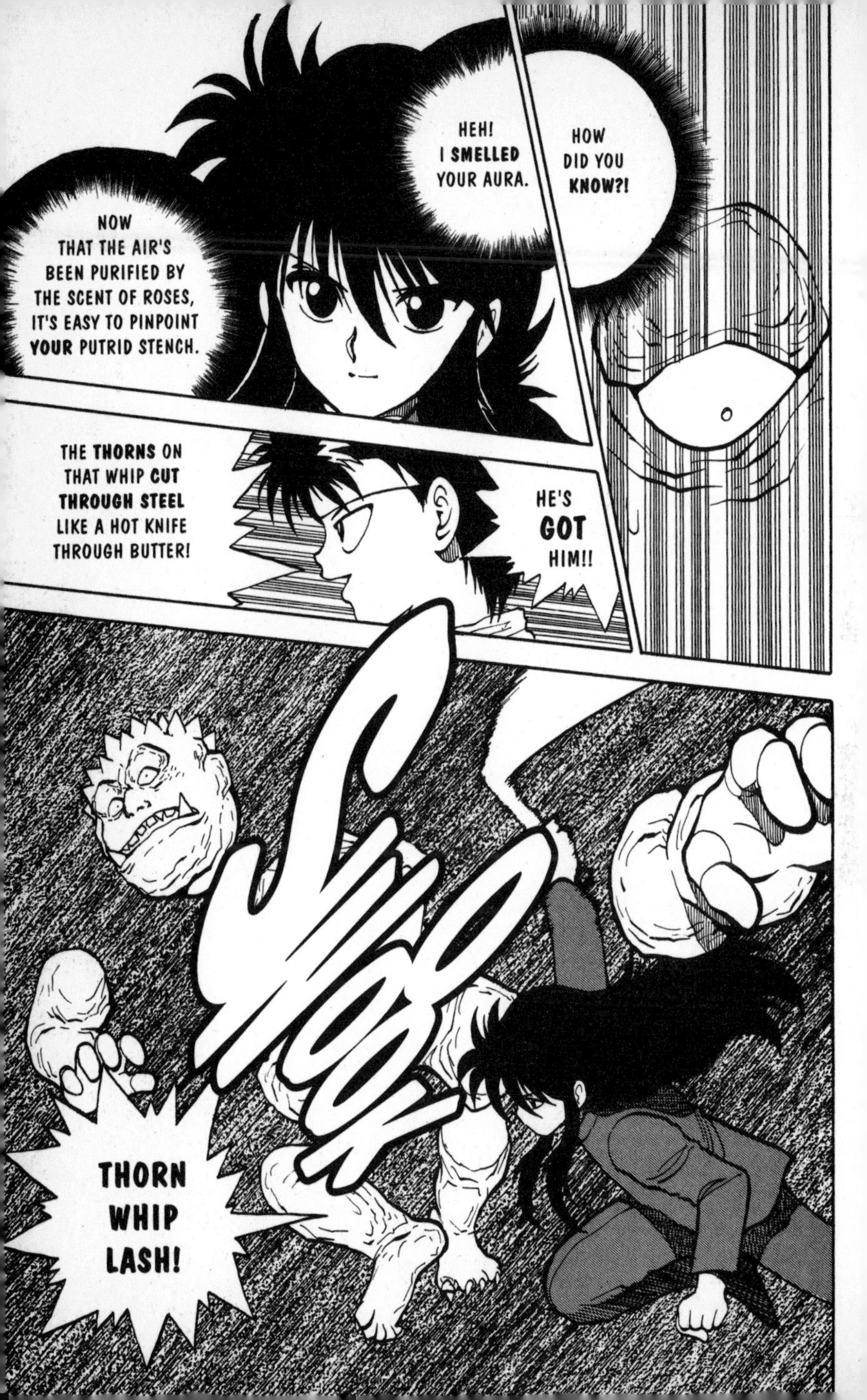
HOW DID YOU KNOW?!
HEH! I SMELLED YOUR AURA.
NOW THAT THE AIR'S BEEN PURIFIED BY THE SCENT OF ROSES, IT'S EASY TO PINPOINT YOUR PUTRID STENCH.
THE THORNS ON THAT WHIP CUT THROUGH STEEL LIKE A HOT KNIFE THROUGH BUTTER!
HE'S GOT HIM!!
THORN WHIP LASH!

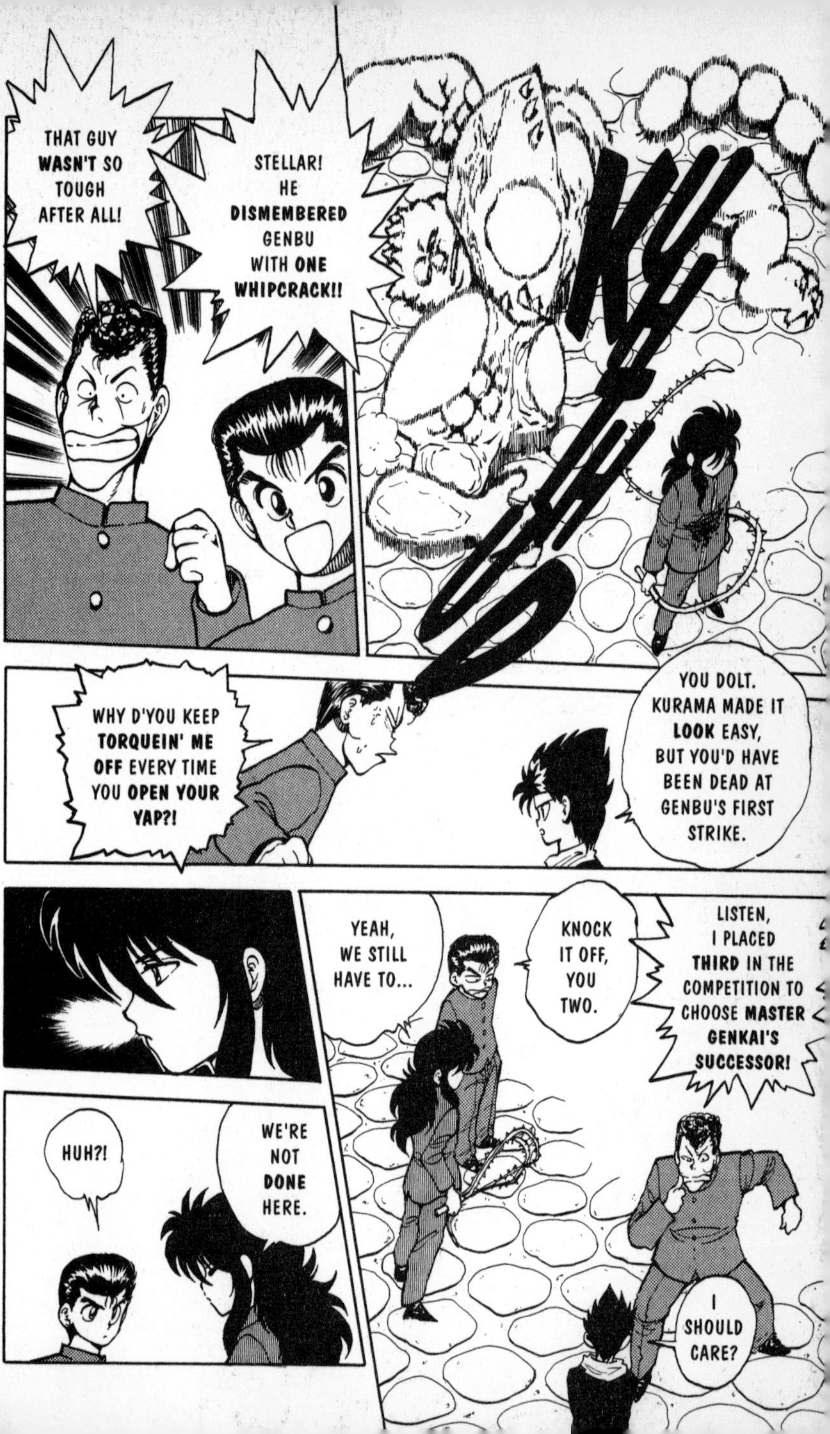
STELLAR! HE **DISMEMBERED** GENBU WITH **ONE WHIPCRACK!!**
THAT GUY **WASN'T** SO TOUGH AFTER ALL!
YOU DOLT. KURAMA MADE IT **LOOK** EASY, BUT YOU'D HAVE BEEN DEAD AT GENBU'S FIRST STRIKE.
WHY D'YOU KEEP **TORQUEIN' ME OFF** EVERY TIME YOU **OPEN YOUR YAP?!**
LISTEN, I PLACED **THIRD** IN THE COMPETITION TO CHOOSE **MASTER GENKAI'S SUCCESSOR!**
I SHOULD CARE?
KNOCK IT OFF, YOU TWO.
YEAH, WE STILL HAVE TO...
WE'RE NOT **DONE** HERE.
HUH?!

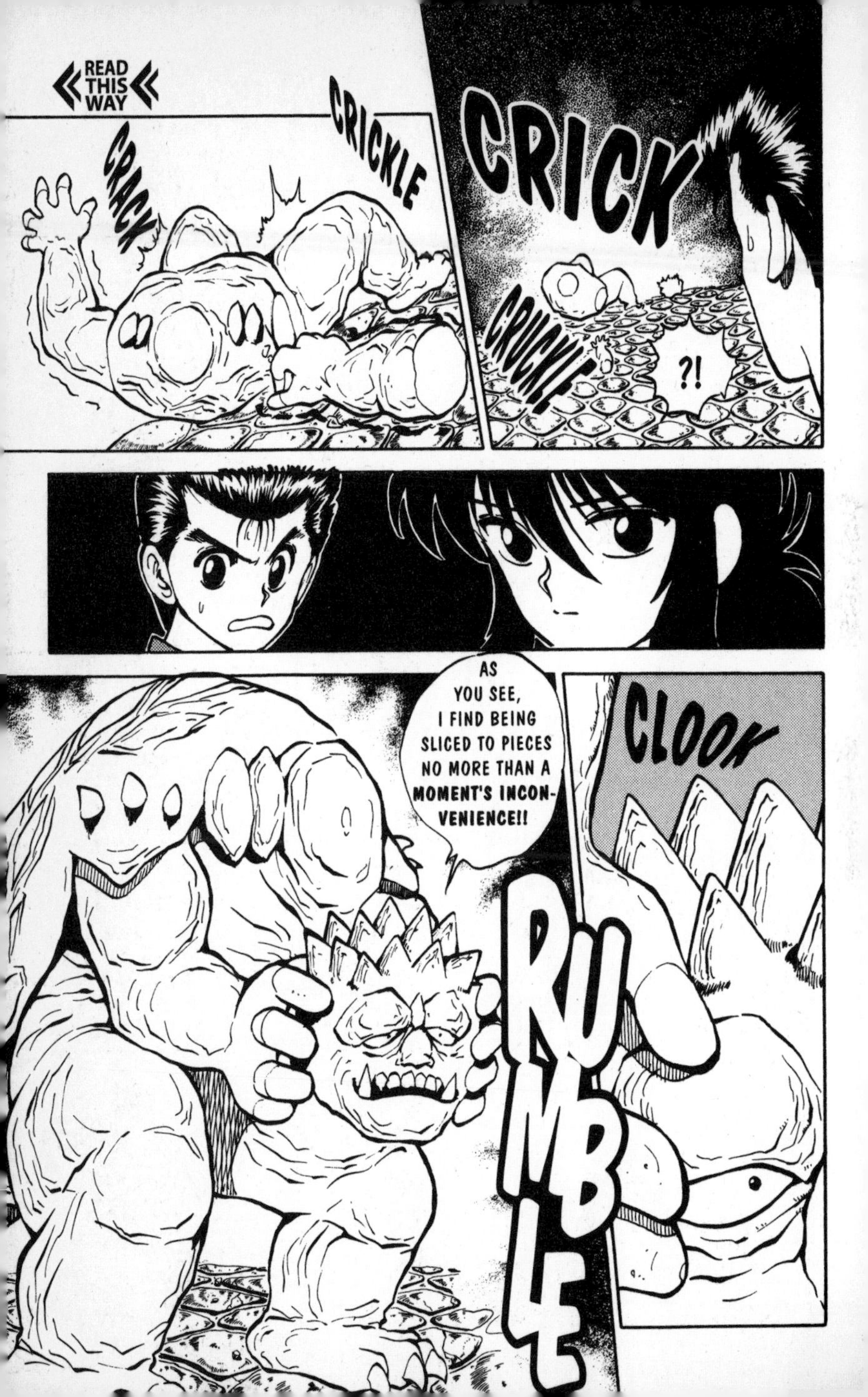
READ THIS WAY
CRICK
CRICKIT
?!
CRICKLE
CRACK
CLOOK
AS YOU SEE, I FIND BEING SLICED TO PIECES NO MORE THAN A **MOMENT'S INCON-VENIENCE!!**
RUMBLE

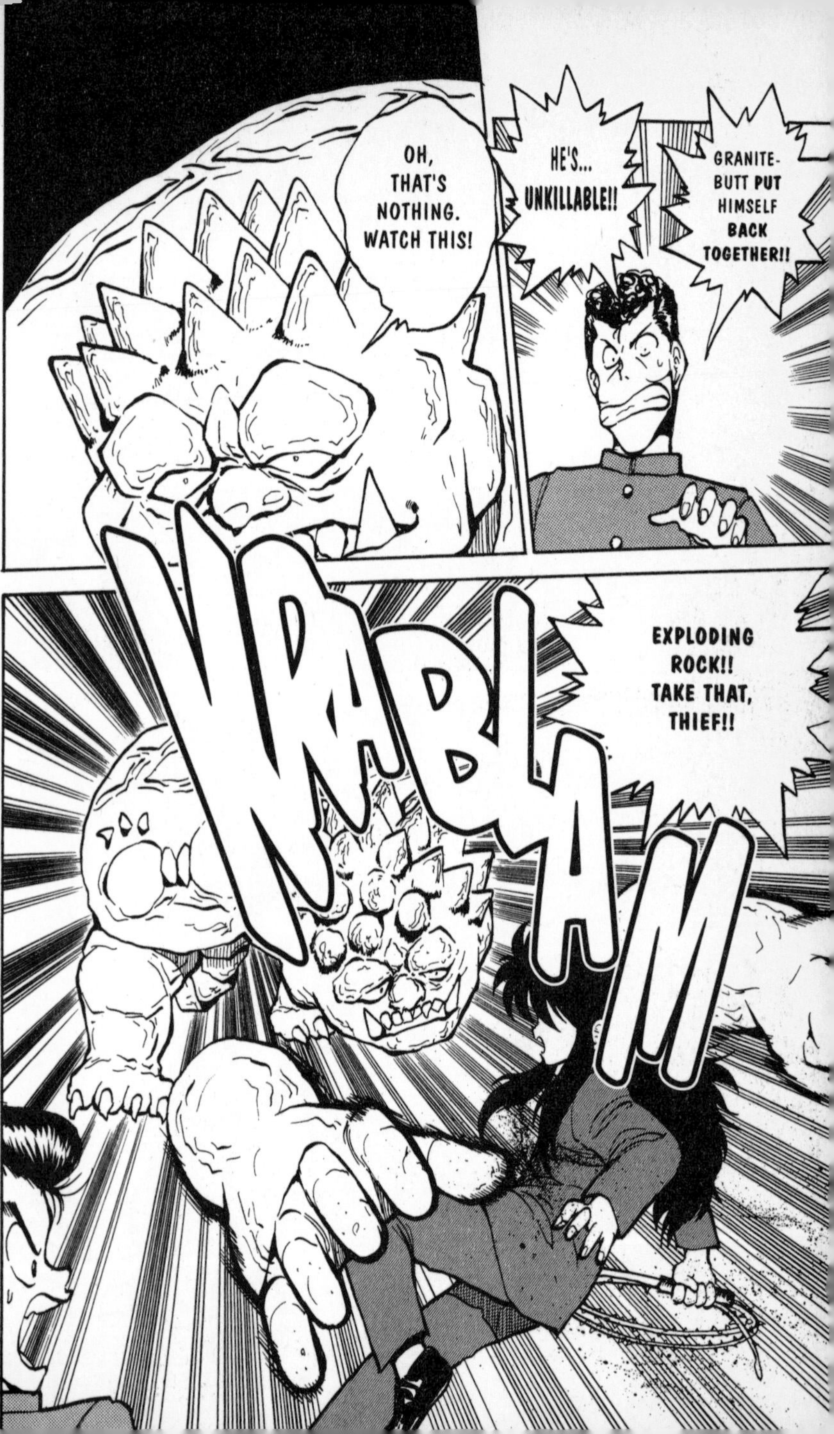
GRANITE-BUTT PUT HIMSELF BACK TOGETHER!!
HE'S... UNKILLABLE!!
OH, THAT'S NOTHING. WATCH THIS!
KRABLAM
EXPLODING ROCK!! TAKE THAT, THIEF!!

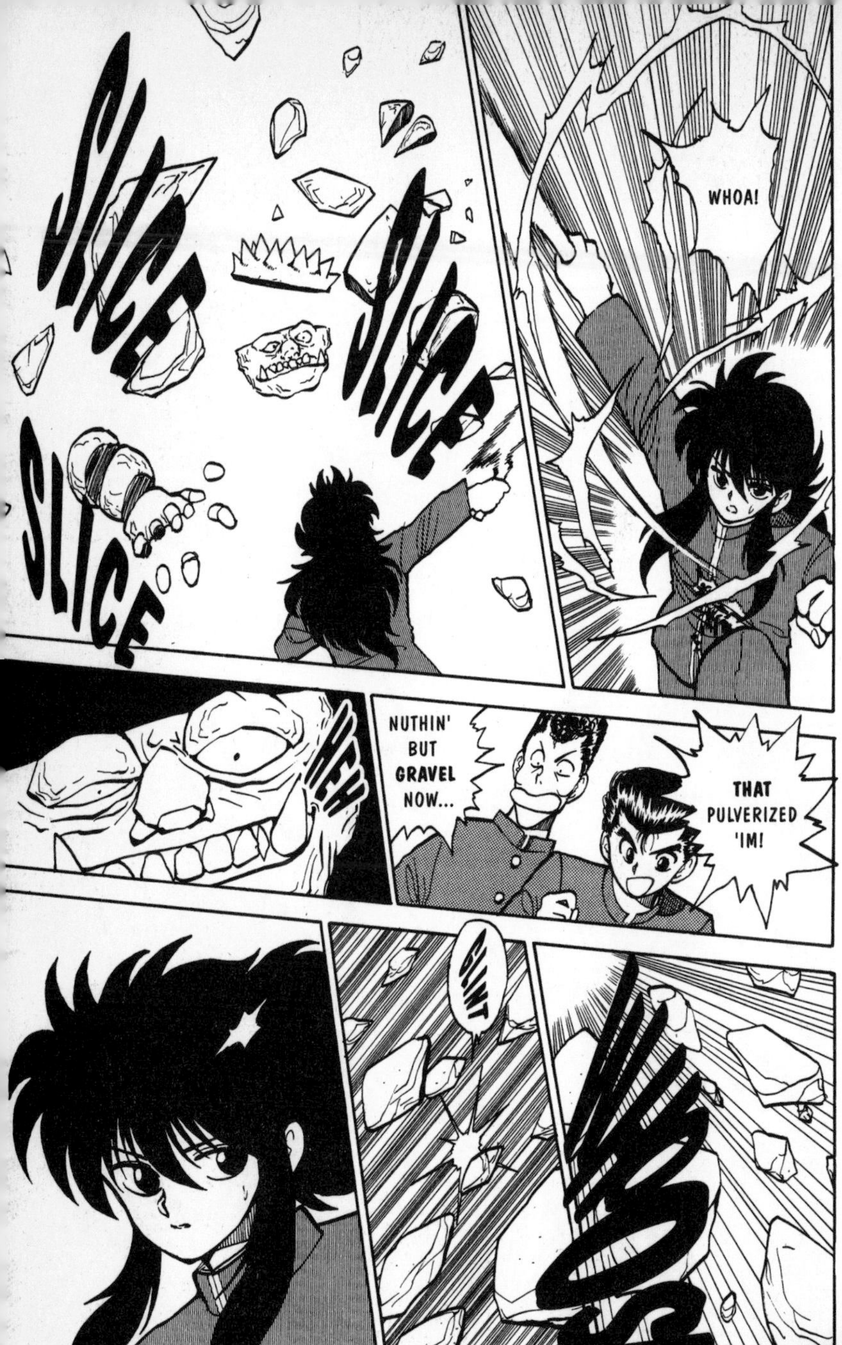
WHOA!
SLICE
SLICE
SLICE
THAT PULVERIZED 'IM!
NUTHIN' BUT GRAVEL NOW...
HEH
GLINT

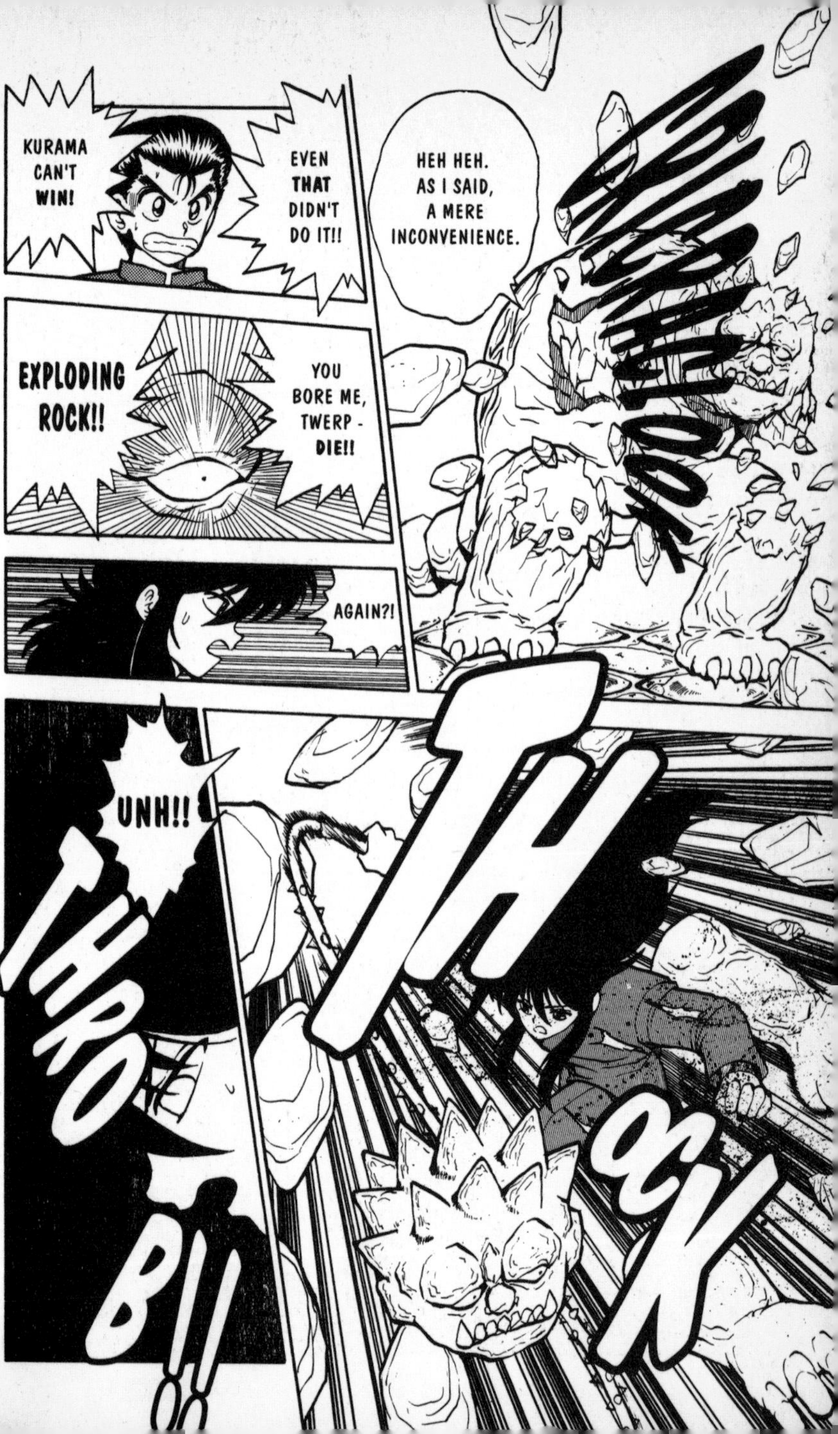
HEH HEH. AS I SAID, A MERE INCONVENIENCE.
EVEN THAT DIDN'T DO IT!!
KURAMA CAN'T WIN!
YOU BORE ME, TWERP - DIE!!
EXPLODING ROCK!!
AGAIN?!
THOCK
UNH!!
THROB!!

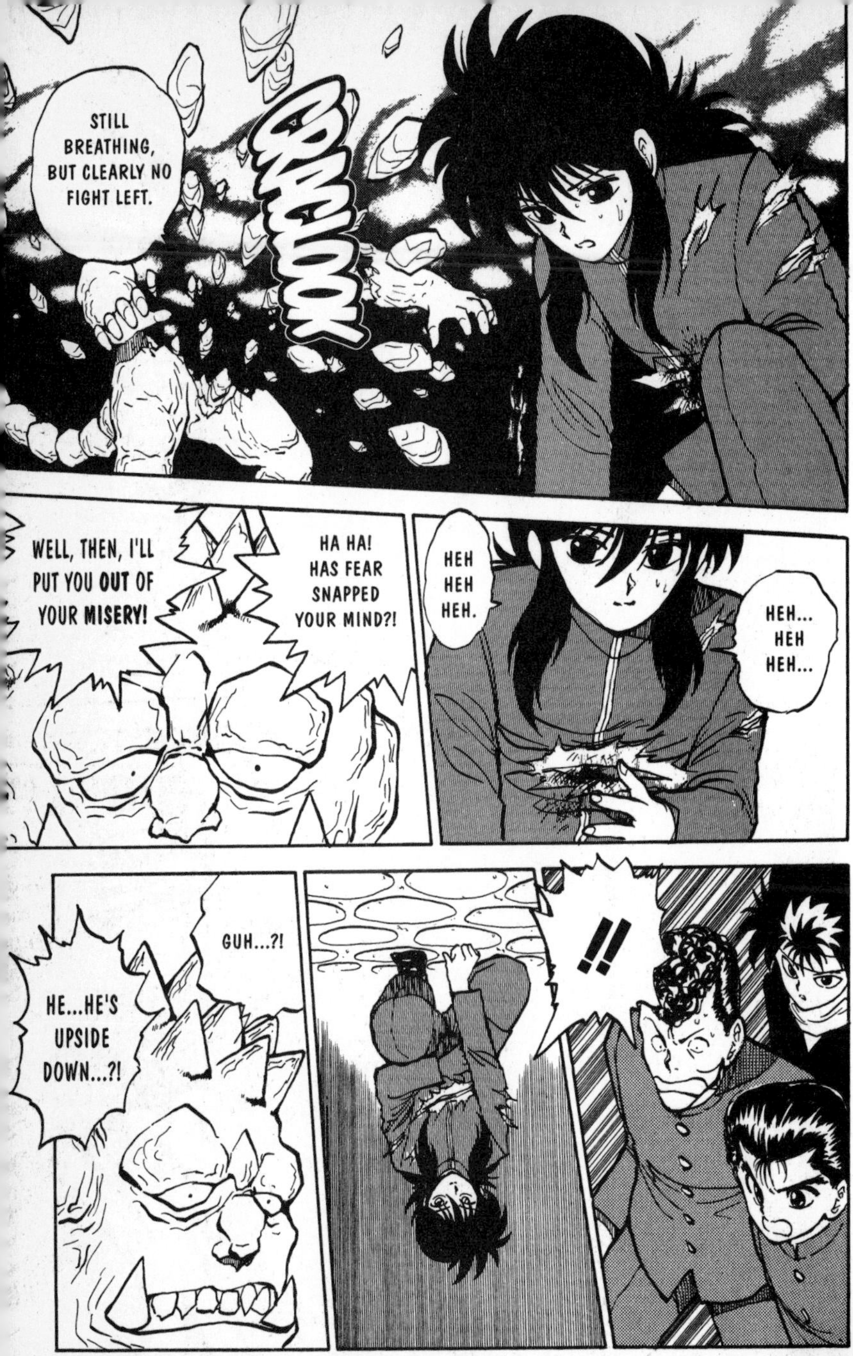
STILL BREATHING, BUT CLEARLY NO FIGHT LEFT.
HEH... HEH HEH...
HEH HEH HEH.
HA HA! HAS FEAR SNAPPED YOUR MIND?!
WELL, THEN, I'LL PUT YOU OUT OF YOUR MISERY!
!!
GUH...?!
HE...HE'S UPSIDE DOWN...?!

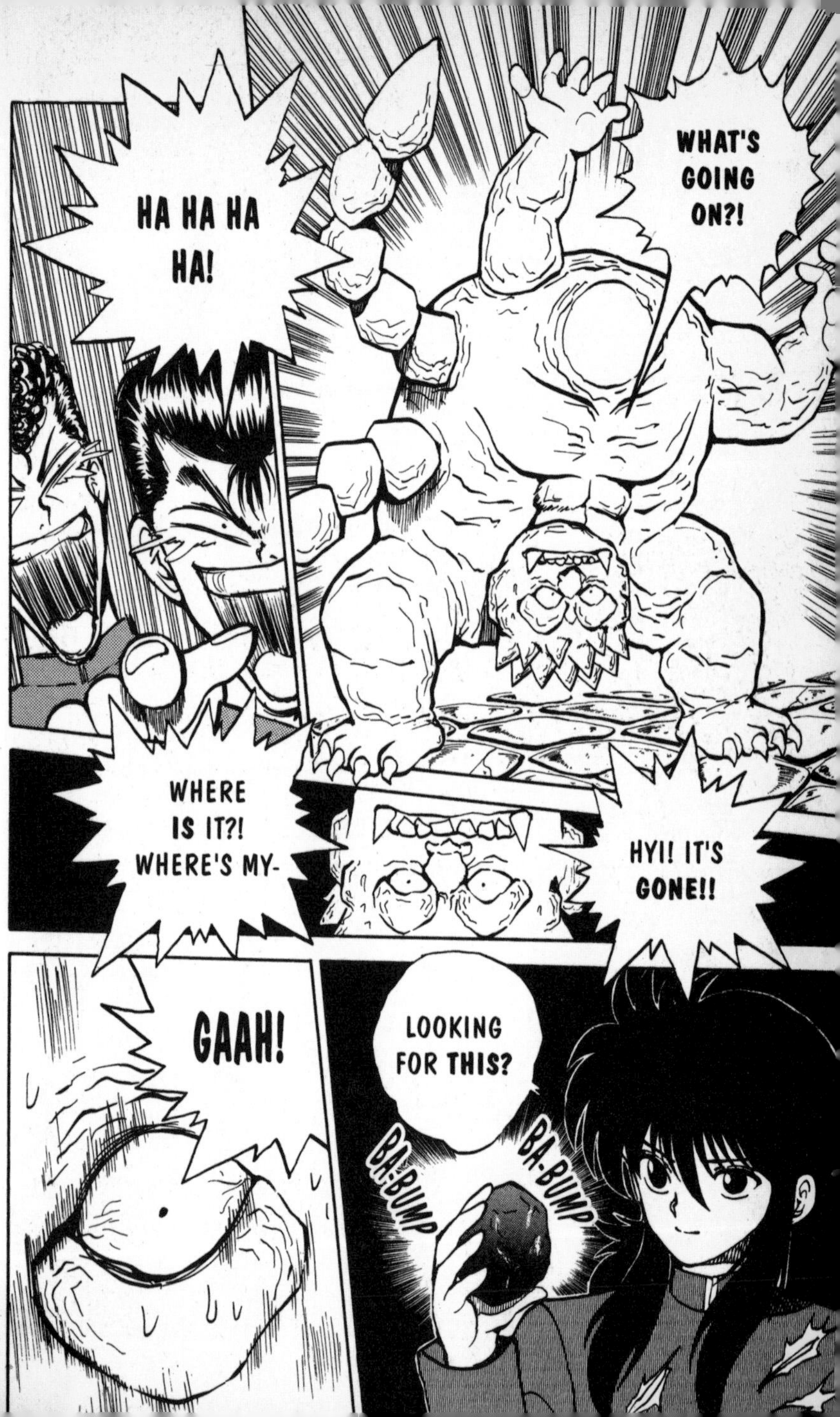
WHAT'S GOING ON?!
HA HA HA HA!
HYI! IT'S GONE!!
WHERE IS IT?! WHERE'S MY-
LOOKING FOR THIS?
BA-BUMP
BA-BUMP
GAAH!

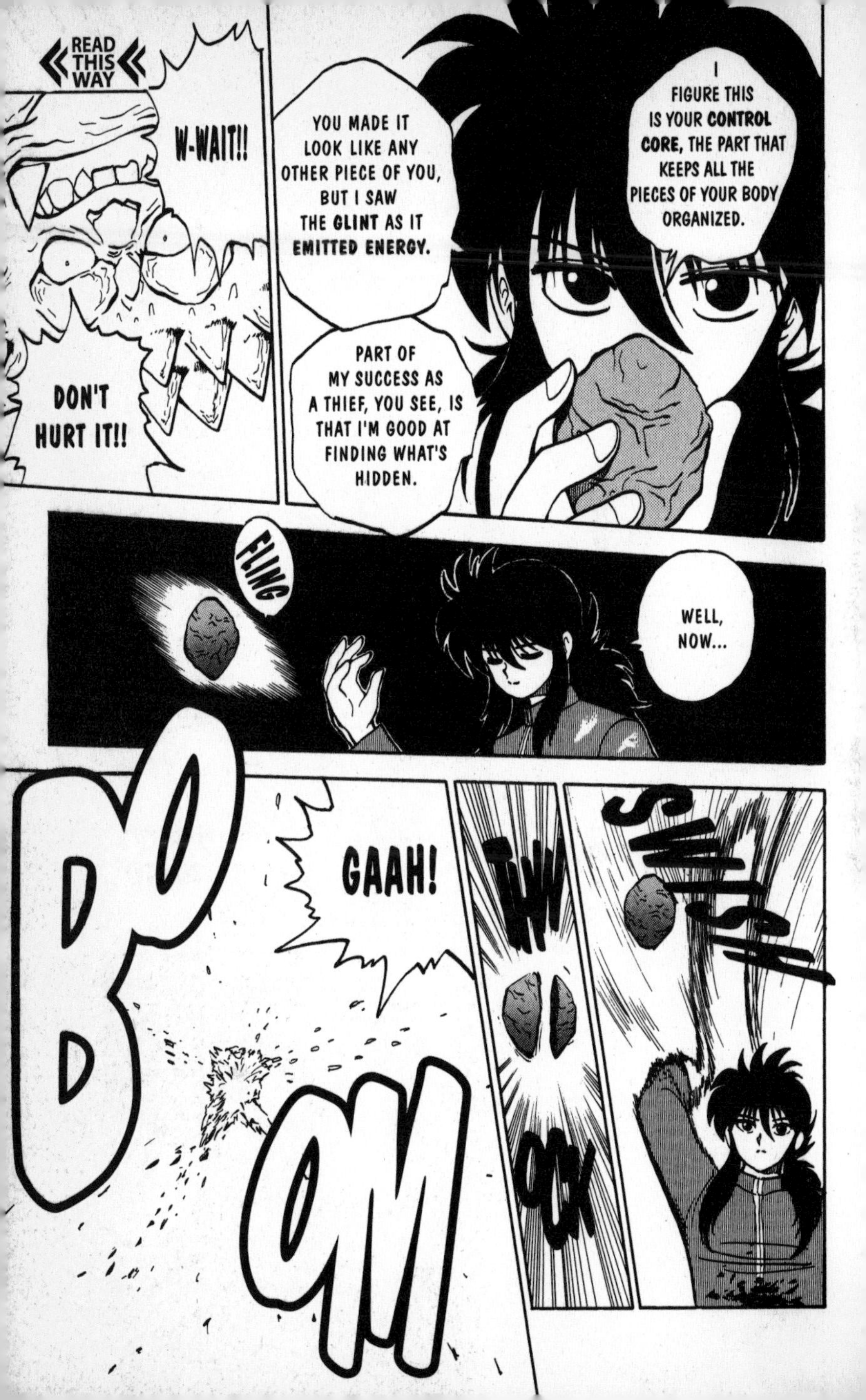
READ THIS WAY
I FIGURE THIS IS YOUR CONTROL CORE, THE PART THAT KEEPS ALL THE PIECES OF YOUR BODY ORGANIZED.
YOU MADE IT LOOK LIKE ANY OTHER PIECE OF YOU, BUT I SAW THE GLINT AS IT EMITTED ENERGY.
PART OF MY SUCCESS AS A THIEF, YOU SEE, IS THAT I'M GOOD AT FINDING WHAT'S HIDDEN.
W-WAIT!!
DON'T HURT IT!!
WELL, NOW...
FLING
SWISH
THWOCK
GAAH!
BOOM

READ THIS WAY

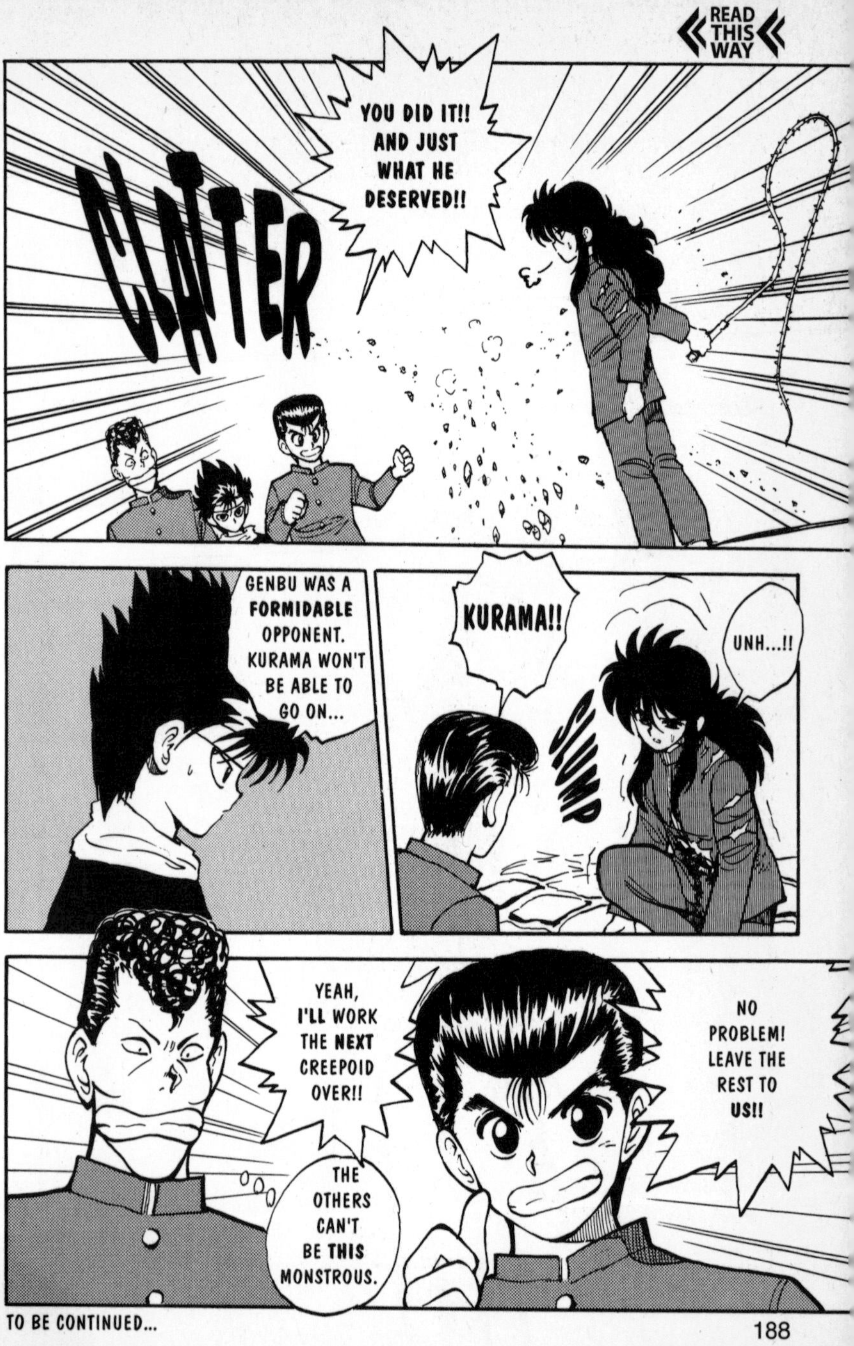
YOU DID IT!! AND JUST WHAT HE DESERVED!!
CLATTER
KURAMA!!
UNH...!!
SLUMP
GENBU WAS A FORMIDABLE OPPONENT. KURAMA WON'T BE ABLE TO GO ON...
NO PROBLEM! LEAVE THE REST TO US!!
YEAH, I'LL WORK THE NEXT CREEPOID OVER!!
THE OTHERS CAN'T BE THIS MONSTROUS.

TO BE CONTINUED...

IN THE NEXT VOLUME...

The battle for Demon City continues, as Yusuke and his partners take on the three remaining Beasts. But time is running out: Suzaku, leader of the Four Beasts, has turned the power of the whistle against Yusuke's friends on Earth. While Keiko and Botan fight off an army of brain-bugged zombies, Yusuke races after the merciless demon crime lord...

COMING October 2004!

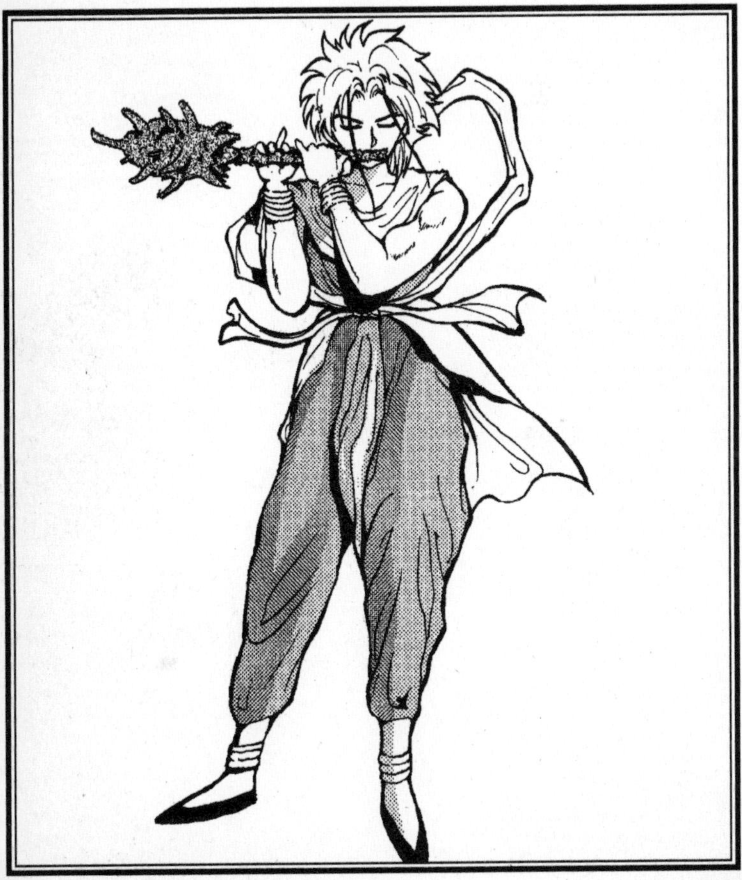

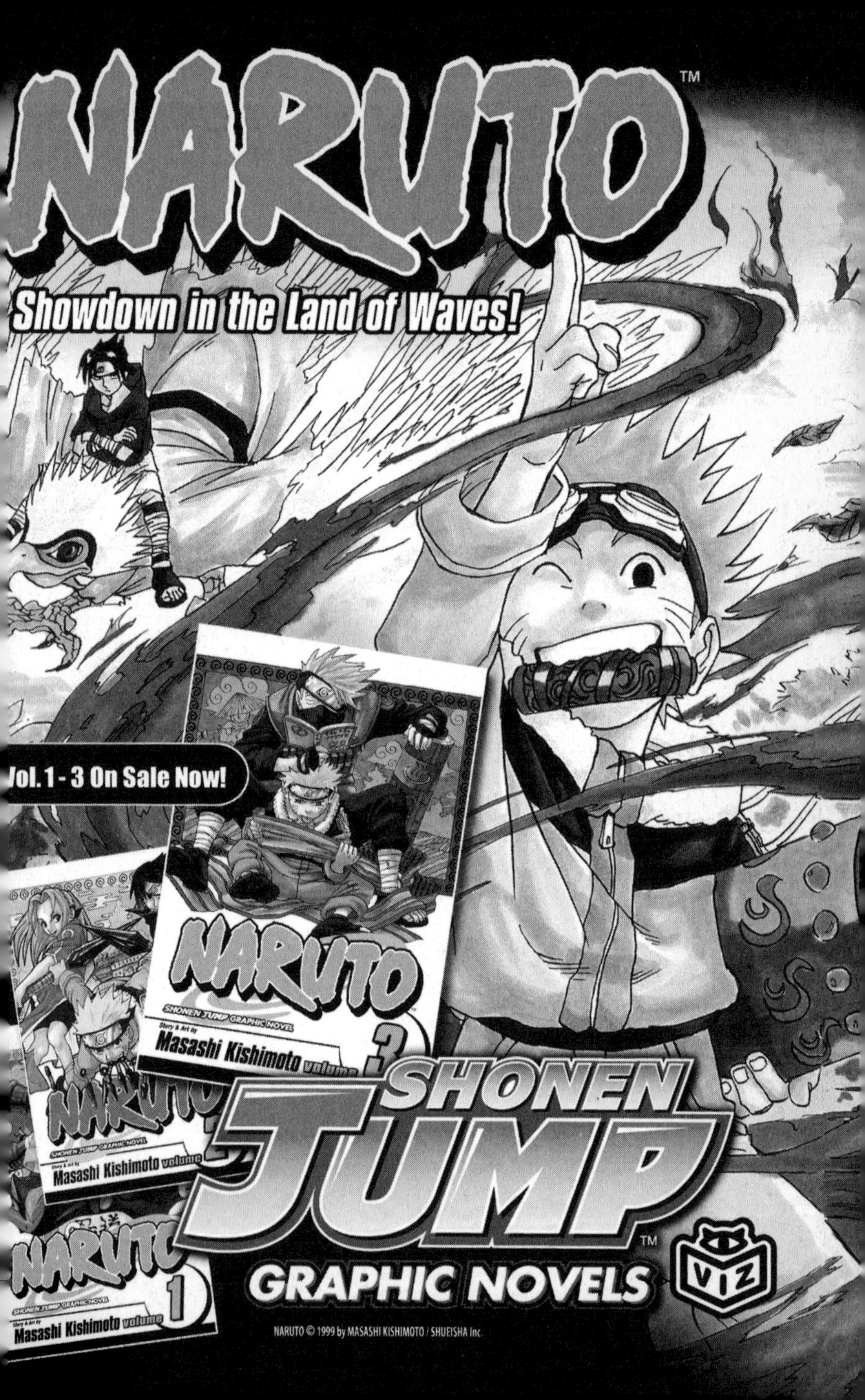

NARUTO™
Showdown in the Land of Waves!
Vol. 1 - 3 On Sale Now!
NARUTO
SHONEN JUMP GRAPHIC NOVEL
Story & Art by
Masashi Kishimoto volume 3
SHONEN JUMP™
GRAPHIC NOVELS
VIZ
Masashi Kishimoto volume
NARUTO 1
Masashi Kishimoto volume
NARUTO © 1999 by MASASHI KISHIMOTO / SHUEISHA Inc.

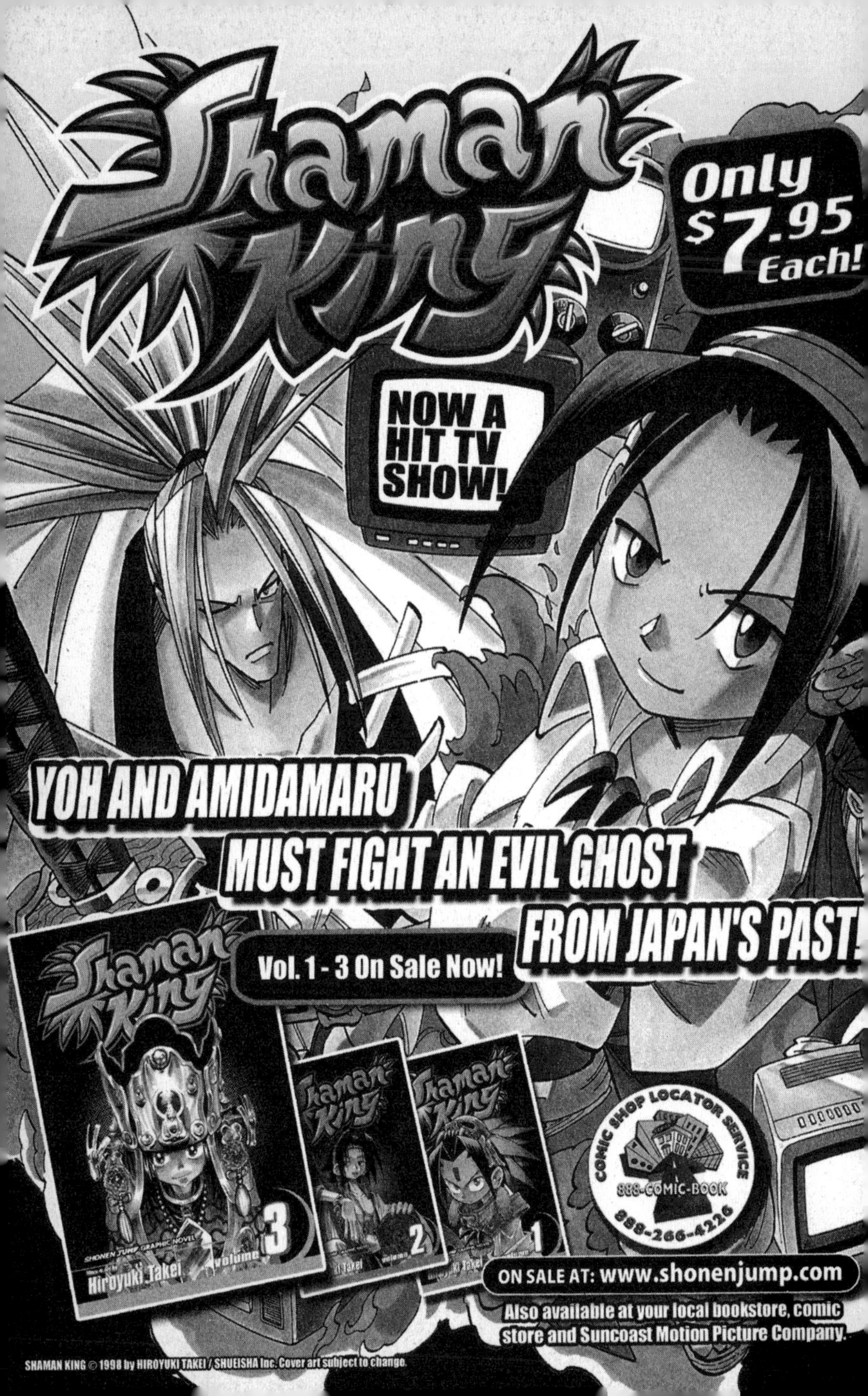
Shaman King
Only $7.95 Each!
NOW A HIT TV SHOW!
YOH AND AMIDAMARU MUST FIGHT AN EVIL GHOST FROM JAPAN'S PAST!
Vol. 1 - 3 On Sale Now!
COMIC SHOP LOCATOR SERVICE
888-COMIC-BOOK
888-266-4226
ON SALE AT: www.shonenjump.com
Also available at your local bookstore, comic store and Suncoast Motion Picture Company.
SHAMAN KING © 1998 by HIROYUKI TAKEI / SHUEISHA Inc. Cover art subject to change.

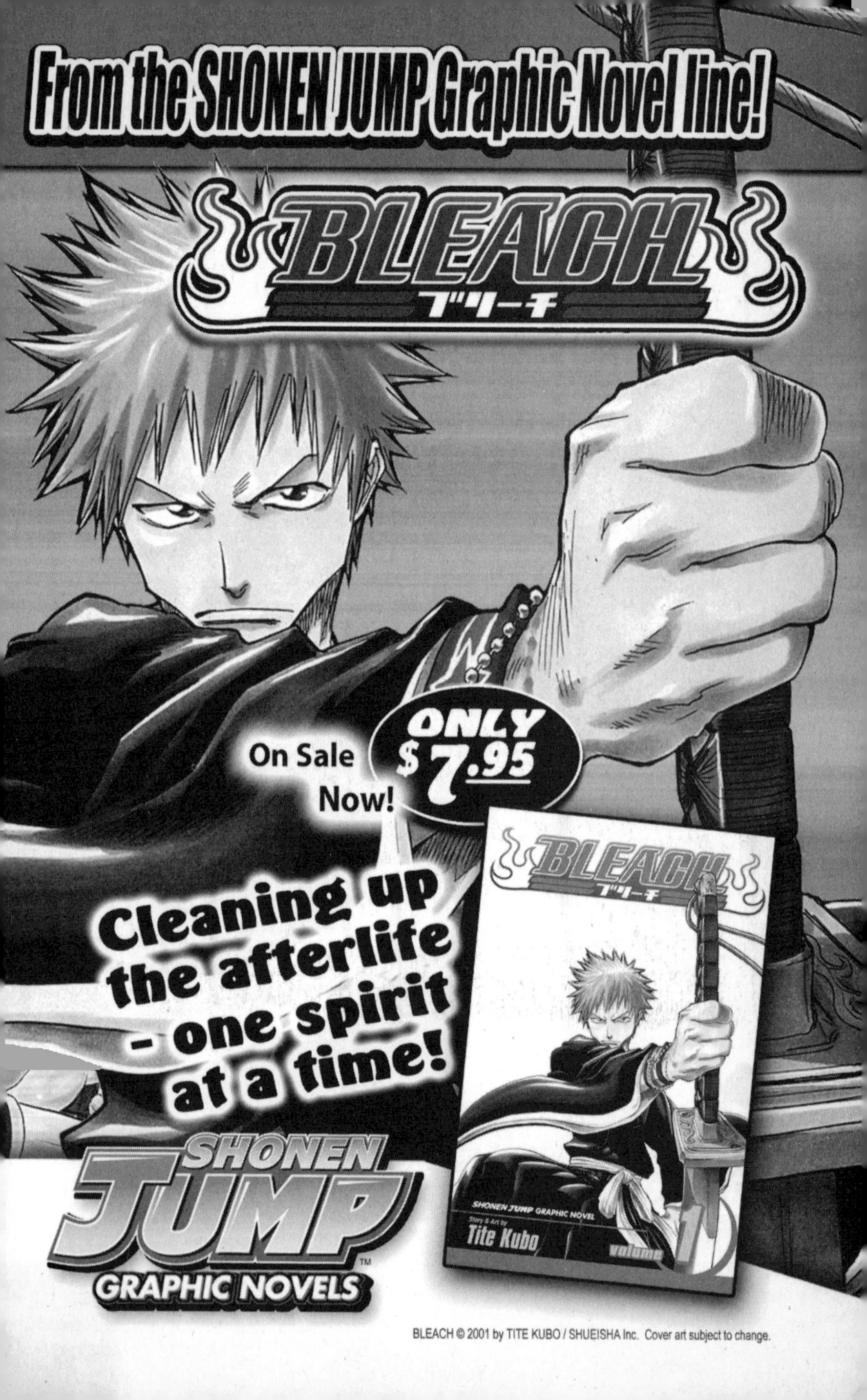
From the SHONEN JUMP Graphic Novel line!
BLEACH
ブリーチ
On Sale Now!
ONLY $7.95
Cleaning up the afterlife - one spirit at a time!
BLEACH
ブリーチ
SHONEN JUMP GRAPHIC NOVEL
Story & Art by
Tite Kubo
volume 1
SHONEN JUMP™
GRAPHIC NOVELS
BLEACH © 2001 by TITE KUBO / SHUEISHA Inc. Cover art subject to change.

COMPLETE OUR SURVEY AND LET US KNOW WHAT YOU THINK!

☐ Please check here if you DO NOT wish to receive information or future offers from VIZ

Name: _____

Address: _____

City: _____ State: _____ Zip: _____

E-mail: _____

☐ Male ☐ Female Date of Birth (mm/dd/yyyy): ___ / ___ / _____ (Under 13? Parental consent required)

What race/ethnicity do you consider yourself? (please check one)

☐ Asian/Pacific Islander ☐ Black/African American ☐ Hispanic/Latino

☐ Native American/Alaskan Native ☐ White/Caucasian ☐ Other: _____

What SHONEN JUMP Graphic Novel did you purchase? (indicate title purchased)

_____

What other SHONEN JUMP Graphic Novels, if any, do you own? (indicate title(s) owned)

_____

_____

Reason for purchase: (check all that apply)

☐ Special offer ☐ Favorite title ☐ Gift

☐ Recommendation ☐ Read in SHONEN JUMP Magazine

☐ Other _____

Where did you make your purchase? (please check one)

☐ Comic store ☐ Bookstore ☐ Mass/Grocery Store

☐ Newsstand ☐ Video/Video Game Store ☐ Other: _____

☐ Online (site: _____)

Do you read SHONEN JUMP Magazine?

☐ Yes ☐ No **(if no, skip the next two questions)**

Do you subscribe?

☐ Yes ☐ No

If you do not subscribe, how often do you purchase SHONEN JUMP Magazine?

☐ 1-3 issues a year

☐ 4-6 issues a year

☐ more than 7 issues a year

What genre of manga would you like to read as a SHONEN JUMP Graphic Novel?
(please check two)

☐ Adventure ☐ Comic Strip ☐ Science Fiction ☐ Fighting

☐ Horror ☐ Romance ☐ Fantasy ☐ Sports

Which do you prefer? (please check one)

☐ Reading right-to-left

☐ Reading left-to-right

Which do you prefer? (please check one)

☐ Sound effects in English

☐ Sound effects in Japanese with English captions

☐ Sound effects in Japanese only with a glossary at the back

THANK YOU! Please send the completed form to:

VIZ Survey
42 Catharine St.
Poughkeepsie, NY 12601

All information provided will be used for internal purposes only. We promise not to sell or otherwise divulge your information.

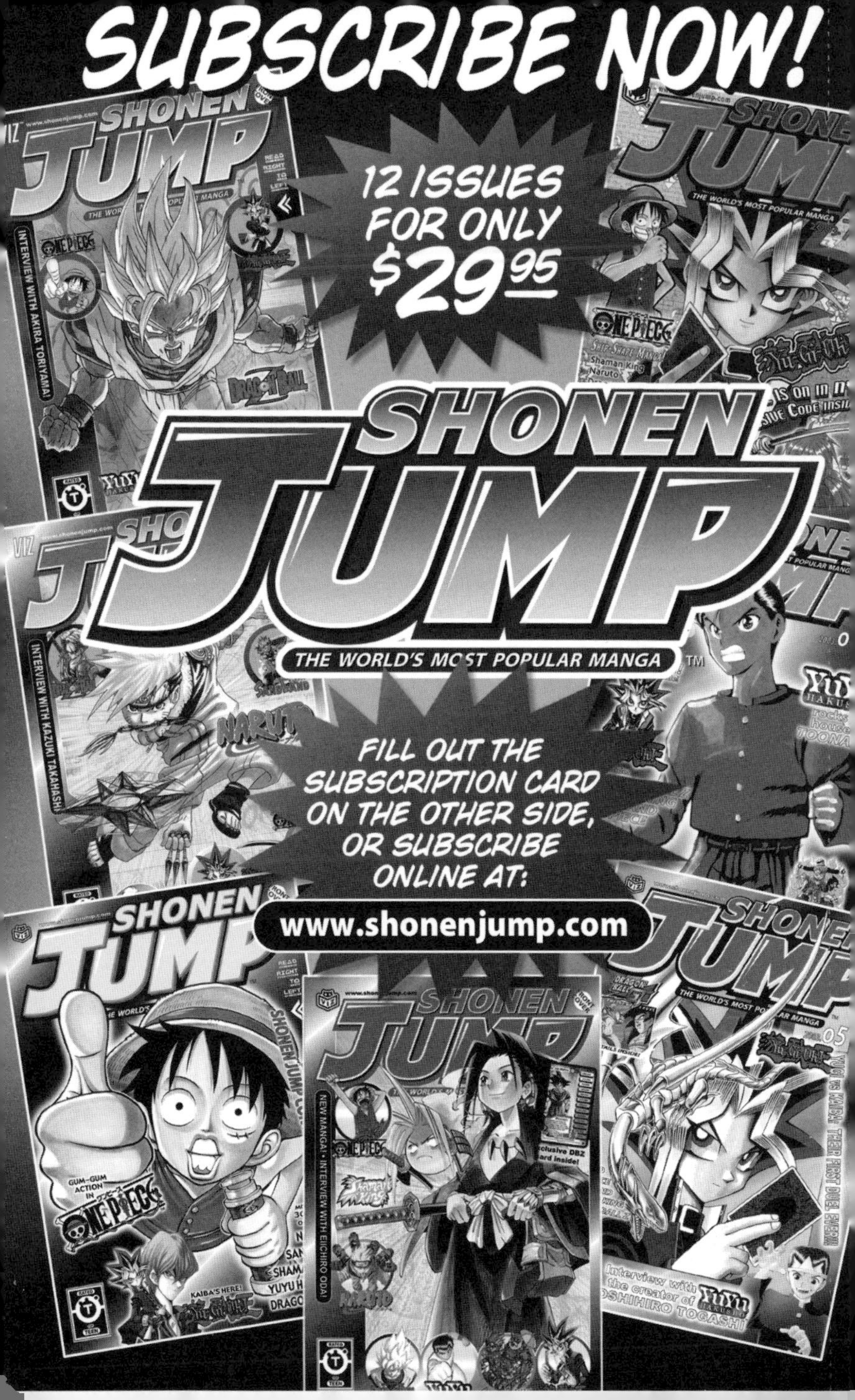
SUBSCRIBE NOW!
12 ISSUES FOR ONLY $29.95
SHONEN JUMP
THE WORLD'S MOST POPULAR MANGA ™
FILL OUT THE SUBSCRIPTION CARD ON THE OTHER SIDE, OR SUBSCRIBE ONLINE AT:
www.shonenjump.com